Unjust Relations:
Aboriginal Rights
in Canadian Courts

Unjust Relations:
Aboriginal Rights in Canadian Courts

Edited by
Peter Kulchyski

Toronto
OXFORD UNIVERSITY PRESS
1994

Oxford University Press
70 Wynford Drive, Don Mills, Ontario M3C 1J9

Toronto Oxford New York
Delhi Bombay Calcutta Madras Karachi
Kuala Lumpur Singapore Hong Kong Tokyo
Nairobi Dar es Salaam Cape Town
Melbourne Auckland Madrid

and associated companies in
Berlin Ibadan

Oxford is a trademark of Oxford University Press

Canadian Cataloguing in Publication Data

Main entry under title:

Unjust relations: aboriginal rights in Canadian courts

Includes index.
ISBN 0-19-540985-X

1. Native peoples - Canada - Legal status, laws,
etc. - Cases.* 2. Canada. Supreme Court.
I. Kulchyski, Peter Keith, 1959-

KE7706.U55 1994   342.71087202643   C94-930068-3
KF8205.U55 1994

Contents

Acknowledgments

While I accept responsibility for my comments and editorial decisions, I am deeply indebted to many friends, students and colleagues for a variety of forms of assistance with this project. In particular, I would like to thank the students of my Native Law course, Arctic College, Yellowknife in the summer of 1990; it was in that class that this project had its genesis. M.J. Patterson, Deborah Simpson and John Simpson were all helpful in the organization of that course. I am greatful to Susan Baer and staff at the NWT Department of Justice library for allowing me to use the library. Two students, Eric Menicoche and Trudy Mowry, took independent studies courses in Native Law at Trent University which were similarly intellectually stimulating. I have also benefited from discussion and support in the very co-operative atmosphere of Native Studies at Trent, and for this I thank Paul Bourgeois, Marlene Brant Castellano, Louise Garrow, Don McCaskill, John Milloy, David Newhouse, Maureen Simpkins and Shirley Williams.

Three research assistants—Andrew Barbour, Art Beaver and Robertson Anderson—were very helpful in the technical aspects of putting together this manuscript. It also gives me great pleasure to thank the very dedicated administrative staff of the Native Studies Department here at Trent—Special Programs Assistant Kathy Fife, Secretary Barb Rivett, and particularly Academic Programs Co-ordinator Joyce Miller—for incalculable assistance and for making daily routines so enjoyable.

I rely on a diverse group of friends to puncture any too large intellectual balloons I blow up and ensure that my thoughts engage with a range of critical perspectives. In the context of this project I would like to thank Sedef Arat-Koc, Himani Bannerji, Shannon Bell, Dorothy Chocolate, Marina Devine, Gad Horowitz, Mustafa Koc, Donna Landry, Gerald Maclean, Lee Selleck, David Simmons, Deborah Lee Simmons, Frank Tester, Frank Tough, Andrew Wernick, and Colleen Youngs.

I would also like to thank Brian Henderson and Phyllis Wilson at Oxford University Press for encouragement and support with this project. Molly Wolf did an extraordinary job in proof-reading and copy-editing the manuscript. I owe her an enormous debt of thanks. Those tortuous sentences and strange textual constructions which remain are a product of my own obstinacy rather than her clear-eyed and careful reading.

Finally, for intellectual guidance on questions of gender relations, which have helped with my interpretation of the Lavell-Bedard case specifically, for an understanding that rigour and creativity are not mutually exclusive, and for intellectual, physical and emotional support beyond all boundaries of duty and pleasure, I thank Julia Emberley.

Theses on Aboriginal Rights

Nothing, today, can be manifested. Except, possibly, the fact that humanity is not yet just. The indecency of a humanism that goes on as if nothing had happened. The task of extremist writing is to put through the call for a justice of the future. Henceforth, Justice can no longer permit itself to be merely backward looking or bound in servility to sclerotic models and their modifications (their "future"). A justice of the future would have to show the will to rupture.

AVITAL RONELL

I. Justice colludes with totalizing power. Aboriginal rights themselves have been oriented as another tool of totalization, but also still contain the hidden promise of something else. For Aboriginal Canadians the law has acted as a vehicle of totalization, colluding with a power that demanded constraint, de-limitation, definition, demarcation. Aboriginal rights have become an elaborate juridical doctrine that legitimates these processes, while at the same time it is the term we give to the remainder, what is left over, the excess of the process of totalizing; unknown and threatening, Aboriginal rights remain just over the horizon of established property relations. Totalization: the process by which objects, people, spaces, times, ways of thinking, and ways of seeing are ordered in accordance with a set of principles conducive to the accumulation of capital and the logic of the commodity form. Wealth piles up; every social product including people is made to be bought and sold, to have an exchange value and a use value; these principles spread as the dominant way of being in the world today: totalization. The order, the underlying rule, of these principles is the order of quantity, of homogeneity, of seriality. Fredric Jameson has written that "the social totality can be sensed, as it were, from the outside, like a skin at which the Other somehow looks, but which we ourselves will never see" (1992: 114). A system that presents itself—or attempts to present itself—as benign and nuturing to those inside of it, as a liberal democracy based on principles of individual rights and equalities, appears totalitarian to those, such as Aboriginal peoples, who experience its limits, its totalizing edges, who experience it as the process of totalization. Struggling against this process, resisting the imposition of this newly established order, Aboriginal Americans—Indians, indigenous peoples, First Nations, Native peoples, Métis, Inuit—find a variety of tools: violence, passive resistance, negotiation, the courts. A legal doctrine, Aboriginal rights, is set in play. Documents are produced, promises made.

It is the job of the courts to interpret these documents. By doing so, the courts take on the role of defining, fixing and circumscribing Aboriginal rights. The courts characterize Aboriginal rights in a way that carries forward the project of totalization. In the Canadian context they do a very good job: Aboriginal title—the ownership of land—becomes constrained in 1888 so that it is defined as a "burden" on underlying crown title. That is, the crown "owns" all the land; Aboriginal people merely have some undefined legal interest in it. This legal fiction becomes the ground of Aboriginal rights jurisprudence, the ground upon which legal struggles in the last few decades have been and continue to be fought. But the battle was already lost over a century ago. What is left but to further circumscribe the remaining remainder, parcel out a few partial victories, a salve for the conscience of the colonizers, and define these as Aboriginal rights. Aboriginal rights: subject of intense legal debate, hence, provider of income to many a jurist.

* * *

II. In his well-known essay "Force of Law: The 'Mystical Foundation of Authority'" Jacques Derrida comments "to address oneself to the other in the language of the other is, it seems, the condition of all possible justice" (17). Later, he adds "the violence of an injustice has begun when all the members of a community do not share the same idiom throughout" (18). The point here is more than that common language is a precondition of justice; language itself already has justice buried within it. In the Drybones case, the fact that Drybones did not speak or understand English lead to an overturning of his initial guilty plea, and ultimately to the case's reaching the Supreme Court of Canada. But, again, Derrida's point has a much broader significance; language and idiom in this context speak to the politics of form, the language or conceptual knowledge of material and social structures that allows one to know, for example, that one is in a court of law. Aboriginal languages and Aboriginal forms have rarely been "addressed" by the courts; Aboriginal people have painstakingly had to learn the process of addressing the courts in order to begin to be heard. It is not insignificant that the two earliest cases cited here—St. Catherine's Milling (1888) and Re: Eskimos (1939)—did not involve direct participation of the people whose lives were most affected by them.

The languages of Aboriginal peoples, not just the verbal patterns and "translatability" but the very grammar implied in the cultural forms, have not been addressed by the courts. Sweetgrass is not burned to cleanse, pipes are not shared. Instead, the dominant cultural form presents itself as Truth: bibles are produced, spectacles are arranged. I have a story from my own experience that in some mediated way speaks to this issue:

It was late March 1989. I was driving on the highway between Saskatoon and Prince Albert, on my way north to teach a group of students in the Saskatchewan Urban Native Teacher Education Program. The drive was monotonous, boring. I was mentally in "automatic', letting the car run on cruise control, about half an hour south of town. Ahead of me I saw what looked like a bright orange rag, blown across the highway by the prairie wind. It turned out to be a person, thumbing a ride. The bright orange colour at first made me think that this person was a road worker. I slowed, then stopped. My new passenger was Cree, and not a road worker at all. He lurched into the car bringing with him a very strong smell of wind, of prairie, of smoke, of alcohol. The smell, like his presence, like the outdoors, entered the car and took over. His face was recently scarred. My first thought, I confess, was "oh oh . . . '

We spoke the whole time in fragments. He's going to Prince Albert. Of course. He peered at me. Deciding. Finally asked: "Are you a man or a woman?" I have long hair. I responded with affronted masculine dignity: "a man." Pause. He decided. Put out a hand: "I'm Percy." I, still driving, shook it: "Peter." "What." "PETER." "Oh." Pause. He took off his hat. Turned it upside down. Pulled something out of the inside of his hatband. Sweetgrass. Suddenly I was not on automatic, but alert as if every fibre of my being had been jump-started because it's sweetgrass and because there was more to this than met the eye. "I've been out all night," he said, "looking for some of this. I'm on my way back home. Funeral. Had to pick some sweetgrass, bring it home for the funeral. I was out all night. Left Saskatoon last night. Got in a fight. They kicked the shit out of me. Lost my glasses. Found sweetgrass. It's my nephew that died. I have to get home. Bring the sweetgrass. You want some?" "Yes." Now I was paying attention. Putting things together as he spoke, making sense of his actions and repetitions as he continued to speak. He couldn't tell if I was a man or a woman because of the lost glasses; he had a reason to be banged up: "it took three of them to hold me down"; he was carrying sweetgrass—used in cleansing ceremonies—so in some way he was a traditional person, held traditional knowledge. He clumsily cut off about four inches of braided sweetgrass, handed it to me, put the rest back in his hatband, said: "I like you. You stopped to pick me up," which made sense. Then: "Would you like me to sing a song for you?" Me: "Yes." It's a "hey-yah" song. So there I was, driving through the rolling hills and scrub prairie, coming into Prince Albert in my small rental car, listening to this voice, these sounds, this breathing sounding singing I've heard before from a distance but rarely so clear and never so close. Then he stopped. He may have sung for one minute, or perhaps five. No more. Dream time. He said something about how he "works the powwow circuit." Then we got into town. He let me know where to drop him; not ordering. Instructing. It wasn't much out of my way and I had lots of time. He said "My father always told me that if I needed help, someone would be there. Someone always comes along." He said "My father died last year." He said "Turn here. These people will give me a ride the rest of the way." How long ago was it? A day? A year? I still have the sweetgrass. I can still hear his song.

What took place could be seen as a kind of gift exchange. I gave a ride, I got a song. Perhaps my telling the story here is another gift, or perhaps I am merely returning what I was given. Some might say it is an appropriation: I am a non-Native. The song, made up more of vocables than words, says as much and more to me than the words of this text, both my own and those I have reproduced. It says, in part: this is not only another language, but another way of being language. A language not addressed by the courts. That version of Aboriginal rights that sees them as carving a space from which to resist totalization would say that Aboriginal rights cannot be comprehended at even the most minimal level if we do not pay attention to cultural difference. A truism of sorts; less obvious, perhaps, is the question of how different this difference is from other differences. A question to which I will return.

*   *   *

III. If we take seriously the notion that Aboriginal rights are a point of negotiation between non-Native and Native societies or realities in Canada today, we must simultaneously acknowledge the impossibility of defining Aboriginal rights. Thus, as against the common charge—self-government: a concept in need of a definition—we must affirm self-government and Aboriginal rights (the relation between these two terms to be discussed below) as the undefinable, fluid line of contact between two social orders. There can be no answer to the question "what are Aboriginal rights?" that is not in the terms of the dominant, non-Native society, a society that strives for fixity, for the definite and for definitions. Or, any answer to the question "what are Aboriginal rights?" is already an attempt to confine, constrain, demarcate, and delimit those rights and consequently part of the process of confining, constraining, demarcating, and delimiting Aboriginal peoples. Aboriginal rights become a growing body of interpretations of a limited set of documents as opposed to a shifting basis for negotiations founded upon the primacy of the notion of mutual respect.

This must be affirmed at the outset. Undefinability must colour and override all the interpretations of these seemingly fixed and canonical texts. The limits of interpretation, of understanding, of western forms of knowledge, of the totalizing dynamic that governs so much of history, must be acknowledged. And, if I stress the alterity of Aboriginal peoples, the "otherness" of the other, rather than reaching that desired point of balance where we can understand that, in the words of Dominick LaCapra, "the comprehensive problem in inquiry is how to understand and to negotiate varying degrees of proximity and distance in the relation to the "other" that is both outside and inside ourselves" (140), it is because in this field of relations between power and knowledge, where the illusion of total understanding has served colonial power very well, where "when an Indian breathes, it's politics" (Cindy Gilday), where being itself is the question in question, we are at a beginning point and must destabilize the comforting narratives that consolidate our selves, our forms of knowledge, our legal claim to be right and to make legal claims.

*   *   *

IV. The discourse of Aboriginal rights, although it speaks the language of justice and although in the Canadian context it has constantly referred to abstract and universal ideals, has been and remains profoundly political. The term "Aboriginal rights" has come into prominence fairly recently, gaining particular currency in the last few decades. In the early 1960s, when as a result of status Indians gaining the vote it became clear that the special status of Indians involved at a minimum equal citizenship rights with a likelihood of additional rights, the concept of "citizens plus" was advanced by H.B. Hawthorne in his *Survey of the Contemporary Indians of Canada.* This concept, embodying the notion that Aboriginal peoples had all of the rights of Canadian citizens plus additional rights by virtue of their status as prior occupants, was endorsed and employed by Native political organizations in their struggle against the proposed White Paper policy of 1969. The White Paper, formally called *Statement of the Government of Canada on Indian Policy 1969,* had proposed removing most forms of special status for Aboriginal peoples in the hopes of ending discrimination against them. While the policy may have been well-intentioned, it amounted to a proposal for wholesale assimilation in the eyes of most Aboriginal leaders and was attacked until it was withdrawn in 1971. Through the 1970s the concept of "citizens plus" continued to evolve; as citizenship rights were secured the "plus" or additional rights became the focus of discussion.

In the late seventies, when constitutional negotiations came to dominate the Canadian and Aboriginal agendas, the term "Aboriginal rights" gained greater prominence. The term "Aboriginal," eventually defined in the Constitution Act (1982), became popular because it could be used to describe all of the many First Nations and categories of Native peoples; these included status and non-status Indians, Métis and Inuit. In Canada it had not acquired the problematic connotations that other jurisdictions, such as Australia, had imposed on it. Thus, the term "Aboriginal rights" quickly replaced the term "citizens plus" in legal and political discourse and remains a focal concept for negotiating the boundary between Aboriginal and non-Aboriginal peoples. This political micro-history was acknowledged by the Supreme Court of Canada in the Sparrow decision, as part of the justification for the argument that the words "existing Aboriginal rights" in the Canadian Constitution, since they were the result of a lengthy and intense political struggle, had to mean *something.*

*   *   *

V. The evolving doctrine of Aboriginal rights grounds itself on a significant historical fiction: what we now want was always already present, what is now desired was there all along. An important article by Brian Slattery on "Understanding Aboriginal Rights", partly inspired by the decision in the Guerin case and itself quoted favourably in the later Sparrow decision, remains the most useful general introduction to the issue of Aboriginal rights from a legal perspective. Slattery attempts to develop an overall theory of Aboriginal rights, whose basic tenets are summarized as follows:

> From early colonial days, the doctrine of Aboriginal rights has formed part of the basic constitutional structure of Canada. It originated in principles of colonial law that defined the relationship between the British Crown and the native peoples of Canada and the status of their lands, laws, and existing political structures. Some of those principles were articulated in the Royal Proclamation of 1763, and were reflected in treaties concluded between the Crown and particular native groups. At Confederation, they passed into the federal sphere, and formed a body of basic common law principles operating across Canada. In principle, these principles were liable to be overridden by legislation. However, they were protected in part by the provisions of constitutional instruments such as the Proclamation of 1763, and the Constitution Act, 1867. With the enactment of the Constitution Act in 1982, they have become constitutionally entrenched. (782-3)

Although I am in sympathy with much of Slattery's argument, which has enormous tactical value in the legal struggle for Aboriginal rights, there is surely something disingenuous in this attempt to forge such a consolidated historical narrative. It seems to me as interesting and important to stress the ways in which Aboriginal rights were as equally ignored "from early colonial days", or through much of the colonial period, as they "formed part of the basic constitutional structure." Slattery's historical narrative presents what appears to me as a story of fits and starts, a fragmented narrative of fundamental injustices, as though it were a seamless narrative that coalesces in a doctrine of Aboriginal rights which have "always already existed" in a "hidden constitution" of Canada. I am more inclined to say that the way the principles of Aboriginal rights were employed in the late nineteenth and early twentieth centuries violated the principles of the Royal Proclamation of 1763. Furthermore, those principles themselves must not be the horizon for how we see or negotiate Aboriginal rights today. I have other criticisms of Slattery—my own emphasis is on culture and political rights as much as Aboriginal title, I would take issue with Slattery's understanding of "Indian Country" in the Proclamation—but do refer the reader to him for an alternative "map" of Aboriginal rights.

*　　*　　*

VI. The dual-sided approach to Aboriginal rights—as a tool of totalization and as what totalization allows outside of itself—is reflected in the question of the origin of Aboriginal rights. When we consider Aboriginal rights in Canada we have, ironically enough, a number of originary moments of historical and textual significance. Two deserve particular attention while I will omit a series of others, such as Papal bulls and documents of the French and Spanish American regimes, which by and large played a secondary role in the legal texts under consideration and represent a more specialized topic. The two originary moments to be examined here are of special importance for British North America and hence for what would become Canada: first, the fact and idea of Aboriginal people's prior occupation of the continent; and second, the Royal Proclamation of 1763.

Prior occupation is the historical ground upon which Aboriginal rights rest. "They were here first" translates into: "at one time, all of this land was theirs. We rarely conquered them by force of arms. Now all this land is ours. We must owe them something." That "something" is Aboriginal rights. Aboriginal rights can be said historically to derive from the prior occupancy of Aboriginal peoples, their occupation from time immemorial—or at least from the time of the coming of the Europeans—of the lands now constituting Canada. Over this ground, Aboriginal rights can be characterized as pre-dating or "pre-existing" European occupation. Aboriginal peoples, of course, did not go around talking about their rights; mostly, they spoke in a discourse of responsibilities and respect. But that discourse was circulated among themselves. When others came and established—or forced—dominance, it became relevant to speak of rights as a way of negotiating relations. In the terms of this origin story, the role of courts and constitutions is to recognize what always already pre-existed: namely that Aboriginal peoples had special rights by virtue of their prior occupancy of the Americas. The history of Aboriginal rights then becomes a history of when and where these rights were recognized and when and where they were ignored.

The second story accounting for the origin of Aboriginal rights is more popular because it has more fixity or discursive certainty. The Royal Proclamation of 1763 can be described as the textual ground of Aboriginal rights. Aboriginal rights were established (or, better, recognized) by a document signed by a British monarch. The Royal Proclamation then became the founding document by which Aboriginal rights were enshrined in British law, which itself came to dominate Canada. The Proclamation itself was an outcome of the Seven Years War (or the French and Indian War) of 1756 to 1763. When the British defeated the French on the Plains of Abraham they established their dominance, as opposed to other European powers, over much of North America. One purpose of the Proclamation, which followed the Treaty of Paris that ended the war, was to establish boundaries and administrations for the new British possessions. Aware that their Aboriginal allies were an important factor in the victory and that those same allies were unhappy with colonists trying to grab the land, the Colonial Office also attempted through the Proclamation to reassure its Indian allies by protecting their lands. About half the matter of the Proclamation deals with new colonies and half deals with Aboriginal rights. The Proclamation has never been revoked; along with the Hudson's Bay Company's Royal Charter (1670), it is one of the first British documents dealing with what would become Canada; it has been characterized as having the legal force of a statute or law; it has also been characterized as having, by convention, constitutional status and as a result could be said to be the first constitution of Canada; it is reaffirmed by name in section 25 of the Constitution Act (1982); lawyers for Aboriginal people and legal scholars have called it an Aboriginal *magna carta*.

The language of the Proclamation is notoriously ambiguous. The section on Aboriginal rights tries to do two basic things: it affirms that territories beyond the boundaries of the colonies were "Indian lands" and could not be settled on; and it establishes a process whereby Aboriginal peoples could surrender their lands only to the Crown. Thus, the Proclamation can be said to have acknowledged that Aboriginal people held title to much of the Americas. The nature, value and limits of such title was in doubt. Two questions were particularly vexing and will crop up in the legal decisions that follow. The first is this: did the Proclamation recognize pre-existing Aboriginal rights or did the King create Aboriginal rights? It is an important question because if the King created these rights then he may have had the power to uncreate them, to take them away. If he recognized them then he was effectively affirming a reality that could not be changed. The document is silent about this question, although at one place it says "until Our further pleasure be known" implying that the King thought he could change his mind about the subject. The second question has to do with the jurisdiction of the Proclamation: where did it apply? Some argue that western Canada, possibly *terra incognita* (unknown territory) at the time of the Proclamation, should not be considered within its framework; but here the literal wording strongly favours a more general applicability. The Proclamation reads "all the lands to the west of the sources of the rivers flowing into the Atlantic" are lands where Indians have title. Literally, "all the lands" would include those in western Canada. There is some debate, as well, about whether much of the Canadian northwest was truly *terra incognita*; for example, see Hall's dissent in the Calder case.

Historically, then, Aboriginal rights can be thought to have two sources. They come from Aboriginal people's prior occupancy of the Americas or from the Royal Proclamation of 1763 or possibly from both. The documentary history of Aboriginal rights, and their evolution, can be traced through a series of policies and acts that followed. The British North America Act of 1867, unlike the Proclamation, contained only one line about Aboriginal peoples, but the line was very important. Section 91 of the BNA Act lists areas of federal responsibility; line 24 on the list of federal responsibilities is "Indians and lands reserved for Indians." Effectively—and consistent with the implicit policy embodied in the Proclamation—the BNA Act entrenched the notion that the highest level of government should have jurisdiction over Aboriginal matters because it would be more likely to see the long-term importance of protecting Aboriginal lands against other interests, including provinces, that would be more likely to appropriate and use those lands. Section 91 (24) thereby implicitly recognized that the federal government had a special responsibility for Aboriginal peoples as well as jurisdiction over them and their land. The nature of this responsibility was one of the central questions in the Guerin case.

Under the authority of section 91 (24) the federal government passed an

Enfranchisement Act (1869) and, eventually, an Indian Act (1876) with many subsequent amendments. One section of the Indian Act, section 88, deals with Aboriginal and treaty rights. Section 88 says that provincial laws of general application apply on reserves and to status Indians unless those laws contradict federal legislation or violate treaty rights. Section 88 ensured that treaty rights were to have precedence over provincial laws of general application although arguably the federal government continued to have the power to override treaty rights.

The treaties themselves are the last major piece in the historical puzzle that constitutes Aboriginal rights. The treaties were negotiated in accordance with the provisions of the Royal Proclamation. Their purpose, from the government's viewpoint, was to extinguish or get rid of any Aboriginal title and rights to land. In exchange, Aboriginal first nations gained reserve lands, annuities, one-time presents of cash and agricultural supplies, and a variety of other, sometimes amorphous, treaty rights. Some first nations, notably the Dene, were convinced that their treaty was a treaty of peace and friendship rather than a land surrender. Other first nations have accepted that their Aboriginal title was extinguished through the treaty process but have insisted that they have treaty rights that go beyond the narrow reading of the written words in the treaty documents. They insist that the spirit of the treaties is their real meaning and that treaty rights are much more valuable than is often thought. The Sioui decision goes some way towards supporting this view.

Together these documents—the Royal Proclamation, the BNA Act, section 88 of the Indian Act, the various treaties—along with the doctrine of prior occupancy, are the crucial locus for legal arguments respecting the nature and origins of Aboriginal rights. The court cases refer consistently to various combinations of these documents as well as to each other.

A new document, the Constitution Act of 1982, was added to this framework within the last decade and has changed how older documents are interpreted. Two sections of the Constitution Act are particularly important: section 25 of the Charter of Rights and Freedoms has determined that equality rights guaranteed by the charter cannot be interpreted in a manner that would diminish Aboriginal rights. Section 25 refers to Aboriginal and treaty rights and specifies as well rights associated with the Royal Proclamation. Section 35 of the Constitution Act says that "existing Aboriginal and treaty rights of the Aboriginal peoples of Canada are hereby recognized and affirmed."

There is no clear, evolutionary logic in the historical development of Aboriginal rights. In spite of after-the-fact stories that have tried to imply a consistent logic in the approach to Aboriginal rights, there was a basic incoherence, an instability and set of contradictions embodied in the approach of various British and Canadian administrations. Sandwiched between two important moments when those rights were affirmed in limited ways—1763 and 1982—was a long period when the rights were sometimes recognized and more often than not ignored outright. The recognition and affirmation of Aboriginal rights cannot be seen as an outcome of a progressive liberalization of society, as the latest step in a process by which every day, in every way, things are getting better and better. It is a history of sustained, often vicious struggle, a history of losses and gains, of shifting terrain, of strategic victories and defeats, a history where the losers often win and the winners often lose, where the rules of the game often change before the players can make their next move, where the players change while the logic remains the same, where the moves imply each other just as often as they cancel each other out. It is a complex history whose end has not been written and whose beginnings are multiple, fragmentary and undecidable.

*   *   *

VII. Without limiting or defining, and hopefully without circumscribing, Aboriginal rights, it is possible to map the terrain of Aboriginal rights as they have been circumscribed by the State and the courts, to describe them and subject them to analysis. The metaphor of mapping was employed by Slattery, who wrote that "the goal, then, is to provide a map for understanding what Aboriginal rights are all about "(732). The notion of cognitive mapping has been deployed by Fredric Jameson in his *Postmodernism, or, The Cultural Logic of Late Capitalism* (1991) as a way of linking particular events to totalizing contexts and of negotiating trajectories through the postmodern world. In this sense Aboriginal rights act more as a kind of compass for Aboriginal peoples, a mechanism for tracing or negotiating a path through the postmodern. Aspects of this trajectory can be mapped through both the historical and structural descriptions I am attempting here, although this can never serve to tell us what Aboriginal rights are "all about".

Structurally, Aboriginal rights can be divided into two main types or categories: property rights and political rights. This boundary is a slippery one. Some rights occupy both fields and it is possible to argue that one type without the other is virtually meaningless. However, the distinction serves a useful function if it allows us to situate and specify Aboriginal rights, to distinguish between them and to understand how different kinds of Aboriginal rights relate to each other.

Aboriginal property rights themselves can be further divided into land rights and resource rights. The term "Aboriginal title" is used legally to specify Aboriginal rights to land. It can be argued that Aboriginal title is the basis of all other Aboriginal rights; that all the other political and property rights flow from the doctrine of prior occupancy and the title to land that the doctrine implies. Aboriginal title may be characterized as that title that Aboriginal peoples have by virtue of their prior occupancy, from time immemorial, of their traditional territory; alternatively, Aboriginal title may derive from occupancy over an extensive period of time of lands within "Indian territory" as that territory was described by the Royal Proclamation. Legally, it has been distinguished from fee simple title and is seen as a lesser form of ownership. It is thought of as a legal burden on Crown title, as an interest of unspecified value that Aboriginal people have in their traditional lands or, more specifically, on the surface of that land. This, at least, is how the courts have come to circumscribe the notion of Aboriginal title. Instead, it is possible to argue that Aboriginal title is Aboriginal ownership, the nature of which has not yet been understood by non-Native institutions—including the courts and the State—but which has some recognizable features. Aboriginal title involves ownership in common; it is not generally thought of as title held by individuals to specific pieces of land but rather as title held by nations to broad territories. Further, Aboriginal title could also be characterized as inalienable. That is, it is not possible to buy or sell Aboriginal title, it exists by virtue of an historical fact—prior occupancy—which cannot be undone. In this view, Aboriginal title would underlie Crown title, rather than the reverse, it would remain even where land claims and treaties pretend to extinguish it, and it would give Aboriginal peoples the fundamental, ongoing basis for negotiating their shifting relationship with non-Native society.

The second form of Aboriginal property rights I specified is to resources. These would include the hunting, fishing, trapping and gathering rights that various Aboriginal nations exercise to differing degrees, depending on whether they have treaties, the nature of those treaties, the historical position of provincial jurisdictions, and so on. Recognition of these kinds of rights varies widely across the country. Aboriginal resource rights are related to Aboriginal title; they usually imply rights to surface resources, the resources Aboriginal people can show they used "since time immemorial". It is possible to argue that resource rights are actually, legally, the form that Aboriginal title takes; that Aboriginal title is itself a usufructuary right guaranteeing access to resources, to use resources on the land, rather than to the land itself. Clearly, I have distanced myself from this kind of interpretation. While resource rights may derive from Aboriginal title, they are not the same: one refers to land itself, the other to resources on it. Legally, while Aboriginal title is seen similarly throughout Canada, Aboriginal resource rights vary dramatically province by province (or territory), First Nation by First Nation, treaty by treaty, and through the complex interplay of each of these factors (and others).

Aboriginal political rights involve a separate complex of laws, doctrines and regions. The most important of these, certainly the most prominent, is the right of Aboriginal self-government. But political rights also include a variety of freedoms: free movement beyond provincial and national borders, freedom of religion or spirituality, freedom from taxation, and so on. Aboriginal political rights, like Aboriginal title, can be thought of as rights deriving from prior occupancy. But in this case, what is fundamental is the notion that prior occupancy implies a right to have no restriction on cultures, ways of life, or traditions. Immigrant peoples, who whether or not of their own choosing leave their homelands, are in a position where they, to a greater or lesser degree, must accept the dominant cultural values of their chosen land. Aboriginal peoples did not choose to join the dominant cultural order; it chose to impose itself on them. Aboriginal political rights are the rights that derive from this situation.

Aboriginal self-government means the right to make decisions that are important to self-constitution. Aboriginal people have the right to be self-determining, to make decisions for themselves, in the forms that are appropriate to their cultural values. This latter point is particularly important. Regardless of the level of power provided to Aboriginal governments, every decision that is made following the dominant logic, in accordance with the hierarchical and bureaucratic structures of the established order, will take Aboriginal peoples further away from their own culture. Every decision that is made in the form appropriate to traditional cultures will be another step in the life of that culture.

Aboriginal people, by and large, never surrendered their right to control their own destiny. Furthermore, the line of contact or negotiation between Natives and non-Natives is a political line. Politics has assumed a crucial place in the lives of Aboriginal peoples. In this context, political control has become the primary concern of many Aboriginal communities; other issues either derive from it or are secondary.

Other political rights like freedom of movement, the right to their own spirituality, freedom from taxation, and so on, can be seen within the same logic, as rights derived from prior occupancy. Some of these political rights might derive from treaties or land claims. The economic advantages that might be conferred as a result of the use of these rights—for example, the employment of free movement across borders to sell goods duty-free—can be said to appropriately belong to First Nations. Whatever economic advantages might derive from these rights are comparatively small compensation for the losses Aboriginal nations have experienced and, given the economic deprivation experienced today by many Aboriginal people, might also offer one of the few practical possibilities for future economic self-sufficiency. It is interesting to note that these are the rights that have been most abused historically, particularly through the Indian Act, which restricted movement of Indians, banned specific cultural practices and limited basic civil liberties. Finally, these political rights in no way limit Aboriginal people's rights as Canadian citizens; they are additional rights that derive from prior occupancy.

Having provided a map of the terrain of Aboriginal rights, it is important to make a few comments about treaty rights, which are also the subject of many of the legal decisions that follow. Treaty rights can be seen as specific rights which different First Nations gained in exchange for limiting their Aboriginal title or agreeing to peaceful relations with non-Natives. Treaty rights can in theory involve anything, including rights to health, education, economic resources, and so on, depending on the terms of the treaty in question. If the treaties are to be seen as meaningful, rather than as outdated examples of near-fraud on the part of non-Natives and foolishness on the part of a generation of Aboriginal leaders, they must be interpreted beyond the literal meaning of the words in the treaty documents. By giving non-Natives access to huge amounts of lands and resources, the Treaty Nations were in effect saying, through the treaties: "you now have our source of economic well-being, our source of health, our books, our source of knowledge. In return, you will ensure that, as long as we need it, we will be given medicine, education, social welfare, and economic support." This interpretation would allow an understanding of the treaties as a good and fair deal for Aboriginal treaty nations. Treaty rights can be specified in the same way as Aboriginal rights: there are both property rights—including title and resource rights—and political rights—including self-government, a variety of freedoms, and so on—as well as any other rights that were promised through the treaties, most of which related to social and economic benefits.

*   *   *

VIII. Aboriginal rights cannot be meaningfully discussed without reference to Aboriginal cultures and their fundamental difference from Euro-Canadian culture. Aboriginal cultures are the waters through which Aboriginal rights swim. The discussion of Aboriginal culture is predicated on an acknowledgment of the difference of Aboriginal difference from other differences. In the spring of 1992 I attended a conference on access to law programs for Aboriginal peoples and Latinos in Albuquerque, New Mexico. The organizers had no sense of the degree to which the theme of the conference and its practical workings violated some basic principles of "asymmetrical equity." Latinos and Aboriginal peoples were collapsed into the category of other, in this instance as significant ethnic minorities (a similar conference on Afro-Americans had been held a year earlier). But the demands of Aboriginal peoples are structured on a fundamentally different ground than the demands of Latinos; while the latter struggle for equality rights, for a proportionately fair share of what the system offers, the former struggle for mechanisms that will allow for a continued assertion of meaningful difference. It was the same collapsing of categories, refusal to recognize the difference of Aboriginal difference from other differences, that led the Canadian government to target discrimination as the basic problem facing Aboriginal peoples and develop the White Paper policy of 1969 that became the focus of so much controversy in Aboriginal communities. One person's end to discrimination is another person's ruthless tool of assimilation.

There are two realities in the country we know as Canada. One of those realities is made up of the complex of social classes, genders, cultures, races, sexual orientations. This reality, or multiplicity of realities, could be called the dominant society. The dominant society is itself dominated by the values and traditions of a particular sector within it; those values can be characterized as western or European. The logic of those values is based on an instrumental rationality. The values and traditions, most especially the material preconditions, of the dominant society are totalizing. By this I mean that dominant Canadian society demands to understand everything as part of a process of shaping everything into a form that suits the basic principles upon which the established order is premised. Every thing, every thought, every human relation is still in the contested process of being reshaped into a modality that suits the commodity form. As long as the material preconditions remain, as long as the necessity for expansion of the commodity form and the accumulation of capital continue as fundamental social forces, the project of totalization will continue without rest.

The existence of an alternative Aboriginal reality can be quantified. Time and again, all of the statistical indices point to a distinctive position for Aboriginal peoples in Canadian society. The indices form what I call a morbid line: higher rates of death due to violence, lower life expectancy, lower levels of education, poorer housing, poorer job prospects, higher rates of infant mortality, higher rates of suicide. Statistically, Aboriginal peoples belong to the dispossessed in Canadian society, the very poor. Here alone, there is a certain call to justice. Of a friend, Drucilla Cornell eloquently wrote "in her death she remains as the limit of the system in which she was killed. In the death that demands redress we will always hear the call of the Other" (1992b: 89). The many deaths premised, not by the existence of this different social reality but by its impossible marginalization and its impossible struggle to survive as a difference, are in themselves a call. However, unlike unemployed workers, recent immigrants, single mothers, visible minorities, and other structural fragments at the margins of society who also call, Aboriginal peoples have a unique cultural claim.

Non-Aboriginal cultures within the multicultural fabric known as Canada almost all have homelands elsewhere. That means that if a recent immigrant from Poland loses her language, while this may be individually sad, it is not a cultural tragedy. Polish will still be spoken in Poland. Thai will still be spoken in Thailand. Jamaican culture will continue to thrive in Jamaica and German culture will continue to thrive in Germany. If the Cree language disappears from Canada, the Cree language disappears from the earth. If the Gitksan culture is erased in northern British Columbia, the Gitksan culture becomes extinct. The fact of prior occupancy implies or embodies the fact of territorial cultural centres or homelands. There is nowhere else for the Kaska-Dene to go. In the fall of 1991, when Angela Sidney died, we lost the last fluent speaker of Tagish; thus continues a legacy that even preceded the death of the last fluent speaker of Beothuk, Shawnadithit.

The positive value of cultural diversity, in a world where "ethnic tensions" seem to pose some new and very real threat, can be discussed with reference to a concrete example. The example, or story, or metaphor, deals with the relation of knowledge to experience: When you walk through the bush, what you see depends on what you know. If you walk down a trail as a trained geologist, while you see the trees, the swamp, the sky, what you are likely to notice is the way glaciers thousands of years old made the landscape, leaving behind striations in the rock, the way this vein of quartz is likely (or not) to be mineral-bearing, and so on. If you walk down the same trail as a botanist, while you would see the same sky and rocks you would be more likely to notice that this is a transition zone between boreal and coniferous forest, that the processes of decay and replenishment are at a specific stage, that certain uncommon species of wildflower can be found on this part of the trail. A hunter might walk down the same trail with quite a different perspective, noting locations for trap settings, animal prints and droppings, the flicker of partridge tails. An artist might see a perspective or view of the relation between trees and sky and rocks that promises a lively canvas. A lover might notice almost nothing, seeing only the eyes or smile of a companion who stayed behind. One way to walk down the trail is to know as much as possible about rocks, about trees, about animals, about air, and perhaps about art and love. The more we know, the more we can gain from our walk, the richer our experience of the walk. As well, the more areas we know about the more likely we are to encounter the one or two features on the trail that stand out (if this trail happens to pass a gold outcrop or the nest of a rare bird). It is useful to remind ourselves, in this era when knowledge has been so intimately connected with the workings of power, that knowledge can also enrich experience and help us see more. Cultures are also ways of seeing and ways of experiencing. The more cultures we have available to us, the more ways we have of seeing, the richer we are as societies and as individuals.

While this argument could be employed to defend the general principle of cultural diversity, Aboriginal cultures in Canada belong to a specific type of culture that deserve special attention. Aboriginal peoples belonged to gathering and hunting cultures. Unlike the agricultural and industrial cultures that make up most of the rest of the multicultural Canadian framework, there is a qualitative break in the nature of gathering and hunting cultures from the other two. Gatherers and hunters viewed themselves, the world around them, the objects they used, and other people they encountered in drastically different ways which we are only beginning to understand today. A single example can be deployed to illustrate this. The way we view objects, things, is drastically different. People from either agricultural or industrial societies have a cognitive relation of desire to objects. We want things. Even if we are not sure whether or not we can use something, we want it. Our desire exists because of a material precondition: we have a place to put things. So, if we encounter a strange object on the trail, if it at all appeals to us, we collect it and take it home. Most gatherers and hunters have quite a different way of looking at objects. They have a cognitive relation of suspicion. The first thing they are likely to think of on seeing an object is "how much does it weigh?". This is because, as nomadic peoples, any object they possess has to be carried. They are more likely than not to leave behind an object that we would take. Agricultural and industrial societies are accumulative; gatherers and hunters are not. So they "see" objects differently.

Furthermore, the argument about prior occupancy joins with my arguments about the substantive character of gathering and hunting cultures. Canada's First Nations occupied this land, even by the most conservative estimates, for thousands of years before the first city-state societies developed in Eurasia or Africa. While I would argue that Aboriginal people lived no closer to "nature" or "the land" than our own societies (how can anyone live closer to nature when nature is inside of each of us? when every society produces its own concepts of what nature is or is not?) they did, through millennia of occupation, develop special understandings of their homelands and special ways of interacting with land-scapes and resources. Their names of, their thoughts about, their knowledge of this land deserve a respect they have not been accorded. This knowledge has been structured so differently from our own concepts, our own way of concep-tualizing in instrumental rationalities, that we have not been able to appreciate it.

What I am trying to specify here is the difference of Aboriginal difference from other differences. Too often, the phrases "pre-industrial" or "pre-capitalist" or "traditional" are used to cover over the importance of the neolithic break, the rupture between gathering and hunting peoples and agriculturalists. In effect, I am suggesting that gatherers and hunters are more different from industrial and agricultural societies than the other two are from each other. The nature of this difference is frequently elided. Substantively, the values of gatherers and hunters, the way of seeing, the forms of language, are so different and in many ways opposed to our own that we have barely begun to comprehend and the very act of comprehending becomes itself political as it draws us away from ourselves.

*   *   *

IX. Another story comes to mind.

It's October and I'm in Yellowknife to begin the process of consulting over a research project I have in mind. My friend Dorothy asks me to drive her out to her parents' bush camp because her partner has to work that weekend. Our drive takes us out of one reality—that of Yellowknife, capital of contradictions—and into another—a small wall tent, one of many strung out along the north shore of Tucho (Great Slave Lake) where Dogrib families are working on caribou hides brought in by the fall hunt.

I feel like I'm being treated as the guest of honour; fed fresh rabbit and wonderful stories told in Dogrib by Dorothy's father (she translates). I help a bit with bringing in wood; Dorothy's mother is the busiest of us, patiently scraping caribou hides to remove the fat. The mood is all relaxed, easy, com-fortable. In spite of a very cool early winter day, the tent gets quite warm. We shift around, moving away from the drum-barrel stove when it gets too hot, moving closer as it cools, adding wood and moving back again; the rhythm of our movements reflected in the rhythm of our conversation.

Through the whole period of my visit the portable radio phone is on. Occa-sionally we hear other families talking with each other. More often than not, these conversations provoke bursts of laughter in the tent: someone is gossiping, someone else is berating her adult children for not coming out to the camp to help. Radio phones, rifles, power saws, potato chips, soft drinks; all an intimate part of this reality, which remains open to being described by that contradictory yet potent, maddeningly ambiguous though politically charged word: tradi-tional.

When I see Dorothy's parents occasionally in Yellowknife, the situation loses its ease. I get tea for them, smile. Unable to speak their language, I wonder if I'm doing the right things, following the right protocols. But they belong there, too.

* * *

X.

Emmanuel Levinas once indicated that we need rights because we cannot have Justice. Rights, in other words, protect us against the hubris that any current conception of Justice or right is the last word.

DRUCILLA CORNELL (1992a: 167)

It is a truism to suggest that Aboriginal cultures, like western cultures, need not be seen as static or preserved in some pure, untainted way. There is as much of the postmodern as there is of the paleolithic in contemporary Aboriginal communities. The point is that, given how little we know about Aboriginal peoples, they themselves should have a greater measure of control over their destinies. While acknowledging what we don't know, we can also acknowledge that their cultural traditions are not outdated or outmoded remainders of a past way of life and need not be assessed by the ethnocentric and racist standards that were common in the past. Rather, Aboriginal cultural traditions should be respected and appreciated for what they have to offer. The first step is probably to acknowledge how little we understand. This is itself a political gesture, a move to resist the illusion of total understanding that totalization gives itself and carries with it. A version of Aboriginal rights that respects this would allow Aboriginal peoples to be placed in a structural position where they do not have to accept the imposition of dominant values and logics as a pregiven context; where instead they have the ability to negotiate their own trajectory through the historical continuum, to resist the continuing onslaughts of totalization. Aboriginal rights act as a principle from which the position of First Nations in Canadian society may be renegotiated on an ongoing basis. Recognition of Aboriginal rights implies that such negotiations might take place based on the principle of mutual respect rather than the principle of structural dominance. Or, at least, that Aboriginal peoples have some ground upon which they can resist totalization.

We would be wise not to ignore the radicality of this call. Derrida has written that "each advance in politicization obliges one to reconsider, and so reinterpret the very foundations of law such as they had previously been calculated or delimited" (28). The call for a version of Aboriginal rights that resists totalization is a call that challenges the established order; it is a call that demands room for that which is not only different, but in many ways opposed.

* * *

XI. The challenge posed by Aboriginal rights, precisely, is that they force us to re-examine the foundations of law. In a powerful indictment of the way in which western courts have circumscribed Aboriginal rights, James Youngblood Henderson observed that:

> The courts became caretakers of the racism of the late nineteenth and twentieth centuries. Such cowardice incurs an enormous cost. When governments act in a disorderly and lawless way, their courts save face by classifying oppression as justice or confiscation as a political question. Either way, they remove the cause of action from their jurisdiction. Their decisions do not pretend to have any generality or stability, nor can they sensibly speak of fixed entitlements and duties. As a result, Aboriginal people are deprived of the rule of law. (220)

Henderson's critique thus moves in a different direction than my own. He argues, effectively, that the basic principles of western law are sound—specifying in particular the tort and restitution principles, and the contract and property principles (186)—but that they were not applied fairly to Aboriginal peoples. From this basis he indicts the Canadian courts: "In its approach to the rights of native peoples the law becomes tyranny at worst and an ineffective apologist at best. The Canadian governments may call it law, but it is racism. It is not founded on the principles that recognize the supremacy of God and the rule of law" (220).

While this argument has a great deal of force, particularly in understanding the history of the legal devolutions of Aboriginal rights, it also gives a great deal away. The ultimate vision here is not one in which Aboriginal cultures continue to maintain their basic integrity and resist totalization, but rather one in which Aboriginal peoples take their place as property holders within the established order, gaining their fair share. While Aboriginal leaders certainly cannot be faulted, given the often desperate circumstances of the people, for trying to improve the material well-being of Aboriginal communities, we should not confuse these efforts with the greater challenge posed by the being of Aboriginal cultures as distinct cultures to the foundations of the established order.

*   *   *

XII. This book provides an overview of how Aboriginal rights have been framed, understood, and often ignored in the legal forum. Most of the cases reproduced here are from the last few decades, when increasing attention to Aboriginal issues developed as a result of a political and cultural renaissance in Aboriginal affairs. Almost all of these cases deal with the issue of Aboriginal title although three deal with what we might call "citizenship" rights. All but one were decided by the Supreme Court of Canada. The exception was appealed beyond the Supreme Court of Canada to the Judicial Committee of the Privy Council in England, when that possibility for appeal still existed. These are the most frequently cited rulings around Aboriginal rights in Canadian jurisprudence. I have left out the voluminous case load dealing with hunting, fishing, and trapping rights in specific provincial jurisdictions. Although there are important Supreme Court of Canada decisions in these areas, they usually are of primary relevance to specific regions only and there are so many cases that it would be difficult to justify the inclusion of some rather than others.

In editing the cases I have been torn between two impulses. On the one hand, I wanted the cases to be as complete as possible so that the whole argument would be available and readers would be free to decide what parts of it are more important. On the other hand, wanting to produce a single volume that included all the most important cases, I needed to be conscious of the size of the volume. In editing decisions, I used a light hand; I chose to remove some technical aspects of the decision that were not related to Aboriginal rights issues. I also removed the official summaries that begin each case, substituting my own less technical introduction. Finally, where in the same case different Supreme Court Justices cited the same document I often removed the later quotations. In sum, the cases presented here are virtually complete and all deletions are indicated with ellipses.

I began this introduction by referring to Avital Ronell's call for a justice of the future which would show a "will to rupture". This is because there seems to me a danger in the project of defining Aboriginal rights—even where these definitions might involve important material gains for Aboriginal communities—with too much fixity. Such definitions will constrain Aboriginal rights and, like the written version of the treaties, may not serve Aboriginal peoples well in an uncertain future. The will to rupture in this context must be a reminder of the necessary fluidity of Aboriginal rights, of Aboriginal rights as a line of negotiation rather than a specific allowance, exception, or lenience. Aboriginal rights: the mark, within the established order, of what has not been established.

Peterborough, Ont.   PETER KULCHYSKI
November 1993

SOURCES

Boldt, Menno and J. Anthony Long, eds. *The Quest for Justice*. Toronto: University of Toronto Press, 1985.

Clark, Bruce. *Native Liberty, Crown Sovereignty*. Montreal and Kingston: McGill-Queen's University Press, 1990.

Cornell, Drucilla. *The Philosophy of the Limit*. New York: Routledge, 1992a.

———. 'The Philosophy of the Limit: Systems Theory and Feminist Legal Reform' in Drucilla Cornell, Michel Rosenfeld and David Gray Carlson, eds. *Deconstruction and the Possibility of Justice*. New York: Routledge, 1992b.

———, Michel Rosenfeld, and David Gray Carlson, eds. *Deconstruction and the Possibility of Justice*. New York: Routledge, 1992.

Cumming, Peter A. and Neil H. Mickenberg. *Native Rights in Canada*. Toronto: General Publishing, 1980.

Derrida, Jacques. "Force of Law: The 'Mystical Foundation of Authority'" in

Drucilla Cornell, Michel Rosenfeld and David Gray Carlson, eds. *Deconstruction and the Possibility of Justice*. New York: Routledge, 1992.

Henderson, James Youngblood. "The Doctrine of Aboriginal Rights in Western Legal Tradition" in Menno Boldt and J. Anthony Long, eds. *The Quest for Justice*. Toronto: University of Toronto Press, 1985.

Jameson, Fredric. *Postmodernism, or, The Cultural Logic of Late Capitalism*. Durham: Duke University Press, 1991.

———. *The Geopolitical Aesthetic*. Bloomington: Indiana University Press, 1992.

LaCapra, Dominick. *History and Criticism*. Ithaca: Cornell University Press, 1989.

Morse, Bradford, ed. *Aboriginal Peoples and the Law*. Ottawa: Carleton University Press, 1985.

Ronell, Avital. *Crack Wars*. Lincoln: University of Nebraska Press, 1992.

Slattery, Brian. "Understanding Aboriginal Rights," *The Canadian Bar Review* Vol. 66, 1987.

———. "The Hidden Constitution: Aboriginal Rights in Canada" in Menno Boldt and J. Anthony Long, eds. *The Quest for Justice*. Toronto: University of Toronto Press, 1985.

Smith, Derek G., ed. *Canadian Indians and the Law*. Toronto: McClelland and Stewart, 1975.

Woodward, Jack. *Native Law*. Toronto: Carswell, 1989.

CHAPTER 1

St. Catherine's Milling

THE FULL title for this case is St. Catherine's Milling and Lumber Company v. The Queen; it was heard by the Judicial Committee of the Privy Council of the House of Lords on appeal from the Supreme Court of Canada and the decision was rendered in 1888. Until 1949, decisions of the Supreme Court of Canada could be appealed, and frequently were, to the Judicial Committee of the Privy Council. Although this was not technically a Canadian decision (that is to say, not a decision of the Canadian courts) it was a Canadian case and the decision of the Privy Council was binding on Canada. Furthermore, this particular decision involved the most important early Canadian court interpretation of the Royal Proclamation of 1763 and it became a crucial precedent, cited in virtually all of the cases that follow in this book.

The case developed when the federal or dominion government granted the St. Catherine's Milling and Lumber Company a permit to cut lumber on land that had been surrendered to the Crown through Treaty 3, though the land was within the boundary of the province of Ontario. Although, technically speaking, the St. Catherine's Milling and Lumber Company was the defendant, charged by the Ontario government with taking lumber without a valid permit (which had to be issued by provincial authorities in their view), the dominion government intervened and effectively took over the defense of the case. Lawyers for the dominion government advanced the key arguments for the defense.

The reason why this case is of such interest to us in this context is that the basis of the dominion argument was that the Ojibway people who had negotiated Treaty 3 had, prior to the signing of the treaty, held full title to their land and therefore the federal government was effectively purchasing the land outright from its owners through the treaty process. In order to make this argument the dominion had to assert that the Aboriginal title guaranteed by the Royal Proclamation of 1763 was full title to the land. Having purchased the land from the Ojibway, the dominion government was fully within its rights in issuing a lumber permit. The provincial government argued that prior to the treaty the land was Crown land; the treaty served merely to extinguish any outstanding interest in the land that the Ojibway may have had, and the "beneficial interest" in Crown land was passed to the province through the British North America

Act of 1867. Hence only the provincial government had the authority to sell licences and derive revenues from resources on the land.

The Supreme Court of Canada had agreed with the provincial interpretation, so the dominion government sponsored the appeal to the Judicial Committee of the Privy Council. The Committee upheld the decision of the Supreme Court, arguing that "the tenure of the Indians was a personal and usufructuary right, dependent upon the good will of the Sovereign" (27). A usufructuary right involves the right to use something owned by someone else, as long as that use does not destroy the thing or interfere with the rightful ownership. Hence, St. Catherine's Milling determined that Aboriginal title was a "burden" on Crown title, that Crown title was underlying and preceded the signing of treaties, and that Aboriginal title could be granted or taken away by the Crown.

The decision includes the single most extensive early discussion of the Royal Proclamation of 1763, the treaties (focusing on Treaty 3), the British North America Act, and the Indian Act as they pertain to Aboriginal title. Three final points are worth stressing. First, the Judicial Committee relied heavily on precedents from the United States, particularly on the well-known Marshall decisions such as Johnson v. McIntosh (1823); hence the case could also be read as writing Justice Marshall's interpretation of Aboriginal rights and titles into Canadian jurisprudence. Second, the case contains one of the most remarkable statements in the history of Canadian jurisprudence; Lord Watson, discussing the question of the nature of Aboriginal rights conferred by the Royal Proclamation, wrote: "There was a great deal of learned discussion at the Bar with respect to the precise quality of the Indian right, but their Lordships do not consider it necessary to express any opinion upon the point" (27). Third, this case resulted in a decision of extraordinary importance to Canada's Aboriginal peoples, drastically circumscribing the nature of their title to their traditional lands, and, at the broadest levels, affecting the course of Canadian history. Both the balance of federal and provincial powers and the value of unextinguished Aboriginal title (and perhaps ultimately the respect accorded Aboriginal peoples by the Canadian state) hung in the balance. Yet the Ojibway and other First Nations had no legal representation, made no intervention and had no direct role in the proceedings at any level. It is unlikely they were made aware that the case was being prosecuted.

The text of the case begins with dominion (Webster) and defense (McCarthy) counsel arguments for overturning the Supreme Court of Canada decision; Mowat and Blake respond with the province's arguments and Webster replies to these. Lord Watson then delivers the judgment, including a summary of the facts of the case. The substantial arguments in the case are here presented in full; some of the references to other cases have been removed.

P.K.

SIR R.E. WEBSTER, A.G., and MCCARTHY, Q.C., contended that the judgment of the Supreme Court should be reversed. It lay on the respondent to make good the title of the Province to these lands. Previous to the treaty of the 3rd of October, 1873, the lands in suit, and the whole area of which they formed part, were occupied by a tribe of the Ojibbeway Indians, who by the treaty ceded the whole area in manner as therein mentioned to the Government of the Dominion. The provincial Government were no party to this treaty, and it was admitted that no surrender had been made of Indian title except to the Dominion. Reference was made to the British North America Act, 1867, sect. 91, sub-sect. 24, which gives to the Dominion exclusive legislative authority over "Indians and lands reserved for the Indians" as compared with sect. 92, sub-sect. 5, which assigns "the management and sale of public lands belonging to the Province, and of the timber and wood thereon" to the legislative authority of the Province. Also to sects. 109 and 117, and to Attorney-General of Ontario v. Mercer.

Documentary evidence was referred to, to shew the nature and character of the Indian title. It was contended that the effect of it was to shew that from the earliest times the Indians had, and were always recognised as having, a complete proprietary interest, limited by an imperfect power of alienation. British and Canadian legislation was referred to, to shew that such complete title had been uniformly recognised: see Royal Proclamation October 7, 1763, held by Lord Mansfield in Campbell v. Hall to have the same force as a statute, under which the lands in suit were reserved to the Indians in absolute proprietary right; . . . The proclamation in 1763 was uniformly acted on and recognised by the Government as well as the legislature, and was regarded by the Indians as their charter. It was not superseded by the Québec Act (14 Geo. 3, c.83, imperial statute); but it was held by the Supreme Court of the United States to be still in force in 1823: see Johnson v. McIntosh. . . .

The absolute title being in the Indians was ceded by them, subject to certain reservations, for valuable consideration to the Dominion, and the treaty to that effect did not enure to the benefit of the Province in any way. The Province could not claim property in the land except by virtue of the Act of 1867, and as regards that Act the lands did not belong to the Province prior thereto within sect. 109; they were not in 1867 public property which the Province could retain under sect. 117; they were not public lands of the Province within sect. 92, sub-sect. 5.

*   *   *

MOWAT, Q.C., and BLAKE, Q.C., for the respondent, contended that both before and after the treaty of 1873 the title to the lands in suit was in the Crown and not in the Indians. The lands being within the limits of the Province, the beneficial interest therein passed to the Province under the Act of 1867, and the Dominion obtained thereunder no such interest as it claims in this suit. Even if they were lands reserved for the Indians within the meaning of the Act the Dominion gained thereunder only a power of legislating in respect to them, it did not gain ownership or a right to become owner by purchase from the Indians. Under sect. 109, whether reserved to the Indians or not the land goes to the Province subject to any interest on the part of the Indians. See also sect. 108 and sect. 91, sub-sect. 9. With regard to the alleged absolute title of the Indians to which the Dominion is said to have succeeded by treaty, no such title existed on their part either as against the King of France before the conquest or against the Crown of England since the conquest. Their title was in the nature of a personal right of occupation during the pleasure of the Crown, and it was not a legal or an equitable title in the ordinary sense. For instance, the Crown made grants of land in every part of British North America both before and after the proclamation of 1763 without any previous extinguishment of the Indian claim. The grantees in those cases had to deal with the Indian claims, but the legal validity of the grants themselves was undeniably recognised both in the Canadian and the American Courts. As regards that proclamation it was argued that it was not intended to divest, and did not divest, the Crown of its absolute title to the lands, and the reservation, upon which so much argument has been rested, was expressed to last only "for the present and until Our further pleasure be known." Further, as regards the lands now in suit the proclamation was superseded by the Imperial Act of 1774, known as the Québec Act, which added that land to the Province. It was not the intention of that Act to give to the Indians any new right over and above the interest which they possessed under the proclamation, and which was a mere licence terminable at the will of the Crown. With regard to the effect of purchases from the Indians, reference was made to Meigs v. McClung's Lessee and Clark v. Smith.

With regard to the application of the British North American Act and the construction to be placed upon it, it was submitted that that Act should be on all occasions interpreted in a large, liberal, and comprehensive spirit, considering the magnitude of the subjects with which it purports to deal in very few words. The general scheme, purpose, and intent of the Act should be borne in mind. The scheme is to create a federal union consisting of several entities. The purpose was at the same time to preserve the Provinces, not as fractions of a unit, but as units of a multiple. The Provinces are to be on an equal footing. The ownership and development of Crown lands and the revenues therefrom are to be left to the Province in which they are situated. As to legislative powers, it is the residuum which is left to the Dominion; as to proprietary rights, the residuum goes to the Provinces. Where property is intended to go to the Dominion it is specifically granted, even though legislative authority over it may already have been vested in the Dominion. It is contrary to the spirit of the Act to hold that the grant of legislative power over lands reserved for the Indians carries with it by implication a grant of proprietary right.

*   *   *

SIR R.E. WEBSTER, A.G., replied:
Upon the question whether the old province of Canada had any right to the lands in suit at the date of the Act of 1867 which passed thereunder, certain legislative duties had been conferred on the province with regard to Indians, and a certain power of bargaining with regard to Indian lands; but no proprietary right had been given: see 2 Vict. c. 15 (U.C.), which was held to apply to unsurrendered lands in The Queen v. Strong and Little v. Keating. There is a series of statutes which shews that prior to 1867 the Province had nothing but some slight legislative rights over the land: see 3 & 4 Vict. c. 35, s. 54; 12 Vict. c. 9; 13 & 14 Vict. c. 74; Cons. Stat. 22 Vict. (U.C.) c. 81; 23 Vict. c. 61, s. 54. The whole

course of legislation before 1867 was that the proceeds of the Indian lands should be kept for the Indians, and not go to the Province. [Lord Selborne: This is the first suggestion to that effect.] Reference was then made to the later Dominion Acts, 31 Vict. c. 42, ss. 6, 7, 8, 10, 11, especially 24; 39 Vict. c. 18; 43 Vict. c. 18. The Crown lands were dealt with by 23 Vict. c. 2; the Indian lands by 23 Vict. c. 151. Reference was made to Vanvleck v. Stewart; Fegan v. McLean, as shewing that the Indians had the right to cut and sell timber in the special reserves, and appropriate proceeds.

* * *

The judgment of their Lordships was delivered by Lord Watson:

On the 3rd of October, 1873, a formal treaty or contract was concluded between commissioners appointed by the Government of the Dominion of Canada, on behalf of her Majesty the Queen, of the one part, and a number of chiefs and headmen duly chosen to represent the Salteaux tribe of Ojibbeway Indians, of the other part, by which the latter, for certain considerations, released and surrendered to the Government of the Dominion, for Her Majesty and her successors, the whole right and title of the Indian inhabitants whom they represented, to a tract of country upward of 50,000 square miles in extent. By an article of the treaty it is stipulated that, subject to such regulations as may be made by the Dominion Government, the Indians are to have right to pursue their avocations of hunting and fishing throughout the surrendered territory, with the exception of those portions of it which may, from time to time, be required or taken up for settlement, mining, lumbering, or other purposes.

Of the territory thus ceded to the Crown, an area of not less than 32,000 square miles is situated within the boundaries of the province of Ontario; and, with respect to the area, a controversy has arisen between the Dominion and Ontario, each of them maintaining that the legal effect of extinguishing the Indian title has been to transmit to itself the entire beneficial interest of the lands, as now vested in the Crown, freed from incumbrance of any kind, save the qualified privilege of hunting and fishing mentioned in the treaty.

Acting on the assumption that the beneficial interest in these lands had passed to the Dominion Government, their Crown Timber Agent, on the 1st of May 1883, issued to the appellants, the St. Catherine's Milling and Lumber Company, a permit to cut and carry away one million feet of lumber from a specified portion of the disputed area. The appellants having availed themselves of that licence, a writ was filed against them in the Chancery Division of the High Court of Ontario, at the instance of the Queen on the information of the Attorney-General of the Province, praying—(1) a declaration that the appellants have no rights in respect of the timber cut by them upon the lands specified in their permit; (2) an injunction restraining them from trespassing on the premises and from cutting any timber thereon; (3) an injunction against the removal of timber already cut; and (4) decree for the damage occasioned by their wrongful acts. The Chancellor of Ontario, on the 10th of June, 1885, decerned with costs against the appellants, in terms of the first three of these conclusions, and referred the amount of damage to the Master in Ordinary. The judgment of the learned Chancellor was unanimously affirmed on the 20th of April, 1886, by the Court of Appeal for Ontario, and an appeal taken from their decision to the Supreme Court of Canada was dismissed on the 20th of June, 1887, by a majority of four of the six judges constituting the court.

Although the present case relates exclusively to the right of the Government of Canada to dispose of the timber in question to the appellant company, yet its decision necessarily involves the determination of the larger question between that government and the province of Ontario with respect to the legal consequences of the treaty of 1873. In these circumstances, her Majesty, by the same order which gave the appellants leave to bring the judgment of the court below under the review of this Board, was pleased to direct that the Government of the Dominion of Canada should be at liberty to intervene in this appeal, or to argue the same upon a special case raising the legal question in dispute. The Dominion Government elected to take the first of these courses, and their Lordships have had the advantage of hearing from their counsel an able and exhaustive argument in support of their claim to that part of the ceded territory which lies within the provincial boundaries of Ontario.

The capture of Québec in 1759, and the capitulation of Montreal in 1760, were followed in 1763 by the cession to Great Britain of Canada and all its dependencies, with the sovereignty, property, and possession, and all other rights which had at any previous time been held or acquired by the Crown of France. A royal proclamation was issued on the 7th of October, 1763, shortly after the date of the Treaty of Paris, by which His Majesty King George erected four distinct and separate Governments, styled respectively, Québec, East Florida, West Florida, and Grenada, specific boundaries being assigned to each of them. Upon the narrative that it was just and reasonable that the several nations and tribes of Indians who lived under British protection should not be molested or disturbed in the "possession of such parts of Our dominions and territories as, not having been ceded to or purchased by us, are reserved to them or any of them as their hunting grounds," it is declared that no governor or commander-in-chief in any of the new colonies of Québec, East Florida, or West Florida, do presume on any pretence to the bounds of their respective governments, or "until Our further pleasure be known," upon any lands whatever which, not having been ceded or purchased as aforesaid, are reserved to the said Indians or any of them. It was further declared "to be Our Royal will, for the present, as aforesaid, to reserve under Our sovereignty, protection, and dominion, for the use of the said Indians, all the land and territories not included within the limits of Our said three new Governments, or within the limits of the territory grant to the Hudson's Bay Company." The proclamation also enacts that no private person shall make any purchase from the Indians of lands reserved to them within those colonies where settlement was permitted, and that all purchases must be on behalf of the Crown, in a public assembly of the Indians, by the governor or commander-in-chief of the colony in which the lands lie.

The territory in dispute has been in Indian occupation from the date of the proclamation until 1873. During that interval of time Indian affairs have been administered successively by the Crown, by the Provincial Governments, and (since the passing of the British North America Act, 1867), by the Government of the Dominion. The policy of these administrations has been all along the same in this respect, that the Indian inhabitants have been precluded from entering into any transaction with a subject for the sale or transfer of their interest in the land, and have only been permitted to surrender their rights to the Crown by a formal contract, duly ratified in a meeting of their chiefs or head men convened for the purpose. Whilst there have been changes in the administrative authority, there has been no change since the year 1763 in the character of the interest which its Indian inhabitants had in the lands surrendered by the treaty. Their possession, such as it was, can only be ascribed to the general provisions made by the royal proclamation in favour of all Indian tribes then living under the sovereignty and protection of the British Crown. It was suggested in the course of the argument for the Dominion, that inasmuch as the proclamation recites that the territories thereby reserved for Indians had never "been ceded to or purchased by" the Crown, the entire property of the land remained with them. That inference is, however, at variance with the terms of the instrument, which shew that the tenure of the Indians was a personal and usufructuary right, dependent upon the good will of the Sovereign. The lands reserved are expressly stated to be "parts of Our dominions and territories"; and it is declared to be the will and pleasure of the sovereign that, "for the present," they shall be reserved for the use of the Indians, as their hunting grounds, under his protection and dominion. There was a great deal of learned discussion at the Bar with respect to the precise quality of the Indian right, but their Lordships do not consider it necessary to express any opinion upon the point. It appears to them to be sufficient for the purposes of this case that there has been all along vested in the Crown a substantial and paramount estate, underlying the Indian title, which became a plenum dominium whenever that title was surrendered or otherwise extinguished.

By an Imperial statute passed in the year 1840 (3 & 4 Vict. c. 35), the provinces of Ontario and Québec, then known as Upper and Lower Canada, were united under the name of the Province of Canada, and it was, inter alia, enacted that, in consideration of certain annual payments which Her Majesty had agreed to accept by way of civil list, the produce of all territorial and other revenues at the disposal of the Crown arising in either of the united Provinces should be paid into the consolidated fund of the new Province. There was no transfer to the Province of any legal estate in the Crown lands, which continued to be vested in the Sovereign; but all moneys realized by sales or in any other manner became the property of the Province. In other words, all beneficial interest in such lands within the provincial boundaries belonging to the Queen, and either producing or capable of producing revenue, passed to the Province, the title still remaining in the Crown. That continued to be the right of the Province until the passing of the British North America Act, 1867. Had the Indian inhabitants of the area in question released their interest in it to the Crown at any time between 1840 and the date of that Act, it does not seem to admit of doubt, and it was not disputed by the learned counsel for the Dominion, that all revenues derived from its being taken up for settlement, mining, lumbering, and other purposes would have been the property of the Province of Canada. The case maintained for the appellants is that the Act of 1867 transferred to the Dominion all interest in Indian lands which previously belonged to the Province.

The Act of 1867, which created the Federal Government, repealed the Act of 1840, and restored the Upper and Lower Canadas to the condition of separate Provinces, under the titles of Ontario and Québec, due provision being made (sect. 142) for the division between them of the property and assets of the United Province, with the exception of certain items specified in the fourth schedule, which are still held by them jointly. The Act also contains careful provisions for the distribution of legislative powers and of revenues and assets between the respective Provinces included in the Union, on the one hand, and the Dominion, on the other. The conflicting claims to the ceded territory maintained by the Dominion and the Province of Ontario are wholly dependent upon these statutory provisions. In construing these enactments, it must always be kept in view that, wherever public land with its incidents is described as "the property of" or as "belonging to" the Dominion or a Province, these expressions merely import that the right to its beneficial use, or to its proceeds, has been appropriated to the Dominion or the Province, as the case may be, and is subject to the control of its legislature, the land itself being vested in the Crown.

Sect. 108 enacts that the public works and undertakings enumerated in Schedule 3 shall be the property of Canada. As specified in the schedule, these consist of public undertakings which might be fairly considered to exist for the benefit of all the Provinces federally united, of lands and buildings necessary for carrying on the customs or postal service of the Dominion, or required for the purpose of national defence, and of "lands set apart for general public purposes." It is obvious that the enumeration cannot be reasonably held to include Crown lands which are reserved for Indian use. The only other clause in the Act by which a share of what previously constituted provincial revenues and assets is directly assigned to the Dominion is sect. 102. It enacts that all "duties and revenues" over which the respective legislatures of the United Provinces had and have power of appropriation, "except such portions thereof as are by this Act reserved to the respective legislatures of the Provinces, or are raised by them in accordance with the special powers conferred upon them by this Act," shall form one consolidated fund, to be appropriated for the public service of Canada. The extent to which duties and revenues arising within the limits of Ontario, and over which the legislature of the old Province of Canada possessed the power of appropriation before the passing of the Act, have been transferred to the Dominion by this clause, can only be ascertained by reference to the two exceptions which it makes in favour of the new provincial legislatures.

The second of these exceptions has really no bearing on the present case, because it comprises nothing beyond the revenues which provincial legislatures are empowered to raise by means of direct taxation for Provincial purposes, in terms of sect. 92(2). The first of them, which appears to comprehend the whole sources of revenue reserved to the provinces, by sect. 109, is of material consequence. Sect. 109 provides that "all lands, mines, minerals, and royalties belonging to the several Provinces of Canada, Nova Scotia, and New Brunswick, in which the same are situate or arise, subject to any trusts existing in respect thereof, and to any interest other than that of the Province in the same." In connection with this clause it may be observed that, by sect. 117, it is declared that the Provinces shall retain their respective public property not otherwise disposed of in the Act, subject to the right of Canada to assume any lands or public property required for fortifications or for the defence of the country. A different form of expression is used to define the subject-matter of the first exception, and the property which is directly appropriated to the Provinces; but it hardly admits of doubt that the interests in land, mines, minerals, and royalties, which by sect. 109 are declared to belong to the Provinces, included, if they are not identical with, the "duties and revenues" first excepted in sect. 102.

The enactments of sect. 109 are, in the opinion of their Lordships, sufficient to give to each Province, subject to the administration and control of its own Legislature, the entire beneficial interest of the Crown in all lands within its boundaries, which at the time of the union were vested in the Crown, with the exception of such lands as the Dominion acquired right to under sect. 108, or might assume for the purposes specified in sect. 117. Its legal effect is to exclude from the "duties and revenues" appropriated to the Dominion, all the ordinary territorial revenues of the Crown arising within the Provinces. That construction of the statute was accepted by this Board in deciding Attorney General of Ontario v. Mercer, where the controversy related to land granted in fee simple to a subject before 1867, which became escheat to the Crown in the year 1871. The Lord Chancellor (Earl Selborne) in delivering judgment in that case, said: It was not disputed, in the argument for the Dominion at the bar, that all territorial revenues arising within each Province from "lands" (in which term must be comprehended all estates in land), which at the time of the union belonged to the Crown, were reserved to the respective Provinces by sect. 109; and it was admitted that no distinction could, in that respect, be made between lands then ungranted, and lands which had previously reverted to the Crown by escheat. But it was insisted that a line was drawn at the date of the union, and that the words were not sufficient to reserve any lands afterwards escheated which at the time of the union were in private hands, and did not then belong to the Crown. Their Lordships indicated an opinion to the effect that the escheat would not, in the special circumstances of that case, have passed to the Province as "lands"; but they held that it fell within the class of rights reserved to the Provinces as "royalties" by sect. 109.

Had its Indian inhabitants been the owners in fee simple of the territory which they surrendered by the treaty of 1873, Attorney-General of Ontario v. Mercer might have been an authority for holding that the Province of Ontario could derive no benefit from the cession, in respect that the land was not vested in the Crown at the time of the union. But that was not the character of the Indian interest. The Crown has all along had a present propriety estate in the land, upon which the Indian title was a mere burden. The ceded territory was at the time of the union, land vested in the Crown, subject to "an interest other than that of the Province in the same," within the meaning of sect. 109; and must now belong to Ontario in terms of that clause, unless its rights have been taken away by some provision of the Act of 1867 other than those already noticed.

In the course of the argument the claim of the Dominion to the ceded territory was rested upon the provisions of sect. 91 (24), which in express terms confer upon the Parliament of Canada power to make laws for "Indians, and the lands reserved for the Indians." It was urged that the exclusive power of legislation and administration carried with it, by necessary implication, any patrimonial interest which the Crown might have had in the reserve lands. In reply to that reasoning, counsel for Ontario referred us to a series of provincial statutes prior in date to the Act of 1867, for the purpose of shewing that the expression "Indian reserves" was used in legislative language to designate certain lands in which the Indians had, after the royal proclamation of 1763, acquired a special interest, by treaty or otherwise, and did not apply to land occupied by them in virtue of the proclamation. The argument might have deserved consideration if the expression had been adopted by the British Parliament in 1867, but it does not occur in sect. 91 (24), and the words actually used are, according to natural meaning, sufficient to include all lands reserved, upon any terms or conditions, for Indian occupation. It appears to be the plain policy of the Act that, in order to ensure uniformity of administration, all such lands, and Indian affairs generally, shall be under the legislative control of one central authority.

Their Lordships are, however, unable to assent to the argument for the Dominion founded on sect. 91 (24). There can be no a priori probability that the British Legislature, in a branch of the statute which professes to deal only with the distribution of legislative power, intended to deprive the Provinces of rights which are expressly given them in that branch of it which relates to the distribution of revenues and assets. The fact that the power of legislating for Indians, and for lands which are reserved to their use, has been entrusted to the Parliament of the Dominion is not in the least degree inconsistent with the right of the Provinces to a beneficial interest in these lands, available to them as a source of revenue whenever the estate of the Crown is disencumbered of the Indian title.

By the treaty of 1873 the Indian inhabitants ceded and released the territory in dispute, in order that it might be opened up for settlement, immigration, and such other purpose as to Her Majesty might seem fit, "to the Government of the Dominion of Canada," for the Queen and Her successors forever. It was argued that a cession in these terms was in effect a conveyance to the Dominion Government of the whole rights of the Indians, with consent of the Crown. That is not the natural import of the language of the treaty, which purports to be from beginning to end a transaction between the Indians and the Crown; and the surrender is in substance made to the Crown. Even if its language had been more favourable to the argument of the Dominion upon this point, it is abundantly clear that the commissioners who represented Her Majesty, whilst they had full authority to accept a surrender to the Crown, had neither authority nor power to take away from Ontario the interest which had been assigned to that province by the Imperial Statute of 1867.

These considerations appear to their Lordships to be sufficient for the disposal of this appeal. The treaty leaves the Indians no right whatever to the timber growing upon the lands which they gave up, which is now fully vested in the Crown, all revenues derivable from the sale of such portions of it as are situate within the boundaries of Ontario being the property of that Province. The fact, that it still possesses exclusive power to regulate the Indians' privilege of hunting and fishing, cannot confer upon the Dominion power to dispose, by issuing permits or otherwise, of that beneficial interest in the timber which has now passed to Ontario. Seeing that the benefit of the surrender accrues to her, Ontario must, of course, relieve the Crown, and the Dominion, of all obligations involving the payment of money which were undertaken by Her Majesty, and which are said to have been in part fulfilled by the Dominion Government. There may be other questions behind, with respect to the right to determine to what extent, and at what periods, the disputed territory, over which the Indians still exercise their avocations of hunting and fishing, is to be taken up for settlement or other purposes, but none of these questions are raised for decision in the present suit.

Their Lordships will therefore humbly advise Her Majesty that the judgment of the Supreme Court of Canada ought to be affirmed, and the appeal dismissed. It appears to them that there ought to be no costs for the appeal.

CHAPTER 2

Re: Eskimos

THIS CASE is cited as Re: Eskimos, S.C.C. (1939). The case arose as a result of a dispute between the government of Québec and the federal (or dominion) government. At issue was the question of relief payments to Inuit in northern Québec. Through the 1920s the Canadian government had been administering relief supplies to Inuit in northern Québec and then billing the Québec government for the costs. Québec willingly paid those bills until, undoubtedly under the influence of the Depression, Premier Taschereau started to question the practice. In the early 1930s the government of Québec argued that Inuit (then called Eskimos) were "Indians" within the meaning of section 91 (24) of the British North America Act (1867), which said that "Indians and lands reserved for Indians" were a federal responsibility. The government of Canada claimed instead that Inuit were not "Indians" but rather ordinary citizens, and therefore relief was a provincial responsibility. In effect, each level of government attempted to get the other to accept jurisdiction over Inuit.

The case was finally referred to the Supreme Court of Canada in 1937. The court was asked to respond to the following question: "Does the term 'Indians' as used in Head 24 of s. 91 of the B.N.A. Act, 1867, include Eskimo inhabitants of the Province of Québec?" The court answered the question in the affirmative, effectively determining that Inuit were a federal responsibility. Of the cases included herein, this is the least cited and has largely been ignored in subsequent Aboriginal rights jurisprudence. In fact, the editors of the *Dominion Law Review*, in publishing the case, felt bound to say the following: "EDITORIAL NOTE: From a legal point of view the chief interest in this case is the process by which the Supreme Court derived the intention of Parliament."

The case deserves more serious attention. Canadian Inuit will be interested in the case, which determined their legal status within the Canadian federation. Indeed, it can be argued that Inuit Aboriginal rights themselves might have been in question had the case been decided the other way. The reasons for the decision, particularly those offered by Lyman Duff, stressed not simply jurisdictional authority but also responsibility. In effect, the policy goals of the Royal Proclamation of 1763—particularly protection—were found to apply to Inuit. Furthermore, Duff's discussion of the relevance of the Proclamation itself is not unimportant to those interested in the question of its geographic jurisdiction.

The decision was handed down on 5 April 1939. The case was heard by the Supreme Court of Canada, consisting of Duff C.J.C., Cannon, Crocket, Davis, Kerwin and Hudson JJ. The lawyers for Canada were J. McGregor Stewart and C.P. Plaxton; for Québec A. Desilets and C.A. Seguin. The decision was unanimous. There was some discussion on the federal side of appealing to the Judicial Committee of the Privy Council in London, but the war intervened. The end of the war led to further delays, as the federal legal team was no longer in place. In 1949 the Supreme Court of Canada became the highest arbiter in the country, and an appeal became impossible. Like St. Catherine's Milling, this case, which involved the legal status of Inuit Canadians, was notable for the absence of direct Inuit testimony and representation. The case is presented in full, with the slight omission of some quotation marks from block quotes.

P.K.

SIR LYMAN P. DUFF C.J.C.: The reference with which we are concerned arises out of a controversy between the Dominion and the Province of Québec touching the question whether the Eskimo inhabitants of that Province are "Indians" within the contemplation of head no. 24 of s. 91 of the B.N.A. Act which is in these words, "Indians and Lands Reserved for Indians"; and under the reference we are to pronounce upon that question. Among the inhabitants of the three Provinces, Nova Scotia, New Brunswick and Canada that, by the immediate operation of the B.N.A. Act became subject to the constitutional enactments of that statute there were few, if any, Eskimo. But the B.N.A. Act contemplated the eventual admission into the Union of other parts of British North America as is explicitly declared in the preamble and for which provision is made by s. 146 thereof. The Eskimo population of Québec, with which we are now concerned, inhabits (in the northern part of the Province) a territory that in 1867 formed part of Rupert's Land; and the question we have to determine is whether these Eskimo, whose ancestors were aborigines of Rupert's Land in 1867 and at the time of its annexation to Canada, are Indians in the sense mentioned.

In 1867 the Eskimo population of what is now Canada, then between four and five thousand in number, occupied, as at the present time, the northern littoral of the continent from Alaska to, and including part of, the Labrador coast within the territories under the control of the Hudson's Bay Co., that is to say, in Rupert's Land and the North-Western Territory which, under the authority given by s. 146 of the B.N.A. Act were acquired by Canada in 1871. In addition to these Eskimo in Rupert's Land and the North-Western Territory, there were some hundreds of them on that part of the coast of Labrador (east of Hudson Strait) which formed part of, and was subject to the Government of, Newfoundland. The B.N.A. Act is a statute dealing with British North America, and, in determining the meaning of the word "Indians" in the statute, we have to consider the meaning of that term as applied to the inhabitants of British North America. In 1867 more than half of the Indian population of British North America were within the boundaries of Rupert's Land and the North-Western Territory; and of the Eskimo population nearly 90% were within those boundaries. It is, therefore, important to consult the reliable sources of information as to the usage of the term "Indian" in relation to the Eskimo in those territories. Fortunately, there is evidence of the most authoritative character furnished by the Hudson's Bay Co. itself.

It will be recalled that the Hudson's Bay Co., besides being a trading company, possessed considerable powers of government and administration. Some years before the passing of the B.N.A. Act complaints having been made as to the manner in which these responsibilities had been discharged, a committee of the House of Commons in 1856 and 1857 investigated the affairs of the company. Among the matters which naturally engaged the attention of the Committee was the company's relations with and conduct towards the aborigines; and for the information of the Committee a census was prepared and produced before it by the officers of the company showing the Indian populations under its rule throughout the whole of the North American continent. This census was accompanied by a map showing the "location" of the various tribes and was included in the Report of the Committee; and was made an appendix to the Committee's Report which was printed and published by the order of the House of Commons. It is indisputable that in the census and in the map the "Esquimaux" fall under the general designation "Indians" and that, indeed, in these documents, "Indians" is used as synonymous with "aborigines." The map bears this description, "An Aboriginal Map of North America denoting the boundaries and locations of various Indian Tribes." Among these "Indian Tribes" the Eskimo are shown inhabiting the northern littoral of the continent from Labrador to Russian America. In the margin of the map are tables. Two are of great significance. The first of these is headed "Statement of the Indian Tribes of the Hudson's Bay Territories." The tribes "East of the Rocky Mountains" are given as "Blackfeet and Sioux groups comprising eight tribes, Algonquins comprising twelve tribes" and "Esquimaux."

The second is headed "Indian Nations once dwelling East of the Mississippi." The list is as follows:

Algonquin	Uchee (extinct)	Kolooch
Dahcotah or Sioux	Natches (extinct)	Athabascan
Huron Iroquois	Mobilian	Sioux
Catawba (extinct)	Esquimaux	Iroquois
Cherokee		

The census concludes with a summary which is in these words: The Indian Races shown in detail in the foregoing census may be classified as follows:

Thickwood Indians on the east side of the Rocky Mountains	35,000
The Plain Tribes (Blackfeet, etc.)	25,000
The Esquimaux	4,000
Indians settled in Canada	3,000
Indian in British Oregon and on the North West Coast	80,000
Total Indians	147,000
Whites and half-breeds in Hudson's Bay Territory	11,000
Souls	158,000

As already observed, the appointment of the Committee was due in part at all events to representations made to the Imperial Government respecting the conduct of the Hudson's Bay Co. towards the Indians and the condition of the Indian population was one of the subjects with which the Committee was principally concerned. They were also concerned with representations made by the Government of Canada urging the desirability of transferring to Canada all the territories of the company, at least as far west as the Rocky Mountains. Chief Justice Draper was present at the sittings of the Committee representing the Government of Canada. The Committee, as is well known, reported in favour of the cession to Canada of the districts of the Red River and the Saskatchewan River.

Seven years later, the scheme of Confederation, propounded in the Québec Resolutions of October 10, 1864, included a declaration that provision should be made "for the admission into the Union on equitable terms of Newfoundland, the North-West Territory, British Columbia, and Vancouver." This declaration was renewed in the Resolutions of the London Conference in December, 1866, and in the B.N.A. Act specific provision was made, as we have seen, in s. 146 for the acquisition of Rupert's Land as well as the North-West Territory and, in 1868, a statute of the Imperial Parliament conferred upon the Queen the necessary powers as respects Rupert's Land.

The B.N.A. Act came into force on July 1, 1867, and, in December of that year, a joint address to Her Majesty was voted by the Senate and House of Commons of Canada praying that authority might be granted to the Parliament of Canada to legislate for the future welfare and good government of these regions and expressing the willingness of Parliament to assume the duties and obligations of government and legislation as regards those territories. In the Resolution of the Senate expressing the willingness of that body to concur in the joint address is this paragraph: "Resolved that upon the transference of the Territories in question to the Canadian Government, it will be the duty of the Government to make adequate provisions for the protection of the Indian Tribes, whose interest and well being are involved in the transfer."

By Order-in-Council of June 23, 1870, it was ordered that from and after July 15, 1870, the North-West Territory and Rupert's Land should be admitted into, and become part of, the Dominion of Canada and that, from that date, the Parliament of Canada should have full power and authority to legislate for the future welfare and good government of the territory. As regards Rupert's Land, such authority had already been conferred upon the Parliament of Canada by s. 5 of the Rupert's Land Act of 1868.

The vast territories which by these transactions became part of the Dominion of Canada and were brought under the jurisdiction of the Parliament of Canada were inhabited largely, indeed almost entirely, by aborigines. It appears to me to be a consideration of great weight in determining the meaning of the word "Indians" in the B.N.A. Act that, as we have seen, the Eskimo were recognized as an Indian tribe by the officials of the Hudson's Bay Co. which, in 1867, as already observed, exercised powers of government and administration over this great tract; and that, moreover, this employment of the term "Indians" is evidenced in a most unequivocal way by documents prepared by those officials and produced before the Select Committee of the House of Commons which were included in the Report of that Committee which, again, as already mentioned, was printed and published by the order of the House. It is quite clear from the material before us that this Report was the principal source of information as regards the aborigines in those territories until some years after Confederation.

I turn now to the Eskimo inhabiting the coast of Labrador beyond the confines of the Hudson's Bay territories and within the boundaries and under the Government of Newfoundland. As regards these, the evidence appears to be conclusive that, for a period beginning about 1760 and extending down to a time subsequent to the passing of the B.N.A. Act, they were by governors, commanders-in-chief of the fleet and other naval officers, ecclesiastics, missionaries and traders who came into contact with them, known and classified as Indians.

First of the official documents. In 1762, General Murray, then Governor of Québec, who afterwards became first Governor of Canada, in an official report of the state of the Government of Québec deals under the sixth heading with "Indian nations residing within the government." He introduces the discussion with this sentence: "In order to discuss this point more clearly I shall first take notice of the Savages on the North shore of the River St. Lawrence from the Ocean upwards, and then of such as inhabit the South side of the same River, as far as the present limits of the Government extend on either side of it."

In the first and second paragraphs he deals with the "Savages" on the North Shore and he says: "The first to be met with on this are the Esquimaux." In the second paragraph he deals with the Montagnais who inhabited a "vast tract" of country from Labrador to the Saguenay.

It is clear that here the Eskimo are classified under the generic term Indian. They are called "Savages," it is true, but so are the Montagnais and so also the Hurons settled at Jeune Lorette. It is useful to note that he speaks in the first paragraph of the Esquimaux as "the wildest and most untamable of any" and mentions that they are "emphatically styled by the other Nations, Savages."

Then there are two reports to His Majesty by the Lords of Trade. The first, dated June 8, 1763, discusses the trade carried on by the French on the coast of Labrador. It is said that they carried on "an extensive trade with the Esquimaux Indians in Oyl, Furs, & ca. [sic] (in which they allowed Your Majesty's Subjects no Share)."

In the second, dated April 16, 1765, in dealing with complaints on the part of the Court of France respecting the French fishery on the coast of Newfoundland and in the Gulf of St. Lawrence, their observations on these complaints are based upon information furnished by Commodore Palliser who had been entrusted with the superintendency of the Newfoundland fishery and the Government of the island. In this report, this sentence occurs: "The sixth and last head of complaint contained in the French Ambassador's letter is, that a captain of a certain French vessel was forbid by your Majesty's Governor from having commerce with the Esquimaux Indians"; and upon that it is observed that the Governor "is to be commended for having forbid the subjects of France to trade or treat with these Indians." "These Indians" are spoken of as inhabitants ". . . who are under the protection of and dependent upon your Majesty."

Then there is a series of proclamations by successive Governors and Commanders-in-Chief in Newfoundland, the first of which was that of Sir Hugh Palliser of July 1, 1764. The proclamation recites, ". . . Advantages would arise to His Majesty's Trading Subjects if a Friendly Intercourse could be Established with the Esquimaux Indians, Inhabiting the Coast of Labrador. . ." and that the Government "has taken measures for bringing about a friendly communication between the said Indians and His Majesty's subjects." All His Majesty's subjects are strictly enjoined "to treat them in the most civil and friendly manner."

The next is a Proclamation by the same governor dated April 8, 1765, which recites the desirability of "friendly intercourse with the Indians on the Coast of Labrador" and that "attempts hitherto made for that purpose have proved ineffectual, especially with the Esquimaux in the Northern Ports without the Straits of Belle Isle" and strictly enjoins and requires "all his Majesty's subjects who meet with any of the said Indians to treat them in a most civil and friendly manner."

On April 10, 1772, Governor Shuldham in a Proclamation of that date requires "all His Majesty's subjects coming upon the coast of Labrador to act towards the Esquimaux Indians in a manner agreeable to the Proclamation issued at St. John's the 8th day of July 1769 respecting the savages inhabiting the coast of Labrador." In this Proclamation it should be noted that "Esquimaux savages" and "Esquimaux Indians" are used as convertible expressions.

In 1774, the boundaries of Québec were extended, and the northeastern coast of Labrador and the Eskimo population therein came under the jurisdiction of the governor of Québec and remained so until 1809. Nevertheless, the Governor and Commander-in-Chief of Newfoundland, who at the date was Admiral Edwards, acting under the authority of that Order in Council of March 9, 1774, took measures to protect the missionaries of the Unitas Fratrum and their settlements on the coast of Labrador from molestation or disturbance and, on May 14, 1779, Admiral Edwards issued a Proclamation requiring "all his Majesty's subjects coming upon the Coast of Labrador to act towards the Esquimaux Indians justly, humanely and agreeably to these laws, by which His Majesty's subjects are bound." Here again it is to be observed that the word "savages" and "Indians" are used as equivalents.

A further Proclamation by Admiral Edwards on January 30, 1781, employs the same phrases, the Eskimo being described as "Esquimaux savages" and as "Esquimaux Indians."

On May 15, 1774, Governor Campbell, as Governor and Commander-in-chief, issued a Proclamation in terms identical with that of 1781.

On December 3, 1821, a Proclamation was issued by Governor Hamilton as Governor and Commander-in-Chief of Newfoundland (now again including the Labrador coast) relating to a "fourth settlement" by the Moravian missionaries requiring all His Majesty's subjects "to act towards the missionaries and the Esquimaux Indians justly and humanely."

There are other official documents. In a report in 1798 by Captain Crofton, addressed to Admiral Waldegrave, Governor and Commander-in-Chief of Newfoundland, the phrase "Esquimaux Indians" occurs several times and the Eskimo are plainly treated as coming under the designation "Indians." A report to Lord Dorchester, Governor and Commander-in-Chief of Québec, Nova Scotia, New Brunswick and their dependencies, in 1788, upon an application by George Cartwright for a grant of land at Touktoke Bay on the coast of Labrador by a special Committee of the Council appointed to consider the same refers to the applicant's exertions in "securing friendly intercourse with the Esquimaux Indians and his success in bringing about a friendly intercourse between that nation and the Mountaineers."

Evidence as to subsequent official usage is adduced in a letter of 1824 from the Advocate General of Canada to the Assistant Civil Secretary on some matter of a criminal prosecution in which "Esquimaux Indians" are concerned; and in a report of 1869 by Judge Pinsent of the Court of Labrador to the Governor of Newfoundland in which this sentence occurs: "In this number about 300 Indians and half-breeds of the Esquimaux and Mountaineer races are included."

Reports from missionaries and clergymen are significant. I refer particularly to two. There is a communication in 1821 by the Unitas Fratrum sent to Admiral Hamilton, Governor and Commander-in-Chief of Newfoundland and Labrador, on a visit by H.M.S. "Clinker" to their settlements. In this the Eskimo are mentioned as "Eskimaux Indians" and "Esquimaux Tribes" and the report concludes with a table giving the numbers of "Esquimaux Indians who have embraced the Christian religion" at the various stations.

In 1849, a report from the Bishop of Newfoundland was printed and published in London for the Society for the Propagation of the Gospel by the Bishop of London with a prefatory letter and seems to have been put into circulation through Rivingtons and other booksellers. Extracts from this report, which describes a visit to Labrador, are produced in the Québec case, and as these passages exemplify in a remarkable way the use of the term Indian, as designating the Eskimo inhabitants of Labrador as well as other classes of Indians there, it is right, I think, to reproduce them in full:

> p. 17.—At St. Francis Harbour, where we next stopped, we celebrated the Lord's Supper, as there were several members of the Church from Newfoundland fishing in the neighbourhood; and the agent and his lady also communicated, (Mr. and Mrs. Saunders). Several Esquimaux Indians were here admitted into the Church, and married. One of them afterwards accompanied us as pilot to Sandwich Bay.
>
> I was obliged very reluctantly to leave the Church ship at St. Francis Harbour (the wind blowing in), and proceeded in a boat twenty-five miles to the Venison Islands, where I remained three days on shore, before the Hank could join us, and, with Mr. Hoyles, was very kindly entertained by Mr. Howe, Messrs. Slade's agent. Here all the females are either Esquimaux or mountaineer Indians, or descended from them. With the exception of Mrs. Saunders, there is not an Englishwomen on the coast, from Battle Harbour to Sandwich Bay; all, or nearly all, are Indians (Esquimaux or mountaineer), or half Indians, and of course the children are the same mixed race.
>
> p. 40.—Wednesday, August 2.—The wind blew so strong last night, with heavy rain, that our captain, who was on shore, could not return to the ship. I had intended to proceed this morning, but, partly on account of the high sea, and partly because there was yet work to be done here, I was persuaded to delay my departure. I went on shore with my Chaplains after breakfast; and while I remained at the house of Mr. Ellis, the merchant of Newfoundland, they visited an Englishman, who was married, or united,

to a poor Indian woman, an Esquimaux, and who we understood, had children to be baptized. . .

p. 49.—Mr. Bendle also informed us of the character &c., of the Indians who dwell in or resort to his neighbourhood. There are three distinct tribes—the Micmacs, Mountaineers and Esquimaux. The first two are generally Roman Catholics, but the Esquimaux owe their instruction and conversion to the Moravian Missionaries. These Missionaries (on the Labrador coast) have four stations and establishments, the nearest about 400 miles to the north of Battle Harbour, and the most distant nearly 400 miles farther, or 800 miles from this place. There are three families of the Moravians at each of their Stations, who live together in a stone house, and have large trading concerns in fish, &c., with the Esquimaux. . . .

p. 63.—Tuesday, August 15.—The wind came round again to the westward this morning, but was very light. We got under way at ten o'clock, and did not reach the Seal Islands till five. Mr. Howe kindly furnished a pilot. Here, as in every other harbour, are several vessels from Newfoundland. Messrs. Hunt also keep a small crew here; that is, a few men dwelling together to prosecute the fishery in the summer and kill seals in the winter. Five Englishmen remained together here last winter, who killed 500 seals. In the first three months of the year they are in the woods, to cut timber and firewood. Besides this crew, the only residents are Indians (Esquimaux) and half Indians, who live together, crowded in two huts, with an Englishman who has taken one of the half Indian women as his wife. Guided by the skipper of Mr. Hunt's crew, we visited these Indians. Nearly all (twenty out of twenty-three) crowded together in one small hut, with our two guides, Messrs. Harvey and Hoyles, and myself. A strange group, or crowd, we were. Indians will compress into the smallest possible compass; but still we were brought into painfully close proximity. . . .

p. 68.—A few years ago the Esquimaux woman, generally wore a cloak, or cape, of seal-skin, with the hair outwards, the tail hanging down behind, and the flippers on their arms; but now all rejoice in European dresses, shawls and gowns of many colours. The only remains of Indian dress is the sealskin boot, which even the smallest children wear; it is of great use in the snow, being quite impervious to wet. In the race of mixed blood, or Anglo-Esquimaux, the Indian characteristics very much disappear, and the children are both lively and comely.

p. 69.—The afternoon service commenced soon after three o'clock, and was not concluded till seven o'clock, in consequence of the number to be christened and added to the Church. I admitted six adults myself, who were able to answer for themselves; three were Esquimaux. All made the proper answers correctly and seriously, and not the least so the poor Indians.

Having regard to the well established usage of designating the Esquimaux of Labrador as Indians or Esquimaux Indians, evidenced by the Proclamations of the Governors of Newfoundland, and other official and unofficial documents, one finds little difficulty in appreciating the significance of the phraseology of the correspondence, in 1879, between Sir John A. Macdonald and Sir Hector Langevin on the subject of the Eskimo on the north shore of the St. Lawrence.

The phrase "Esquimaux Indians" is employed in this correspondence as it had been employed for a hundred years in official and other documents to designate the Labrador Esquimaux. In 1882, three years after the date of this correspondence, the sale of intoxicating liquors to "Esquimaux Indians" was prohibited by an Act of the Legislature of Newfoundland.

Newfoundland, including the territory inhabited by these Labrador Eskimo was, as already pointed out, one of the British North American Colonies the union of which with Canada was contemplated by the B.N.A. Act. Thus it appears that, through all the territories of British North America in which there were Eskimo, the term "Indian" was employed by well established usage as including these as well as the other aborigines; and I repeat the B.N.A. Act, in so far as it deals with the subject of Indians must, in my opinion, be taken to contemplate the Indians of British North America as a whole.

As against this evidence, the Dominion appeals to the Royal Proclamation of 1763 as furnishing the clue to the true meaning and application of the term "Indians" in s. 91. The Indians therein referred to are said to be the same type of aborigines as are described in that Proclamation as "the several nations or tribes of Indian with whom We are connected and who lived under Our protection."

First, it is said that the terms "nation" and "tribe" are not employed in relation to the Eskimo. That is a proposition which finds no support in the documents produced dealing with the Labrador Eskimo; and, as regards the Eskimo inhabiting the Hudson's Bay Co.'s territories, they, as already pointed out, are (in the tables in the margin of the Hudson's Bay Co.'s aboriginal map) included in the statement of "Indian tribes" in those territories and they are in the list of "Indian nations" once dwelling east of the Mississippi.

Then it is said they were never "connected" with the British Crown or "under the protection" of the Crown. I find some difficulty in affirming that the Eskimo and other Indians ruled by the Hudson's Bay Co., under either charter or license from the Crown, were never under the protection of the Crown, and in understanding how, especially in view of the Proclamations cited, that can be affirmed of the Esquimaux of north-eastern Labrador. I cannot give my adherence to the principle of interpretation of the B.N.A. Act which, in face of the ample evidence of the broad denotation of the term "Indian" as employed to designate the aborigines of Labrador and the Hudson's Bay territories as evidenced by the documents referred to, would impose upon that term in the B.N.A. Act a narrower interpretation by reference to the recitals of and the events leading up to the Proclamation of 1763. For analogous reasons I am unable to accept the list of Indian tribes attached to the Instructions to Sir Guy Carleton as controlling the scope of the term "Indians" in the B.N.A. Act. Here it may be observed parenthetically that if this list of tribes does not include Eskimo, as apparently it does not, neither does it appear to include the Montagnais Indians inhabiting the north shore of the St. Lawrence east of the Saguenay or the Blackfeet or the Cree or the Indians of the Pacific Coast.

Another argument advanced by counsel for the Crown is based upon the supposed contrast between the language used in arts. 31 and 32 of the Instructions to Sir Guy Carleton and that used in relation to the Eskimo in art. 37. It has already been pointed out that, in the official documents relating to the Labrador Eskimo, the words "savages" and "Indians" are used convertibly; that in General

Murray's Report in 1762 the Montagnais, the Hurons and the Eskimo are all spoken of as "savages"; and in art. 31 of Sir Guy Carleton's instructions, the term "savages" is applied to the Indians of Illinois, the straits of Detroit, Michilmackinak and Gaspé; and, in art. 32, the term "savages" is applied to the Indians affected by the Royal Proclamation in 1763 and within the scope of the plan of 1764. I can find nothing in the language of these Instructions which militates against the inference which, as already explained, seems to me to arise from the documents mentioned above having relation to the Labrador Eskimo.

Nor do I think that the fact that British policy in relation to the Indians, as evidenced in the Instructions to Sir Guy Carleton and the Royal Proclamation of 1763, did not contemplate the Eskimo (along with many other tribes and nations of British North American aborigines) as within the scope of that policy is either conclusive or very useful in determining the question before us. For that purpose, for construing the term "Indians" in the B.N.A. Act in order to ascertain the scope of the provisions of that Act defining the powers of the Parliament of Canada, the Report of the Select Committee of the House of Commons in 1857 and the documents relating to the Labrador Eskimo are, in my opinion, far more trustworthy guides.

Nor can I agree that the context (in head no. 24) has the effect of restricting the term "Indians." If "Indians" standing alone in its application to British North America denotes the aborigines, then the fact that there were aborigines for whom lands had not been reserved seems to afford no good reason for limiting the scope of the term "Indians" itself.

For these reasons I think the question referred to us should be answered in the affirmative.

*　　*　　*

CANNON J.: The question referred to us for hearing and consideration pursuant to s. 55 of the Supreme Court Act, R.S.C. 1927, c. 35 is: Does the term "Indians" as used in Head 24 of s. 91 of the B.N.A. Act, 1867, include Eskimo inhabitants of the Province of Québec? I answer the question in the affirmative. In the evidence given by Sir George Simpson before the Select Committee on the Hudson Bay Co., it appears that in 1857, the Eskimos were included amongst the so-called Indian races classified in the census prepared by the company and the report of the Committee must have been known to the Legislature at Westminster in 1867. The correspondence between Sir John Macdonald and Sir Hector Langevin with reference to the relief to be given to the Montagnais and Eskimo Indians of the Lower St. Lawrence would show that these two Fathers of the Confederation always understood that the English word "Indians" was to be construed and translated as "sauvages" which admittedly did include all the aborigines living within the territories in North America under British authority, whether Imperial, Colonial, or subject to the administrative powers of the Hudson Bay Co.

I do not insist on these two points which have been well treated by my brother Kerwin with whom I agree. I would like to add the following considerations.

As to the exact meaning of the word "Indians" at the time of Confederation, I believe that we have in the official documents "respecting the Proposed Union of the British North American Provinces" presented to both houses of Parliament of the United Kingdom, on February 8, 1867, all we need to form an opinion of the significance of this word and its scope.

In the English Text of the Report of the Resolutions adopted at a Conference of Delegates from the Provinces of Canada, Nova Scotia and New Brunswick, and the Colonies of Newfoundland and Prince Edward Island, held at the City of Québec, October 10, 1864, as the basis of a proposed Confederation of those Provinces and Colonies, Resolution 29 reads as follows:

> The General Parliament shall have power to make Laws for the peace, welfare and good Government of the Federated Provinces (saving the Sovereignty of England), and especially Laws respecting the following subjects: [. . .]
>
> 29. Indians and Lands Reserved for the Indians.

The official French translation of this resolution, as I find it in "Débats Parlementaires sur la Question de la Confédération des Provinces de l'Amérique Britannique du Nord," imprimés par Ordre de la Legislature par Hunter, Rose et Lemieux, Imprimeurs Parlementaires, 1865, follows:

> 29. Le parlement général aura le pouvoir de faire des lois pour la paix, le bien-être et le bon gouvernement des provinces fédérées (sans, toutefois, pouvoir porter atteinte à la souveraineté de l'Angleterre), et en particulier sur les sujets suivants: [. . .]
>
> 29. Les Sauvages et les terres réservées pour les Sauvages.

The petition to the Queen passed on March 13, 1865, by the Legislature reproduces, as to this sub-paragraph, word for word the Québec resolutions, and the French translation also gives to the General Parliament under s. 29—"Les Sauvages et les terres réservées pour les Sauvages."

This, I think, disposes of the very able argument on behalf of the Dominion that the word "Indians" in the B.N.A. Act must be taken in a restricted sense. The Upper and Lower Houses of Upper and Lower Canada, petitioners to the Queen, understood that the English word "Indians" was equivalent to or equated the French word "Sauvages" and included all the present and future aborigines native subjects of the proposed Confederation of British North America, which at the time was intended to include Newfoundland.

The official French version of the B.N.A. Act also translates "Indians" by "Sauvages." See Statute du Canada 1er Parlement, 31 Victoria, 1867-1868, Imprime par Malcolm Cameron, Imprimeur de Sa Très Excellente Majesté la Reine—Ottawa, 1867, Page 24, Section 91, sous-paragraphe 24.

I therefore, according to statute, certify that the above contains my opinion upon the question referred to us with the reasons for my answer.

*   *   *

CROCKET J.: I am of opinion that the question submitted to us should be answered in the affirmative for the reasons stated by my Lord the Chief Justice and my brothers Cannon and Kerwin.

*   *   *

DAVIS J., concurs with SIR LYMAN P. DUFF C.J.C.

*   *   *

KERWIN J.: The question should be answered in the affirmative. In my opinion, when the Imperial Parliament enacted that there should be confided to the Dominion Parliament power to deal with "Indians and lands reserved for the Indians," the intention was to allocate to it authority over all the aborigines within the territory to be included in the Confederation. The fact that there were no Eskimos within the boundaries of the Provinces that first constituted the Dominion is beside the point as provision was made by the B.N.A. Act to include the greater part, if not all, of the territory belonging to the Hudson's Bay Co. And whether the Eskimos as now known emigrated directly from Asia or inhabited the interior of America (originally coming from Asia) and subsequently migrated north, matters not, however interesting it may be to follow the opinions of those who have devoted time and study to that question. From the date of the visit of Champlain to this country in 1625 when he discovered "une nation de sauvages qui habitent ces pays, qui s'appellent Esquimaux," and of Radisson who in an account of his travels and experiences refers to "Indians called Esquimos"; through the reports of the missionaries and the correspondence between France and New France, the Indians are referred to as "sauvages" and the Eskimos as "sauvages esquimaux." Later we find by referring to such books as might be expected to be known to the Fathers of Confederation and to the British Parliament statements indicating that the Eskimos was considered as one of the Indian tribes. The following is a partial list of such books:

1855.—Webster's American Dictionary of the English language defines the Esquimaux: "A nation of Indians inhabiting the northwestern parts of North America."

1855.—Adrien Guibert in his Geographical Dictionary classifies the Eskimos among the Indians of America.

1856.—In "The Indian Races of North and South America," Charles de Wolf Brownell, an American author, speaks of the Esquimaux Indians and devotes a chapter to the study of their manners and personal appearance.

1857.—In the "Gazetteer of the World," published in London by A. Fullerton & Co., the Eskimos are dealt with as Indians, who are the aboriginal people of the New Continent; mentions are made of Eskimos in opposition to "common Indian" and to "other Indians."

1857.—In an Imperial Blue Book is a Report from the Select Committee on the Hudson's Bay Co. in which the Eskimos are enumerated among the Indians, are classified with the Indian races and are shown on a map denoting the boundaries and locations of various Indian tribes.

1857.—In the evidence given before a Select Committee of the House of Commons (Imperial), appointed to consider the state of the British Possessions in North America, Sir George Simpson, Governor of the territories of the Hudson's Bay Co., includes the Eskimos in the Indian population.

1869.—In an "Esquisse sur le Nord-Ouest de l'Amerique" by Mgr. Taché, Bishop of St. Boniface, Manitoba, reference is made to the aboriginal tribes being called Indians (Sauvages) and the Esquimaux are dealt with at length as one of the five linguistic Indian families.

A word should be added as to Webster's Dictionary. Counsel for the Dominion pointed out that in the 1913 edition of Webster's New International Dictionary, as well as the 1923, 1925, and 1927 editions, "Indian" is defined as being "a member of any of the aboriginal American stocks excepting the Eskimauan." However, in the earlier 1855 edition, then known as the American Dictionary of the English Language, appears the following: "'Indian,' M.A. General name of any native of the Indies; as an East Indian or West Indian. It is particularly applied to any native of the American continent."

In the 1865 edition of what had then become the Dictionary of the English Language, "Indians" were defined as "Indians are the aboriginal inhabitants of America so called originally from the idea on the part of Columbus and the early navigators of the identity of America with India." It was only in the 1913, 1923 and 1927 editions that the earlier definition was departed from while in the 1934 edition of Webster's International Dictionary, "Indian" is defined as follows:

> Indian 5. A member of the aboriginal American race; an American, or Red, Indian; an Amerind . . . . About 75 linguistic families or stocks are recognized in North America, and about 75 more in South America and the West Indies. Some stocks comprise many tribes speaking distinct, but related, languages. The 16 stocks listed below occupied more than half the area of the continent and comprised a large majority of the Indians at the time of the discovery of North America, Algonquian, Athapaskan, Eskimauan, Iroquoian, Mayan, Muskhegian, Siouian, and Uto-Aztecan.

It is true that in the New English (Oxford) Dictionary, Volume 5, under the heading "Indian" appears the following:

> A. . . . 2. Belonging or relating to the race of original inhabitants of America and the West Indies.
> B. . . . 2. A member of any of the aboriginal races of America or the West Indies; an American Indian.
> The Eskimos, in the extreme north, are usually excluded from the term; as are sometimes the Patagonians and Fuegians in the extreme south.

There are also a few other publications to which our attention has been called where "Indians" and "Esquimaux" are differentiated but the majority of authoritative publications, and particularly those that one would expect to be in common use in 1867, adopt the interpretation that the term "Indians" includes all the aborigines of the territory subsequently included in the Dominion. As pointed out in a memorandum of November 1, 1918, by the Deputy Superintendent General of Indian Affairs to the Minister, the Eskimos had never been mentioned in any legislation up to that time but by c. 47 (s. 1) of 14-15 Geo. V., assented to July, 1924, s. 4 of the Indian Act, c. 81, R.S.C. 1906, was amended by adding thereto the following subsection: "(2) The Superintendent General of Indian Affairs shall have charge of Eskimo affairs." This was afterwards repealed and even if the repeal had never occurred perhaps no argument could be adduced from the provisions of the amending statute but it is significant that in 1879 a letter from the Very Reverend Edmond Langevin to the Postmaster General of Canada, referring to the necessitous condition of "the Montagnais and Esquimaux Indians on the north coast of the St. Lawrence below the Saguenay" was sent by the addressee to Sir John A. Macdonald as Superintendent General of Indian Affairs with the following covering letter:

> Ottawa, 20 January, 1879.
> The enclosed letter from the Very Reverend Edmond Langevin, Vicar General of Rimouski, calls my attention to the position of the Montagnais and Esquimaux Indians on the north coast of the St. Lawrence, below the Saguenay. He says that the amount that used to be given to these Indians was seventy-eight cents a head, and that now it is only thirty-eight cents. These poor people are starving they can't cultivate the land, which in that region is hardly cultivable, and have had no provision made for them by the Government, and he requires on their behalf that we should come to their help. Will you kindly see that they are treated as well as we treat the Indians of our new territories. Of course I leave the whole matter in your hands.

The matter referred to was commented upon by the Deputy Superintendent General of Indian Affairs in the following report:

> To the Right Hon. Sir John A. Macdonald, K.C.B., Supt. General of Indian Affairs

> Ottawa, 24 jany [sic] 1879.
> With reference to the letter of the 20th Instant (placed Herewith) from the Honourable Hector Langevin, enclosing a letter of the 13th Instant, from the Very Reverand Edmond Langevin, of Rimouski, in the Province of Québec, relative to the insufficient relief give to the Montagnais and Esquimaux Indians of the Lower St. Lawrence, the undersigned has the honour to report that frequent representations to the same effect have been made to the Department and that last year he endeavoured to induce the then Superintendent General of Indian Affairs to ask Parliament for a larger grant, but that when the proposed estimates for the year 1878-79 were submitted to Council for revision, the proposed increase of $2000 to the Parliamentary Grant for these Indians was struck out.
> The present Government has however sanctioned the Supplementary Estimates for 1878-9 which will be submitted to Parliament at the approaching session being anticipated by granting the said sum of $2000.00, and the undersigned has moreover increased the grant for those Indians by that amount in the proposed estimates for the year 1879-80, with the hope that the Government will sanction and Parliament confirm the same.

All respectively submitted,
L. Van Koughnet, Deputy Supt. General of Indian Affairs.

That so soon after Confederation the position of Eskimos should be treated in this manner is significant. It not only more than counter balances any reference made later as to the Department's attitude but, to my mind, is conclusive as to what was in the minds of those responsible for the drafting of the Resolutions leading to the passing of the B.N.A. Act, at that time and shortly thereafter.

Special attention should also be paid to the report of the Select Committee on the Hudson's Bay Co. to the Houses of Parliament of Great Britain and Ireland, presented in 1857. As appears from the Imperial Blue Books on Affairs Relating to Canada, the Committee reported:

> It is a matter of great difficulty to obtain reliable information respecting the Indian population, their migratory habits, and the vast extent of country over which they are spread, misleading the calculations, and rendering it almost impracticable to prepare a satisfactory census. The following estimates have been compiled with great care, from a mass of documents and the actual personal knowledge of several of the Company's officers, tested by comparison with published statements, especially those presented to Government in 1816 by Messrs. Warre and Vavasour, and those of Colonel Lefroy, R.A., contained in a paper read before the Canadian Institute.

The estimates referred to are headed "Establishments of the Hudson's Bay Company in 1856 and number of Indians frequenting them." After a long list of the names of the posts and localities and of the number of Indians frequenting each post is appended the following:

Add Whites and half breeds in Hudson's Bay Territory, not included	6,000
Add Esquimaux not enumerated	4,000
Total	158,960

The Indian Races shown in detail in the foregoing Census may be classified as follows:

Thickwood Indians on the east side of the Rocky Mountains	35,000
The Plain Tribes (Blackfeet, &c)	25,000
The Esquimaux	4,000
Indians settled in Canada	3,000
Indian in British Oregon and on the North-west Coast	80,000
Total Indians	147,000
Whites and half-breeds in Hudson's Bay Territory	11,000
Souls	158,000

The Esquimaux, it will be seen, are included among the Indian races and this is based apparently upon the evidence of Sir George Simpson, which had been taken before the Committee. Questions 1062 and 1472, together with the answers, are as follows:

1062. Mr. Cregson: What mode have you of ascertaining of the population of the Indians?—We have lists of the Indians belonging to various posts; we have compared and checked them with the report of the Government officers who went to Vancouver's Island some years ago, as regards the tribes to the west of the mountains, and with Colonel Lefroy's lists, as regards those on the east side, and we have arrived at this estimate of the population.

1472. Mr. Roebuck: Will you state the total? The Indians, east of the mountains, 55,000; West of the mountains, 80,000; Esquimaux, 4000.

While counsel for the Dominion sought to draw from the answer to Q. 1472 the inference that Sir George Simpson had not treated the Esquimaux as one of the Indian tribes, I think the answer is not susceptible of that interpretation and it is certainly not the one that the Committee adopted. After considering the reports of missionaries, explorers, agents, cartographers and geographers, included in the cases submitted on behalf of the Dominion and Province of Québec, I do not believe anything further may be usefully added. The weight of opinion favours the construction which I have indicated is the proper one of head 24 of s. 91 of the B.N.A. Act but the deciding factor, in my view, is the manner in which the subject was considered in Canada and in England at or about the date of the passing of the Act.

*   *   *

HUDSON J., concurs with SIR LYMAN P. DUFF C.J.C.

*   *   *

Question answered in affirmative.

CHAPTER 3

Drybones

THIS CASE is cited as "Regina v. Drybones", S.C.C. (1969). Joseph Drybones had been found intoxicated at the Old Stope Hotel in Yellowknife, Northwest Territories on April 8, 1967. He was charged under the Indian Act, section 94. Since the Indian Act varied significantly from the territorial Liquor Ordinance, particularly in that the punishments under the Indian Act were stronger, Drybones's lawyers argued that his equality rights as a Canadian citizen were being violated. The crux of the case was the question of which piece of federal legislation had precedence: the Indian Act or the Canadian Bill of Rights (1960).

Drybones was acquitted by Justice Morrow in spite of the fact that he had pleaded guilty when arraigned before a magistrate. Drybones was "allowed to withdraw that plea," as Ritchie noted in his decision below, because "there was some serious doubt as to whether he fully appreciated his plea in the lower Court" (51); Drybones did not speak English. The Crown appealed Morrow's decision to the NWT Court of Appeal and then to the Supreme Court of Canada.

The Justices at the Supreme Court were divided over the case and rendered a split decision. Chief Justice Cartwright, along with Justices Abbott and Pigeon argued that the appeal should be successful, while the majority of Supreme Court Justices—Fauteux, Martland, Judson, Ritchie, Hall and Spence—successfully argued that the appeal should fail. Ritchie wrote the leading judgment, arguing that the relevant section of the Bill of Rights:

> means at least that no individual or group of individuals is to be treated more harshly than another under that law, and I am therefore of the opinion that an individual is denied equality before the law if it is made an offense punishable at law, on account of his race, for him to do something which his fellow Canadians are free to do without having committed any offense or having been made subject to any penalty. (54-5)

Much of the debate focused on the question of whether the courts actually had the power, through interpreting the Bill of Rights, to render pieces of federal legislation such as Section 94 of the Indian Act inoperative. The focus of both sides was on this question rather than on the question of the nature of Aboriginal citizenship, which is our interest in this context. Thus, Cartwright and Abbott's dissenting opinions are based on the general view that the Bill of Rights, which said that "there have existed and shall continue to exist in Canada" certain rights and freedoms, can only be used to interpret other pieces of legislation which appear to limit those rights or freedoms. Pigeon made this argument as well, but he was also the only justice who saw the broader impact on Indian citizenship of Ritchie's liberal perspective:

> If one of the effects of the Canadian Bill of Rights is to render inoperative all legal provisions whereby Indians as such are not dealt with in the same way as the general public, the conclusion is inescapable that Parliament, by the enactment of the Bill, has not only fundamentally altered the status of the Indians in that indirect fashion but has also made any future use of federal legislative authority over them subject to the requirement of expressly declaring every time "that the law shall operate notwithstanding the Canadian Bill of Rights." (58)

The decision should be compared to that rendered in the Lavell/Bedard case a few years later, when a growing awareness of Aboriginal rights made the court's dealing with what was effectively the same issue much more complex. In Lavell/Bedard, a long list of intervenors got involved in the case to defend the priority of the Indian Act over the Bill of Rights in the name of Aboriginal rights; there were no such intervenors at Drybones, and it is only in Pigeon's dissenting opinion that the argument is even—albeit indirectly—broached.

The Drybones case was heard by Cartwright, then Chief Justice, Fauteux, Abbott, Martland, Judson, Ritchie, Hall, Spence, and Pigeon. G. Brian Purdy was Drybones' lawyer, with D.H. Christie and C.D. MacKinnon acting for the Crown. The case has been edited slightly, removing some of the sources of the arguments and discussions of the relation of the Bill of Rights to other federal legislation.

P.K.

CARTWRIGHT C.J.C. (dissenting): The relevant facts, which are undisputed, and the course of the proceedings in the Courts below, are set out in the reasons of my brothers Ritchie and Pigeon which I have had the advantage of reading. There is no doubt that, on the facts, the respondent was guilty of a breach of s. 94(b) of the Indian Act, R.S.C. 1952, c. 149, and the question to be decided is whether that provision is rendered inoperative by the terms of the Canadian Bill of Rights, 1960 (Can.), c. 44, hereinafter referred to as the "Bill".

In approaching this question I will assume the correctness of the view that s. 94(b) infringes the right of the respondent to equality before the law declared by s. 1(b) of the Bill, in that because he is an Indian it renders him guilty of a punishable offence by reason of conduct which would not have been punishable if indulged in by any person who was not an Indian.

This is, I believe, the first occasion on which it has become necessary for this

Court to decide this question. In Robertson and Rosetanni v. The Queen, 41 D.L.R. (2d) 485, [1964] 1 C.C.C. 1, [1963] S.C.R. 651, the majority were of the view that the impugned provisions of the Lord's Day Act, R.S.C. 1952, c. 171, did not infringe the right to freedom of religion declared by s. 1(c) of the Bill, and consequently did not deal with the opinion which I expressed in my dissenting reasons as to the effect of the Bill on a provision of an Act of Parliament which does infringe one of the declared rights.

In the case at bar s. 94(b) of the Indian Act is expressed in plain and unequivocal words. It is not possible by the application of any rule of construction to give it a meaning other than that an Indian who is intoxicated off a reserve is guilty of an offence.

In these circumstances the choice open to us is to give effect to the section according to its plain meaning or to declare it inoperative, that is to say, to declare that the Indian Act is pro tanto repealed by the Bill. . . .

The question is whether or not it is the intention of Parliament to confer the power and impose the responsibility upon the Courts of declaring inoperative any provision in a statute of Canada although expressed in clear and unequivocal terms the meaning of which after calling in aid every rule of construction including that prescribed by s. 2 of the Bill is perfectly plain, if in the view of the Court it infringes any of the rights or freedoms declared by s.1 of the Bill.

In approaching this question it must not be forgotten that the responsibility mentioned above, if imposed at all, is imposed upon every Justice of the Peace, Magistrate and Judge of any Court in the country who is called upon to apply a statute of Canada or any order, rule or regulation made thereunder.

If it were intended that the question should be answered in the affirmative there would, in my opinion, have been added after the word "declared" in the seventh line of the opening paragraph of s. 2 of the Bill some such words as the following "and if any law of Canada cannot be so construed and applied it shall be regarded as inoperative or pro tanto repealed".

What now appears to me to have been the error in my reasoning . . . is found in the statement that the Bill requires the Courts to refuse to apply any law of Canada which is successfully impugned as infringing one of the declared rights or freedoms whereas on the contrary, as Davey, J.A., had pointed out, the Bill directs the Courts to apply such a law, not to refuse to apply it.

For these reasons I would dispose of the appeal as proposed by my brother Pigeon.

* * *

FAUTEUX J., concurs with RITCHIE J.

* * *

ABBOTT J. (dissenting): The relevant facts, which are undisputed, are set out in the reasons of my brothers Ritchie and Pigeon which I have had the advantage of reading.

The interpretation of the Canadian Bill of Rights, 1960 (Can.), c. 44, adopted by the Courts below, necessarily implies wide delegation of the legislative authority of Parliament to the Courts. The power to make such a delegation cannot be questioned but, in my view, it would require the plainest words to impute to Parliament an intention to extend to the Courts, such an invitation to engage in judicial legislation. I cannot find that intention expressed in s. 2 of the Bill. On the contrary, I share the opinion expressed by the Chief Justice, by my brother Pigeon and by Davey, J.A., as he then was, in R. v. Gonzales (1962), 32 D.L.R. (2d) 290, 2 C.C.C. 237, 37 C.R. 56, that, with respect to existing legislation, the section provides merely a canon or rule of interpretation for such legislation.

I would dispose of the appeal as proposed by my brother Pigeon.

* * *

MARTLAND and JUDSON JJ., concur with RITCHIE J.

* * *

RITCHIE J.: This is an appeal brought with leave of this Court from a judgment of the Court of Appeal for the Northwest Territories dismissing an appeal by the Crown from a judgment of Morrow, J., of the Territorial Court of the Northwest Territories by which he had acquitted Joseph Drybones of being "unlawfully intoxicated off a reserve" contrary to s. 94(b) of the Indian Act, R.S.C. 1952, c. 149, after having heard an appeal by way of trial de novo from a judgment of Magistrate Anderson-Thompson who had convicted the respondent of this offence and sentenced him to be fined $10 and costs and in default to spend three days in custody. The full charge against Drybones was that he,

On or about the 8th of April, 1967 at Yellowknife in the Northwest Territories, being an Indian, was unlawfully intoxicated off a reserve, contrary to s. 94(b) of the Indian Act.

The respondent is an Indian and he was indeed intoxicated on the evening of April 8, 1967, on the premises of the Old Stope Hotel in Yellowknife in the Northwest Territories where there is no "reserve" with the meaning of the Indian Act.

When he was first arraigned before Magistrate Anderson-Thompson, Drybones, who spoke no English, pleaded guilty to this offence, but on appeal to the Territorial Court, Mr. Justice Morrow found that there was some serious doubt as to whether he fully appreciated his plea in the lower Court and he was allowed to withdraw that plea whereafter the appeal proceeded as a trial de novo with a plea of not guilty. Section 94 of the Indian Act reads as follows:

94. An Indian who
   (a) has intoxicants in his possession,
   (b) is intoxicated, or
   (c) makes or manufactures intoxicants off a reserve, is guilty of an offence and is liable on summary conviction to a fine of not less than ten dollars and not more than fifty dollars or to imprisonment for a term not exceeding three months to both fine and imprisonment.

I agree with the Court of Appeal that the use of the words "off a reserve" creates [64 D.L.R. (2d) 260 at p. 264, [1968] 2 C.C.C. 69 at p. 73, 61 W.W.R. 370]:

. . . an essential element to be proved in any charge laid under s. 94. But once it is proved, as it was in the present case, that the offence was not committed upon a reserve, the requirement of the section was satisfied. The fact that there are no reserves in the Territories is quite irrelevant.

The important question raised by this appeal has its origin in the fact that in the Northwest Territories it is not an offence for anyone except an Indian to be intoxicated otherwise than in a public place. The Liquor Ordinance, R.O.N.W.T. 1956, c. 60, s. 19(1)(a) which is of general application in the Territories, provides that: "No person shall be in an intoxicated condition in a public place . . ." but unlike s. 94 of the Indian Act, there is no provision for a minimum fine and the maximum term of imprisonment is only 30 days as opposed to three months under the Indian Act.

The result is that an Indian who is intoxicated in his own home "off a reserve" is guilty of an offence and subject to a minimum fine of not less than $10 or a term of imprisonment not exceeding three months or both, whereas all other citizens in the Territories may, if they see fit, become intoxicated otherwise than in a public place without committing any offence at all. And even if such other citizen is convicted of being intoxicated in a public place, the only penalty provided by the Ordinance is "a fine not exceeding $50 or . . . imprisonment for a term not exceeding 30 days or . . . both fine and imprisonment".

The argument which was successfully advanced by the respondent before Mr. Justice Morrow and before the Court of Appeal was that because of this legislation, Indians in the Northwest Territories, by reason of their race, are denied "equality before the law" with their fellow Canadians, and that s. 94(b) of the Indian Act therefore authorizes the abrogation, abridgement or infringement of one of the human rights and fundamental freedoms recognized and declared as existing in Canada without discrimination by reason of race, pursuant to the provisions of the Canadian Bill of Rights, 1960 (Can.), c. 44 (hereinafter sometimes referred to as "the Bill of Rights" or "the Bill") which provides, inter alia:

1. It is hereby recognized and declared that in Canada there have existed and shall continue to exist without discrimination by reason of race, national origin, colour, religion or sex, the following human rights and fundamental freedoms, namely,
   (b) the right of the individual to equality before the law and the protection of the law;
2. Every law of Canada shall, unless it is expressly declared by an Act of the Parliament of Canada that it shall operate notwithstanding the Canadian Bill of Rights, be so construed and applied as not to abrogate, abridge or infringe or to authorize the abrogation, abridgement or infringement of any of the rights or freedoms herein recognized and declared . . .
5 (2). The expression "law of Canada" in Part 1 means an Act of the Parliament of Canada enacted before or after the coming into force of this act, any order, rule or regulation thereunder, and any law in force of Canada or in any part of Canada at the commencement of this Act that is subject to be repealed, abolished or altered by the Parliament of Canada.

The Court of Appeal agreed with Mr. Justice Morrow that s. 94(b) of the Indian Act is rendered inoperative by reason of this legislation and the notice to appeal to this Court is limited to the single ground

That the Court of Appeal in the Northwest Territories in upholding the decision of the Territorial Court of the Northwest Territories erred in acquitting the respondent of "an offence contrary to s. 94(b) of the Indian Act, R.S.C. 1952 Ch. 149 on the ground that s. 94 of the Indian Act is rendered inoperative by reason of the Canadian Bill of Rights, Stat. Can. 1960 Ch. 44."

It was contended on behalf of the appellant that the reasoning and conclusion of the Courts below makes the question of whether s. 94 has been rendered inoperative by the Bill of Rights dependent upon whether or not the law of any Province or Territory makes it an offence to be intoxicated otherwise than in a public place and that its operation could therefore not only vary from place to place in Canada but also from time to time, depending upon amendments which might be made to the provincial or territorial legislation. I can, however, find no room for the application of this argument in the present case as the ordinance in question is a law of Canada within the meaning of s. 5 (2) of the Bill of Rights (see Northwest Territories Act, R.S.C. 1952, c. 331, s. 15), and it is a law of general application in the Territories, whereas the Indian Act is, of course, also a law of Canada although it has special application to Indians alone.

The question of whether s. 94 of the Indian Act is rendered inoperative by reason of the provisions of the Bill of Rights on the ground that it abrogates, abridges or infringes the right of Canadians of the Indian race to "equality before the law" was considered by the Court of Appeal of British Columbia in R. v. Gonzales (1962), 32 D.L.R. (2d) 290 at p. 298, 132 C.C.C. 237 at p. 245, 37 C.R. 56, where Tysoe, J.A., speaking for the majority of the Court, concluded that:

Section 94(a) of the Indian Act does not abrogate or infringe the right of the appellant to "equality before the law" as I understand it. Section 2 of the Canadian Bill of Rights does not therefore affect it.

In reaching the same conclusion, Davey, J.A. (as he then was), who wrote separate reasons for judgment from the other two members of the Court, took the view that s. (1) of the Bill of Rights should be treated as merely providing a canon of construction for the interpretation of legislation existing at the time when the statute was enacted. The learned Judge said [at p. 292 D.L.R., p. 239 C.C.C.]:

In so far as existing legislation does not offend against any of the matters specifically mentioned in clauses (a) to (g) of s. 2, but is said to otherwise infringe upon some of the human rights and fundamental freedoms declared in s. 1, in my opinion the section does not repeal such legislation either expressly or by implication. On the contrary, it expressly recognizes the continued existence of such legislation, but provides that it shall be construed and applied so as not to derogate from those rights and freedoms. By that it seems merely to provide a canon or rule of interpretation for such legislation. The very language of s. 2, "be so construed and applied as not to abrogate" assumes that the prior Act may be sensibly construed and applied in a way that will avoid derogating from the rights and freedoms declared in s. 1. If the prior legislation cannot be so construed and applied sensibly, then the effect of s. 2 is exhausted, and the prior legislation must prevail according to its plain meaning.

The application of that rule of construction to existing legislation may require a change in the judicial interpretation of some statutes where the language permits and thus change the law.

The difficulty with s. 94(a) of the Indian Act is that it admits of no construction or application that would avoid conflict with s. 1(b) of the Canadian Bill of Rights as appellant's counsel interprets it. Since the effect of the Canadian Bill of Rights is not to repeal such legislation, it is the duty of the Courts to apply s. 94(a) in the only way its plain language permits, and that the learned Magistrate did when he convicted.

This proposition appears to me to strike at the very foundations of the Bill of Rights and to convert it from its apparent character as a statutory declaration of the fundamental human rights and freedoms which it recognizes, into being little more than a rule for the construction of federal statutes, but as this approach has found favour with some eminent legal commentators, it seems to me to be important that priority should be given to a consideration of it. . . .

In any event, it was not necessary to decide this question in Robertson and Rosetanni because it was found that the impugned provisions of the Lord's Day Act and the Bill of Rights were not in conflict, and I accordingly do not consider that case to be any authority for the suggestion that the Bill of Rights is to be treated as being subject to federal legislation existing at the time of its enactment, and more particularly I do not consider that the provisions of s. 1(b) of the Bill of Rights are to be treated as being in any way limited or affected by the terms of s. 94(b) of the Indian Act.

The right which is here at issue is "the right of the individual to equality before the law and the protection of the law". Mr. Justice Tysoe, who wrote the reasons for judgment on behalf of the majority of the Court of Appeal of British Columbia in the Gonzales case, supra, expressed the opinion [at p. 296 D.L.R., p. 243 C.C.C.] that as these words occur in the Bill of Rights they mean

> . . . a right of every person *to whom a particular law relates or extends*, no matter what may be a person's race, national origin, colour, religion or sex, to stand on an equal footing with every other person to whom that particular law relates or extends, and a right to the protection of the law.
> (The italics are Mr. Justice Tysoe's.)

Like the members of the Courts below, I cannot agree with this interpretation pursuant to which it seems to me that the most glaring discriminatory legislation against a racial group would have to be construed as recognizing the right of each of its individual members "to equality before the law", so long as all the other members are being discriminated against in the same way.

I think that the word "law" as used in s. 1(b) of the Bill of Rights is to be construed as meaning "the law of Canada" as defined in s. 5(2) (i.e., Acts of the Parliament of Canada and any orders, rules or regulations thereunder) and without attempting any exhaustive definition of "equality before the law" I think that s. 1(b) means at least that no individual or group of individuals is to be treated more harshly than another under that law, and I am therefore of opinion that an individual is denied equality before the law if it is made an offence punishable at law, on account of his race, for him to do something which his fellow Canadians are free to do without having committed any offence or having been made subject to any penalty.

It is only necessary for the purpose of deciding this case for me to say that in my opinion s. 94(b) of the Indian Act is a law of Canada which creates such an offence and that it can only be construed in such manner that its application would operate so as to abrogate, abridge or infringe one of the rights declared and recognized by the Bill of Rights. For the reasons which I have indicated, I am therefore of opinion that s. 94(b) is inoperative.

For the purpose of determining the issue raised by this appeal it is unnecessary to express any opinion respecting the operation of any other section of the Indian Act.

For all the above reasons I would dismiss this appeal.

Since writing the above I have had the advantage of reading the reasons for judgment prepared by the Chief Justice and by Mr. Justice Pigeon which, when read together, appear to me to lead to the conclusion that, even on the assumption that the application of the provisions of prior federal legislation has the effect of denying equality before the law, and thus discriminating against, a sector of the population "by reason of race", they must nevertheless be given full effect notwithstanding the provisions of the Bill of Rights. In view of this conclusion, I find it necessary to restate the position which I take in the matter. . . .

It may well be that the implementation of the Canadian Bill of Rights by the Courts can give rise to great difficulties, but in my view full effect must be given to the terms of s. 2 thereof.

The present case discloses laws of Canada which abrogate, abridge and infringe the right of an individual Indian to equality before the law and in my opinion if those laws are to be applied in accordance with the express language used by Parliament in s. 2 of the Bill of Rights, then s. 94(b) of the Indian Act must be declared to be inoperative.

It appears to me to be desirable to make it plain that these reasons for judgment are limited to a situation in which, under the laws of Canada, it is made an offence punishable at law on account of race, for a person to do something which all Canadians who are not members of that race may do with impunity; in my opinion the same considerations do not by any means apply to all the provisions of the Indian Act.

*   *   *

HALL J.: I agree with the reasons of my brother Ritchie and wish only to add some observations regarding the decision in R. v. Gonzales (1962), 32 D.L.R. (2d) 290, 132 C.C.C. 237, 37 C.R. 56.

The concept that the Canadian Bill of Rights, 1960 (Can.), c. 44, is operative in the face of a law of Canada only when that law does not give equality to all persons within the class to whom that particular law extends or relates, as it was expressed by Tysoe, J.A., at p. 296 D.L.R., p. 243 C.C.C.:

Coming now to s. 1(b) of the Canadian Bill of Rights. The meaning of the word "equality" is well known. In my opinion, the word "before" in the expression "equality before the law", in the sense in which that expression is used in s. 1(b) means "in the presence of ". It seems to me this is the key to the correct interpretation of the expression and makes it clear that "equality before the law" has nothing to do with the application of the law equally to everyone and equal laws for everyone in the sense for which appellant's counsel contends, namely, the same laws for all persons, but to the position occupied by persons to whom a law relates or extends. They shall be entitled to have the law as it exists applied equally and without fear or favour to all persons to whom it relates or extends.

is analogous to the position taken by the Supreme Court of the United States in Plessy v. Ferguson (1896),153 U.S. 537, and which was wholly rejected by the same Court in its historic desegregation judgment, Brown v. Board of Education of Topeka (1953), 347 U.S. 483.

In Plessy v. Ferguson the Court had held that under the "separate but equal" doctrine, equality of treatment is accorded when the races are provided substantially equal facilities even though these facilities be separate. In Brown v. Board of Education the Court held the "separate but equal" doctrine to be totally invalid.

The social situations in Brown v. Board of Education and in the instant case are, of course, very different, but the basic philosophic concept is the same. The Canadian Bill of Rights is not fulfilled if it merely equates Indians with Indians in terms of equality before the law, but can have validity and meaning only when, subject to the single exception set out in s. 2, it is seen to repudiate discrimination in every law of Canada by reason of race, national origin, colour, religion, or sex in respect of the human rights and fundamental freedoms set out in s. 1 in whatever way that discrimination may manifest itself not only as between Indian and Indian, but as between all Canadians whether Indian or non-Indian.

* * *

SPENCE J., concurs with RITCHIE J.

* * *

PIGEON J. (dissenting): The respondent is an Indian and the following charge was made against him before a Magistrate in the Northwest Territories, namely, that he,

> On or about the 8th of April, 1967 at Yellowknife in the Northwest Territories, being an Indian, was unlawfully intoxicated off a reserve, contrary to s. 94(b) of the Indian Act.

Respondent pleaded guilty and was sentenced to a fine of $10 and costs. On his appeal to the Territorial Court, he was allowed to withdraw his plea of guilty. Having then pleaded not guilty, he raised the contention that s. 94(b) of the Indian Act, R.S.C. 1952, c. 149, has been rendered inoperative by the Canadian Bill of Rights, 1960 (Can.), c. 44 (hereinafter called the "Bill"). This contention was accepted by Morrow, J., and the charge dismissed [60 W.W.R. 321].

On appeal by the Crown to the Court of Appeal for the Northwest Territories, that Court refused to follow the contrary decision of the Court of Appeal of British Columbia in R. v. Gonzales (1962), 32 D.L.R. (2d) 290, 132 C.C.C. 237, 37 C.R.

56, and affirmed the acquittal [64 D.L.R. (2d) 260, [1968] 2 C.C.C. 69, 61 W.W.R. 370].

The Crown now appeals to this Court by special leave.

The question before us is essentially whether, in respect of existing federal legislation, s. 2 of the Bill enacts a canon of construction or casts upon the Courts the task of removing therefrom, whenever the question is raised, every provision that may be considered as being in conflict with the enumerated rights and freedoms. In thus stating the question I am not unmindful of the fact that, due to the definition in s. 5(2) of the expression "law of Canada", s. 2 applies to subsequent federal statutes equally as to existing legislation. However, because different considerations may conceivably apply in the case of subsequent statutes, I find it desirable to go no further than necessary for the decision of the case at hand which has to do with existing legislation.

Before considering any enacting clause I must note that the Bill is prefaced by a preamble, as follows:

> The Parliament of Canada, affirming that the Canadian Nation is founded upon principles that acknowledge the supremacy of God, the dignity and worth of the human person and the position of the family in a society of free men and free institutions;
>
> Affirming also that men and institutions remain free only when freedom is founded upon respect for moral and spiritual values and the rule of law;
>
> And being desirous of enshrining these principles and the human rights and fundamental freedoms derived from them, in a Bill of Rights which shall reflect the respect of Parliament for its constitutional authority and which shall ensure the protection of these rights and freedoms in Canada:

Then, after the enacting formula and the title "Part I, Bill of Rights", s. 1 is in the following terms:

> 1. It is hereby recognized and declared that in Canada there have existed and shall continue to exist without discrimination by reason of race, national origin, colour, religion or sex, the following human rights and fundamental freedoms, namely,
> (a) the right of the individual to life, liberty, security of the person and enjoyment of property, and the right not to be deprived thereof except by due process of law;
> (b) the right of the individual to equality before the law and the protection of the law;
> (c) freedom of religion;
> (d) freedom of speech;
> (e) freedom of assembly and association; and
> (f) freedom of the press.

In considering the provisions just quoted, one must observe that the Bill itself begins by a solemn declaration by Parliament in the form of an enactment that, in Canada, the enumerated rights and freedoms "have existed and shall continue to exist". This statement is the essential element of the very first provision of the Bill and it is absolutely unqualified. It is the starting point of that legislation and I have great difficulty in reconciling it with the contention that in fact those rights and freedoms were not wholly and completely existing but were restricted by any number of statutory and other provisions infringing thereon.

There can be no doubt that in enacting legislation Parliament is presumed to be aware of the state of the law: Walker v. The King, [1939] 2 D.L.R. 353, 71 C.C.C. 305, [1939] S.C.R. 214. A fortiori must it be so when the enactment itself has reference thereto. Where is the extent of existing human rights and fundamental freedoms to be ascertained if not by reference to the statute books and other legislative instruments as well as to the decisions of the Courts?

It must also be considered that the rights and freedoms enumerated in s. 1 are not legal concepts of precise and invariable content. If those words were to be taken by themselves, a great deal would be left undefined. However, by declaring those rights and freedoms as they existed a large measure of precision was supplied. Is this not an important purpose of s. 1 and a very effective way of defining some keywords of the enactment?

In the instant case, the question whether all existing legislation should be considered as in accordance with the nondiscrimination principle cannot fail to come immediately to mind seeing that it arises directly out of s. 91(24) of the B.N.A. Act, 1867 whereby Parliament has exclusive legislative authority over "Indians, and lands reserved for the Indians". As was pointed out by Riddell, J., in R. v. Martin (1917), 39 D.L.R. 635 at pp. 638-9, 29 C.C.C. 189 at p. 192, 41 O.L.R. 79, this provision confers legislative authority over the Indians qua Indians and not otherwise. Its very object in so far as it relates to Indians, as opposed to lands reserved for the Indians, is to enable the Parliament of Canada to make legislation applicable only to Indians as such and therefore not applicable to Canadian citizens generally. This legislative authority is obviously intended to be exercised over matters that are, as regards persons other than Indians, within the exclusive legislative authority of the Provinces. Complete uniformity in provincial legislation is clearly not to be expected, not to mention the fact that further diversity must also result from special legislation for the territories. Equality before the law in the sense in which it was understood in the Courts below would require the Indians to be subject in every Province to the same rules of law as all others in every particular, not merely on the question of drunkenness. Outside the territories, provincial jurisdiction over education and health facilities would make it very difficult for federal authorities to provide such facilities to Indians without "discrimination" as understood in the Courts below.

If one of the effects of the Canadian Bill of Rights is to render inoperative all legal provisions whereby Indians as such are not dealt with in the same way as the general public, the conclusion is inescapable that Parliament, by the enactment of the Bill, has not only fundamentally altered the status of the Indians in that indirect fashion but has also made any future use of federal legislative authority over them subject to the requirement of expressly declaring every time "that the law shall operate notwithstanding the Canadian Bill of Rights". I find it very difficult to believe that Parliament so intended when enacting the Bill. If a virtual suppression of federal legislation over Indians as such was meant, one would have expected this important change to be made explicitly, not surreptitiously, so to speak.

In s. 2, the crucial words are that every law of Canada shall, subject to the exception just noted, "be so construed and applied as not to abrogate, abridge or infringe" any of the rights and freedoms recognized and declared in the Bill. The question is whether those words enact something more than a rule of construction. Of themselves, it seems to me that they do not. Certainly the word "construed" implies nothing else. Does the word "applied" express a different intention? I do not think so and, even if this may appear a trite saying, I must point out that what respondent asks the Court to do and what the Courts below have effectively done is not to apply the statute, the Indian Act, but to decline to apply it.

The strongest argument against viewing s. 2 as a canon of construction is undoubtedly that the exception "unless it is expressly declared by an Act of the Parliament of Canada that it shall operate notwithstanding the Canadian Bill of Rights" is thereby deprived of any practical meaning. It cannot be denied that the operation of a rule of construction is not normally subject to such a qualification. On the contrary, the principle is that it has no effect against the clearly expressed will of Parliament in whatever form it is put.

On the other hand, in seeking to give effect to some words in s. 2 that cannot for obvious reasons be applicable to any existing law, one must always bear in mind the very starting point of the Bill, namely, that the rights and freedoms therein recognized are declared as existing, not as being introduced or expanded. If in s.1 the Act means what it says and recognizes and declares existing rights and freedoms only, nothing more than proper construction of existing laws in accordance with the Bill is required to accomplish the intended result. There can never be any necessity for declaring any of them inoperative as coming in conflict with the rights and freedoms defined in the Bill seeing that these are declared as existing in them. Thus, it appears to me that s. 2 cannot be construed as suggested by respondent without coming in conflict with s. 1.

If, with respect to existing legislation, we had to choose between reading s. 1 as written and failing to adopt a construction of s. 2 that gives some meaningful effect to the exception, it seems to me that the choice should be in favour of giving paramount effect to s. 1. It is the provision establishing the principle on which the whole Act rests.

Another compelling reason is the presumption against implicit alteration of the law; Parliament must not be presumed to have intended to depart from the existing law any further than expressly stated: *Maxwell on Interpretation of Statutes*, 9th ed., p. 84, cited in Duchesneau v. Cook, [1955] S.C.R. 207 at p. 215. In the present case, the judgments below hold in effect that Parliament in enacting the Bill has implicitly repealed not only a large part of the Indian Act but also the fundamental principle that the duty of the Courts is to apply the law as written and they are in no case authorized to fail to give effect to the clearly expressed will of Parliament. It would be a radical departure from this basic British constitutional rule to enact that henceforth the Courts are to declare inoperative all enactments that are considered as not in conformity with some legal principles stated in very general language, or rather merely enumerated without any definition.

The meaning of such expressions as "due process of law", "equality before the law", "freedom of religion", "freedom of speech", is in truth largely unlimited and undefined. According to individual views and the evolution of current ideas, the actual content of such legal concepts is apt to expand and to vary as is strikingly apparent in other countries. In the traditional British system that is our own by virtue of the B.N.A. Act, 1867, the responsibility for updating the statutes in this changing world rests exclusively upon Parliament. If the Parliament of Canada intended to depart from that principle in enacting the Bill, one would expect to find clear language expressing that intention. On the contrary, what do we find in s. 1 but an apparent desire to adhere to the traditional principle and to avoid the uncertainties inherent in broadly worded enactments by tying the broad words to the large body of existing law and in effect declaring the recognized human rights and fundamental freedoms to be as existing in the laws of Canada.

I fail to see how it can be considered that by taking this to be the fundamental intention, the apparent character of the Bill is not fully recognized. I also fail to see how it can be said that to read s. 2 as little more than a rule of construction is to fail to give effect to the Bill. On what basis is it assumed that anything else was intended in an Act that is not of a constitutional character?

That canons of construction are of less importance than constitutional rules does not mean that they are of minimal importance. For instance, in our legal system, the rule against retrospective operation of enactments as well as the principle that a criminal offence requires *mens rea* are nothing more than canons of construction. It certainly does not mean that they are of secondary importance. Decisions such as Beaver v. The Queen, 118 C.C.C. 129, [1957] S.C.R. 531, 26 C.R. 193; R. v. King, 35 D.L.R. (2d) 386, 133 C.C.C. 1, [1962] S.C.R. 746, clearly show how far-reaching such principles are. If the Canadian Parliament should consider it desirable to enshrine them in a statute, would it be contended that those who subsequently read it as not altering their fundamental nature and letting them remain canons of construction are failing to give it effect?

On the whole, I cannot find in the Canadian Bill of Rights anything clearly showing that Parliament intended to establish concerning human rights and fundamental freedoms some overriding general principles to be enforced by the Courts against the clearly expressed will of Parliament in statutes existing at the time. In my opinion, Parliament did nothing more than instruct the Courts to construe and apply those laws in accordance with the principles enunciated in the Bill on the basis that the recognized rights and freedoms did exist, not that they were to be brought into existence by the Courts.

For those reasons I would allow the appeal, reverse the judgments of the Court of Appeal and of the Territorial Court of the Northwest Territories, and re-establish the conviction and sentence. In view of the terms of the order granting leave to appeal, it is presumed that suitable arrangements have been made for the costs of representation of the respondent and therefore no order requires to be made in that regard.

Since writing the above I have had the advantage of reading the reasons of the Chief Justice and I wish to add that I agree with his observations entirely.

$$* \quad * \quad *$$

Appeal dismissed.

CHAPTER 4

Calder

THIS CASE is cited as Calder v. Attorney-General of British Columbia, S.C.C. (1973). The Nishga Indian Tribal Council had gone to the courts in search of a declaration that they held an unextinguished Aboriginal title to their traditional territories. Both the lower court and the British Columbia Court of Appeal ruled against them, so they appealed to the Supreme Court of Canada. The decision was handed down on January 31, 1973.

The Supreme Court decision was a complex and divided one. Judson wrote the decision, with Hall writing the dissenting opinion. Ritchie and Martland concurred with Judson, while Laskin and Spence concurred with Hall. The deciding vote was cast by Pigeon, who ignored the substantive issues of the case and voted to dismiss the appeal on a technicality not directly related to the issue of Aboriginal title.

Both Judson's and Hall's opinions in the case contain extensive discussions of the Royal Proclamation of 1763, the St. Catherine's Milling case, the Marshall decisions, and the nature of Aboriginal title and the process of extinguishing it. While the Supreme Court Justices were divided on the question of whether the policies of the Royal Proclamation had jurisdiction in British Columbia, Judson wrote:

> Although I think it is clear that Indian title in British Columbia cannot owe its origin to the Proclamation of 1763, the fact is that when the settlers came, the Indians were there, organized in societies and occupying the land as their forefathers had done for centuries. This is what Indian title means and it does not help one in the solution of this problem to call it a 'personal or usufructuary right'. (69)

This meant that all of the justices excluding Pigeon, who did not express an opinion on the matter, believed that Aboriginal title existed in law. The question then became whether or not the Aboriginal title of the Nishga had been extinguished in spite of the fact that there was no treaty, no agreement with the Nishga surrendering their title and no explicit federal or provincial legislation that said their title was extinguished.

Judson thought that title had been extinguished, and he dismissed the appeal.

Hall's dissenting opinion is frequently cited in the chapters which follow and aspects of it have now been adopted in later Supreme Court majority decisions. Hall thought that the Royal Proclamation did have jurisdiction, arguing that the lands west of the Rocky Mountains were known to the British at the time of the Proclamation and that the literal wording of the Proclamation supported a view that it should be applied. On the question of whether title recognized either by common law or the Proclamation had been extinguished, Hall wrote: "it would . . . appear beyond question that the onus of proving that the Sovereign intended to extinguish the Indian title lies on the respondent and that intention must be 'clear and plain'. There is no such proof in the case at bar; no legislation to that effect" (117).

Pigeon's tie-breaking vote dismissed the appeal on a technicality. He argued that "I have to hold that the preliminary objection that the declaration prayed for, being a claim of title against the Crown in the right of the Province of British Columbia, the Court has no jurisdiction to make it in the absence of a fiat of the Lieutenant-Governor of that Province" (126). Some of the discussion of sources for this argument has been edited.

In spite of the fact that the Nishga lost the case, the Calder decision was seen by many as a major victory in the struggle for Aboriginal title. Six Supreme Court Justices had agreed that Aboriginal title existed in law and, where it was not extinguished, continued to have force. A persuasive defense of the concept of Aboriginal title, including a powerful argument that title could not be extinguished unless the Sovereign showed a clear and plain intent to do so, was recorded in Hall's dissenting opinion; these are views which were eventually adopted by the Supreme Court (see Sparrow).

The case helped convince the Canadian government to begin negotiating comprehensive land claims where Aboriginal title had not been extinguished through the treaty process. It is worth noting that among the lawyers for the Nishga was Thomas Berger, who acted with D.J. Rosenbloom and J.M. Baigent. Douglass McK. Brown and A.W. Hobbs acted for British Columbia. Among the key witnesses, cited extensively by both Judson and Hall, was the anthropologist Wilson Duff. The case has been lightly edited, removing long quotes used more than once and some of the technical arguments around whether a fiat was needed from the Crown.

P.K.

MARTLAND J., concurs with JUDSON J.

*   *   *

JUDSON J.: The appellants sue, as representatives of the Nishga Indian Tribe, for a declaration "that the aboriginal title, otherwise known as the Indian title, of the Plaintiffs . . . has never been lawfully extinguished". The action was dismissed at trial. The Court of Appeal rejected the appeal. The appellants appeal from both decisions.

The appellants are members of the Nishga Nation, which is made up of four bands: Gitlakdami, Canyon City, Greenville and Kincolith. They are officers of the Nishga Tribal Council and councillors of each of the four Indian bands. They are descendants of the Indians who have inhabited since time immemorial the territory in question, where they have hunted, fished and roamed. It was agreed for purposes of this litigation that this territory consisted of 1,000 square miles in and around the Nass River Valley, Observatory Inlet, Portland Inlet and the Portland Canal, all located in north-western British Columbia. No other interest has intervened in this litigation to question the accuracy of this agreed statement of facts.

The Crown in right of the Province has made certain grants in this territory, some in fee simple; in other cases rights of pre-emption, mineral and mining rights, petroleum permits, forestry rights and titles, and tree farm licences. However, the vast bulk of the area remains still unalienated.

No treaty or contract with the Crown or the Hudson's Bay Company has ever been entered into with respect to the area by anyone on behalf of the Nishga Nation. Within the area there are a number of reserves but they comprise only a small part of the total land. The Nishga Nation did not agree to or accept the creation of these reserves. The Nishgas claim that their title arises out of aboriginal occupation; that recognition of such a title is a concept well embedded in English law; that it is not dependent on treaty, executive order or legislative enactment. In the alternative they say that if executive or legislative recognition ever was needed, it is to be found in the Royal Proclamation of 1763, in Imperial statutes acknowledging that what is now British Columbia was "Indian Territory", and in Royal instructions to the Governor of British Columbia. Finally, they say that their title has never been extinguished.

All these claims, at one point or another, were rejected in the judgments under appeal.

In the agreed statement of facts, the mode of life of the Indians is set out in rather bald terms. This description is amplified in the material filed at the hearing. I refer to the *Indian History of British Columbia*, chapter 8, by Wilson Duff, published in 1964:

> It is not correct to say that the Indians did not "own" the land but only roamed over the face of it and "used" it. The patterns of ownership and utilization which they imposed upon the lands and waters were different from those recognized by our system of law, but were nonetheless clearly defined and mutually respected. Even if they didn't subdivide and cultivate the land, they did recognize ownership of plots used for village sites, fishing places, berry and root patches, and similar purposes. Even if they didn't subject the forests to wholesale logging, they did establish ownership of tracts used for hunting, trapping, and food-gathering. Even if they didn't sink mine shafts into the mountains, they did own peaks and valleys for mountain goat hunting and as sources of raw materials. Except for barren and inaccessible areas which are not utilized even today, every part of the Province was formerly within the owned and recognized territory of one or other of the Indian tribes.

The Nishga answer to Government assertions of absolute ownership of the land within their boundaries was made as early as 1888 before the first Royal Commission to visit the Nass Valley. Their spokesman said:

> David Mackay—What we don't like about the Government is their saying this: "We will give you this much land." How can they give it when it is our own? We cannot understand it. They have never bought it from us or our forefathers. They have never fought and conquered our people and taken the land in that way, and yet they say now that they will give us so much land—our own land. These chiefs do not talk foolishly, they know the land is their own; our forefathers for generations and generations past had their land here all around us; chiefs have had their own hunting grounds, their salmon streams, and places where they got their berries; it has always been so. It is not only during the last four or five years that we have seen the land; we have always seen and owned it; it is no new thing, it has been ours for generations. If we had only seen it for twenty years and claimed it as our own, it would have been foolish, but it has been ours for thousands of years. If any strange person came here and saw the land for twenty years and claimed it, he would be foolish. We have always got our living from the land; we are not like white people who live in towns and have their stores and other business, getting their living in that way, but we have always depended on the land for our food and clothes; we get our salmon, berries, and furs from the land.

Any Canadian inquiry into the nature of the Indian title must begin with R. v. St. Catherine's Milling & Lumber Co. v. The Queen (1885), 10 O.R. 196; affd (1886), 13 O.A.R. 148; affd (1887), 13 S.C.R. 577; affd (1888), 14 App. Cas. 46. This case went through the Ontario Courts, the Supreme Court of Canada and ended in the Privy Council. The Crown in right of the Province sought to restrain the milling company from cutting timber on certain lands in the District of Algoma. The company pleaded that it held a licence from the Dominion Government which authorized the cutting. In 1873, by a treaty known as the North-West Angle Treaty No. 3, the Dominion had extinguished the Indian title.

The decision throughout was that the extinction of the Indian title enured to the benefit of the Province and that it was not possible for the Dominion to preserve that title so as to oust the vested right of the Province to the land as part of the public domain of Ontario. It was held that the Crown had at all times a present proprietary estate, which title, after Confederation, was in the Province, by virtue of s.109 of the B.N.A. Act. The Indian title was a mere burden upon that title which, following the cession of the lands under the treaty, was extinguished.

The reasons for judgment delivered in the Canadian Courts in the St. Catherine's case were strongly influenced by two early judgments delivered in the Supreme Court of the United States by Chief Justice Marshall—Johnson and Graham's Lessee v. M'Intosh (1823), 8 Wheaton 543, 21 U.S. 240, and Worcester v. State of Georgia (1832), 6 Peters 515, 31 U.S. 530. In Johnson v. M'Intosh the actual decision was that a title to lands, under grants to private individuals, made by Indian tribes or nations north-west of the river Ohio, in 1773 and 1775, could not be recognized in the Courts of the United States. In Worcester v. Georgia, the plaintiff, who was a missionary, was charged with residing among the Cherokees without a licence from the State of Georgia. His defence was that his residence was in conformity with treaties between the United States and the Cherokee nation and that the law under which he was charged was repugnant to the constitution, treaties and laws of the United States. The Supreme Court made a declaration to this effect. Both cases raised the question of aboriginal title to land. The following passage from 8 Wheaton at pp. 587-8 gives a clear summary of the views of the Chief Justice:

> The United States, then, have unequivocally acceded to that great and broad rule by which its civilized inhabitants now hold this country. They hold, and assert in themselves, the title by which it was acquired. They maintain, as all others have maintained, that discovery gave an exclusive right to extinguish the Indian title of occupancy, either by purchase or by conquest; and gave also a right to such a degree of sovereignty, as the circumstances of the people would allow them to exercise.
>
> The power now possessed by the government of the United States to grant lands, resided, while we were colonies, in the crown, or its grantees. The validity of the titles given by either has never been questioned in our Courts. It has been exercised uniformly over territory in possession of the Indians. The existence of this power must negative the existence of any right which may conflict with, and control it. An absolute title to lands cannot exist, at the same time in different persons, or in different governments. An absolute, must be an exclusive title, or at least a title which excludes all others not compatible with it. All our institutions recognise the absolute title of the crown, subject only to the Indian right of occupancy, and recognise the absolute title of the crown to extinguish that right. This is incompatible with an absolute and complete title in the Indians.

The description of the nature of Indian title in the Canadian Courts in the St. Catherine's case is repeated in the reasons delivered in the Privy Council. I quote from 14 App. Cas. at pp. 54-5:

> The territory in dispute has been in Indian occupation from the date of the proclamation until 1873. During that interval of time Indian affairs have been administered successively by the Crown, by the Provincial Government, and (since the passing of the British North America Act, 1867), by the Government of the Dominion. The policy of these administrations has been all along the same in this respect, that the Indian inhabitants have been precluded from entering into any transaction with a subject for the sale or transfer of their interest in the land, and have only been permitted to surrender their rights to the Crown by a formal contract, duly ratified in a meeting of their chiefs or head men convened for the purpose. Whilst there have been changes in the administrative authority, there has been no change since the year 1763 in the character of the interest which its Indian inhabitants had in the lands surrendered by the treaty. Their possession, such as it was, can only be ascribed to the general provisions made by the royal proclamation in favour of all Indian tribes then living under the sovereignty and protection of the British Crown. It was suggested in the

course of the argument for the Dominion, that inasmuch as the proclamation recites that the territories thereby reserved for Indians had never "been ceded to or purchased by" the Crown, the entire property of the land remained with them. That inference is, however, at variance with the terms of the instrument, which shew that the tenure of the Indians was a personal and usufructuary right, dependent upon the good will of the Sovereign. The lands reserved are expressly stated to be "parts of Our dominions and territories"; and it is declared to be the will and pleasure of the sovereign that, "for the present," they shall be reserved for the use of the Indians, as their hunting grounds, under his protection and dominion. There was a great deal of learned discussion at the Bar with respect to the precise quality of the Indian right, but their Lordships do not consider it necessary to express any opinion upon the point. It appears to them to be sufficient for the purposes of this case that there has been all along vested in the Crown a substantial and paramount estate, underlying the Indian title, which became a plenum dominium whenever that title was surrendered or otherwise extinguished.

There can be no doubt that the Privy Council found that the Proclamation of 1763 was the origin of the Indian title —"Their possession, such as it was, can only be ascribed to the . . . royal proclamation in favour of all Indian tribes then living under the sovereignty and protection of the British Crown."

I do not take these reasons to mean that the Proclamation was the exclusive source of Indian title. The territory in the St. Catherine's appeal was clearly within the geographical limits set out in the Proclamation. It is part of the appellants' case that the Proclamation does apply to the Nishga territory and that they are entitled to its protection. They also say that if it does not apply to the Nishga territory, their Indian title is still entitled to recognition by the Courts. These are two distinct questions.

I say at once that I am in complete agreement with judgments of the British Columbia Courts in this case that the Proclamation has no bearing upon the problem of Indian title in British Columbia. I base my opinion upon the very terms of the Proclamation and its definition of its geographical limits and upon the history of the discovery, settlement and establishment of what is now British Columbia.

Following the Treaty of Paris, General Murray was appointed the first Governor of Quebec. By Royal Proclamation, dated October 7, 1763 [see R.S.C. 1952, vol. VI, p. 6127], which accompanied his commission, he was directed with respect to Indians that he should "upon no account molest or disturb them in the possession of such parts of the said province as they at present occupy or possess".

The Crown created four distinct and separate Governments, styled, respectively, Quebec, East Florida, West Florida and Grenada, specific boundaries being assigned to each of them. Upon the recital that it was just and reasonable that the several nations and tribes of Indians, who lived under British protection, should not be molested or disturbed in the "Possession of such Parts of Our Dominions and Territories as, not having been ceded to or purchased by Us, are reserved to them or any of them, as their Hunting Grounds", it is declared that no Governor or Commander-in-Chief in any of the new Colonies of Quebec, East Florida or West Florida, do presume on any pretence to grant warrants of survey or pass any patents for lands beyond the bounds of their respective Governments or, "until our further Pleasure be Known," upon any lands whatever which, not having been ceded or purchased as aforesaid, are reserved to the said Indians or any of them. It was further declared "to be Our Royal Will and Pleasure, for the present as aforesaid, to reserve under our Sovereignty, Protection, and Dominion, for the use of the said Indians, all the Lands and Territories not included . . . within the Limits of the Territory granted to the Hudson's Bay Company". The Proclamation also provides that no private person shall make any purchase from the Indians of lands reserved to them within those Colonies where settlement was permitted, and that all purchases must be on behalf of the Crown, in a public assembly of the Indians, by the Governor or Commander-in-Chief of the Colony in which the lands lie.

It is clear, as the British Columbia Courts have held, and whose reasons I adopt, that the Nishga bands represented by the appellants were not any of the several nations or tribes of Indians who lived under British protection and were outside the scope of the Proclamation.

The British Columbia Courts have dealt with the history of the discovery and settlement of their Province. This history demonstrates that the Nass Valley, and, indeed, the whole of the Province could not possibly be within the terms of the Proclamation.

As to the establishment of British sovereignty in British Columbia in 1818 by a Convention of Commerce between His Majesty and the United States of America, the British Crown and the United States settled the boundary to the height of land in the Rockies, referred to in the Convention as the "Stoney Mountains". The boundary was the 49th parallel of latitude. The Convention provided for the joint occupancy of the lands to the west of that point for a term of 10 years. This Convention was extended indefinitely by a further Convention in 1827.

The area in question in this action never did come under British sovereignty until the Treaty of Oregon in 1846. This treaty extended the boundary along the 49th parallel from the point of termination, as previously laid down, to the channel separating the Continent from Vancouver Island, and thus through the Gulf Islands to Fuca's Straits. The Oregon Treaty was, in effect, a treaty of cession whereby American claims were ceded to Great Britain. There was no mention of Indian rights in any of these Conventions or the treaty.

As to establishment of the northern boundary of what became British Columbia, the Courts below relied on the evidence of Dr. Willard Ireland, Provincial Archivist, who had published a work on the evolution of the boundaries of the Province. He begins with the Imperial ukase of the Czar, dated September 16, 1821, asserting exclusive rights of trade on the Pacific coast as far south as the 51st parallel. There was opposition to this pretension immediately both from Great Britain and the United States. The United States proposed a tri-partite treaty under the terms of which no settlements should be made by Russia south of 55 degrees, by the United States north of 51 degrees or by Great Britain north of 55 degrees or south of 51 degrees. The United States was prepared, if necessary, to accept the 49th parallel as the northern limit for its settlements. This proposal was rejected by the British Government, which preferred to negotiate separately with Russia and the United States. The discussions with Russia culminated in the Convention of February 28, which laid down a line of demarcation.

It was the opinion of Dr. Ireland that although the exact interpretation of these terms became a matter of serious dispute after Russian America was purchased by the United States, this Convention, broadly speaking, established the boundary as it exists today between Canada and Alaska. In other words, it determined the northern limit of British territory on the Pacific coast.

The Colony of Vancouver Island was established by the British Crown in 1849. James Douglas was appointed Governor in 1851. The Colony of British Columbia, being the mainland of what is now the Province, was established by the British Crown in 1858 and the same James Douglas was the first Governor of the Colony with full executive powers. Douglas remained Governor of both Colonies until 1864. On November 17, 1866, the two Colonies were united as one Colony under the British Crown and under the name of British Columbia. This Colony entered Confederation on July 20, 1871, and became the Province of British Columbia and part of the Dominion of Canada.

When the Colony of British Columbia was established in 1858, there can be no doubt that the Nishga territory became part of it. The fee was in the Crown in right of the Colony until July 20, 1871, when the Colony entered Confederation, and thereafter in the Crown in light of the Province of British Columbia, except only in respect of those lands transferred to the Dominion under the Terms of Union.

The political and social conditions prevailing in these two Colonies are described in some detail in the reasons of Tysoe, J.A., 13 D.L.R. (3d) at pp. 80-1:

> Prior to the establishment of the territories of Vancouver Island and the mainland of British Columbia as British colonies they had been governed by the Hudson's Bay Company, of which company James Douglas was for some time the chief factor. It had been his responsibility to see to the orderly settlement of the lands and to control the native Indians, some tribes of which were of a warlike and aggressive nature. Douglas had to keep law and order. The responsibility continued to rest upon his shoulders after the establishment of the colonies and until executive councils were appointed, as in due course they were. Douglas had his difficulties with the Indians on Vancouver Island. In 1862 the white settlers with their children numbered only about one thousand and they were surrounded by an Indian population of nearly thirty thousand. On the mainland he had like troubles but in aggravated form. The territory was much larger and the discovery of gold exacerbated the situation. Vancouver Island had been the scene of an influx of foreigners and it was fear of this that led to the setting up of the Colony of Vancouver Island. On the mainland conditions in this regard were worse. Gold was first discovered on the Fraser River and this resulted in a great number of Americans from the California gold fields entering the territory. They were men who had "a hankering in their minds after annexation to the United States" and they did not have the same respect for the native Indians as did the British colonists. The first white child was born at Fort Langley on the mainland on November 1, 1857. The precious metal was the lure that brought the Kanakas from Hawaii in 1858,

and it is said that in that year there were ten thousand men engaged in gold mining in the Colony of British Columbia. In the years 1859 and 1860 the mining population was being added to by small parties of men who had travelled overland from Eastern Canada. That was the commencement of a slow but steady stream of immigrants from beyond the Rocky Mountains. See Margaret Ormsby, "British Columbia", p. 145, and Cicely Lyons, "Salmon, our Heritage", pp. 80, 81, 82, 85. In the late fifties and early sixties roads were being built into the mining areas. Frequent clashes with the Indians occurred. As immigration increased Douglas became concerned about the danger of Indian warfare spreading into the interior from Washington territory and alarmed about the great hazards of disrespect for Imperial rights and law and order. The search for gold spread further and further north and east. White settlers were spreading out and some were encroaching upon the village lands and other occupied lands of the Indians. The need for protection to the Indians and protection to the settlers against the Indians increased immeasurably. Such protection and an orderly system of settlement became of paramount consideration. Douglas had these matters very much in mind in the year 1858 and in succeeding years.

Although I think that it is clear that Indian title in British Columbia cannot owe its origin to the Proclamation of 1763, the fact is that when the settlers came, the Indians were there, organized in societies and occupying the land as their forefathers had done for centuries. This is what Indian title means and it does not help one in the solution of this problem to call it a "personal or usufructuary right". What they are asserting in this action is that they had a right to continue to live on their lands as their forefathers had lived and that this right has never been lawfully extinguished. There can be no question that this right was "dependent on the goodwill of the Sovereign".

It was the opinion of the British Columbia Courts that this right, if it ever existed, had been lawfully extinguished, that with two societies in competition for land—the white settlers demanding orderly settlement and the Indians demanding to be let alone—the proper authorities deliberately chose to set apart reserves for Indians in various parts of the territory and open up the rest for settlements. They held that this had been done when British Columbia entered Confederation in 1871 and that the Terms of Union recognized this fact.

As to Vancouver Island, we have before us a collection of dispatches between the Colonial Office and Governor Douglas in connection with the Indian problem that was confronting him. The first, dated July 31, 1858, contains an admonition that it should be an invariable condition in all bargains or treaties with the natives for the cession of lands possessed by them that subsistence should be supplied in some other shape. It is in the following terms.

July 31, 1858

I have to enjoin upon you to consider the best and most humane means of dealing with the Native Indians. The feelings of this country would be strongly opposed to the adoption of any arbitrary or oppressive measures towards them. At this distance, and with the imperfect means of knowledge which I possess, I am reluctant to offer, as yet, any suggestion as to the prevention of affrays between the Indians and the immigrants. This question is of so local a character that it must be solved by your knowledge and experience, and I commit it to you, in the full persuasion that you will pay every regard to the interests of the Natives which an enlightened humanity can suggest. Let me not omit to observe, that it should be an invariable condition, in all bargains or treaties with the natives for the cession of lands possessed by them, that subsistence should be supplied to them in some other shape, and above all, that it is the earnest desire of Her Majesty's Government that your early attention should be given to the best means of diffusing the blessings of the Christian Religion and of civilization among the natives.

These dispatches are detailed and informative on both sides. They set out the difficulties and problems as they arose and suggestions for their solution. I quote from the last dispatch of the Governor, which conveniently summarizes his efforts:

Victoria, 25th March, 1861

My Lord Duke,—I have the honour of transmitting a petition from the House of Assembly of Vancouver Island to your Grace, praying for the aid of Her Majesty's Government in extinguishing the Indian title to the public lands in this Colony; and setting forth, with much force and truth, the evils that may arise from the neglect of that very necessary precaution.

2. As the native Indian population of Vancouver Island have distinct ideas of property in land, and mutually recognize their several exclusive possessory rights in certain districts, they would not fail to regard the occupation of such portions of the Colony by white settlers, unless with the full consent of the proprietary tribes, as national wrongs; and the sense of injury might produce a feeling of irritation against the settlers, and perhaps disaffection to the Government that would endanger the peace of the country.

3. Knowing their feelings on that subject, I made it a practice up to the year 1859, to purchase the native rights in the land, in every case prior to the settlement of any district; but since that time in consequence of the termination of the Hudson's Bay Company's Charter, and the want of funds, it has not been in my power to continue it. Your Grace must, indeed, be well aware that I have, since then, had the utmost difficulty in raising money enough to defray the most indispensable wants of Government.

He then went on to point out the need for further purchases, totalling in all three thousand pounds, and asked for a loan of this amount from the Imperial Government. The reply was that the problem was essentially local in character and the money would have to be raised in the Colony. The full reply is as follows:

Downing Street, 19th October, 1861

Sir.—I have had under my consideration your despatch No. 24, of the 25th of March last, transmitting an Address from the House of Assembly of Vancouver Island, in which they pray for the assistance of Her Majesty's Government in extinguishing the Indian title to the public lands in the Colony, and set forth the evils that may result from a neglect of this precaution.

I am fully sensible of the great importance of purchasing without loss of time the native title to the soil of Vancouver Island; but the acquisition of the title is a purely colonial interest, and the Legislature must not entertain any expectation that the British taxpayer will be burthened to supply the funds or British credit pledged for the purpose. I would earnestly recommend therefore to the House of Assembly, that they should enable you to procure the requisite means, but if they should not think proper to do so, Her Majesty's Government cannot undertake to supply the money requisite for an object which, whilst it is essential to the interests of the people of Vancouver Island, is at the same time purely Colonial in its character, and trifling in the charge that it would entail.

The reasons for judgment next deal with a series of Proclamations by James Douglas as Governor of the Colony of British Columbia. The first is dated December 2, 1858, and it is stated to be a Proclamation having the force of law to enable the Governor of British Columbia to have Crown lands sold within the said Colony. It authorized the Governor to grant any land belonging to the Crown in the Colony.

The second Proclamation is dated February 14, 1859. It declared that all lands in British Columbia and all mines and minerals thereunder belonged to the Crown in fee. It provided for the sale of these lands after surveys had been made and the lands were ready for sale, and that due notice should be given of such sales.

The third Proclamation is dated January 4, 1860. It provided for British subjects and aliens who take the oath of allegiance acquiring unoccupied and unreserved and unsurveyed Crown land, and for the subsequent recognition of the claim after the completion of the survey.

The fourth Proclamation is dated January 20, 1860. It provided for the sale of certain lands by private contract and authorized the Commissioner of Land and all Magistrates and Gold Commissioners to make these sales at certain prices.

The fifth Proclamation of January 19, 1861, dealt with further details of land sales.

The sixth Proclamation, dated January 19, 1861, reduced the price of land.

The seventh Proclamation, dated May 28, 1861, dealt with conditions of pre-emption and limited the right to 160 acres per person.

The eighth Proclamation, dated August 27, 1861, was a consolidation of the laws affecting the settlement of unsurveyed Crown lands in British Columbia.

The ninth Proclamation, dated May 27, 1863, dealt with the establishment of mining districts.

Then follow four Ordinances enacted by the Governor by and with the consent of the Legislative Council of British Columbia. The first is dated April 11, 1865. It repeats what the Proclamation had previously said, namely, that all lands in British Columbia and all mines and minerals therein, not otherwise lawfully appropriated, belong the Crown in fee. It goes on to provide for the public sale of lands and the price; that unless otherwise specially announced at the time of the sale, the conveyance of the lands shall include all trees and all mines and minerals within and under the same (except mines of gold and silver). It also deals with rights of pre-emption of unoccupied, unsurveyed and unreserved Crown lands "not being the site of an existent or proposed town, or auriferous land or an Indian reserve or settlement under certain conditions".

The next Ordinance, dated March 31, 1866, restricts those who may acquire lands by pre-emption under the Ordinance of April 11, 1865. British subjects or aliens who take the oath of allegiance have this right but it does not extend without special permission of the Governor to companies or "to any of the Aborigines of this Colony or the Territories neighbouring thereto".

The third Ordinance is dated March 10, 1869. It deals with the payment of purchase money for pre-emption claims.

The last Ordinance is dated June 1, 1870, and is one to amend and consolidate the laws affecting Crown lands in British Columbia.

The result of these Proclamations and Ordinances was stated by Gould, J., at the trial in the following terms [8 D.L.R. (3d) at pp. 81-2]. I accept his statement, as did the Court of Appeal:

> The various pieces of legislation referred to above are connected, and in many instances contain references inter se, especially XIII. They extend back well prior to November 19, 1866, the date by which, as a certainty, the delineated lands were all within the boundaries of the Colony of British Columbia, and thus embraced in the land legislation of the Colony, where the words were appropriate. All thirteen reveal a unity of intention to exercise, and the legislative exercising, of absolute sovereignty over all the lands of British Columbia, a sovereignty inconsistent with any conflicting interest, including one as to "aboriginal title, otherwise known as the Indian title", to quote the statement of claim. The legislation prior to November 19, 1866, is included to show the intention of the successor and connected legislation after that date, which latter legislation certainly included the delineated lands.

The same opinion is expressed in a letter dated January 29, 1870, from Governor Musgrave to the Colonial Office, which had received certain representations from the Aborigines Protection Society relative to the conditions of the Indians on Vancouver Island. He had a memorandum prepared by the Commissioner of Lands and Works and Surveyor-General, Mr. Trutch. When the Colony entered Confederation on July 20, 1871, Mr. Trutch was appointed its first Lieutenant Governor. He had served as the Colony's chief negotiator, both in Ottawa and London, of the terms of entry into Confederation, and he had resided in the Colony since it was established in 1858. He said in part:

> The Indians have, in fact, been held to be the special wards of the Crown, and in the exercise of this guardianship Government has, in all cases where it has been desirable for the interests of the Indians, set apart such portions of the Crown lands as were deemed proportionate to, and amply sufficient for, the requirements of each tribe; and these Indian Reserves are held by Government, in trust, for the exclusive use and benefit of the Indians resident thereon.
>
> But the title of the Indians in the fee of the public lands, or of any portion thereof, has never been acknowledged by Government, but, on the contrary, is distinctly denied. In no case has any special agreement been made with any of the tribes of the Mainland for the extinction of their claims of

possession; but these claims have been held to have been fully satisfied by securing to each tribe, as the progress of the settlement of the country seemed to require, the use of sufficient tracts of land for their wants for agricultural and pastoral purposes.

The terms used in this letter bring to mind what was said on the subject of extinguishment of Indian title in United States v. Santa Fe Pacific R. Co. (1941), 314 U.S. 339 at p. 347:

Nor is it true, as respondent urges, that a tribal claim to any particular lands must be based upon a treaty, statute, or other formal government action. As stated in the Cramer case, "The fact that such right of occupancy finds no recognition in any statute or other formal governmental action is not conclusive." 261 U.S. at 229.

Extinguishment of Indian title based on aboriginal possession is of course a different matter. The power of Congress in that regard is supreme. The manner, method and time of such extinguishment raise political, not justiciable, issues. Buttz v. Northern Pacific Railroad, supra [119 U.S. 55], p. 66. As stated by Chief Justice Marshall in Johnson v. M'Intosh, supra [8 Wheaton 543], p. 586, "the exclusive right of the United States to extinguish" Indian title has never been doubted. And whether it be done by treaty, by the sword, by purchase, by the exercise of complete dominion adverse to the right of occupancy, or otherwise, its justness is not open to inquiry in the courts. Beecher v. Wetherby, 95 U.S. 517, 525.

To the same effect are the reasons delivered in the Privy Council in Re Southern Rhodesia, [1919] A.C. 211.

The Terms of Union under which British Columbia entered into Confederation with the Dominion of Canada are also of great significance in this problem. These terms were approved by Imperial Order in Council dated May 16, 1871 [see R.S.C. 1952, vol. VI, p. 6259; R.S.B.C. 1960, vol. V, p. 5223], which has, under s. 146 of the B.N.A. Act, the force of an Imperial statute. Term 13 reads:

13. The charge of the Indians, and the trusteeship and management of the lands reserved for their use and benefit, shall be assumed by the Dominion Government, and a policy as liberal as that hitherto pursued by the British Columbia Government shall be continued by the Dominion Government after the Union.

To carry out such policy, tracts of land of such extent as it has hitherto been the practice of the British Columbia Government to appropriate for that purpose, shall from time to time be conveyed by the Local Government to the Dominion Government in trust for the use and benefit of the Indians on application of the Dominion Government; and in case of disagreement between the two Governments respecting the quantity of such tracts of land to be so granted, the matter shall be referred for the decision of the Secretary of State for the Colonies.

On the question of reserves, it is convenient to mention at this point, though it is out of chronological order, the McKenna-McBride Commission, its Report and the Dominion legislation which followed on its recommendations.

The Commission was established in 1913 to settle all differences between the Dominion and the Province of British Columbia respecting Indian lands and Indian affairs generally in the Province. Seven years later, the recommendations of this Commission were followed by Dominion legislation, 1920 (Can. 2nd Sess.), c. 51. This legislation is entitled "An Act to provide for the Settlement of Differences between the Governments of the Dominion of Canada and the Province of British Columbia respecting Indian Lands and certain other Indian affairs in the said Province." It recites the establishment of the Commission, the receipt of its report and recommendations as to lands reserved and to be reserved for Indians in the Province of British Columbia, and otherwise for the settling of all differences between the said Governments respecting Indian lands and Indian affairs generally in the Province. Section 2 of the Act reads:

> 2. To the full extent to which the Governor in Council may consider it reasonable and expedient the Governor in Council may do, execute, and fulfil every act, deed, matter or thing necessary for the carrying out of the said Agreement between the Governments of the Dominion of Canada and the Province of British Columbia according to its true intent, and for giving effect to the report of the said Royal Commission, either in whole or in part, and for the full and final adjustment and settlement of all differences between the said Governments respecting Indian lands and Indian affairs in the Province.

The recommendations of the Commission resulted in the establishment of new or confirmation of old Indian reserves in the Nass area. They are over thirty in number. Frank Calder, one of the appellants, says that this was done over Indian objections. Nevertheless, the federal authority did act under its powers under s. 91(24) of the B.N.A. Act, 1867. It agreed, on behalf of the Indians, with the policy of establishing these reserves.

In the Department of Indian Affairs and Northern Development there exists a Nass River Agency that administers the area in question. The reserves generally correspond with the fishing places that the Indians had traditionally used. The Government of the original Crown colony and, since 1871, the Government of British Columbia have made alienations in the Nass Valley that are inconsistent with the existence of an aboriginal title. These have already been referred to and show alienations in fee simple and by way of petroleum and natural gas leases, mineral claims and tree farm licences.

Further, the establishment of the railway belt under the Terms of Union is inconsistent with the recognition and continued existence of Indian title. Term 11 reads:

> 11. The Government of the Dominion undertake to secure the commencement simultaneously, within two years from the date of the Union, of the construction of a railway from the Pacific towards the Rocky Mountains, and from such point as may be selected, east of the Rocky Mountains, towards the Pacific, to connect the seaboard of British Columbia with the railway system of Canada; and, further, to secure the completion of such railway within ten years from the date of the Union.

And the Government of British Columbia agree to convey to the Dominion Government, in trust, to be appropriated in such manner as the Dominion Government may deem advisable in furtherance of the construction of the said railway, a similar extent of public lands along the line of railway, throughout its entire length in British Columbia (not to exceed however, twenty (20) miles on each side of said line), as may be appropriated for the same purpose by the Dominion Government from the public lands of the North-West territories and the Province of Manitoba: Provided that the quantity of land which may be held under pre-emption right or by Crown grant within the limits of the tract of land in British Columbia to be so conveyed to the Dominion Government shall be made good to the Dominion from contiguous public lands; and provided further, that until the commencement, within two years, as aforesaid, from the date of the Union, of the construction of the said railway, the Government of British Columbia shall not sell or alienate any further portions of the public lands of British Columbia in any other way than under right of pre-emption requiring actual residence of the pre-emptor on the land claimed by him. In consideration of the land to be conveyed in aid of the construction of the said railway, the Dominion Government agree to pay to British Columbia, from the date of the Union, the sum of 100,000 dollars per annum, in half yearly payments in advance.

There was no reservation of Indian rights in respect of the railway belt to be conveyed to the Dominion Government.

From what I have already said, it is apparent that before 1871 there were no treaties between the Indian tribes and the Colony relating to lands on the mainland. From the material filed, it appears that on Vancouver Island there were, in all, fourteen purchases of Indian lands in the area surrounding Fort Victoria. These are the ones referred to in the correspondence between James Douglas and the Colonial Office. In 1899, Treaty 8 was negotiated and certain tribes of northeastern British Columbia were grouped with the Cree, Beaver, Chipewyan, Alberta and Northwest Territories' tribes, and included in the treaty. The area covered by this treaty is vast—both in the Northwest Territories and northeastern British Columbia. There can be no doubt that by this treaty the Indians surrendered their rights in both areas.

The appellants submit that this treaty constituted a recognition of their rights by the Dominion in 1899. Whether this involved a recognition of similar rights over the rest of the Province of British Columbia is another matter. The territorial limitations of the treaty and the fact that the Indians of north-eastern British Columbia were included with those in the Northwest Territories may have some significance. But the answer of the Province is still the same—that original Indian title had been extinguished in the Colony of British Columbia prior to Confederation and that there were no Indian claims to transfer to the Dominion beyond those mentioned in term 13 of the Terms of Union.

In the United States an issue closely comparable with the one now before us was dealt with in three fairly recent cases in the Supreme Court. These cases are: United States v. Alcea Band of Tillamooks et al. (1946), 329 U.S. 40; United States

v. Alcea Band of Tillamooks et al. (1951), 341 U.S. 48; Tee-Hit-Ton Indians v. United States (1955), 348 U.S. 272.

In these cases the Indians were claiming compensation for the taking of their lands outside their reserves and not covered by any treaty. The facts in the first Tillamooks case were these: After creating a Government for the Territory of Oregon by Act of 1848, Congress in 1850 authorized the negotiation of treaties with Indian tribes in the area. The official designated by the legislation concluded a treaty providing for the cession of Indian lands in return for certain money payments, and the creation of a reservation which by the very terms of its creation might be subject to future diminution. This treaty was only to be operative upon ratification. It was not submitted to the Senate until 1857 and it was never ratified. The reservation itself in subsequent years was reduced in size either by executive order or Act of Congress in order to open up more land for public settlement. Eventually, in 1894 Congress approved of the reservation as it then existed, i.e., at its reduced size, and from then on did not take reservation lands without compensation.

The Tillamooks tribe brought action against the United States under an Act of 1935, which gave the Court of Claims jurisdiction to hear and adjudicate cases involving any and all legal and equitable claims arising under or growing out of the original Indian title, claims or rights in the lands described in the unratified treaties. The judgment of the majority was that on proof of their original Indian title to the designated lands, and that their interest in these lands was taken without their consent and without compensation, the Tillamooks were entitled to recover compensation without showing that the original Indian title was ever formally recognized by the United States.

This was the first time that such a claim had been accepted and paid for in the United States. There had been previous cases where lands which had been re-served for Indians pursuant to treaty had been taken by the United States without the consent of the Indians. Such cases were Shoshone Tribe of Indians v. United States (1937) 299 U.S. 476 and United States v. Klamath and Moadoc Tribes of Indians (1938), 304 U.S. 119.

In the Shoshone case the Indians, by a treaty made in 1868, had a reservation set apart for their exclusive use. Ten years later the Commissioner of Indian Affairs settled another band of Indians on the reservation and from then on treated the two tribes as equal beneficiaries of the reservation. Acts of Congress subsequently adopted the policy initiated by the Commissioner. The Shoshones protested for a long time against this invasion of their rights, and eventually, in 1927, secured from Congress a jurisdictional Act which permitted them to claim compensation for the taking of an undivided one-half interest in their tribal lands.

In view of the subsequent developments in the Tillamooks and Tee-Hit-Ton cases, the basis of the award for compensation is of great interest. The Shoshones were awarded not only the value of their property rights at the time of taking, but also such additional amount as might be necessary to award just compensation, [p. 496] "the increment to be measured either by interest on the value or by such other standard as might be suitable in the light of all the circumstances".

In the Klamath case, a similar award was made for the taking of part of their reserve.

The significance of the Tillamooks case [329 U.S. 40] is that the Court held that the principle of awarding compensation for the taking of Indian Reserves applied equally to claims arising out of original Indian title. The ratio of the majority appears in the following paragraph from the reasons of Vinson, C.J. [p. 51]:

> Nor do other cases in this Court lend substance to the dichotomy of "recognized" and "unrecognized" Indian title which petitoner urges. Many cases recite the paramount power of Congress to extinguish the Indian right of occupancy by methods the justice of which "is not open to inquiry in the courts." United States v. Santa Fe Pacific R. Co., supra [314 U.S.], at 347. Lacking a jurisdictional act permitting judicial inquiry, such language cannot be questioned where Indians are seeking payment for appropriated lands; but here in the 1935 statute Congress has authorized decision by the courts upon claims arising out of original Indian title. Furthermore, some cases speak of the unlimited power of Congress to deal with those Indian lands which are held by what petitioner would call "recognized" title; yet it cannot be doubted that, given the consent of the United States to be sued, recovery may be had for an involuntary, uncompensated taking of "recognized" title. We think the same rule applicable to a taking of original Indian title. "Whether this tract . . . was properly called a reservation . . . or unceded Indian country, . . . is a matter of little moment . . . the Indians' right of occupancy has always been held to be sacred: something not to be taken from him except by his consent, and then upon such consideration as should be agreed upon." Minnesota v. Hitchcock, 185 U.S. 373 (1902) 388-9.

Mr. Justice Black agreed with the majority in the result but was of the opinion that the legislation of 1935, which permitted the bringing of the action, also created the obligation on the part of the Government to pay the Tillamooks for all lands for which their ancestors held an "original Indian title". Three Judges dissented. They would have dismissed the claim for the reasons summarized in the following paragraph [p. 64]:

> As we are of the opinion that the jurisdictional act permitted judgment only for claims arising under or growing out of the original Indian title and are further of the opinion that there were no legal or equitable claims that grew out of the taking of this Indian title, we would reverse the judgment of the Court of Claims and direct that the bill of the respondents should be dismissed. Cf. Shoshone Indians v. United States, 324 U.S. 335.

The original Tillamooks case, 329 U.S., cannot be dealt with without its sequel, United States v. Alcea Band of Tillamooks et al. (1951), 341 U.S. 48. In the interval the Court of Claims had heard evidence on the amount of recovery and had given judgment for the value of the lands as of 1855, plus interest from that date. On appeal to the Supreme Court, the award of interest was unanimously set aside. The ground for this decision was that the special jurisdictional Act of 1935 did not expressly provide for the payment of interest, the only exception to this rule being when the taking entitles the claimant to just compensation under the Fifth Amendment [p. 49]:

Looking to the former opinions in this case, we find that none of them expressed the view that recovery was grounded on a taking under the Fifth Amendment. And, since the applicable jurisdictional Act, 49 Stat. 801 (1935), contains no provision authorizing an award of interest, such award must be

Reversed.

This, to me, amounts to an affirmance of the opinion of Mr. Justice Black, above noted, that the jurisdictional Act of 1935 created the obligation to pay. In the first Tillamooks case, the majority had clearly said that there was no difference between compensation for the taking of reserves (Shoshone and Klamath) and for claims under original Indian title, and that both claims came under the Fifth Amendment. The second Tillamooks case receded from this position and held that the claim had to be dealt with under the legislation of 1935 and not under the Fifth Amendment.

The next case is Tee-Hit-Ton Indians v. United States (1955), 348 U.S. 27. The United States had taken certain timber from Alaskan lands which the Indians said belonged to them. They asked for compensation. In this case compensation claimed did not arise from any statutory direction to pay. The petition was founded on the Fifth Amendment and the aboriginal claim against the lands upon which the timber stood. The suit was one which could be brought as a matter of procedure under a jurisdictional Act of 1946 permitting suits for Indian claims accruing after that date. The Court held that the recovery in the Tillamooks cases (329 U.S. 40 and 341 U.S. 48) was based upon a statutory direction to pay for the aboriginal title in the special jurisdictional Act for the purpose of equalizing the Tillamooks with the neighbouring tribes and not that there had been a compensable taking under the Fifth Amendment.

Again, I say this was, in effect, an adoption of the opinion of Mr. Justice Black in the Tillamooks case that the basis of recovery was statutory.

The relevant portion of the Fifth Amendment provides as follows: ". . . nor shall private property be taken for public use, without just compensation." The finding of the Court in the second Tillamooks case was therefore that aboriginal title did not constitute private property compensable under the Amendment.

This position is spelled out in the Tee-Hit-Ton case. In the opinion of the Court, at p. 279, in discussing the nature of aboriginal Indian title, it is said:

> This is not a property right but amounts to a right of occupancy which the sovereign grants and protects against intrusion by third parties but which right of occupancy may be terminated and such lands fully disposed of by the sovereign itself without any legally enforceable obligation to compensate the Indians.

In my opinion, in the present case, the sovereign authority elected to exercise complete dominion over the lands in question, adverse to any right of occupancy which the Nishga Tribe might have had, when, by legislation, it opened up such lands for settlement, subject to the reserves of land set aside for Indian occupation.

We were not referred to any cases subsequent to Tee-Hit-Ton on the problem of compensation for claims arising out of original Indian title. The last word on the subject from the Supreme Court of the United States is, therefore, that there is no right to compensation for such claims in the absence of a statutory direction to pay. An Indian Claims Commission Act was, in fact, passed by Congress in 1946. I note the concluding paragraph in the reasons for judgment in Tee-Hit-Ton [348 U.S. at pp. 290 - 1]. In my opinion, it has equal application to the appeal now before us:

> In the light of the history of Indian relations in this Nation, no other course would meet the problem of the growth of the United States except to make congressional contributions for Indian lands rather than to subject the Government to an obligation to pay the value when taken with interest to the date of payment. Our conclusion does not uphold harshness as against tenderness toward the Indians, but it leaves with Congress, where it belongs, the policy of Indian gratuities for the termination of Indian occupancy of Government-owned land rather than making compensation for its value a rigid constitutional principle.

For the foregoing reasons I have reached the conclusion that this action fails and that the appeal should be dismissed.

There is the further point raised by the respondent that the Court did not have jurisdiction to make the declaratory order requested because the granting of a fiat under the Crown Procedure Act, R.S.B.C. 1960, c. 89, was a necessary prerequisite to bringing the action and it had not been obtained. While it is not necessary, in view of my conclusion as to the disposition of this appeal, to determine this point, I am in agreement with the reasons of my brother Pigeon dealing with it.

I would dismiss the appeal and would make no order as to costs.

* * *

RITCHIE J., concurs with JUDSON J.

* * *

HALL J. (dissenting): This appeal raises issues of vital importance to the Indians of northern British Columbia and, in particular, to those of the Nishga tribe. The Nishga tribe has persevered for almost a century in asserting an interest in the lands which their ancestors occupied since time immemorial. The Nishgas were never conquered nor did they at any time enter into a treaty or deed of surrender as many other Indian tribes did throughout Canada and in southern British Columbia. The Crown has never granted the lands in issue in this action other than a few small parcels later referred to prior to the commencement of the action.

The claim as set out in the statement of claim reads as follows:

> WHEREFORE the Plaintiffs claim a declaration that the aboriginal title, otherwise known as the Indian title, of the Plaintiffs to their ancient tribal territory hereinbefore described, has never been lawfully extinguished.

The Attorney-General of Canada, although given notice under the Constitutional Questions Determination Act, R.S.B.C. 1960, c. 72, elected not to intervene in the action (ex. 3).

It was stated and agreed to by counsel at the hearing in this Court that Parliament had not taken any steps or procedures to extinguish the Indian right of title after British Columbia entered Confederation. The appeal was argued on this basis and on the representation of counsel that no constitutional question was involved.

Consideration of the issues involves the study of many historical documents and enactments received in evidence, particularly exs. 8 to 18 inclusive and exs. 25 and 35. The Court may take judicial notice of the facts of history whether past or contemporaneous: Monarch Steamship Co. Ltd. v. A/B Karlshamns Oljefabriker, [1949] A.C. 196 at p. 234, and the Court is entitled to rely on its own historical knowledge and researches: Read et al. v. Lincoln, [1892] A.C. 644, per Lord Halsbury at pp. 652-4.

The assessment and interpretation of the historical documents and enactments tendered in evidence must be approached in the light of present-day research and knowledge disregarding ancient concepts formulated when understanding of the customs and culture of our original people was rudimentary and incomplete and when they were thought to be wholly without cohesion, laws or culture, in effect a subhuman species. This concept of the original inhabitants of America led Chief Justice Marshall in his otherwise enlightened judgment in Johnson and Graham's Lessee v. M'Intosh (1823), 8 Wheaton 543, 21 U.S. 240, which is the outstanding judicial pronouncement on the subject of Indian rights to say [p. 590], "But the tribes of Indians inhabiting this country were fierce savages, whose occupation was war . . .". We now know that that assessment was ill-founded. The Indians did in fact at times engage in some tribal wars but war was not their vocation and it can be said that their preoccupation with war pales into insignificance when compared to the religious and dynastic wars of "civilized" Europe of the 16th and 17th centuries. Chief Justice Marshall was, of course, speaking with the knowledge available to him in 1823. Chief Justice Davey in the judgment under appeal [13 D.L.R. (3d) 64, 74 W.W.R. 481], with all the historical research and material available since 1823 and notwithstanding the evidence in the record which Gould, J. [8 D.L.R. (3d) 59, 71 W.W.R. 81], found was given "with total integrity", said of the Indians of the mainland of British Columbia [p. 66]:

> ...they were undoubtedly at the time of settlement a very primitive people with few of the institutions of civilized society, and none at all of our notions of private property.

In so saying this in 1970, he was assessing the Indian culture of 1858 by the same standards that the Europeans applied to the Indians of North America two or more centuries before.

The case was tried in part upon written admissions, including the following:

> 1. The Defendant admits that the Plaintiff Frank Calder is the President of the Nishga Tribal Council and that the Plaintiffs James Gosnell, Nelson Azak, William McKay, Anthony Robinson, Robert Stevens, Hubert Doolan and Henry McKay are the officers of the Nishga Tribal Council.
> 6. The Defendants admit that the bands referred to in paragraphs 2, 3, 4 and 5 of the Statement of Claim are the descendants of Indians who have inhabited since time immemorial the area delineated in the map annexed

hereto and signed by counsel for the Plaintiffs and the Defendant.

7. The Defendant admits that the ancestors of persons referred to in paragraphs 2, 3, 4 and 5 of the Statement of Claim in this action had obtained a living since time immemorial from the lands and waters delineated in the map annexed hereto.

Paragraphs 6 and 7 constitute the basis of the claim founded on possession from time immemorial. Further admissions were made at the trial as follows:

MR. BERGER: The Defendant has admitted that the plaintiffs are the officers of the Nishga Tribal Council and members of the Band Councils of each of the bands. The Defendant has also admitted that these bands are the descendants of Indians who have inhabited since time immemorial the area delineated in the map annexed hereto, prepared by Professor Wilson Duff of U.B.C. which has been signed by Counsel for the Plaintiff and Counsel for the Defendant. The Defendant also admits that the ancestors of the persons who are members of the band in the Naas River today had obtained a living since time immemorial from the lands and waters delineated in the map.

The admissions of fact have been signed by my friend, Mr. Brown.

THE COURT: That will be exhibit 1.

The map referred to by Mr. Berger was received in evidence as ex. 2 and the lands in question in this action are those delineated in ex. 2. This is the map referred to in para. 6 of the admissions previously quoted.

All the area outlined in ex. 2 is now internationally recognized as being in Canada, but Canadian sovereignty over part (the greater part of Pearce Island) was not confirmed until the United States-Canadian boundary was fixed by the Alaskan Boundary Commission in 1903. This historical fact cannot be overlooked in considering whether, as the respondent alleges, the Indian right or title, if any, was extinguished between 1858 and when British Columbia entered Confederation in 1871.

The boundary line separating the Territory of Alaska from the Province of British Columbia was in doubt at the time of Confederation. This is borne out by a petition from the Legislative Assembly of British Columbia dated March 12, 1872, which reads in part as follows:

. . . inasmuch as the boundary line between the adjoining Territory of Alaska and the said Province of British Columbia has never been properly defined, and insomuch as it will materially assist in maintaining peace, order, and good government within the said Province to have the boundary line properly laid down—to take such steps as may call the attention of the Dominion Government to the necessity of some action being taken at an early date, to have the boundary line properly defined.

This was followed by attempts to have the boundary line surveyed and there followed extensive communications between the Governments of the United States and of England but no definite action was taken to settle the boundary until a treaty was signed in Washington on January 24, 1903, setting up the Alaska Boundary Commission charged with fixing the boundary.

The appellant Calder described the area as follows:

Q Can you tell his lordship whether the Nishgas today make use of the lands and waters outlined in the map, exhibit 2?
A Put it this way, in answer to your question, from time immemorial the Nishgas have used the Naas River and all its tributaries within the boundaries so submitted, the lands in Observatory Inlet, the lands in Portland Canal, and part of Portland Inlet. We still hunt within those lands and fish in the waters, streams and rivers, we still do, as in time past, have our campsites in these areas and we go there periodically, seasonally, according to the game and the fishing season, and we still maintain these sites and as far as we know, they have been there as far back as we can remember.
 We still roam these territories, we still pitch our homes there whenever it is required according to our livelihood and we use the land as in times past, we bury our dead within the territory so defined and we still exercise the privilege of free men within the territory so defined.
Q Mr. Calder, do you know whether the Indian tribes that live in the area adjacent to the territory outlined in the map, exhibit 2, acknowledged the rights of the Nishga people within the territory?
A Yes, we have a very friendly relationship within the neighbouring tribes to the extent the Nishgas have even allowed historical rights within the area like the famous candle fish.
Q On the map there is a line circling part of the Nass River—
A Just above Naas Bay. You are referring to this?
Q No, I am referring to the circle, the dotted line that encircles the Naas River just above Naas Bay.
A Yes.
THE COURT: That is where it encircles the Naas River?
THE WITNESS: Just above Naas Bay, above and opposite and below. Northeast, I should say, my lord.
MR. BERGER:
Q Does that circle indicate the Ooligchan grounds?
A Yes.
Q Are the rights of any other tribes besides the Nishga people recognized there?
A The Port Simpson people, the Tsimshian tribes have their own locations in which they have their supply of Ooligchans.

The area described by Calder covers all the lands outlined in ex. 2 other than a small parcel granted by the Government of British Columbia for the townsite of Stewart as well as tree farm licence 1 and possibly some mineral leases and timber dispositions of indefinite duration. These parcels total but a fraction of the area in ex. 2. The appellants now make no claim in respect of these parcels but it will be noted that in paras. 19, 20 and 21 of the statement of claim the appellants allege as follows:

19. No part of the said territory was ever ceded to or purchased by Great Britain or the United Kingdom, and no part of the said territory was ever ceded to or purchased by the Colony of British Columbia.

20. No part of the said territory has been ceded to or purchased by the Crown in right of the Province of British Columbia and no part thereof has been purchased from the said Nishga tribe or the Plaintiffs or any of them by the Crown or by any person acting on behalf of the Crown, at a public meeting or assembly or otherwise, or by any person whomsoever.

21. The Plaintiffs say that the Land Act and other statutes of the Province of British Columbia do not apply to the lands comprising the tribal territory of the Nishga tribe so as to confer any title or interest in the said lands unencumbered by the aboriginal title of the Nishga tribe, and that if the Land Act and other statutes of the Province of British Columbia have purported to purport to confer any title or interest unencumbered by the aboriginal title of the Nishga tribe, in any of the land comprising the tribal territory of the Nishga nation, the same are ultra vires the Province of British Columbia.

Paragraph 21 alleges that any disposition by the Province of British Columbia purporting to have been made under the Land Act or other statutes of the Province are ultra vires the Province and also by paras. 1 and 2 of the reply the appellants plead that all the Proclamations and enactments set out and referred to in paras. 12 and 13 of the statement of defence were ultra vires the Colony of British Columbia and of the Province of British Columbia.

The nature of the title of the interest being asserted on behalf of the Nishgas was stated in evidence by Calder in cross-examination as follows:

From time immemorial the Naas River Nishga Indians possessed, occupied and used the Naas Valley, Observatory Inlet, and Portland Inlet and Canal, and within this territory the Nishgas hunted in its woods, fished in its waters, streams and rivers. Roamed, hunted and pitched their tents in the valleys, shores and hillsides. Buried their dead in their homeland territory. Exercised all the privileges of free men in the tribal territory. The Nishgas have never ceded or extinguished their aboriginal title within this territory.

which is actually a quotation from ex. 7.

When asked to state the nature of the right being asserted and for which a declaration was being sought, counsel for the appellants described it as "an interest which is a burden on the title of the Crown; an interest which is usufructuary in nature; a tribal interest inalienable except to the Crown and extinguishable only by legislative enactment of the Parliament of Canada". The exact nature and extent of the Indian right or title does not need to be precisely stated in this litigation. The issue here is whether any right or title the Indians possess as occupants of the land from time immemorial has been extinguished. They ask for a declaration that there has been no extinguishment. The precise nature and value of that right or title would, of course, be most relevant in any litigation that might follow extinguishment in the future because in such an event, according to common law, the expropriation of private rights by the Government under the prerogative necessitates the payment of compensation: Newcastle Breweries Ltd. v. The King, [1920] 1 K.B. 854. Only express words to that effect in an enactment would authorize a taking without compensation. This proposition has been extended to Canada in City of Montreal v. Montreal Harbour Com'rs, [1926] 1 D.L.R. 840, 47 Que. K.B. 163, [1926] A.C. 299. . . . This is not a claim to title in fee but is in the nature of an equitable title or interest (see Cherokee Nation v. State of Georgia (1831), 5 Peters 1, 30 U.S. 1), a usufructuary right and a right to occupy the lands and to enjoy the fruits of the soil, [of] the forest and of the rivers and streams which does not in any way deny the Crown's paramount title as it is recognized by the law of nations. Nor does the Nishga claim challenge the federal Crown's right to extinguish that title. Their position is that they possess a right of occupation against the world except the Crown and that the Crown has not to date lawfully extinguished that right. The essence of the action is that such rights as the Nishgas possessed in 1858 continue to this date. Accordingly, the declaratory judgment asked for implies that the status quo continues and this means that if the right is to be extinguished it must be done by specific legislation in accordance with the law.

The right to possession claimed is not prescriptive in origin because a prescriptive right presupposes a prior right in some other person or authority. Since it is admitted that the Nishgas have been in possession since time immemorial, that fact negatives that anyone ever had or claimed prior possession.

The Nishgas do not claim to be able to sell or alienate their right to possession except to the Crown. They claim the right to remain in possession themselves and to enjoy the fruits of that possession. They do not deny the right of the Crown to dispossess them but say the Crown has not done so. There is no claim for compensation in this action. The action is for a declaration without a claim for consequential relief as contemplated by British Columbia O. 25, r. 5 (M.R. 285) quoted later. However, it must be recognized that if the Nishgas succeed in establishing a right to possession, the question of compensation would remain for future determination as and when proceedings to dispossess them should be taken. British Columbia's position has been that there never was any right or title to extinguish, and alternatively, that if any such right or title did exist it was extinguished in the period between 1858 and Confederation in 1871. The respondent admits that nothing has been done since Confederation to extinguish the right or title.

The appellants do challenge the authority of British Columbia to make grants in derogation of their rights, but because the grants made so far in respect of Nishga lands are so relatively insignificant the appellants have elected to ignore them while maintaining that they were ultra vires.

Unlike the method used to make out title in other contexts, proof of the Indian title or interest is to be made out as a matter of fact. In Amodu Tijani v. Secretary, Southern Nigeria, [1921] 2 A.C. 399, Lord Haldane said at pp. 402-4:

> Their Lordships make the preliminary observation that in interpreting the native title to land, not only in Southern Nigeria, but other parts of the British Empire, much caution is essential. *There is a tendency, operating at times unconsciously, to render that title conceptually in terms which are appropriate only to systems which have grown up under English law. But this tendency has to be held in check closely.* As a rule, in the various systems of native jurisprudence throughout the Empire, there is no such full division between property and possession as English lawyers are familiar with. *A*

very usual form of native title is that of a usufructuary right, which is a mere qualification of or burden on the radical or final title of the Sovereign where that exists. In such cases the title of the Sovereign is a pure legal estate, to which beneficial rights may or may not be attached. But this estate is qualified by a right of beneficial user which may not assume definite forms analogous to estates, or may, where it has assumed these, have derived them from the intrusion of the mere analogy of English jurisprudence. Their Lordships have elsewhere explained principles of this kind in connection with the Indian title to reserve lands in Canada. (See [St. Catherine's Milling & Lumber Co. v. The Queen (1888),] 14 App. Cas. 46 and [A.-G. Que. v. A.-G. Can., 56 D.L.R. 373,] [1920] 1 A.C. 401.) But the Indian title in Canada affords by no means the only illustration of the necessity for getting rid of the assumption that the ownership of land naturally breaks itself up into estates, conceived as creatures of inherent legal principle. Even where an estate in fee is definitely recognized as the most comprehensive estate in land which the law recognizes, it does not follow that outside England it admits of being broken up. In Scotland a life estate imports no freehold title, but is simply in contemplation of Scottish law a burden on a right of full property that cannot be split up. In India much the same principle applies. The division of the fee into successive and independent incorporeal rights of property conceived as existing separately from the possession is unknown. In India, as in Southern Nigeria, there is yet another feature of the fundamental nature of the title to land which must be borne in mind. The title such as it is, may not be that of the individual, as in this country it nearly always is in some form, but may be that of a community. Such a community may have the possessory title to the common enjoyment of a usufruct, with customs under which its individual members are admitted to enjoyment, and even to a right of transmitting the individual enjoyment as members by assignment inter vivos or by succession. To ascertain how far this latter development of right has progressed involves the study of the history of the particular community and its usages in each case. Abstract principles fashioned a priori are of but little assistance, and are as often as not misleading.

(Emphasis added.)

The appellant Calder who is a member of the Legislature of British Columbia testified as follows:

Q Are you on the band list?
A I am.
Q Would you tell his lordship where you were born?
A I was born in Naas Bay, near the mouth of the Naas River.
Q Where were you raised?
A I was raised at Naas Bay and mostly at Greenville.
Q Were your parents members of the Greenville Indian Band?
A Yes they are.
Q Going back beyond your own parents, are you able to say whether your forefathers lived on the Naas River?

A Yes, they did.

Q Now, Mr. Calder, are you a member of the Nishga Tribe?

A Yes, I am.

Q What Indians compose the Nishga Tribe?

A The Nishga Indians that live in the four inlets of the Naas River.

Q What are the names of the four Indians?

A Kincolith.

Q Kincolith?

A That's correct, Greenville, Canyon City and Aiyansh.

Q Can you tell his lordship, Mr. Calder, whether all of the Indians who live in the four communities on the Naas River are members of the Nishga Tribe?

A Yes, they are members of the Nishga Tribe.

Q Do you include not only the men and women but the children as well?

A Yes.

Q What language do the members of the Nishga Tribe speak?

A They speak Nishga, known as Nishga today.

Q Is that language related to any other languages that are spoken on the North Pacific Coast?

A It is not the exact—our neighbouring two tribes, we more or less understand each other, but Nishga itself is in the Naas River, and there is no other neighbouring tribe that has that language.

Q What are the names of the two neighbouring tribes who have a limited understanding of your language?

A Gitskan and Tsimshian.

Q Do you regard yourself as a member of the Nishga Tribe?

A Yes, I do.

Q Do you know if the Indian people who are members of the four Indian bands on the Naas River regard themselves as members of the Nishga Tribe?

A Yes, they do.

Q Apart from their language, do they share anything else in common?

A Besides the language they share our whole way of life.

Q Now, Mr. Calder, I am showing you exhibit 2, which is a map Mr. Brown and I have agreed upon. Does the territory outlined in the map constitute the ancient territory of the Nishga people?

A Yes, it does

Q Have the Nishga people, Mr. Calder, ever surrendered their aboriginal title to the land in exhibit 2?

A They have not.

THE COURT: Isn't that what I have to decide?

MR. BERGER: I don't think the—

MR. BROWN: My friend can ask him what he knows. I think your lordship has summed it up correctly.

THE COURT: That earlier question you phrased, would you repeat it please?

MR. BERGER: The ancient territory of the Nishga people.

THE COURT: Your next question was objected to.

MR. BROWN: I don't object to it, if my friend is using his question in the sense of have there been documents or treaties under which they have surrendered some right. That is a legitimate fact, I think; I withdraw my objection to that extent.

MR. BERGER:

Q You have told the court you were born and raised in the Naas Valley and you were a member of the Nishga Tribe. Are you in fact the President of the Nishga Tribal Council?

A I am the elected President.

Q Have you been President of the Nishga Tribal Council since 1955?

A Yes, since its formation. I have been elected annually as President of the Council, yes.

Q Are you acquainted with the territory outlined in the map, exhibit 2?

A Yes.

Q Have the Nishga people ever signed any document or treaty surrendering their aboriginal title to the territory outlined in the map, exhibit 2?

A The Nishgas have not signed any treaty or any document that would indicate extinguishment of the title.

Gosnell, Chief Councillor of the Gitlakdamix band, said:

Q Mr. Gosnell, have the Nishga people ever signed any treaty or document giving up their Indian title to the lands and the waters comprised in the area delineated on the map Exhibit 2 which I am showing you?

A No.

MR. BROWN: I think I can save my friend some trouble, I think the Attorney-General is prepared to say while denying there is such a thing as an Indian title in the area, that the inhabitants never did give up or purport to give up that right.

The witnesses McKay, Nyce and Robinson confirmed the evidence of Calder and Gosnell.

W. E. Ireland, Archivist for British Columbia, produced the private papers of Governor Douglas as well as despatches between the Secretary of State for the Colonies and Governor Douglas and many other historic documents, including the Nishga petition to the Privy Council in 1913. There were received in evidence extracts from testimony given at hearings of two Royal Commissions, the first being in 1888 when David Mackay, speaking for the Nishgas, said in part:

[see above, p. 64].

At the second Royal Commission hearing in 1915 (the McKenna-McBride Commission), Gideon Minesque for the Nishgas said:

We haven't got any ill feelings in our hearts but we are just waiting for this thing to be settled and we have been waiting for the last five years—we have been living here from time immemorial—it has been handed down in legends from the old people and that is what hurts us very much because the white people have come along and taken this land away from us. I myself am an old man and as long as I have lived, my people have been telling me stories about the flood and they did not tell me that I was only to live here on this land for a short time. We have heard that some white men, it must have been in Ottawa; this white man said that they must be dreaming when they say they own the land upon which they live. It is not a dream—we are certain that this land belongs to us. Right up to this day the government never made any treaty, not even to our grandfathers or our great-grandfathers.

Wilson Duff, associate professor of anthropology at the University of British Columbia, testified as to the nature of the Nishga civilization and culture in great detail. The trial Judge said of this witness and of Dr. Ireland [8 D.L.R. (3d) at p. 63]: "Drs. Ireland and Duff are scholars of renown, and authors in the field of Indian history, and records." And on the question of credibility, he said:

> I find that all witnesses gave their respective testimony as to facts, opinions, and historical and other documents, with total integrity. Thus there is no issue of credibility as to the witnesses in this case, and an appellate Court, with transcript and exhibits in hand, would be under no comparative disadvantage in evaluating the evidence from not having heard the witnesses in personam.

Dr. Duff is the author of vol. I of the *Indian History of British Columbia* published by the Government of British Columbia and admitted in evidence as ex. 25. Dr. Duff testified as follows, quoting from ex. 25 and related quotations applicable to the Nishgas:

> Q Did you, Professor Duff, in fact prepare for counsel the map that has been marked Exhibit 2 in this case?
> A Yes, I did.
> Q Are you familiar with the anthropological history of the Indian people who inhabited the area delineated in the map and the surrounding areas?
> A Yes, I am.
> Q Who has, since time immemorial, inhabited the area delineated on the map?
> A The Nishga Indians.
> Q Can you tell the Court what position the Indians in the areas adjacent to that delineated on the map took regarding the occupancy of the Nishga Tribe of that area?
> A All of the surrounding tribes knew the Nishga as the homogeneous group of Indians occupying the area delineated on the map. They knew of them collectively under the term Nishga. They knew that they spoke their own dialect, that they occupied and were owners of that territory and they respected these tribal boundaries of the territory.
> Q By the tribal boundaries do you mean the boundaries delineated on the map?
> A Yes. . . .
> Q Now, are you able to tell the Court whether the Nishga Tribe made use of the land and the waters delineated on the map beyond the limits of the reserve that appear on this map in the McKenna-McBride report?
> A Yes.
> Q Is there any significance to the location of the reserves on the Portland Canal and Observatory Inlet and the Nass River?
> A Yes, I think that I can say that in many cases these small reserves were

located, for example, on the Portland Canal at the mouth of the tributary stream, at the mouth of a valley. The reserve is a small piece of land at the mouth of the stream which, to a degree, protects the Indian fishing rights to the stream.

Q Now, prior to the establishment of these reserves what use would the Indian people have made of the areas which flow into the mouths of the streams and rivers?

A The general pattern in these cases would be that the ownership of the mouth of the stream and the seasonal villages, or habitations that were built there, signify the ownership and use of the entire valley. It would be used as a fishing site itself and a fishing site on the river, but in addition to that the people who made use of this area would have the right to go up the valley for berry picking up on the slopes, for hunting and trapping in the valley and up to forest slopes, usually for the hunting of mountain goats. In other words they made use, more or less intensive use of the entire valley rather than just the point at the mouth of the stream.

Q So that in the case of each of those Indian Reserves situated at the mouth of a stream use would have been made by the Indians—

MR. BROWN: Oh, would my friend not lead quite so much.

MR. BERGER: No, I won't. I won't pursue that matter, anyway.

Q Now, in your book which has been marked as an exhibit you say on page 8:

At the time of contact the Indians of this area were among the world's most distinctive peoples. Fully one-third of the native population of Canada lived here. They were concentrated most heavily along the coastline and the main western rivers, and in these areas they developed their cultures to higher peaks, in many respects, than in any other part of the continent north of Mexico. Here, too, was the greatest linguistic diversity in the country, with two dozen languages spoken, belonging to seven of the eleven language families represented in Canada. The coastal tribes were, in some ways, different from all other American Indians. Their languages, true enough, were members of American families, and physically they were American Indians, though with decided traits of similarity to the peoples of Northeastern Asia. Their cultures, however, had a pronounced Asiatic tinge, evidence of basic kinship and long continued contact with the peoples around the North Pacific rim. Most of all, their cultures were distinguished by a local richness and originality, the product of vigorous and inventive people in a rich environment.

Would that paragraph apply to the people who inhabited the area delineated on the map, Exhibit 2?

A Yes.

Q The next paragraph reads:

It is not correct to say that the Indians did not own the land but only roamed over the face of it and used it. The patterns of ownership and utilization which they imposed upon the lands and waters were different from those recognized by our system of law, but were nonetheless clearly defined and mutually respected. Even if they didn't subdivide and cultivate the land, they did recognize ownership of plots used for village sites, fishing places, berry and root patches, and similar purposes. Even if they didn't subject the forest to wholesale logging, they did establish ownership of tracts used for hunting, trapping and food gathering. Even if they didn't sink mine shafts into the mountains, they did own peaks and valleys for mountain goat hunting and as sources of raw materials. Except for barren and inaccessible areas which are not utilized even today, every part of the province was formerly within the owned and recognized territory of one or other of the Indian Tribes.

Does that paragraph apply to the people who inhabited the area delineated on the map, Exhibit 2?

A Yes, it does.

Q Does it apply to the Nishga Tribe?

A Yes, it does.

Q Now, you have said that the paragraph that I have just read to you applies to the Nishga Tribe. Can you tell his lordship the extent of the use to which the Nishgas have put the lands and waters in the area delineated on Exhibit 2 and how intensive that use was?

A This could be quite a long statement.

Q Well, I think we can live with it.

A And much of it has already been said. However, the territories in general were recognized by the people themselves and by other tribes as the territory of the Nishga Tribe. Certain of these territories were used in common for certain purposes, for example, obtaining of logs and timber for houses, and canoes, totem poles, and the other parts of the culture that were made of wood, like the dishes and the boxes and masks and a great variety of other things, and the obtainment of bark which was made into forms of cloth and mats and ceremonial gear. These would tend to be used in common.

Other areas weren't tribal territories, would be allotted or owned by family groups of the tribe and these would be used, different parts, with different degrees of intensity. For example, the beaches where the shell fish were gathered would be intensively used. The salmon streams would be most intensively used, sometimes at different times of the year, because different kinds of salmon can run at different times of the year.

The lower parts of the valley where hunting and trapping were done would be intensively used, not just for food and the hides and skins and bone and horn material that was used by the Indian culture, but for furs of different kinds of large and small animals which were either used by the Indians or traded by them.

These people were great traders and they exploited their territories to a great degree for materials to trade to other Indians and later to the white man.

The farther slopes up the valleys, many of them would be good mountain goat hunting areas. This was an important animal for hunting. Other slopes would be good places for trapping of marmots, the marmot being equally important, and there are a great number of lesser resources, things like minerals of certain kinds for tools and lichen and mosses of certain kinds that were made into dyes. It becomes a very long list.

Q Go ahead.

A Now, in addition to this, the waterways were used for the hunting of sea animals as well as fishing of different kinds. They were used also as highways, routes of travel for trade amongst themselves and for their annual migration from winter to summer villages, and a great variety of minor resources from water, like shell fish of different kinds, fish eggs, herring eggs—there is a great list of such minor resources in addition.

Q To what extent would the use and exploitation of the resources of the Nishga territory have extended in terms of that territory? Would it have extended only through a limited part of the territory or through the whole territory?

A To a greater or lesser degree of intensity it would extend through a whole territory except for the most barren and inaccessible parts, which were not used or wanted by anyone. But the ownership of an entire drainage basin marked out by the mountain peaks would be recognized as resting within one or other groups of Nishga Indians and these boundaries, this ownership would be respected by others.

Q Now, can you make any comparison between the area that is represented by the Indian Reserves in the map, in the third volume of the McKenna-McBride Report; can you make any comparison between that area represented by those reserves and the area of the whole Nishga territory that was used and exploited by the Nishgas before their confinement to reserves?

A Well, I think the comparison is simply here, and these are several tiny plots of land, whereas on the map the entire tract was used for some purpose or other with some greater or lesser degree of intensity.

Q Well, by the map do you mean the map, Exhibit 2?

A That's right, yes.

On cross-examination he said:

A May I tell you the nature of my information on which I am working because I think this needs to be said?

THE COURT: Yes.

A All right. I am, of course, familiar with the great bulk of the published material on the Indians of this area, some of which will be entered into evidence. I have myself discussed these matters with many Indians, both Nishga and their neighbours, but my main source of information is the great, abundant body of unpublished anthropological and historical material which was assembled in the National Museum of Canada by the anthropologist Marius Barbeau, who worked in this area between 1914 and the late '40s, and continued to assemble it until just a couple of years ago. He died this past year. Also, a Tsimshian gentleman who actually thought of himself as a Nishga chief, William Beynon who lived the greater part of his life at Port Simpson, who was an interpreter and assistant of Barbeau and other anthropologists and who, himself, until his death in 1967, recorded hundreds and hundreds of pages of anthropological information and family traditions and narratives having to do with the Nishga and the Gitksan people. I have had access to this great body of unpublished material. I spent a year at the National Museum working with it ten years ago and this has provided me with the detailed information upon which I can make these statements. Unfortunately I haven't worked it up into a publishable form as yet and it is such a vast body of material that I don't have it all at the tip of my tongue.

Q Yes. Now, the fact is that the members of these bands did reside from time to time in communities and those communities would appear to have been within some of the present reserves?

A Yes, that's right.

Q Well, now, I was asking you as to what documentary or other evidence there was that justifies you in using the word "ownership". I suggest that that was a concept that was foreign to the Indians of the Nass Agency?

A I am an anthropologist, sir, and the kind of evidence with which I work is largely not documentary evidence. It is verbal evidence given by people who didn't produce documents and it is turned into documentary form in anthropological and historical reports and in the reports of various Commissions.

Q All right. Well, that is what I want now.

A Yes, okay.

Q I want you to state, so I can go and look them up, the documents you rely upon to support your statement, your use of the word "ownership", as "belonging" in the Indian concept.

A Anthropological reports which I understand Mr. Berger is going to enter into the record, one of them by Philip Drucker, is a general book on the Indians of the Northwest Coast and it would use the term. Another is a book by Viola Garfield as to the Tsimshian Indians in general and in this sense it includes the Nishga which would use a concept of ownership.

Q Now, are you suggesting that this is anything other than a tribal concept?

A It includes the tribal concept and it is more besides, yes.

Q Well, perhaps if my learned friend would give me the book you can indicate just what you mean. What was the book you referred to, Drucker?

A Drucker or Docker.

MR. BERGER: Yes, I have it, my lord.

THE COURT: It is enmeshed in the toils of your papers, is that right?

MR. BERGER: That's right.

I think those are two of them.

MR. BROWN:

Q Would you indicate what you had in mind?

A May I read it? Do you want me to read a section?

Q Yes. Just direct our attention, will you, to the particular points?

A This is Viola Garfield's book, "The Tsimshian, Their Arts and Music."
On page 14—

THE COURT: Now, tell me something about the author first.

A Yes. The authoress is an anthropologist who studied at the University of Washington in Seattle and who is still a professor of Anthropology there and who did her field work and much of her writing on the Tsimshian Indians. These would be primarily the Tsimshian, in the narrower sense of people who live at Port Simpson, now Metlakatla, but the concepts would apply to the Nishga as well.

On page 14 she writes:

It was characteristic of the Tsimshian, as of other Northwest Coast Tribes, that exclusive rights to exploit the resource districts were claimed by kin. Lineages of the Tsimshian were the owners of rights to hunt, fish, pick berries or gather raw materials from geographically defined territory. Lineage properties were listed at an installation potlatch of a new head, hence were in his name. Lineage heads could and did designate certain areas as actually his and pass them on as private property to successors. This is the concept of ownership that—

Q Well, the basis of any statement about ownership would lie in the fact that the Nishgas had exclusive possession of the area, it was unchallenged, isn't that true?

A For the area marked on the map?

Q Yes.

A Yes.

Q So that anyone has to be careful about what word you apply because of the legal implications and to speak of ownership simply because someone has an unchallenged possession is to confuse two things, would you not agree?

A The point I was trying to make in the second paragraph that Mr. Berger read out was that although their concepts of ownership were not the same as our legal concept of ownership, they nevertheless existed and were recognized and that is the point I was trying to make.

Q Well, anyway, you are unable to find any documentary evidence in support other than conclusions drawn by anthropologists?

A And also verbatim statements by Indians at the various Commissions, and I think Mr. Berger is going to enter some of this.

MR. BERGER: They have been entered.

MR. BROWN: Yes.

Q Well, in other words the Indians would speak of the fact that when they attended before a Commission, that they owned the land?

A Yes.

Q They would speak in those terms as "We" as a group.

A Yes.

Q "Own the land".

A I think they would go beyond that and say, "And the chief owned that certain territory up Portland Inlet where we used to get this and that," and the whole list of things that I referred to before.

Q Would one family defend its right like that against other families?

A It could, yes.

Q Well, is there evidence of that?

A   There are narratives to that effect, yes.
Q   In the Nishga Valley, in the territory you have marked off there?
A   Yes.
Q   Where? Can you point to that?
A   They are in the unpublished material that I have been referring to.

Possession is of itself at common law proof of ownership: Cheshire, *Modern Law of Real Property*, 10th ed. (1967), p. 659, and Megarry and Wade, *Law of Real Property*, 3rd ed. (1966), p. 999. Unchallenged possession is admitted here.

Dr. Duff also went into the details of the Nishga system of succession to property based on a matrilineal line, showing that the Nishgas had a well-developed and sophisticated concept of property. Regarding the general state of development and sophistication of the culture of the Nishga, he testified, quoting from his book as follows:

Q   I will go on to something else for the time being, then. Now, at page 17 of your book you say in the last paragraph:
There were some incipient or tentative groupings of tribes into larger units. In some cases clusters of closely related tribes bore collective names; for example, Cowichan.
And you mentioned some others,
In other cases such a cluster was acknowledged to be closely inter-related but had no joint names; for example, the Haida of Cumshewa, Skedans and Tanoo. A number of descriptive names for regional groups have appeared in print so often that they have become established by usage; for example, Upper Thompson, Lower Kootenay, Northern Kwakiutl, and Coast Tsimshian. Though not native names, these have been included in the table. These larger groupings had no internal organization, with two interesting exceptions. After the establishment of Fort Rupert the Southern Kwakiutl Tribes arranged themselves in a definite order of rank in order to control their ceremonial relations and potlaching organizations, and after the establishment of Port Simpson the nine Lower Skeena Tsimshian Tribes did much the same thing.
Now, is that what we are talking about, the organization of these groups for potlaching purposes?
A   Which groups?
Q   Well, what you are talking about there was this organization of family groups basically related to the potlaching arrangements.
A   The potlaching was the mechanism by which the family groups maintained their relative ranking, yes.
Q   Yes.
A   Within the tribes.
Q   Now, you say, going back to page 16:
On the Northern Coast, where kinship ties were most rigidly defined, matrilineal households or lineages were the basic units that united in each locality to form tribal groups, which usually assembled for part of the year in a common village.

Now, was that a characteristic in the Nishga group, and if so, where did they assemble in a common village?

A There was no single common village in which all of the Nishga groups assembled at any one time.

Q No, I didn't understand that from the councillors. Now, you say:

Among the Tsimshian these tribes hardened into firmly knit political
units (this was somewhat less the case among the Gitksan, Niska—

Now, those two peoples we are talking about, the people within the area you have delineated, are they not?

A The Gitksan are just outside of the area and the Nishga are inside the area.

Q Yes. So Niska means Nishga there?

A That is correct, yes.

Q And is that a correct statement, that this was somewhat less the case among the Nishga?

A Yes, that is correct.

and reverting to the question of ownership, he said, quoting with approval from Drucker, a well-known American anthropologist:

Q Yes, please.

A This is the chapter on social and political organization of the peoples of the North Pacific Coast. The section that is relevant here concerns the localized groups of kin. The localized groups of kin define who lived together, worked together and who jointly considered themselves exclusive owners of the tracts from which food and other prime materials were obtained.

Q Jointly considered themselves, is that the word?

A Jointly considered themselves, yes.

The whole group owned not only lands and their produce but all other forms of wealth, material treasures and intangible rights usually referred to as privileges, names for persons, houses, canoes, houseboats and even for dogs and slaves. I emphasize the phrases that I wanted to emphasize there.

Q So that there was a form, again, of a communal approach?

A In that sense.

Q Yes.

A It belonged to the group, yes.

Q Thank you.

A And on page 49, the last eight or so lines, this is dealing with wealth in these cultures and I quote:

Distinctive of North Pacific Coast culture is the inclusion of natural
resources and items of wealth; the foodstuffs, the materials for dress,
shelter and transport and the places from which these things were
obtained. Each group regarded the areas utilized as the exclusive
property of the group. Group members used habitation sites, fishing
grounds, clam beaches, hunting and burying grounds, that is in the
sense of getting buried, forest areas where timber and bark were

obtained through right. Outsiders entered by invitation or in trespass.

   Bounds were defined by natural landmarks with a precision remarkable for people with no surveying equipment.

THE COURT: Read me the last sentence again, please.

   Bounds were defined by natural landmarks with a precision remarkable for people with no surveying equipment.

Now, these are the only two specific specimens in this book.

MR. BROWN:

Q Thank you. Now, what is he discussing there? Is he discussing a particular group?

A He is discussing the Northwest Coast groups in general, of which the
Nishga are one.

An interesting and apt line of questions by Gould, J., in which he endeavoured
to relate Duff's evidence as to Nishga concepts of ownership of real property to
the conventional common law elements of ownership must be quoted here as
they disclose that the trial Judge's consideration of the real issue was inhibited
by a preoccupation with the traditional indicia of ownership. In so doing, he
failed to appreciate what Lord Haldane said in Amodu Tijani, supra [[1921] 2
A.C. at p. 402]:

> Their Lordships make the preliminary observation that in interpreting the
> native title to land, not only in Southern Nigeria, but other parts of the
> British Empire, much caution is essential. There is a tendency, operating
> at times unconsciously, to render that title conceptually in terms which are
> appropriate only to systems which have grown up under English law. But
> this tendency has to be held in check closely.

The trial Judge's questions and Duff's answers were as follows:

THE COURT:

Q I want to discuss with you the short descriptive concept of your modern
ownership of land in British Columbia, and I am going to suggest to you
three characteristics (1) specific delineation of the land, we understand is
the lot.

A Yes.

Q Specifically delineated down to the lot, and the concept of the survey;
(2) exclusive possession against the whole world, including your own
family. Your own family, you know that, you want to keep them off or kick
them off and one can do so; (3) to keep the fruits of the barter or to leave
it or to have your heirs inherit it, which is the concept of wills. Now, those
three characteristics—are you with me?

A Yes.

Q Specific delineation, exclusive possession, the right of alienation, have
you found in your anthropological studies any evidence of that concept
being in the consciousness of the Nishgas and having them executing such
a concept?

A My lord, there are three concepts.

Q Yes, or a combination of them.

A Could we deal with them one at a time?

Q Yes, you can do it any way you like. You deal with it.

A Specific delineation, I think, was phrased by Dr.—

Q Touched upon by landmarks.

A Physical landmarks, physical characteristics. The exclusive occupation did not reside in an individual. It rested in a group of people who were a sub-group of the tribe.

Q The third one was alienation.

A The owners in this sense had certain rights of alienation. They could give up the tract of land, lose it in warfare, but in practice it would not go to anybody outside of the tribe, that is, a tract of Nishga land might change hands but it wouldn't go to other than a Nishga family.

Q So am I correct in assuming that there are similarities in the Nishga civilization in the first two characteristics, but not the third? All that alien-ation means, of course, is that you can sell it to anybody you like?

A Yes.

Q Generally speaking, I mean, that is what it does. Two of the three the Nishga Tribe—I don't want to put words in your mouth, now, I want you to tell me. I don't want to tell you anything.

A Delineation but not by modern surveying methods.

Q Of course, I understand, yes.

A Exclusive ownership resting not in an individual.

Q Possession or occupancy, not ownership?

A Oh, I see. Possession or occupancy resting in a specific group rather than an individual. The right of alienation, which in practice would leave the land within the same tribe. It was limited.

Q Could the group having exclusive occupancy select within the tribe, if they chose, another group to whom they wanted to either, to use the modern word, convey it, or would that go by general communal habit, custom or even law?

A The group could do the thing you suggest. For example, in some cases the chief of a group might convey a property to his son, which would not be the normal way; it would be to his nephew in the normal way.

Q Yes.

A And that would, on rare occasions, be accepted.

Q Always subject to the acceptance of what, the tribe?

A The tribe, yes.

RE-EXAMINED BY MR. BERGER:

Q His lordship put to you three characteristics of modern day real prop-erty concepts. Having regard to the territory of the Nishga Tribe outlined on the map, Exhibit 2, can you say whether or not there would have been specific delineation of that area in the sense in which it was put to you by his lordship?

A Of the boundaries of that area?

Q Yes.

A Yes.

Q What would the means of delineation have been?

A As Dr. Drucker has described them here, landmarks.

Q By landmarks. Do you mean the mountain tops?

A Yes, geographical locations.

Q Now, his lordship put to you the notion of exclusive possession. As regards the territory delineated on the map, Exhibit 2, the Nishga territory, what would have been the application of that concept if it had any in the time before the coming of the white man?

A It would be recognized by all as Nishga territory. They would exercise exclusive possession of it.

MR. BERGER: I have no further questions.

THE COURT: I have some more now.

Q I will give two more characteristics of ownership, the right to destroy it at your own whim, if you like, and the other, that the exclusive possession should be of indeterminable time, that is, cannot be terminated by a person's life, that is, can be passed on to one's heirs. That makes five. Now, you have dealt with three. Now, the right to destroy at whim, set fire to your own house; these matters you have been dealing with, would a group within the Nishga have the right, if the buildings at the mouth of a certain river had been in their exclusive use some time and they will say, "Let's set fire to it," would the tribe prohibit that?

A I would think that they would have that right.

Q You would think they would have that right?

A Yes.

Q Now, what about the duration of the right, not to destroy, but the right of exclusive ownership, would it go to their heirs?

A Yes.

Q Or go back to the tribe for distribution?

A In theory it belongs within that kinship group through time, with no duration in theory. It always remains with that same kinship group.

Q There is the matrilineal line?

A Yes.

THE COURT: Thank you.

In enumerating the indicia of ownership, the trial Judge overlooked that possession is of itself proof of ownership. Prima facie, therefore, the Nishgas are the owners of the lands that have been in their possession from time immemorial and, therefore the burden of establishing that their right has been extinguished rests squarely on the respondent.

What emerges from the foregoing evidence is the following: the Nishgas in fact are, and were from time immemorial a distinctive cultural entity with concepts of ownership indigenous to their culture and capable of articulation under the common law having, in the words of Dr. Duff, "developed their culture to higher peaks in many respects than in any other part of the continent north of Mexico". A remarkable confirmation of this statement comes from Captain Cook who, in 1778, at Cape Newenham claimed the land for Great Britain. He reported having gone ashore and entered one of the native houses which he said was 150 ft. in length, 24 to 30 ft. wide and 7 to 8 ft. high and that "there were no native buildings to compare with these north of Mexico". The report continues that Cook's officers were full of admiration for the skill and patience required to erect these buildings which called for a considerable knowledge of engineering.

While the Nishga claim had not heretofore been litigated, there is a wealth of jurisprudence affirming common law recognition of aboriginal rights to possession and enjoyment of lands of aborigines precisely analogous to the Nishga situation here.

Strong, J. (later C.J.C.), in St. Catherine's Milling & Lumber Co. v. The Queen (1887), 13 S.C.R. 577, said at pp. 608-9:

> In the Commentaries of Chancellor Kent and in some decisions of the Supreme Court of the United States we have very full and clear accounts of the policy in question. *It may be summarily stated as consisting in the recognition by the crown of a usufructuary title in the Indians to all unsurrendered lands. This title, though not perhaps susceptible of any accurate legal definition in exact legal terms, was one which nevertheless sufficed to protect the Indians in the absolute use and enjoyment of their lands, whilst at the same time they were incapacitated from making any valid alienation otherwise than to the crown itself, in whom the ultimate title was, in accordance with the English law of real property, considered as vested.* This short statement will, I think, on comparison with the authorities to which I will presently refer, be found to be an accurate description of the principles upon which the crown invariably acted with reference to Indian lands, at least from the year 1756, when Sir William Johnston was appointed by the Imperial Government superintendent of Indian affairs in North America, being as such responsible directly to the crown through one of the Secretaries of State, or the Lords of Trade and Plantation, and thus superseding the Provincial Governments, down to the year 1867, when the confederation act constituting the Dominion of Canada was passed. So faithfully was this system carried out, that I venture to say that there is no settled part of the territory of the Province of Ontario, except perhaps some isolated spots upon which the French Government had, previous to the conquest, erected forts, such as Fort Frontenac and Fort Toronto, which is not included in and covered by a surrender contained in some Indian treaty still to be found in the Dominion Archives. These rules of policy being shown to have been well established and acted upon, and the title of the Indians to their unsurrendered lands to have been recognized by the crown to the extent already mentioned, it may seem of little importance to enquire into the reasons on which it was based.

(emphasis added) and at pp. 610-11:

> The American authorities, to which reference has already been made, consist (amongst others) of passages in the commentaries of Chancellor Kent (*Kent's Commentaries* 12 ed. by Holmes, vol. 3 p. 379 et seq. and in editor's notes), in which the whole doctrine of Indian titles is fully and elaborately considered, and of several decisions of the Supreme Court of the United States, from which three, Johnson v. McIntosh (8 Wheaton 543), Worcester v. State of Georgia (6 Peters 515), and Mitchell v. United States (9 Peters 711), may be selected as leading cases. *The value and importance of these authorities is not merely that they show that the same doctrine as that already*

propounded regarding the title of the Indians to unsurrendered lands prevails in the United States, but, what is of vastly greater importance, they without exception refer its origin to a date anterior to the revolution and recognise it as a continuance of the principles of law or policy as to Indian titles then established by the British government, and therefore identical with those which have also continued to be recognized and applied in British North America. Chancellor Kent, referring to the decision of the Supreme Court of the United States in Cherokee Nation v. State of Georgia (5 Peters 1), says:—

> The court there held that the Indians were domestic, dependent nations, and their relations to us resembled that of a ward to his guardian; and they had an unquestionable right to the lands they occupied until that right should be extinguished by a voluntary cession to our government (3 Kent Comms. 383).

(Emphasis added.) [pp. 612-13:]

It thus appears, that in the United States a traditional policy, derived from colonial times, relative to the Indians and their lands has ripened into well established rules of law, and that the result is that the lands in the possession of the Indians are, until surrendered, treated as their rightful though inalienable property, so far as the possession and enjoyment are concerned; in other words, that the *dominium utile* is recognized as belonging to or reserved for the Indians, though the *dominium directum* is considered to be in the United States. Then, if this is so as regards Indian lands in the United States, which have been preserved to the Indians by the constant observance of a particular rule of policy acknowledged by the United States courts to have been originally enforced by the crown of Great Britain, how is it possible to suppose that the law can, or rather could have been, at the date of confederation, in a state any less favourable to the Indians whose lands were situated within the dominion of the British crown, the original author of this beneficent doctrine so carefully adhered to in the United States from the days of the colonial governments? *Therefore, when we consider that with reference to Canada the uniform practice has always been to recognize the Indian title as one which could only be dealt with by surrender to the crown,* I maintain that if there had been an entire absence of any written legislative act ordaining this rule as an express positive law, we ought, just as the United States courts have done, to hold that it nevertheless existed as a rule of the unwritten common law, which the courts were bound to enforce as such, and consequently, that the 24th sub-section of section 91, as well as the 109th section and the 5th subsection of section 92 of the British North America Act, must all be read and construed upon the assumption that these territorial rights of the Indians were strictly legal rights which had to be taken into account and dealt with in that distribution of property and proprietary rights made upon confederation between the federal and provincial governments.

(Emphasis added.) [pp. 615-16 :]

To summarize these arguments, which appear to me to possess great force, we find, that at the date of confederation the Indians, by the constant usage and practice of the crown. [sic] were considered to possess a certain proprietary interest in the unsurrendered lands which they occupied as hunting grounds, that this usage had either ripened into a rule of the common law as applicable to the American Colonies, or that such a rule had been derived from the law of nations and had in this way been imported into the Colonial law as applied to Indian Nations; that such property of the Indians was usufructuary only and could not be alienated, except by surrender to the crown as the ultimate owner of the soil; . . .

Strong, J., with whom Gwynne, J., agreed, was dissenting in the case but the dissent was on the question of whether the Dominion or provincial Government acquired title when the Indian title was extinguished as it had been in that case by treaty. The majority held that the Crown in the right of the Province became the owner and Strong and Gwynne, JJ., held that the Dominion became the owner. However, on the point of Indian title there was no disagreement between the majority and minority views. Ritchie, C.J., for the majority agreed substantially with Strong, J., in this respect, saying at pp. 599-600:

I am of opinion, that all ungranted lands in the province of Ontario belong to the crown as part of the public domain, *subject to the Indian right of occupancy [in] cases in which the same has not been lawfully extinguished*, and when such right of occupancy has been lawfully extinguished absolutely to the crown, and as a consequence to the province of Ontario. I think the crown owns the soil of all the unpatented lands, the Indians possessing only the right of occupancy, and the crown possessing the legal title subject to that occupancy, with the absolute exclusive right to extinguish the Indian title either by conquest or by purchase . . .

(Emphasis added.)

The St. Catherine's Milling case was affirmed in the Privy Council, 14 App. Cas. 46. The judgment was given by Lord Watson who, in referring to Indian aboriginal interests, said at pp. 54 - 5:

It was suggested in the course of the argument for the Dominion that inasmuch as the proclamation recites that the territories thereby reserved for Indians had never "been ceded to or purchased by" the Crown, the entire property of the land remained with them. That inference is, however, at variance with the terms of the instrument, which shew that the tenure of the Indians was a personal and usufructuary right, dependent upon the good will of the Sovereign. The lands reserved are expressly stated to be "parts of Our dominions and territories," and it is declared to be the will and pleasure of the sovereign that, "for the present," they shall be reserved for the use of the Indians, as their hunting grounds under his protection and dominion. *There was a great deal of learned discussion at the Bar with respect to the precise quality of the Indian right, but their Lordships do not consider it necessary to express any opinion upon the point. It appears to them to be sufficient for the purposes of this case that there has been all along vested in the Crown a substantial and paramount estate, underlying the Indian title, which became a plenum dominium whenever that title was surrendered or otherwise extinguished.*

(Emphasis added.)

The case most frequently quoted with approval dealing with the nature of aboriginal rights is Johnson and Graham's Lessee v. M'Intosh (1823), 8 Wheaton 543, 21 U.S. 240. It is the locus classicus of the principles governing aboriginal title. Gould, J., in his reasons said of this case at p. 69:

> The most cogent one of these is the argument based upon a classic and definitive judgment of Chief Justice Marshall of the United States, in 1823, in the case of Johnson and Graham's Lessee v. M'Intosh (1823), 8 Wheaton 541, wherein that renowned jurist gives an historical account of the British Crown's attitude towards the rights of aboriginals over land originally occupied by them, and an enunciation of the law of the United States on the same subject.

and on p. 71 he said:

> For more than 150 years this strong judgment has at various times been cited with approval by such authorities as the House of Lords, Tamaki v. Baker, [1901] A.C. 561 at p. 580; the Supreme Court of Canada, St. Catherine's Milling & Lumber Co. v. The Queen (1887), 13 S.C.R. 577, per Strong, J., at p. 610; Court of Appeal for Ontario (in the same case), 13 O.A.R. 148, per Burton, J.A. at pp. 159-60; Ontario High Court, Chancery Division (in the same case), 10 O.R. 196, per Boyd, C., at p. 209; Court of Appeal for British Columbia, R v. White and Bob (1964), 50 D.L.R. (2d) 613 at pp. 646-7, 52 W.W.R. 193; Supreme Court of New Brunswick, Warman v. Francis (1958), 20 D.L.R. (2d) 627, 43 M.P.R. 197, per Anglin, J., at p. 630.

Chief Justice Marshall said in Johnson v. M'Intosh [pp. 572-4]:

> On the discovery of this immense continent, the great nations of Europe were eager to appropriate to themselves so much of it as they could respectively acquire. Its vast extent offered an ample field to the ambition and enterprise of all and the character and religion of its inhabitants afforded an apology for considering them as a people over whom the superior genius of Europe might claim as [sic] ascendency. The potentates of the old world found no difficulty in convincing themselves that they made ample compensation to the inhabitants of the new, by bestowing on them civilization and Christianity, in exchange for unlimited independence. But, as they were all in pursuit of nearly the same object, it was necessary, in order to avoid conflicting settlements, and consequent war with each other, to establish a principle which all should acknowledge as the law by which the right of acquisition, which they all asserted, should be regulated as between themselves. This principle was, that discovery gave title to the government by whose subjects, or by whose authority it was made, against all other European governments, which title might be consummated by possession.
> The exclusion of all other Europeans necessarily gave to the nation

making the discovery the sole right of acquiring the soil from the natives and establishing settlements upon it. It was a right with which no Europeans could interfere. It was a right which all asserted for themselves, and to the assertion of which, by others, all assented.

Those relations which were to exist between the discoverer and the natives, were to be regulated by themselves. The rights thus acquired being exclusive, no other power could interpose between them.

In the establishment of these relations, the rights of the original inhabitants were, in no instance, entirely disregarded; but were necessarily, to a considerable extent, impaired. *They were admitted to be the rightful occupants of the soil, with a legal as well as just claim to retain possession of it, and to use it according to their own discretion*; but their rights to complete sovereignty, as independent nations were necessarily diminished, and their power to dispose of the soil at their own will, to whomsoever they pleased, was denied by the original fundamental principle, that discovery gave exclusive title to those who made it.

While the different nations of Europe respected the right of the natives, as occupants, they asserted the ultimate dominion to be in themselves, and claimed and exercised, as a consequence of this ultimate dominion, a power to grant the soil, while yet in possession of the natives. These grants have been understood by all to convey a title to the grantees, subject only to the Indian right of occupancy.

(Emphasis added.) It is pertinent to quote here what Norris J.A. said of Johnson v. M'Intosh in R. v. White and Bob (1964), 50 D.L.R. (2d) 613 at pp. 631-2, 52 W.W.R. 193 [affd 52 D.L.R. (2d) 481n, [1965] S.C.R. vi]:

> . . . The judgment in Johnson v M'Intosh, supra, was delivered at an early stage of exploration of this continent and when controversy as to those rights was first becoming of importance. Further, on the consideration of the subject-matter of this appeal, it is to be remembered that it was delivered only 6 years after the Convention of 1818 between Great Britain and the United States (erroneously referred to by counsel as the Jay Treaty) providing that the northwest coast of America should be free and open for the term of 10 years to the vessels, citizens, and subjects of both powers in order to avoid disputes between the powers. The rights of Indians were naturally an incident of the implementation of a common policy which was perforce effective as applying to what is now Vancouver Island and the territory of Washington and Oregon, all of which were then Hudson's Bay territories. For these reasons and because the judgment in Johnson v. M'Intosh, supra, was written at a time of active exploration and exploitation of the West by the Americans, it is of particular importance.

The dominant and recurring proposition stated by Chief Justice Marshall in Johnson v. M'Intosh is that on discovery or on conquest the aborigines of newly-found lands were conceded to be the rightful occupants of the soil with a legal as well as a just claim to retain possession of it and to use it according to their own discretion, but their rights to complete sovereignty as independent nations were necessarily diminished and their power to dispose of the soil on their own will to whomsoever they pleased was denied by the original fundamental principle that discovery or conquest gave exclusive title to those who made it.

Chief Justice Marshall had occasion in 1832 once more to adjudicate upon the question of aboriginal rights in Worcester v. State of Georgia (1832), 6 Peters 515, 31 U.S. 530, 8 L. Ed. 483. He said at pp. 542-4 Peters:

America, separated from Europe by a wide ocean, was inhabited by a distinct people, divided into separate nations, independent of each other and of the rest of the world, *having institutions of their own, and governing themselves by their own laws*. It is difficult to comprehend the proposition, that the inhabitants of either quarter of the globe could have rightful original claims of dominion over the inhabitants of the other, or over the lands they occupied; or that the discovery of either by the other should give the discoverer rights in the country discovered, which annulled the pre-existing right of its ancient possessors.

After lying concealed for a series of ages, the enterprise of Europe, guided by nautical science, conducted some of her adventurous sons into this western world. They found it in possession of a people who had made small progress in agriculture or manufactures and whose general employment was war, hunting and fishing.

Did these adventurers, by sailing along the coast, and occasionally landing on it, acquire for the several governments to whom they belonged, or by whom they were commissioned, a rightful property in the soil from the Atlantic to the Pacific; or rightful dominion over the numerous people who occupied it? Or has nature, or the great Creator of all things, conferred these rights over hunters and fishermen, on agriculturalists and manufacturers?

But power, war, conquest, give rights, which after possession, are conceded by the world; and which can never be controverted by those on whom they descend. We proceed, then, to the actual state of things, having glanced at their origin, because holding it in our recollection might shed some light on existing pretensions.

The great maritime powers of Europe discovered and visited different parts of this continent at nearly the same time. The object was too immense for anyone of them to grasp the whole; and the claimants were too powerful to submit to the exclusive or unreasonable pretensions of any single potentate. To avoid bloody conflicts, which might terminate disastrously to all it was necessary for the nations of Europe to establish some principle which all would acknowledge, and which should decide their respective rights as between themselves. This principle, suggested by the actual state of things, was, "that discovery gave title to the government by whose subjects or by whose authority it was made, against all other European governments, which title might be consummated by possession." 8 Wheat. 673.

This principle, acknowledged by all Europeans, because it was the interest of all to acknowledge it, gave to the nation making the discovery, as its inevitable consequence, the sole right of acquiring the soil and of making settlements on it. It was an exclusive principle which shut out the right of competition among those who had agreed to it, not one which could annul the previous rights of those who had not agreed to it. It regulated the right given by discovery among the European discoverers; *but could not affect the rights of those already in possession, either as aboriginal occupants, or as occupants by virtue of a discovery made before the memory of man. It gave the exclusive right to purchase, but did not found that right on a denial of the right of the possessor to sell.*

(Emphasis added.) See also Chancellor Kent in his *Commentaries on American Law*, rev. ed. (1889), vol. 3, p. 411.

The view that the Indians had a legal as well as a just claim to the territory they occupied was confirmed as recently as 1946 by the Supreme Court of the United States in the case of United States v. Alcea Band of Tillamooks et al. (1946), 329 U.S. 40. In that case it was held that the Indian claims legislation of 1935 did not confer any substantive rights on the Indians, that is, it did not convert a moral claim for taking their land without their consent and without compensation into a legal claim, because they already had a valid legal claim, and there was no necessity to create one. The statute simply removed the necessity that previously existed for the Indians to obtain the consent of the Government of the United States to sue for an alleged wrongful taking. The judgment is based squarely on the recognition by the Court of "original Indian title" founded on their previous possession of the land. It was held that "the Indians have a cause of action for compensation arising out of an involuntary taking of lands held by original Indian title". Vinson, C.J., said at pp. 45-8:

The language of the 1935 Act is specific, and its consequences are clear. By this Act Congress neither admitted or denied liability. The Act removes the impediments of sovereign immunity and lapse of time and provides for judicial determination of the designated claims. No new right or cause of action is created. A merely moral claim is not made a legal one. . . .

It has long been held that by virtue of discovery the title to lands occupied by Indian tribes vested in the sovereign. This title was deemed subject to a right of occupancy in favour of Indian tribes, because of their original and previous possession. It is with the content of this right of occupancy, this original Indian title, that we are concerned here.

As against any but the sovereign, original Indian title was accorded the protection of complete ownership; but it was vulnerable to affirmative action by the sovereign, which possessed exclusive power to extinguish the right of occupancy at will. Termination of the right by sovereign action was complete and left the land free and clear of Indian claims. Third parties could not question the justness or fairness of the methods used to extinguish the right of occupancy. Nor could the Indians themselves prevent a taking of tribal lands or forestall a termination of their title. However, it is now for the first time asked whether the Indians have a cause of action for compensation arising out of an involuntary taking of lands held by original Indian title. . . .

A contrary decision would ignore the plain import of traditional methods of extinguishing original Indian title. The early acquisition of Indian lands, in the main, progressed by a process of negotiation and treaty. The first treaties reveal the striking deference paid to Indian claims, as the analysis in Worcester v. Georgia, supra, clearly details. It was usual policy not to coerce the surrender of lands without consent and without compensation. *The great drive to open western lands in the 19th Century, however productive of sharp dealing, did not wholly subvert the settled practice of negotiated extinguishment of original Indian title. In 1896, this Court noted that ". . . nearly every tribe and band of Indians within the territorial limits of the United States was under some treaty relations with the Government."* Marks v. United States, 161 U.S. 297, 302 (1896). Something more than sovereign grace prompted the obvious regard given to original Indian title.

(Emphasis added.) The same considerations applied in Canada. Treaties were made with the Indians of the Canadian West covering enormous tracts of land. See Kerr's *Historical Atlas of Canada* (1961), p. 57 (map 81). These treaties were a recognition of Indian title.

In Re Southern Rhodesia, [1919] A.C. 211, Lord Sumner said at pp. 233 - 4:

In any case it was necessary that the argument should go the length of showing that the rights, whatever they exactly were, belonged to the category of rights of private property, such that upon a conquest it is to be presumed, in the absence of express confiscation or of subsequent expropriatory legislation, that the conqueror has respected them and forborne to diminish or modify them.

The estimation of the rights of aboriginal tribes is always inherently difficult. Some tribes are so low in the scale of social organization that their usage and conceptions of rights and duties are not to be reconciled with the institutions or the legal ideas of civilized society. Such a gulf cannot be bridged. It would be idle to impute to such people some shadow of the rights known to our law and then to transmute it into the substance of transferable rights of property as we know them. In the present case it would make each and every person by a fictional inheritance a landed proprietor "richer than all his tribe." *On the other hand, there are indigenous peoples whose legal conceptions, though differently developed, are hardly less precise than our own. When once they have been studied and understood they are no less enforceable than rights arising under English law.*

(Emphasis added.)

Chief Justice Marshall in his judgment in Johnson v. M'Intosh referred to the English case of Campbell v. Hall (1774), 1 Cowp. 204, 98 E.R. 1045. This case was an important and decisive one which has been regarded as authoritative throughout the Commonwealth and the United States. It involved the rights and status of residents of the Island of Grenada which had recently been taken by British arms in open war with France. The judgment was given by Lord Mansfield. In his reasons he said at pp. 208-9:

A great deal has been said, and many authorities cited relative to propositions, in which both sides seem to be perfectly agreed; and which, indeed are too clear to be controverted. The stating some of those propositions which we think quite clear, will lead us to see with greater perspicuity, what is the question upon the first point, and upon what hinge it turns. I will state the propositions at large, and the first is this:

A country conquered by the British arms becomes a dominion of the

King in the right of his Crown; and, therefore, necessarily subject to the Legislature, and Parliament of Great Britain.

The 2d is, that the conquered inhabitants once received under the King's protection, become subjects, and are to be universally considered in that light, not as enemies or aliens.

The 3d, that the articles of capitulation upon which the country is surrendered and the articles of peace by which it is ceded, are sacred and inviolable according to their true intent and meaning.

The 4th, that the law and legislative government of every dominion, equally affects all persons and all property within the limits thereof; and is the rule of decision for all questions which arise there. Whoever purchases, lives, or sues there, puts himself under the law of the place. An Englishman in Ireland, Minorca, the Isle of Man, or the plantations, has no privilege distinct from the natives.

The 5th, that the laws of a conquered country continue in force, until they are altered by the conqueror: the absurd exception as to pagans, mentioned in Calvin's case [(1608), 7 Co. Rep. la, Moore (R.B.) 790 sub nom. Case del Union, del Realm D'Escose, ove Angleterre, 72 E.R. 908], shews the universality and antiquity of the maxim. For that distinction could not exist before the Christian era; and in all probability arose from the mad enthusiasm of the Crusades. In the present case the capitulation expressly provides and agrees, that they shall continue to be governed by their own laws, until His Majesty's further pleasure be known.

The 6th, and last proposition is, that if the King (and when I say the King, I always mean the King without the concurrence of Parliament,) has a power to alter the old and to introduce new laws in a conquered country, this legislation being subordinate, that is, subordinate to his own authority in Parliament, he cannot make any new change contrary to fundamental principles: he cannot exempt an inhabitant from that particular dominion; as for instance, from the laws of trade, or from the power of Parliament or give him privileges exclusive of his other subjects; and so in many other instances which might be put.

A fortiori the same principles, particularly Nos. 5 and 6, must apply to lands which become subject to British sovereignty by discovery or by declaration.

It is of importance that in all those areas where Indian lands were being taken by the Crown treaties were negotiated and entered into between the Crown and the Indian tribe on land then in occupation. The effect of these treaties was discussed by Davey, J.A. (as he then was), for the majority in White and Bob as follows at pp. 617-8:

It was also the long standing policy of the Imperial Government and of the Hudson's Bay Co. that the Crown or the company should buy from the Indians their land for settlement by white colonists. In pursuance of that policy many agreements, some very formal, others informal, *were made with various bands and tribes of Indians for the purchase of their lands.* These agreements frequently conferred upon the grantors hunting rights over the unoccupied lands so sold. Considering the relationship between the Crown and the Hudson's Bay Co. in the colonization of this country, and the

Imperial and corporate policies reflected in those agreements, I cannot regard ex. 8 as a mere agreement for the sale of land made between a private vendor and a private purchaser. In view of the notoriety of these facts, I entertain no doubt that Parliament intended the word "Treaty" in s. 87 [Indian Act, R.S.C. 1952, c. 149] to include all such agreements, and to except their provisions from the operative part of the section.

(Emphasis added.) The Crown appealed White and Bob to this Court. Cartwright, J. (as he then was), delivered the oral judgment of the Court dismissing the appeal as follows (52 D.L.R. (2d) 481n):

> Mr. Berger, Mr. Sanders and Mr. Christie. We do not find it necessary to hear you. We are all of the opinion that the majority in the Court of Appeal were right in their conclusion that the document, Exhibit 8, was a 'treaty' within the meaning of that term as used in s. 87 of the Indian Act [R.S.C. 1952, c. 149]. We therefore think that in the circumstances of the case, the operation of s. 25 of the Game Act [R.S.B.C. 1960, c. 160] was excluded by reason of the existence of that treaty.

In A.-G. Que. v. A.-G. Can. (Re Indian Lands) (1920), 56 D.L.R. 373, [1921] 1 A.C. 401, Duff, J. (as he then was), speaking for the Privy Council said at p. 377 D.L.R., p. 408 A.C., that the Indian right was a "usufructuary right only and a personal right in the sense that it is in its nature inalienable except by surrender to the Crown".

The aboriginal Indian title does not depend on treaty, executive order or legislative enactment. Sutherland, J., delivering the opinion of the Supreme Court of the United States in Cramer et al. v. United States (1923), 67 L. Ed. 622, 261 U.S., 219, dealt with the subject as follows [p. 626]:

> The fact that such right of occupancy finds no recognition in any statute or other formal governmental action is not conclusive. The right, under the circumstances here disclosed, flows from a settled governmental policy. Broder v. Natoma Water & Min. Co. 101 US 274, 276, 25 L ed 790, 791, furnishes an analogy. There this Court, holding that the Act of July 26, 1866, 14 Stat. at L. 251, chap. 262 9, Comp. Stat. 4647, 9 Fed. Stat. Anno. 2d ed p. 1349, acknowledging and confirming, rights of way for the construction of ditches and canals, was in effect declaratory of a pre-existing right, said: "It is the established doctrine of this court that rights of . . . persons who had constructed canals and ditches . . . are rights which the government had, by its conduct, recognized and encouraged and was found to protect, before the passage of the Act of 1866. We are of opinion that the section of the act which we have quoted was rather a voluntary *recognition of a pre-EXISTING RIGHT OF POSSESSION*, constituting a valid claim to its continued use, than the establishment of a new one."

[Italic capitalization added.]

The Court of Appeal in its judgment cited and purported to rely on United States v. Santa Fe Pacific R. Co. (1941), 86 L. Ed. 260, 314 U.S. 339. This case must be considered to be the leading modern judgment on the question of aboriginal rights. In my view the Court of Appeal misapplied the Santa Fe decision.

This becomes clear when the judgment of Douglas, J., in Santa Fe is read. He said [pp. 269-70]:

> Occupancy necessary to establish aboriginal possession is a question of fact to be determined as any other question of fact. If it were established as a fact that the lands in question were, or were included in, the ancestral home of the Walapais in the sense that they constituted definable territory occupied exclusively by the Walapais (as distinguished from lands wandered over by many tribes), then the Walapais had "Indian title" which, unless extinguished, survived the railroad grant of 1866. Buttz v. Northern P.R. Co., supra [119 US 55, 30 L ed 1275, 7 S Ct. 100].
>
> . . .
>
> Whatever may have been the rights of the Walapais under Spanish law, the Cramer Case assumed that lands within the Mexican Cession were not excepted from the policy to respect Indian right of occupancy. Though the Cramer Case involved the problem of individual Indian occupancy, this Court stated that such occupancy was not to be treated differently from "the original nomadic tribal occupancy." (261 US p. 227, 67 L ed 625, 43 S Ct 342.) Perhaps the assumption that aboriginal possession would be respected in the Mexican Cession was, like the generalizations in Johnson v. M'Intosh, 8 Wheat. (US) 543, 5 L ed 681, supra, not necessary for the narrow holding of the case. But such generalizations have been so often and so long repeated as respects land under the prior sovereignty of the various European nations including Spain, that, like other rules governing titles to property United States v. Title Ins. & T. Co. 265 US 472, 486, 487, 68 L ed 1110, 1114, 44 S Ct 621) they should now be considered no longer open.
>
> . . .
>
> *Nor is it true, as respondent urges that a tribal claim to any particular lands must be based upon a treaty, statute, or other formal government action.* As stated in the Cramer Case, "The fact that such right of occupancy finds no recognition in any state or other formal governmental action is not conclusive". 261 U.S. at 229, 67 L ed 626, 43 S Ct 342.

It is apparent also that the Court of Appeal misapprehended the issues involved in United States v. Alcea Band of Tillamooks et al. (1946), 329 U.S. 40. This is clear from the judgment of Davis, J., in Lipan Apache Tribe et al. v. United States (1967), 180 Ct. Cl. 487. In that case it was argued unsuccessfully that affirmative recognition by Texas prior to entering the Union was essential to any legal assertion of Indian title. The Court said [pp. 491-2]:

> On this motion to dismiss we must accept the factual allegation that the claimant tribes had used and occupied designated lands in Texas to the exclusion of other peoples for many years. Such continuous and exclusive use of property is sufficient, unless duly extinguished, to establish Indian or aboriginal title. See, e.g., Sac and Fox Tribe v. United States, 179 Ct. Cl.8, 21-22 (1967), and cases cited. We know that, prior to the creation of the Republic of Texas in 1836, the previous sovereigns, Spain and Mexico (and France, to some extent), did not cut off the aboriginal rights of the

Indian within their territories on the North American continent. The Supreme Court has clearly indicated that lands formerly under Spanish, Mexican, or French sovereignty are not to be treated differently, for purposes of determining Indian title, from other property within this nation. United States v. Santa Fe Pac. R.R., 314 U.S. 339, 345-6 (1941). In each instance, Indian possession, when proved, must be accorded proper respect. Johnson v. M'Intosh, 21 U.S. (8 Wheat.) 543, 571, 574, 592 (1823); Mohave Tribe v. United States, 7 Ind. Cl. Comm. 219, 260-1 (1959); Washoe Tribe v. United States, 7 Ind. Cl. Comm. 266, 288 (1959).

The Claims Commission has found, however, that, even if the claimants had once possessed aboriginal title to the lands, that right of occupancy was lost after 1836 when Texas became an independent country. The Commission appeared to believe that the survival of aboriginal title depends upon affirmative recognition by the sovereign and that the Republic "did not accord the Indian[s] the right of occupancy . . ."; without such a right to lands in Texas, at the time of annexation, the tribes failed to prove a necessary element of their cause of action and were barred from recovery.

To the extent that the Commission and the appellee believe that affirmative governmental recognition or approval is a prerequisite to the existence of original title, we think they err. Indian title based on aboriginal possession does not depend on sovereign recognition or affirmative acceptancy for its survival. Once established in fact, it endures until extinguished or abandoned. United States v. Santa Fe Pac. R.R., supra, 314 U.S. at 345, 347. It is "entitled to the respect of all courts until it should be legitimately extinguished..." Johnson v. M'Intosh, supra, 21 U.S. (8 Wheat.) at 592. See Clark v. Smith, 38 U.S. (13 Pet.) 195, 201 (1839); Worcester v. State of Georgia, 31 U.S. (6 Pet.) 405, 420, 439 (1832); Mohave Tribe v. United States, supra, 7 Ind. Cl. Comm. at 262.

The correct inquiry is, not whether the Republic of Texas accorded or granted the Indians any rights, but whether that sovereign extinguished their pre-existing occupancy rights. Extinguishment can take several forms; it can be effected "by treaty, by the sword, by purchase, by the exercise of complete dominion adverse to the right of occupancy, or otherwise . . .". United States v. Santa Fe Pac. R.R., supra, 314 U.S. at 347. While the selection of a means is a governmental prerogative, the actual act (or acts) of extinguishment must be plain and unambiguous. *In the absence of a "clear and plain indication" in the public records that the sovereign "intended to extinguish all of the [claimants'] rights" in their property, Indian title continues.* Id. at 353.

(Emphasis added.)

Surely the Canadian treaties, made with much solemnity on behalf of the Crown, were intended to extinguish the Indian title. What other purpose did they serve? If they were not intended to extinguish the Indian right, they were a gross fraud and that is not to be assumed. Treaty 8 made in 1899 was entered into on behalf of Queen Victoria and the representatives of Indians in a section of British Columbia and the Northwest Territories. The treaty was ratified by the Queen's

Privy Council in Canada. Certain statements in the treaty are entirely inconsistent with any argument or suggestion that such rights as the Indians may have had were extinguished prior to Confederation in 1871. The treaty reads in part:

> And whereas the said Commissioners have proceeded to negotiate a treaty with the Cree, Beaver, Chipewyan, and other Indians, inhabiting the district hereinafter defined and described, and the same has been agreed upon and concluded by the respective bands at the dates mentioned hereunder, the Said Indians DO HEREBY CEDE, RELEASE, SURRENDER AND YIELD UP to the Government of the Dominion of Canada, for Her Majesty the Queen and her successors for ever, all their rights, titles and privileges whatsoever, to the lands included within the following limits, that is to say...
>
> . . .
>
> *And also the said Indian rights, title and privileges whatsoever to all other lands wherever situated in the North-West Territories, British Columbia, or in any other portion of the Dominion of Canada.*
> To have and to hold the same to Her Majesty the Queen and her successors forever.

(Emphasis added.) If there was no Indian title extant in British Columbia in 1899, why was the treaty negotiated and ratified?

Paralleling and supporting the claim of the Nishgas that they have a certain right or title to the lands in question is the guarantee of Indian rights contained in the Proclamation of 1763. This Proclamation was an Executive Order having the force and effect of an Act of Parliament and was described by Gwynne, J., in St. Catherine's Milling case at p. 652 as the "Indian Bill of Rights": see also Campbell v. Hall. Its force as a statute is analogous to the status of Magna Carta which has always been considered to be the law throughout the Empire. It was a law which followed the flag as England assumed jurisdiction over newly-discovered or acquired lands or territories. It follows, therefore, that the Colonial Laws Validity Act, 1865 (U.K.), c. 63, applied to make the Proclamation the law of British Columbia. That it was regarded as being the law of England is clear from the fact that when it was deemed advisable to amend it the amendment was affected by an Act of Parliament, namely the Quebec Act of 1774 [1774 (U.K.) (14 Geo. III), c. 83].

In respect of this Proclamation, it can be said that when other exploring nations were showing a ruthless disregard of native rights England adopted a remarkably enlightened attitude towards the Indians of North America. The Proclamation must be regarded as a fundamental document upon which any just determination of original rights rests. Its effect was discussed by Idington, J., in this Court in Province of Ontario v. Dominion of Canada (1909), 42 S.C.R. 1 at pp. 103-4 [affd [1910] A.C. 637], as follows:

> A line of *policy* begotten of prudence, humanity and justice adopted by the British Crown to be observed in all future dealings with the Indians in respect of such rights as they might suppose themselves to possess was outlined in the Royal Proclamation of 1763 erecting, after the Treaty of Paris in that year, amongst others, a separate government for Quebec, ceded by that treaty to the British Crown.

> That policy adhered to thenceforward, by those responsible for the honour of the Crown led to many treaties whereby Indians agreed to surrender such rights as they were supposed to have in areas respectively specified in such treaties.
>
> In these surrendering treaties there generally were reserves provided for Indians making such surrenders to enter into or be confined to for purposes of residence.
>
> The history of this mode of dealing is very fully outlined in the judgment of the learned Chancellor Boyd in the case of The Queen v St. Catherine's Milling Co., 10 O.R. 196 [affirmed 13 O.A.R. 148].

[Italics added.]

The question of the Proclamation's applicability to the Nishgas is, accordingly, relevant in this appeal. The point has been before provincial Courts in Canada on a number of occasions but never specifically dealt with by this Court.

It is necessary, therefore, to face the issue as one of first impression and to decide it with due regard to the historical record and the principles of the common law.

The Judges of the Court of Appeal of British Columbia have disagreed on this important question. Norris, J.A., in White and Bob dealt exhaustively with the subject at pp. 638 to 648 [50 D.L.R. (2d)] of his reasons, saying in part at p. 638:

> The Royal Proclamation of 1763 was declaratory and confirmatory of the aboriginal rights and applied to Vancouver Island.
>
> For the British, the Proclamation of 1763 dealt with a new situation arising from the war with the French, in North America in which Indians to a greater or less degree took an active part on both sides, and incidentally from the Treaty of Paris of 1763 which concluded that war. The problem which then faced the British was the management of a continent by a power, the interests of which had theretofore been confined to the sea coast. As exploration advanced, the natives of the interior and the western reaches must be pacified, trade promoted, sovereignty exercised and justice administered, even if only in a general way, until such time as British settlement could be established. It was a situation which was to face the Imperial power in varying degree and in various parts of the continent until almost the close of the 19th century. In the circumstances it was vital that aboriginal rights be declared and the policy pertaining thereto defined. This was the purpose and the substance of the Royal Proclamation of 1763. The principles there laid down continued to be the charter of Indian rights through the succeeding years to the present time—recognized in the various Treaties with the United States in which Indian rights were involved and in the successive land Treaties made between the Crown and the Hudson's Bay Co. with the Indians.

concluding correctly that the Proclamation was declaratory of the aboriginal rights and applied to Vancouver Island. It follows that if it applied to Vancouver Island it also applied to the Indians of the mainland. Sheppard, J.A., with whom Lord, J.A., agreed, held that the Proclamation did not apply to Vancouver Island. This Court upheld the majority judgment but did not deal with the question of

whether or not the Proclamation extended to include territory in British Columbia.

In the judgment under appeal, Gould, J., accepted the views of Sheppard and
Lord, JJ.A., in preference to that of Norris, J.A. In my view the opinion of
Sheppard, J.A., in White and Bob was based on incomplete research as to the state
of knowledge of the existence of the land mass between the Rocky Mountains
and the Pacific Ocean in 1763.

In R. v. Sikyea, 43 D.L.R. (2d) 150 at p. 152, [1964] 2 C.C.C. 325, 46 W.W.R.
65, Johnson, J.A., said:

> The right of Indians to hunt and fish for food on unoccupied Crown lands
> has always been recognized in Canada—in the early days as an incident of
> their "ownership" of the land, and later by the treaties by which the Indians
> gave up their ownership right in these lands. McGillivray, J.A., in R. v.
> Wesley, [1932] 4 D.L.R. 774, 58 C.C.C. 269, 26 A.L.R. 433, [1932] 2 W.W.R.
> 337, discussed quite fully the origin, history and nature of the right of the
> Indians both in the lands and under the treaties by which these were sur-
> rendered and it is unnecessary to repeat what he has said. It is sufficient to
> say that these rights had their origin in the Royal Proclamation, R.S.C. 1952,
> vol. 6, App. III, p. 6127, that followed the Treaty of Paris in 1763. By that
> Proclamation it was declared that the Indians "should not be molested or
> disturbed in the Possession of such Parts of Our Dominions and Territories
> as, not having been ceded to or purchased by Us, are reserved to them or
> any of them, as their Hunting Grounds". The Indians inhabiting Hudson
> Bay Company lands were excluded from the benefit of the Proclamation,
> and it is doubtful, to say the least, if the Indians of at least the western part
> of the Northwest Territories could claim any rights under the Proclamation,
> for these lands at the time were terra incognita and lay to the north and not
> "to the westward of the Sources of the rivers which fall into the Sea from
> the West and North West" (from the 1763 Proclamation describing the area
> to which the Proclamation applied). That fact is not important because the
> Government of Canada has treated all Indians across Canada, including
> those living on lands claimed by the Hudson Bay Company, as having an
> interest in the lands that required a treaty to effect its surrender.

This Court expressed its agreement with the views of Johnson, J.A., in Sikyea v.
The Queen, 50 D.L.R. (2d) 80 at p. 84, [1965] 2 C.C.C. 129, [1964] S.C.R. 642,
where, speaking for the Court, I said

> On the substantive question involved, I agree with the reasons for judg-
> ment and with the conclusions of Johnson, J.A., in the Court of Appeal.
> He has dealt with the important issues fully and correctly in their historical
> and legal settings, and there is nothing which I can usefully add to what
> he has written.

The wording of the Proclamation itself seems quite clear that it was intended
to include the lands west of the Rocky Mountains. The relevant paragraph reads
[p. 6130]:

> And We do further declare it to be Our Royal Will and Pleasure, for the

present as aforesaid, to reserve under our Sovereignty, Protection, and Dominion, for the use of the said Indians, all the Lands and Territories not included within the Limits of Our Said Three New Governments, or within the Limits of the Territory granted to the Hudson's Bay Company, as also all the Lands and Territories lying to the Westward of the Sources of the Rivers which fall into the Sea from the West and North West as aforesaid;

The only territories not included were: (1) Those within the limits of the three new Governments; and (2) within the limits of the territory granted to the Hudson's Bay Company. The concluding sentence of the paragraph just quoted, "as also all the Lands and Territories lying to the Westward of the Sources of the Rivers which fall into the Sea from the West and North West as aforesaid"; shows clearly that the framers of the paragraph were well aware that there was territory to the west of the sources of the rivers which ran from the west and north-west.

Sheppard, J.A., in White and Bob founded his opinion that the Proclamation did not extend to the lands west of the Rockies in part upon the statement that in 1763 the areas of British Columbia west of the Rockies were terra incognita. Such a view is not at all flattering to the explorers and rulers of England in 1763. The knowledgeable people in England were not unaware that the Russians were by 1742 carrying on a fur-trading business with the natives of what we now know as the Alaskan Panhandle. In 1721 a Dane, Captain Bering, under orders from the Emperor of Russia, had sailed from Kamtschatka to determine if Asia and America were joined or separate. He did determine that the two continents were separate, and in so doing gave his name to Bering Strait. Arctic explorers from Europe and England had been trying to find the fabled Northwest Passage for a considerable time prior to 1763; amongst them Frobisher in 1576-78 and Hudson prior to his disappearance in 1610. The Hudson's Bay Company had been operating in the area west of Hudson Bay and to the Rockies for almost a century prior to 1763, and although it was 30 years more before Alexander Mackenzie crossed the Rockies to the Pacific, the thought of so doing had intrigued explorers for many years. Anthony Hendry for Hudson's Bay Company travelled to the Rockies by way of the Red Deer River in 1754 and into the mountains in 1759. The west coast of the continent was not unknown nor was the fact that it extended very far to the north. Drake in 1579, in an attempt to find a passage from west to east, had sailed northward to a point where the bitter cold caused him to return southward. According to Hakluyt's Voyages, Drake sailed "in a climate zone where his rigging froze, where the trees on the coast were lifeless and where the natives lived in houses covered with earth. Behind the shore rose ridges of snow-capped peaks." It would seem that he reached substantially the same latitude that Cook did two centuries later. Coronado's lieutenant, as early as 1550, stood on the east rim of the Grand Canyon but found it impossible to cross. LaVerendrye's sons sighted the Rockies near Lethbridge in 1743. After LaVerendrye's death in 1749 his sons sought permission to continue their father's explorations into and beyond the mountains but were denied authorization. However, one Legardeur de SaintPierre undertook to reach and cross the mountains. In 1750 he sent an associate, one de Niverville, who, following the South Saskatchewan River and the Bow River, reached a point near the present site of Calgary where he built a stockade in 1751 within the territory of the Blackfoot nation. De Niverville learned from his Indian hosts that trading was done by other Indians to the west with white men on the far side of the mountains. These white men were probably Spaniards for it is known that the Spanish were exploring the west coast of America north from California. The names of several localities in British Columbia attest to that fact. Further confirmation of Spanish trading on the west coast was found by Cook when he put into Nootka Sound in 1778. He reports meeting with a native who had come into Nootka with a group of Indians from a distant area. This native was wearing around his neck as an ornament two silver table spoons which were assumed to have come from Spaniards. These spoons were taken by Cook and, after his death, were presented to the artist, Sir Joseph Banks, who had painted a portrait of Cook in 1776. Accordingly it cannot be challenged that while the west coast lands were mostly unexplored as of 1763 they were certainly known to exist and that fact is borne out by the wording of the paragraph in the Proclamation previously quoted.

This important question remains: were the rights either at common law or under the Proclamation extinguished? Tysoe, J.A., said in this regard at p. 95 [13 D.L.R. (3d)] of his reasons: "It is true, as the appellants have submitted, that *nowhere can one find express words extinguishing Indian title...*" (emphasis added).

The parties here agree that if extinguishment was accomplished, it must have occurred between 1858 and when British Columbia joined Confederation in 1871. The respondent relies on what was done by Governor Douglas and by his successor, Frederick Seymour, who became Governor in 1864.

Once aboriginal title is established, it is presumed to continue until the contrary is proven. This was stated to be the law by Viscount Haldane in Amodu Tijani v. Secretary, Southern Nigeria, [1921] 2 A.C. 399 at pp. 409-10, as follows:

> Their Lordships think that the learned Chief Justice in the judgment thus summarised, which virtually excludes the legal reality of the community usufruct, has failed to recognize the real character of the title to land occupied by a native community. That title, as they have pointed out, is prima facie based, not on such individual ownership as English law has made familiar, but on a communal usufructuary occupation, which may be so complete as to reduce any radical right in the Sovereign to one which only extends to comparatively limited rights of administrative interference. In their opinion there is no evidence that this kind of usufructuary title of the community was disturbed in law, either when the Benin Kings conquered Lagos or when the cession to the British Crown took place in 1861. The general words used in the treaty of cession are not in themselves to be construed as extinguishing subject rights. *The original native right was a communal right, and it must be presumed to have continued to exist unless the contrary is established by the context or circumstances.* There is, in their Lordships' opinion, no evidence which points to its having been at any time seriously disturbed or even questioned. Under these conditions they are unable to take the view adopted by the Chief Justice and the full Court.

(Emphasis added.)

The appellants rely on the presumption that the British Crown intended to respect native rights; therefore, when the Nishga people came under British sovereignty (and that is subject to what I said about sovereignty over part of the lands not being determined until 1903) they were entitled to assert, as a legal right, their Indian title. It being a legal right, it could not thereafter be extinguished except by surrender to the Crown or by competent legislative authority, and then only by specific legislation. There was no surrender by the Nishgas and neither the Colony of British Columbia nor the Province, after Confederation, enacted legislation specifically purporting to extinguish the Indian title nor did Parliament at Ottawa. The following quotation from Lord Denning's judgment in Oyekan et al. v. Adele, [1957] 2 All E.R. 785 at p. 788, states the position clearly. He said:

> In order to ascertain what rights pass to the Crown or are retained by the inhabitants, the courts of law look, not to the treaty, but to the conduct of the British Crown. It has been laid down by their Lordships' Board that

>> Any inhabitant of the territory can make good in the municipal courts established by the new sovereign only such rights as that sovereign has, through his officers, recognised. Such rights as he had under the rule of his predecessors avail him nothing.

> See Vajesingji Joravarsingji v. Secretary of State for India ((1924), L.R. 51 Ind. App. 357 to p. 360 per LORD DUNEDIN), Hoani Te Heuheu Tikino v. Aotea District Maori Land Board ([1941] 2 All E.R. 93 at p. 98). *In inquiring, however, what rights are recognised, there is one guiding principle. It is this: The courts will assume that the British Crown intends that the rights of property of the inhabitants are to be fully respected.* Whilst, therefore, the British Crown, as Sovereign, can make laws enabling it compulsorily to acquire land for public purposes, it will see that proper compensation is awarded to every one of the inhabitants who has by native law an interest in it; and the courts will declare the inhabitants entitled to compensation according to their interests, even though those interests are of a kind unknown to English law: see Amodu Tijani v. Southern Nigeria (Secretary) ([1921] 2 A.C. 399, Sakariyawo Oshodi v. Moriamo Dakolo ([1930] A.C. 667).

(Emphasis added.) Reference should also be made to The Queen v. Symonds (1847), N.Z.P.C.C. 387, approved in Tamaki v. Baker, [1901] A.C. 561 at p. 579. In Symonds, Chapman, J., said at p. 390:

> The practice of extinguishing Native titles by fair purchases is certainly more than two centuries old. It has long been adopted by the Government in our American colonies, and by that of the United States. It is now part of the law of the land, and although the Courts of the United States, in suits between their own subjects, will not allow a grant to be impeached under pretext that the Native title has not been extinguished, yet they would certainly not hesitate to do so in a suit by one of the Native Indians. In the case of the Cherokee Nation v. State of Georgia, (1831) 5 Peters 1, the Supreme Court threw its protective decision over the plaintiff-nation, against a gross attempt at spoliation; calling to its aid, throughout every portion of its judgment, the principles of the common law as applied and adopted from the earliest times by the colonial laws: Kent's Comm. vol. ii, lecture 61. Whatever may be the opinion of jurists as to the strength or weakness of the Native title, whatsoever may have been the past vague

notions of the Natives of this country, whatever may be their present clearer and still growing conception of their own dominion over land, it cannot be too solemnly asserted that it is entitled to be respected, that it cannot be extinguished (at least in times of peace) otherwise than by the free consent of the Native occupiers. But for their protection, and for the sake of humanity, the Government is bound to maintain, and the Courts to assert, the Queen's exclusive right to extinguish it. It follows from what has been said, that in solemnly guaranteeing the Native title, and in securing what is called the Queen's pre-emptive right, the Treaty of Waitangi, confirmed by the Charter of the Colony, does not assert either in doctrine or in practice any thing new and unsettled.

and to the statement of Davis, J., in Lipan Apache previously quoted that:

. . . In the absence of a "clear and plain indication" in the public records that the sovereign "intended to extinguish all of the (claimants') rights" in their property, Indian title continues . . .

It would, accordingly, appear to be beyond question that the onus of proving that the Sovereign intended to extinguish the Indian title lies on the respondent and that intention must be "clear and plain". There is no such proof in the case at bar; no legislation to that effect.

The Court of Appeal also erred in holding that there "is no Indian Title capable of judicial interpretation . . . unless it has previously been recognized either by the Legislature or the Executive Branch of Government" [see p. 70]. Relying on Cook et al. v. Sprigg, [1899] A.C. 572, and other cases, the Court of Appeal erroneously applied what is called the Act of State Doctrine. This doctrine denies a remedy to the citizens of an acquired territory for invasion of their rights which may occur during the change of sovereignty. English Courts have held that a municipal Court has no jurisdiction to review the manner in which the Sovereign acquires new territory. The Act of State is the activity of the Sovereign by which he acquires the property. Professor D. P. O'Connell in his work International Law, 2nd ed. (1970), at p. 378 says:

This doctrine, which was affirmed in several cases arising out of the acquisition of territory in Africa and India, has been misinterpreted to the effect that the substantive rights themselves have not survived the change. In fact English courts have gone out of their way to repudiate the construction, and it is clear that the Act of State doctrine is no more than a procedural bar to municipal law action, and as such is irrelevant to the question whether in international law change of sovereignty affects acquired rights.

The Act of State doctrine has no application in the present appeal for the following reasons: (a) It has never been invoked in claims dependent on aboriginal title. An examination of its rationale indicates that it would be quite inappropriate for the Courts to extend the doctrine to such cases: (b) It is based on the premise that an Act of State is an exercise of the Sovereign power which a municipal Court has no power to review: see Salaman v. Secretary of State in Council of India, [1906] 1 K.B. 613 at pp. 639-40; Cook v. Sprigg, supra, at p. 578.

When the Sovereign, in dealings with another Sovereign (by treaty of cession or conquest) acquires land, then a municipal Court is without jurisdiction to the extent that any claimant asserts a proprietary right inconsistent with acquisition of property by the Sovereign—i.e., acquisition by Act of State. The ratio for the cases relied upon by the Court of Appeal was that a municipal Court could not review the Act of State if in so doing the Court would be enforcing a treaty between two Sovereign States: see Cook v. Sprigg, supra, at p. 578; Vajesingji Joravarsingji v. Secretary of State for India (1924), L.R. 51 Ind. App. 357 at p. 360; Salaman, supra, at p. 639. In all the cases referred to by the Court of Appeal the origin of the claim being asserted was a grant to the claimant from the previous Sovereign. In each case the claimants were asking the Courts to give judicial recognition to that claim. In the present case the appellants are not claiming that the origin of their title was a grant from any previous Sovereign, nor are they asking this Court to enforce a treaty of cession between any previous Sovereign and the British Crown. The appellants are not challenging an Act of State—they are asking this Court to recognize that settlement of the north Pacific coast did not extinguish the aboriginal title of the Nishga people—a title which has its origin in antiquity—not in a grant from a previous Sovereign. In applying the Act of State doctrine, the Court of Appeal completely ignored the rationale of the doctrine which is no more than a recognition of the Sovereign prerogative to acquire territory in a way that cannot be later challenged in a municipal Court.

Once it is apparent that the Act of State doctrine has no application, the whole argument of the respondent that there must be some form of "recognition" of aboriginal rights falls to the ground.

On the question of extinguishment, the respondent relies on what was done by Governors Douglas and Seymour and the Council of British Columbia. The appellants, as I have previously mentioned, say that if either Douglas or Seymour or the Council of the Colony of British Columbia did purport to extinguish the Nishga title that any such attempt was beyond the powers of either the Governors or of the Council and that what, if anything, was attempted in this respect was ultra vires.

Douglas' powers were clearly set out in his Commission. A Governor had no powers to legislate other than those given in the Commission: 5 Hals., 3rd ed., p. 558, para. 1209; Commercial Cable Co. v. Government of Newfoundland, 29 D.L.R. 7 at p. 11, [1916] 2 A.C. 610; Musgrave v. Pulido (1879), 5 App. Cas. 102. Sir Arthur Berridale Keith in his *Responsible Government in the Dominions*, rev. 2nd ed. (1927), said at p. 83 [quoting Musgrave v. Pulido]:

> the Governor of a colony in ordinary cases cannot be regarded as a Viceroy, nor can it be assumed that he possesses general sovereign power. His authority is derived from his commission and limited to the powers thereby expressly or impliedly entrusted to him.

and at pp. 83-4:

> There can be no doubt of the doctrine of the Privy Council; a Governor has no special privilege like that of the Crown; he must show in any court that he has authority by law to do an act, and what is more important for our purpose, he must show not merely that the Crown might do the act, but that he personally had authority to do the act. . . .

There is therefore no alternative but to hold that, apart from statutory powers, the Governor has a delegation of so much of the executive power as enables him effectively to conduct the Executive Government of the territory.

The Letters Patent under which Douglas acted authorized him in part:

> ... and whereas We have, in pursuance of the said Act, by Our Order made by Us in Our Privy Council, bearing date this 2d instant, ordered, authorized, empowered, and commanded Our Governor of Our said Colony to make provision for the administration of justice in Our said Colony, and generally to make, ordain, and establish all such laws, institutions, and ordinances as may be necessary for the peace, order, and good government of Our subjects and others residing therein, wherein the said Governor *is to conform to and exercise the directions, powers, and authorities given and granted to him by Our Commission, subject to all such rules and regulations as shall be prescribed in and by Our Instructions under Our Signet and Sign Manual accompanying Our said Commission, or by any future instructions, as aforesaid;* . . .

(emphasis added) and also the following:

> IV. And We do by these presents further give and grant unto you, the said James Douglas, full power and authority, by Proclamation or Proclamations to be by you from time to time for that purpose issued under the Public Seal of Our said Colony, to make, ordain, and establish all such laws, institutions, and ordinances as may be necessary for the peace, order, and good government of Our subjects and others residing in Our said Colony and its Dependencies: *Provided that such laws, institutions, and ordinances are not to be repugnant, but, as near as may be, agreeable to the Laws and Statutes of Our United Kingdom of Great Britain and Ireland:* Provided also, that all such laws, institutions, and ordinances, of what nature or duration soever, be transmitted under the Public Seal of Our said Colony for Our approbation or disallowance, as in Our said Order provided: And We do by these presents require and enjoin you that in making all such laws, institutions, and ordinances you do strictly conform to and observe the rules, regulations, and restrictions which are or shall be in that respect prescribed to you by Our Instructions under Our Royal Sign Manual and Signet accompanying this Our Commission, or by any future Instructions, as aforesaid.

(Emphasis added.) Attached to Douglas' Commission and forming an integral part thereof were "Instructions" by which he was to govern the Colony. Regarding those Instructions, the Letters Patent said:

> VII. You are, as much as possible, to observe, in the passing of all laws, that each different matter be provided for by a different law, without intermixing in one and the same law such things as have no proper relation to each other; and you are more especially to take care that no clause or clauses be inserted in or annexed to any law which shall be foreign to what the title of such law imports, and that no perpetual clause be part of any temporary law, *and that no law whatever be suspended, altered, continued, revived, or*

repealed by general words, but that the title and date of such law so suspended, altered, continued, revived, or repealed be particularly mentioned and expressed in the enacting part.

(Emphasis added.)

Further Instructions were sent from time to time by the Colonial Secretary in London, including one dated July 31, 1858, which read:

[see above, pp. 69-70]

to which Douglas replied:

16. *I shall not fail to give the fullest scope to your humane consideration for the improvement of the native Indian tribes and shall take care that all their civil and agrarian rights be protected.* I have in fact already taken measures, as far as possible, to prevent collisions between those tribes and the whites, *and have impressed upon the miners the great fact that the law will protect the Indian equally with the white man and regard him in all respects as a fellow subject.* That principle being admitted will go far towards the wellbeing of the Indian tribes, and securing the peace of the country.

(Emphasis added.) Another despatch from the then Colonial Secretary, Sir E. B. Lytton, reads:

2. *To open land for settlement gradually; not to sell beyond the limits of what is either surveyed or ready for immediate survey and to prevent, as far as in you lies squatting on unsold land.* Mineral lands will require a special care and forethought and I request your views thereon.

(Emphasis added.) There is nothing in the record indicating that the Nishga lands have even yet been surveyed or made ready for immediate survey excepting, perhaps, the land given for the townsite of Stewart. The boundary line with Alaska was not surveyed until after the boundary settlement. Consequently, I cannot see how anything can be derived from the fact that surveys were made on Vancouver Island or on the lower mainland that would lead to the conclusion that the rights of the Nishgas in the north-west corner of the Colony were being dealt with by implication or at all.

Specific declarations by Douglas and by the Council of the Colony of British Columbia relied on by the respondent include:

(a) Proclamation dated February 14, 1859, which contained the following paragraph:
1. All the lands in British Columbia, and all the Mines and Minerals therein, belong to the Crown in fee.
(b) Ordinance dated April 11, 1865, in which is found:
3. All the lands in British Columbia, and all the mines and minerals therein, not otherwise lawfully appropriated belong to the Crown in fee.
(c) Ordinance of March 31, 1866, which provided:
The aborigines of this colony or the territories neighbouring thereto could not pre-empt or hold land in fee simple without obtaining special permission of the Governor in writing.

The appellants do not dispute the Province's claim that it holds title to the lands in fee. They acknowledge that the fee is in the Crown. The enactments just referred to merely state what was the actual situation under the common law and add nothing new or additional to the Crown's paramount title and they are of no assistance in this regard to the respondent. In relying so heavily on these enactments, the respondent is fighting an issue that does not arise in the case and is resisting a claim never made in the action. As to the Ordinance of March 31, 1866, the limitation on the right of an aborigine to hold land in fee simple has no bearing whatsoever on the right of the aborigine to remain in possession of the land which has been in the possession of his people since time immemorial. Governor Douglas knew that he had no right to take Indian lands without some form of compensation. He understood his Instructions in that regard. This is clear from paragraphs of his letter to the Colonial Secretary dated March 25, 1861. He said in part:

[For 2. and 3., see above p. 70]

4. All the settled districts of the Colony, with the exception of Cowichan, Chemainus, and Barclay Sound, have been already bought from the Indians, at a cost in no case exceeding 2 pounds 10s. sterling for each family. As the land has since then, increased in value, the expense would be relatively somewhat greater now, but I think that their claims might be satisfied with a payment of 3 pounds to each family; so that taking the native population of those districts at 1,000 families, the sum of 3,000 pounds would meet the whole charge.

The Colonial Secretary replied on October 19, 1861, as follows:
[see above, pp. 70-1]

This reply, while refusing funds to acquire the native rights in land, did not authorize Douglas to take or extinguish those rights without compensation. If the lands were to be taken they had to be paid for by the Colony and not by the British taxpayer. If the Colony had intended extinguishing the Indian title to public lands as referred to in the foregoing letter, it could easily have said, "Indian title to public lands in the Colony is hereby extinguished". No such enactment or one with language to like effect was ever passed.

A number of other Acts, Ordinances and Proclamations were passed or issued between February 14, 1859, and June 1, 1870. All of these were repealed and consolidated by an Ordinance passed July 1, 1870. That Consolidation contained in part the following:

PRE-EMPTION

3. From and after the date of the proclamation in this Colony of Her Majesty's assent to this Ordinance, any male person being a British Subject, of the age of eighteen years or over, may acquire the right to pre-empt any tract of unoccupied, unsurveyed, and unreserved Crown Lands (not being an Indian settlement) not exceeding three hundred and twenty acres in extent in that portion of the Colony situate to the northward and eastward of the Cascade or Coast Range of Mountains, and one hundred and sixty acres in extent in the rest of the Colony. Provided that such right

of pre-emption shall not be held to extend to any of the Aborigines of this Continent, except to such as shall have obtained the Governor's special permission in writing to that effect.

This is the provision chiefly relied on by Gould, J., and by the Court of Appeal in making the finding that the Indian title in British Columbia had been extinguished. It is obvious that this enactment did not apply to the Nishga lands on the Naas River. The north-west boundary of the Colony in that area was still in dispute. In any event, this provision is expansive and permissive in so far as it enables aborigines to get title in fee with the Governor's written permission.

If in any of the Proclamations or actions of Douglas, Seymour or of the Council of the Colony of British Columbia there are elements which the respondent says extinguish by implication the Indian title, then it is obvious from the Commission of the Governor and from the Instructions under which the Governor was required to observe and neither the Commission nor the Instructions contain any power or authorization to extinguish the Indian title, then it follows logically that if any attempt was made to extinguish the title it was beyond the power of the Governor or of the Council to do so and, therefore, ultra vires.

A further observation in respect of the Letter of Instructions of July 31, 1858, must be made of the phrase, "Let me not omit to observe, that it should be an invariable condition, in all bargains or treaties with the Natives for the cession of land possessed by them . . . ". Having in mind the use of the word "cession" in this context, how can it logically be said that the Imperial Government was not at the time recognizing that the natives had something to cede? What they had to cede was their aboriginal right and title to possession of the lands, subject to the Crown's paramount title.

Having reviewed the evidence and cases in considerable detail and having decided that if the Nishgas ever had any right or title that it had been extinguished, Tysoe, J.A., was inexorably driven to the conclusion which he stated as follows [p. 94]:

> As a result of these pieces of legislation the Indians of the Colony of British Columbia *became in law trespassers* on and liable to actions of ejectment from lands in the Colony other than those set aside as reserves for the use of Indians.

(Emphasis added.) Any reasoning that would lead to such a conclusion must necessarily be fallacious. The idea is self-destructive. If trespassers, the Indians are liable to prosecution as such, a proposition which reason itself repudiates.

Following the hearing, the Court's attention was drawn to a recent Australian decision in which judgment was handed down on April 27, 1971, but the report of the judgment was not available until after the appeal was argued. The case is Milirrpum et al. v. Nabalco Pty. Ltd. (1971),17 F.L.R. 141. It is a judgment at trial by Blackburn, J., and involved a consideration of the rights of aborigines and whether the common law recognized a doctrine of "communal native title". The direct issue was the interpretation to be given to the phrase "interest in the land" contained in s. 5(1) of the Lands Acquisition Act, 1955-1966 relating to the acquisition of land on just terms. The issue was to this degree different from the issue here. It dealt with the validity of a grant made under the Lands Acquisition Act.

Blackburn, J., after an extensive review of the facts and historical records involving some 50 pages, held as follows [p 198]:

> This question of fact has been for me by far the most difficult of all the difficult questions of fact in the case. I can, in the last resort, do no more than express that degree of conviction which all the evidence has left upon my mind, and it is this: that I am not persuaded that the plaintiffs' contention is more probably correct than incorrect. In other words, I am not satisfied, on the balance of probabilities, that the plaintiffs' predecessors had in 1788 the same links to the same areas of land as those which the plaintiffs now claim.

That finding necessarily disposed of the claim being made. However, the learned Justice proceeded with a very comprehensive review of much of the case law regarding the rights of aborigines and the questions of the recognition and extinguishment of aboriginal title. It is obvious that all of the observations contained in his judgment following the finding of fact above set out were obiter dicta. In his review he dealt with the trial and appeal judgments in this case and said [p. 223]:

> I consider, with respect, that Calder's case, though it is not binding on this Court, is weighty authority for these propositions:
> 1. In a settled colony there is no principle of communal native title except such as can be shown by prerogative or legislative act, or a course of dealing.
> 2. In a settled colony a legislative and executive policy of treating the land of the colony as open to grant by the Crown, together with the establishment of native reserves, operates as an extinguishment of aboriginal title, if that ever existed.

It will be seen that he fell into the same errors as did Gould, J., and the Court of Appeal. The essence of his concurrence with the Court of Appeal judgment lies in his acceptance of the proposition that after conquest or discovery the native peoples have no rights at all except those subsequently granted or recognized by the conqueror or discoverer. That proposition is wholly wrong as the mass of authorities previously cited, including Johnson v. M'Intosh and Campbell v. Hall, establishes.

One last issue remains to be dealt with. The respondent by way of preliminary objections argued that the Court had no jurisdiction to grant the declaration asked for because it impugns the Crown's title to the land by seeking to have it declared that there is a cloud on the title, namely, aboriginal or Indian title, and secondly that the Court has no jurisdiction to make the declaration as it would affect the rights of persons who have had no opportunity to be heard, and thirdly, that the Court has no jurisdiction to grant a declaration if the declaration cannot have any practical result. Neither Gould, J., nor the Court of Appeal found it necessary to deal with these objections because they dismissed the action on other grounds. As I take the view that the action succeeds, I now deal with the objections.

Dealing with them in reverse order, it seems clear to me that if the declaration can be made it will have a most practical result, namely, the right of the Nishgas to compensation if and when extinguishment should be attempted or takes place. As to the second objection, the appellants' position is that the Nishgas are not asking to disturb the rights of any persons or corporations which had been given grants or rights even though such grants were ultra vires. They are prepared to accept things as they are.

That leaves the first objection, and there are, in my view, two valid answers to it. It is a fact that British Columbia does not have a Crown Proceedings Act, which virtually all the other Provinces have, which confers on the citizen the right to commence an action to have his rights vis-à-vis the Crown determined. Actions against the Crown in British Columbia are governed by the Crown Procedure Act, R.S.B.C. 1960, c. 89, and this Act provides for the historic petition of right procedure. Accordingly, it is argued by the respondent that actions against the Crown must have the consent of the Crown evidenced by a fiat in respect of the petition of right, but it was argued by the appellants that a writ claiming declaratory relief only does not fall within the provisions of the Crown Procedure Act. . . .

. . . it cannot be said that when the petition of right jurisprudence was being formulated that it was contemplated that it should apply to declaratory remedies. The declaratory remedy in the absence of concomitant consequential relief emerged only in the 19th century. The application of the ancient common law rule then would have to be one of deliberate judicial policy to constrain the remedies of the subject against the Crown, a policy of dubious validity today. It is much too late for the Courts to place obstructions in the path of citizens seeking redress against Government by resort to ancient judicial procedures. . . .

. . . The validity of what was done by Governors Douglas and Seymour and by the Council of the Colony of British Columbia is a vital question to be decided in this appeal and the Province cannot be permitted to deny access by the Nishgas to the Courts for the determination of that question.

I would, therefore, allow the appeal with costs throughout and declare that the appellants' right to possession of the lands delineated in ex. 2 with the exceptions before mentioned and their right to enjoy the fruits of the soil, of the forest, and of the rivers and streams within the boundaries of said lands have not been extinguished by the Province of British Columbia or by its predecessor, the Colony of British Columbia, or by the Governors of that Colony.

*　　*　　*

SPENCE J., concurs with HALL J.

*　　*　　*

PIGEON J.: This is an appeal by special leave of this Court from a judgment of the Court of Appeal of British Columbia [13 D.L.R. (3d) 64, 74 W.W.R. 481] affirming the judgment of Gould, J., in the Supreme Court of British Columbia [8 D.L.R. (3d) 59, 71 W.W.R. 81] dismissing an action in that Court claiming "a declaration that the aboriginal title, otherwise known as the Indian title, of the plaintiffs to their ancient tribal territory hereinbefore described, has never been lawfully extinguished".

In his reasons for judgment, Gould, J., after reviewing the facts and referring to St. Catherine's Milling & Lumber Co. v. The Queen (1888),14 App. Cas. 46, said [p. 83]:

> In the instant case sovereignty over the delineated lands came by exploration of terra incognita (see Johnson and Graham's Lessee v. M'Intosh (1823), 8 Wheaton 543), no acknowledgement at any time of any aboriginal rights and specific dealings with the territory so inconsistent with any Indian claim as to constitute the dealings themselves a denial of any Indian or aboriginal title. As the Crown had the absolute right to extinguish, if there was anything to extinguish, the denial amounts to the same thing, sans the admission that an Indian or aboriginal title had ever existed. There is nothing to suggest that any ancient rights, if such had ever existed prior to 1871 and had been extinguished, were revived by British Columbia's entry into Confederation and becoming subject to the B.N.A. Act, 1867.
>
> It is convenient here to deal with the third preliminary objection of defendant referred to earlier, that this matter required the granting of a fiat as a prerequisite to adjudication. In the light of opinions already expressed it is not necessary to decide on this question so interestingly argued by both counsel. It is not the usual judicial course to decide on the merits and then deal with the preliminary objections, but I think the comity of our Courts as an institution would have suffered had these plaintiffs been told judicially that their clearly enunciated claim would get no adjudication because it had been brought in the wrong form.

In the Court of Appeal, the finding adverse to the plaintiffs on the merits was upheld without any reference to the preliminary objections, save in the reasons of Maclean, J.A., at the end of which he said [p. 110]:

> In view of the decision I have arrived at, I do not consider it necessary to deal with the three formidable preliminary objections raised by the respondent as follows:
>
> > "1. The Court does not have jurisdiction to grant the declaration sought because it impugns the Crown's title to the land by seeking to have it declared that there is a cloud on the title, i.e. Indian title.
> > "2. The Court has no jurisdiction to make the declaration because it will affect the rights of others who have had no opportunity to be heard. Audi Alteram Partem.
> > "3. The Court ought not to grant a declaration if it can have no practical consequences."

If the objection that the granting of a fiat is a prerequisite to adjudication merely meant that the proceedings were instituted "in the wrong form", it certainly should not be considered for a moment, especially in this Court and at its stage. However, I feel bound by high authority to hold that the granting of a fiat, when required, is a condition of jurisdiction. Furthermore, the decision of the Executive to withhold the granting of a fiat is one from which there is no appeal: Lovibond v. Governor-General of Canada, [1930] A.C. 717. . . .

. . .Concerning the contention that the making of the declaration prayed for could be considered as an exercise of equitable jurisdiction, I must say that I fail to see how it could be so and how this could be reconciled with the decision above referred to. The substance of the claim is that the Crown's title to the subject land is being questioned, its assertion of an absolute title in fee being challenged on the basis of an adverse title which is said to be a burden on the fee.

It has been pointed out that in their statement of claim the plaintiffs alleged that some pre-Confederation B.C. legislation by Proclamations and statutes was ultra vires and reference was made to authorities holding that there is jurisdiction to issue, without a fiat obtained on a petition of right, declaratory judgments respecting the invalidity of legislation. The answer to this contention is that plaintiffs do not pray for any such declaration. Assuming the Court had jurisdiction to make it, this would not give it jurisdiction to make another quite different declaration. Furthermore, in view of s. 129, B.N.A. Act, I doubt very much that the constitutional validity of pre-Confederation legislation affecting Indians or Indian lands can be made in proceedings instituted against the provincial Attorney-General. . . .

. . .For all those reasons, I have to hold that the preliminary objection that the declaration prayed for, being a claim of title against the Crown in the right of the Province of British Columbia, the Court has no jurisdiction to make it in the absence of a fiat of the Lieutenant-Governor of that Province. I am deeply conscious of the hardship involved in holding that the access to the Court for the determination of the plaintiffs' claim is barred by sovereign immunity from suit without a fiat. However, I would point out that in the United States, claims in respect of the taking of lands outside of reserves and not covered by any treaty were not held justiciable until legislative provisions had removed the obstacle created by the doctrine of immunity. In Canada, immunity from suit has been removed by legislation at the federal level and in most Provinces. However, this has not yet been done in British Columbia.

I would therefore dismiss the appeal and make no order as to costs.

*   *   *

Laskin J., concurs with Hall J.

*   *   *

Appeal dismissed.

CHAPTER 5

Lavell / Bedard

THIS CASE is cited as Attorney-General of Canada v. Lavell / Isaac et al. v. Bedard, S.C.C. (1973). It involves the question of Aboriginal citizenship. Both Jeannette Lavell, from the Wikwemikong Band, and Yvonne Bedard, from the Six Nations Band, were women who lost their legal status as Indians through marriage to non-Indians, in accordance with section 12(1)(b) of the then Indian Act. Though the circumstances of the women were quite different, particularly in regard to their respective needs to live on reserve, the central question was the same in both cases: did section 12(1)(b) deprive the women of their equality rights as guaranteed by the Bill of Rights? As in Drybones (see Chapter Three), at issue was the relationship between the Indian Act and the Bill of Rights.

On the surface, the Drybones precedent could be read as having resolved the issue. However, Lavell/Bedard was a few years later, following both the struggle over the White Paper policy of 1969 and the Calder case of early 1973 (see Chapter Four). The Supreme Court justices' thinking on the question of Aboriginal rights had grown more complex. Pigeon's dissent in Drybones fore-shadowed concerns that would become central here: in using the Bill of Rights to overturn discriminatory sections of the Indian Act, there was a danger of applying the Bill in a manner which would limit or remove any Aboriginal rights. The emerging complexity of the issues was reflected in the number of intervenors in the case; unlike Drybones, where there were no outside inter-venors, Lavell/Bedard included many. Lavell and Bedard each had their own lawyers (Clayton Ruby acted for Lavell); the Attorney General of Canada had a battery of lawyers; the Six Nations Band had separate representation, as did Richard Isaac. As well, a variety of Native women's and women's organizations had representation along with the Treaty Voice of Alberta, most of the existing provincial status Indian groups (whose lawyers included James O'Reilly and Douglas Sanders), the National Indian Brotherhood, and the Native Council of Canada.

The decision was split and mirrored the complexity of the issues. Ritchie wrote the decision, which was agreed to by Martland, Judson, and Fauteux. Pigeon agreed with the effect of the decision, which was consistent with his view in Drybones. Laskin wrote the dissenting opinion, which was supported by Hall,

Spence, and Abbott, with the latter adding a few words of his own. Ritchie made two key arguments in the case. First, he argued that the conflict between the two pieces of legislation had to be interpreted in light of the British North America Act (1867), section 91(24) which made "Indians and lands reserved for Indians" a federal responsibility. Ritchie wrote: "to suggest that the provisions of the Bill of Rights have the effect of making the whole Indian Act inoperative as discriminatory is to assert that the Bill has rendered Parliament powerless to exercise the authority entrusted to it under the Constitution of enacting legislation which treats Indians living on reserves differently from other Canadians in relation to their property and civil rights" (134). Secondly, Ritchie argued that the case could be distinguished from Drybones because the Indian Act generally deals with relations among Indians on reserve and this had to be distinguished from relations between Indians and others off-reserve: "the Drybones case can . . . have no application to the present appeals as it was in no way concerned with the internal regulation of the lives of Indians on reserves or their right to the use and benefit of Crown lands thereon . . . " (141).

Justice Laskin, in a farsighted dissenting opinion, argued that the logic of the Drybones decision was perfectly suited to the situations of Lavell and Bedard, writing "if for the words 'on account of race' there are substituted the words 'on account of sex' the result must surely be the same" (147). Laskin also made the interesting point that the sexism embodied in section 12(1)(b) of the Indian Act could also be interpreted as racism, effectively creating an alliance between two forms of struggle against discrimination: "the contention that a differentiation on the basis of sex is not offensive to the Canadian Bill of Rights where that differentiation operates only among Indians under the Indian Act is one that compounds racial inequality even beyond the point that the Drybones case found unacceptable " (147). As against Ritchie's first argument, Laskin contended that "discriminatory treatment on the basis of race or colour or sex does not inhere in that grant of legislative power" (150).

The appeals were allowed and the lower court decisions favourable to the women overturned. It would be another twelve years of struggle before Bill C-31 would amend the Indian Act and replace section 12(1)(b), with less than satisfactory results for many Aboriginal women. In the post-1985 era, many Indians who regained legal status could not gain band membership, others found they were not eligible for legal status, and all found that government cutbacks to two crucial programs—the post-secondary education funding and off-reserve housing—meant that the benefits of legal status were reduced. The issue of Indian citizenship would continue to be a complex and enormously troubling one for those concerned with Aboriginal self-government. Editing has been confined to removing some of the discussion about the relation of the Bill of Rights to other federal legislation.

P.K.

Fauteux, C.J.C., concurs with Ritchie, J.

* * *

Abbott, J. (dissenting): The facts which are not in dispute are set out in the reasons of Ritchie and Laskin, JJ., which I have had the advantage of reading. I am in agreement with the reasons of Laskin, J., and wish to add only a few observations.

I share his view that the decision of this Court in R. v. Drybones (1969), 9 D.L.R. (3d) 473, [1970] 3 C.C.C. 355, [1970] S.C.R. 282, cannot be distinguished from the two cases under appeal although in these two appeals the consequences of the discrimination by reason of sex under s. 12(1)(b) of the Indian Act, R.S.C. 1970, c. I-6, are more serious than the relatively minor penalty for the drinking offence under s. 94 of the Act which was in issue in Drybones.

In that case, this Court rejected the contention that s. 1 of the Canadian Bill of Rights provided merely a canon of construction for the interpretation of legislation existing when the Bill was passed. With respect I cannot interpret "equality before the law" as used in s. 1(b) of the Bill as meaning simply "the equal subjection of all classes to the ordinary law of the land as administered by the ordinary courts" to use the language of Dicey which is quoted in the reasons of Ritchie, J.

Unless the words "without discrimination by reason of race, national origin, colour, religion or sex" used in s. 1 are to be treated as mere rhetorical window dressing, effect must be given to them in interpreting the section. I agree with Laskin, J., that s. 1(b) must be read as if those words were recited therein.

In my view the Canadian Bill of Rights has substantially affected the doctrine of the supremacy of Parliament. Like any other statute it can of course be repealed or amended, or a particular law declared to be applicable notwithstanding the provisions of the Bill. In form the supremacy of Parliament is maintained but in practice I think that it has been substantially curtailed. In my opinion that result is undesirable, but that is a matter for consideration by Parliament not the Courts.

Ritchie, J., said in his reasons for judgment in Drybones that the implementation of the Bill of Rights by the Courts can give rise to great difficulties and that statement has been borne out in subsequent litigation. Of one thing I am certain the Bill will continue to supply ample grist to the judicial mills for some time to come.

I would dismiss both appeals with costs.

* * *

Martland and Judson, JJ., concur with Ritchie, J.

* * *

Ritchie, J.: I have had the advantage of reading the reasons for judgment prepared for delivery by my brother Laskin.

These appeals, which were heard together, are from two judgments holding that the provisions of s. 12(1)(b) of the Indian Act, R.S.C. 1970, c. I-6, are rendered inoperative by s. 1(b) of the Canadian Bill of Rights, R.S.C. 1970, App. III, as denying equality before the law to the two respondents.

Both respondents were registered Indians and "Band" members within the meaning of s. 11(b) of the Indian Act when they elected to marry non-Indians and thereby relinquished their status as Indians in conformity with the said s. 12(1)(b) which reads as follows:

12(1) The following persons are not entitled to be registered, namely,
(b) a woman who married a person who is not an Indian, unless that woman is subsequently the wife or widow of a person described in section 11.

It is contended on behalf of both respondents that s. 12(1)(b) of the Act should be held to be inoperative as discriminating between Indian men and women and as being in conflict with the provisions of the Canadian Bill of Rights and particularly s. 1 thereof which provides:

1. It is hereby recognized and declared that in Canada there have existed and shall continue to exist without discrimination by reason of race, national origin, colour, religion or sex, the following human rights and fundamental freedoms, namely,
    (b) the right of the individual to equality before the law and the protection of the law;

I think it desirable at the outset to outline the facts concerning the two respondents separately.

1. Mrs. Lavell—This woman was a member of the Wikwemikong Band of Indians who married a non-Indian and whose name was deleted from the Indian Register by the Registrar in charge thereof pursuant to the provisions of s. 12(1)(b) of the Act. An appeal was taken from the Registrar's decision and was heard before His Honour Judge Grossberg, acting as persona designata under the Indian Act before whom evidence was taken which disclosed that at the time of the hearing and for some nine years before her marriage Mrs. Lavell had not lived on any reserve except for sporadic visits to her family, and the learned Judge declined to accept the suggestion that she could not visit her family on the reserve whenever she wished [see 22 D.L.R. (3d) 182, [1972] 1 O.R. 390]. Mrs. Lavell did not claim to have been deprived of any property rights on the reserve except those incidental to her right as a band member.

Judge Grossberg having found that in his opinion s. 12(1)(b) of the Indian Act was not rendered inoperative by the Bill of Rights, an appeal was taken from his judgment to the Federal Court of Appeal where a judgment was rendered by Mr. Justice Thurlow who concluded his opinion by saying of s. 12(1)(b) of the Indian Act [22 D.L.R. (3d) 188 at p.193, [1971] F.C. 347, [1972] 1 O.R. 396n]:

These provisions are thus laws which abrogate, abridge and infringe the right of an individual Indian woman to equality with other Indians before the law. Though this is not a situation in which an act is made punishable at law on account of race or sex, it is one in which under the provisions here in question the consequences of the marriage of an Indian woman to a person who is not an Indian are worse for her than for other Indians who marry non-Indians and than for other Indians of her band who marry persons who are not Indians. *In my opinion this offends the right of such an Indian woman as an individual to equality before the law* and the Canadian Bill of Rights therefore applies to render the provisions in question inoperative.

(The italics are my own.) It is from this judgment that the Crown now appeals.

2. Mrs. Bedard—In this case the respondent sought an injunction restraining the members of the Six Nations Council from expelling her and her two infant children from the home she occupied on the Six Nations Indian Reserve in the County of Brant, and an order setting aside a resolution passed by the Council ordering her to dispose of such property. By agreement an additional claim was added for a declaratory judgment concerning the respective rights of the parties.

Mrs. Bedard was born on the Six Nations Indian reserve of Indian parents and she married a non-Indian in May, 1964, by whom she had two children and with whom she resided off the reserve until June 23, 1970, when, having separated from her husband, she returned to the reserve to live in a house on a property to which her mother had held a certificate of possession under s. 20 of the Indian Act and which had been bequeathed to her under her mother's will which had been approved by the Council of the Six Nations and on behalf of the Minister of Indian Affairs as required by the Indian Act (s. 45(3)), on August 7,1969.

When Mrs. Bedard returned to the reserve with her children in 1970 to occupy her mother's house, the Council passed a series of resolutions giving her permission to reside on the reserve for a period of six months during which she was to dispose of the property, and extending this permission for a further eight months, after which any further requests for her continued residence would be denied. In accordance with these resolutions this respondent conveyed her interest in the property in question to her brother who was a registered member of the Six Nations Band, and to whom a certificate of possession of the property was granted on March 15, 1971, by the Minister. Her brother, however, permitted Mrs. Bedard and her infant children to continue occupying the premises without rent, but the Band Council passed a further resolution on September 15, 1971, by which it was resolved that the Brant District Supervisor should be requested to serve a notice to quit the reserve upon this respondent. It should be noted that the writ instituting this action was issued on September 14, 1971, more than a year after the brother had obtained his certificate of possession and that no notice to quit has been served on Mrs. Bedard pursuant to the resolution which was passed after the writ was issued.

Mrs. Bedard's case was heard by Mr. Justice Osler in the Supreme Court of Ontario where it was contended that the Council's request to the District Supervisor and any action taken by the Supervisor pursuant to such request, and the removal of her name from the band list simply because of her marriage to a non-Indian, are actions that discriminate against her by reason of her race and sex and deny her "equality before the law". Mr. Justice Osler, basing his decision on the judgment of the Federal Court of Appeal in the Lavell case, concluded that [25 D.L.R. (3d) 551 at p. 557, [1972] 2 O.R. 391]:

Section 12(1)(b) of the Act is . . . inoperative and all acts of the Council Band and of the District Supervisor purporting to be based on the provisions of that section can be of no effect.

Leave to appeal from this judgment was granted by order of this Court on January 25, 1972.

The contention which formed the basis of the argument submitted by both respondents was that they had been denied equality before the law by reason of sex, and I propose to deal with the matter on this basis.

In considering the impact of the Bill of Rights on the provisions of the Indian Act, I think it desirable to reproduce the portions of the Bill which I consider to be relevant and which are:

Preamble

The Parliament of Canada, affirming that the Canadian Nation is founded upon principles that acknowledge the supremacy of God, the dignity and worth of the human person *and the position of the family in a society of free men and free institutions;*

Affirming also that *men and institutions remain free only when freedom is founded upon respect for moral and spiritual values and the rule of law;*

And being desirous of enshrining these principles and the human rights and fundamental freedoms derived from them, *in a Bill of Rights which shall reflect the respect of Parliament for its constitutional authority* and which shall ensure the protection of these rights and freedoms in Canada:

Therefore Her Majesty, by and with the advice and consent of the Senate and House of Commons of Canada, enacts as follows:

BILL OF RIGHTS

Recognition and declaration of rights and freedoms

1. It is hereby recognized and declared that in Canada there have existed and shall continue to exist without discrimination by reason of race, national origin, colour, religion or sex, the following human rights and fundamental freedoms, namely,

(a) the right of the individual to life, liberty, security of the person and enjoyment of property, and the right not to be deprived thereof except by due process of law;

(b) the right of the individual to equality before the law and the protection of the law;

(c) freedom of religion;

(d) freedom of speech;

(e) freedom of assembly and association; and

(f) freedom of the press.

Construction of law

2. Every law of Canada shall, unless it is expressly declared by an Act of the Parliament of Canada that it shall operate notwithstanding the Canadian Bill of Rights, be so construed and applied as not to abrogate, abridge or infringe or to authorize the abrogation, abridgment or infringement of any of the rights or freedoms herein recognized and declared, and in particular, no law of Canada shall be construed or applied so as to

(a) authorize or effect the arbitrary detention, imprisonment or exile of any person;

(b) impose or authorize the imposition of cruel and unusual treatment or punishment;

(c) deprive a person who has been arrested or detained

(i) of the right to be informed promptly of the reason for his arrest or detention,

(ii) of the right to retain and instruct counsel without delay, or

(iii) of the remedy by way of habeas corpus for the determination of the validity of his detention and for his release if the detention is not lawful;

(d) authorize a court, tribunal, commission, board or other authority to compel a person to give evidence if he is denied counsel, protection against self crimination or other constitutional safeguards;

(e) deprive a person of the right to a fair hearing in accordance with the principles of fundamental justice for the determination of his rights and obligations;

(f) deprive a person charged with a criminal offence of the right to be presumed innocent until proved guilty according to law in a fair and public hearing by an independent and impartial tribunal, or of the right to reasonable bail without just cause; or

(g) deprive a person of the right to the assistance of an interpreter in any proceedings in which he is involved or in which he is a party or a witness, before a court, commission, board or other tribunal, if he does not understand or speak the language in which such proceedings are conducted.

5(2) The expression "law of Canada" in Part I means an Act of the Parliament of Canada enacted before or after the coming into force of this Act, any order, rule or regulation thereunder, and any law in force in Canada or in any part of Canada at the commencement of this Act that is subject to be repealed, abolished or altered by the Parliament of Canada.

(3) The provisions of Part I shall be construed as extending only to matters coming within the legislative authority of the Parliament of Canada.

(The italics are my own.)

There cannot, in my view, be any doubt that whatever may have been achieved by the Bill of Rights, it is not effective to amend or in any way alter the terms of the British North America Act, 1867 and it is clear from the third recital in the preamble that the Bill was intended to "reflect the respect of Parliament for its constitutional authority . . ." so that wherever any question arises as to the effect of any of the provisions of the Bill, it is to be resolved within the framework of the British North America Act, 1867.

It follows, in my view, that the effect of the Bill of Rights on the Indian Act can only be considered in light of the provisions of s. 91(24) of the British North America Act, 1867 whereby the subject of "Indians, and Lands reserved for Indians" is assigned exclusively to the legislative authority of the Parliament of Canada.

It is true that under s. 88 of the Indian Act laws of general application in any Province are made applicable to and in respect of Indians in the Province *except to the extent that such laws make provision for any matter for which provision is made by or under the Indian Act.* But the incorporation of these laws as a part of the Act in no way signifies a relinquishment of Parliament's exclusive legislative authority over Indians, and in any event, the property and civil rights of members of Indian bands living on reserves, which is what we are here concerned with, are matters for which express provision is made by the Indian Act and which can only apply to Indians as distinct from other Canadians.

In my opinion the exclusive legislative authority vested in Parliament under s. 91(24) could not have been effectively exercised without enacting laws establishing the qualifications required to entitle persons to status as Indians and to the use and benefit of Crown "lands reserved for Indians". The legislation enacted to this end was, in my view, necessary for the implementation of the authority so vested in Parliament under the Constitution.

To suggest that the provisions of the Bill of Rights have the effect of making the whole Indian Act inoperative as discriminatory is to assert that the Bill has rendered Parliament powerless to exercise the authority entrusted to it under the Constitution of enacting legislation which treats Indians living on reserves differently from other Canadians in relation to their property and civil rights. The proposition that such a wide effect is to be given to the Bill of Rights was expressly reserved by the majority of this Court in the case of R. v. Drybones (1969), 9 D.L.R. (3d) 473 at pp. 485-6, [1970] 3 C.C.C. 355, [1970] S.C.R. 282, to which reference will hereafter be made, and I do not think that it can be sustained.

What is at issue here is whether the Bill of Rights is to be construed as rendering inoperative one of the conditions imposed by Parliament for the use and occupation of Crown lands reserved for Indians. These conditions were imposed as a necessary part of the structure created by Parliament for the internal administration of the life of Indians on reserves and their entitlement to the use and benefit of Crown lands situate thereon, they were thus imposed in discharge of Parliament's constitutional function under s. 91(24) and in my view can only be changed by plain statutory language expressly enacted for the purpose. It does not appear to me that Parliament can be taken to have made or intended to make such a change by the use of broad general language directed at the statutory proclamation of the fundamental rights and freedoms enjoyed by all Canadians, and I am therefore of opinion that the Bill of Rights had no such effect.

The responsibility of the Parliament of Canada in relation to the [internal] administration of the life of Indians on reserves is succinctly stated by Rand, J., in St. Ann's Island Shooting & Fishing Club Ltd. v. The King, [1950] 2 D.L.R. 225 at p. 232, [1950] S.C.R. 211, where he was dealing with the effect of s. 51 of the Indian Act, R.S.C. 1906, c. 81, in relation to the "surrender" of lands on Indian reserves and said:

> The language of the statute embodies the accepted view that these aborigines are, in effect, wards of the state, whose care and welfare are a political trust of the highest obligation. . . .

. . . The contention that the Bill of Rights is to be construed as overriding all of the special legislation imposed by Parliament under the Indian Act is, in my view, fully answered by Pigeon, J., in his dissenting opinion in the Drybones case where he said, at pp. 489-90:

> If one of the effects of the Canadian Bill of Rights is to render inoperative all legal provisions whereby Indians as such are not dealt with in the same way as the general public, the conclusion is inescapable that Parliament, by the enactment of the Bill, has not only fundamentally altered the status of the Indians in that indirect fashion but has also made any future use of federal legislative authority over them subject to the requirement of expressly declaring every time "that the law shall operate notwithstanding the Canadian Bill of Rights". I find it very difficult to believe that Parliament so intended when enacting the Bill. If a virtual suppression of federal legislation over Indians as such was meant, one would have expected this important change to be made explicitly, not surreptitiously, so to speak.

That it is membership in the band which entitles an Indian to the use and benefit of lands on the reserve is made plain by the provisions of ss. 2 and 18 of the Indian Act. Section 2(1) (a) reads as follows:

> 2(1) In this Act
> "band" means a body of Indians
> (a) for whose use and benefit in common, lands, the legal title to which is vested in Her Majesty, have been set apart before, on or after the 4th day of September 1951,

Section 18 reads as follows:

> 18(1) Subject to this Act, reserves are held by Her Majesty for the use and benefit of the respective bands for which they were set apart; and subject to this Act and to the terms of any treaty or surrender, the Governor in Council may determine whether any purpose for which lands in a reserve are used or are to be used is for the use and benefit of the band.

In considering the meaning to be given to s. 1(b) of the Bill of Rights, regard must of course be had to what was said by Mr. Justice Laskin, speaking in this regard for the whole of the Court in Curr v. The Queen (1972), 26 D.L.R. (3d) 603 at p. 611, 7 C.C.C. (2d) 181, [1972] S.C.R. 889, where he interpreted s. 1(a) and (b) of the Bill in the following passage:

> In considering the reach of s. 1(a) and s. 1(b), and, indeed, of s. 1 as a whole, I would observe, first, that the section is given its controlling force over federal law by its referential incorporation into s. 2; and, secondly, that I do not read it as making the existence of any of the forms of prohibited discrimination a sine qua non of its operation. Rather, the prohibited discrimination is an additional lever to which federal legislation must respond. Putting the matter another way, federal legislation which does not offend s. 1 in respect of any of the prohibited kinds of discrimination may none the less be offensive to s. 1 if it is violative of what is specified in any of the paras. (a) to (f) of s. 1. It is, a fortiori, offensive if there is discrimination by reason of race so as to deny equality before the law. That is what this Court decided in R. v. Drybones and I need say no more on this point.
> It is, therefore, not an answer to reliance by the appellant on s.1(a) and

s.1(b) of the Canadian Bill of Rights that s. 223 does not discriminate against any person by reason of race, national origin, colour, religion or sex. The absence of such discrimination still leaves open the question whether s. 223 can be construed and applied without abrogating, abridging or infringing the rights of the individual listed in s. 1(a) and s. 1(b).

My understanding of this passage is that the effect of s. 1 of the Bill of Rights is to guarantee to all Canadians the rights specified in paras. (a) to (f) of that section, irrespective of race, national origin, colour or sex. This interpretation appears to me to be borne out by the French version which reads:

> 1. Il est par les présentes reconnu et déclaré que les droits de l'homme et les libertés fondamentales ci-après énoncés ont existé et continueront à exister pour tout individu au Canada quels que soient sa race, son origine nationale, sa couleur, sa religion ou son sexe:

It was stressed on behalf of the respondents that the provisions of s. 12(1)(b) of the Indian Act constituted "discrimination by reason of sex" and that the section could be declared inoperative on this ground alone even if such discrimination did not result in the infringement of any of the rights and freedoms specifically guaranteed by s. 1 of the Bill.

I can find no support for such a contention in the Curr case in which, in any event, no question of any kind of discrimination was either directly or indirectly involved. My own understanding of the passage which I have quoted from that case was that it recognized the fact that the primary concern evidenced by the first two sections of the Bill of Rights is to ensure that the rights and freedoms thereby recognized and declared shall continue to exist for all Canadians, and it follows, in my view, that those sections cannot be invoked unless one of the enumerated rights and freedoms has been denied to an individual Canadian or group of Canadians. Section 2 of the Bill of Rights provides for the manner in which the rights and freedoms which are recognized and declared by s. 1 are to be enforced and the effect of this section is that every law of Canada shall "be so construed and applied as not to abrogate, abridge or infringe or authorize the abrogation, abridgment or infringement of any of the rights and freedoms herein recognized and declared . . ." (i.e., by s. 1). There is no language anywhere in the Bill of Rights stipulating that the laws of Canada are to be construed without discrimination unless the discrimination involves the denial of one of the guaranteed rights and freedoms, but when, as in the case of R. v. Drybones, denial of one of the enumerated rights is occasioned by reason of discrimination, then, as Mr. Justice Laskin has said, the discrimination affords an "additional lever to which federal legislation must respond".

The opening words of s. 2 of the Bill of Rights are, in my view, determinative of the test to be applied in deciding whether the section here impugned is to be declared inoperative. The words to which I refer are:

> 2. Every law of Canada shall, unless it is expressly declared by an Act of Parliament of Canada that it shall operate notwithstanding the Canadian Bill of Rights, be so construed and applied as not to abrogate, abridge or infringe or authorized the abrogation, abridgement or infringement of any of the rights or freedoms herein recognized and declared . . .

In the course of the reasons for judgement rendered on behalf of the majority of this Court in R. v. Drybones, supra, this language was interpreted in the following passage at p. 482:

> It seems to me that a more realistic meaning must be given to the words in question and they afford, in my view, the clearest indication that s. 2 is intended to mean and does mean that if a law of Canada cannot be "sensibly construed and applied" so that it does not abrogate, abridge or infringe one of the rights and freedoms recognized and declared by the Bill, then such law is inoperative "unless it is expressly declared by an Act of the Parliament of Canada that it shall operate notwithstanding the Canadian Bill of Rights".

Accordingly, in my opinion, the question to be determined in these appeals is confined to deciding whether the Parliament of Canada in defining the prerequisites of Indian status so as not to include women of Indian birth who have chosen to marry non-Indians, enacted a law which cannot be sensibly construed and applied without abrogating, abridging or infringing the rights of such women to equality before the law.

In my view the meaning to be given to the language employed in the Bill of Rights is the meaning which it bore in Canada at the time when the Bill was enacted, and it follows that the phrase "equality before the law" is to be construed in light of the law existing in Canada at that time.

In considering the meaning to be attached to "equality before the law" as those words occur in s. 1(b) of the Bill, I think it important to point out that in my opinion this phrase is not effective to invoke the egalitarian concept exemplified by the 14th Amendment of the U.S. Constitution as interpreted by the Courts of that country: see R. v. Smythe (1971), 19 D.L.R. (3d) 480, 3 C.C.C. (2d) 366, [1971] S.C.R. 680, per Fauteux, C.J.C., at pp. 482 and 484 -5. I think rather that, having regard to the language employed in the second paragraph of the preamble to the Bill of Rights, the phrase "equality before the law" as used in s. 1 is to be read in its context as a part of "the rule of law" to which overriding authority is accorded by the terms of that paragraph.

In this connection I refer to *Stephen's Commentaries on the Laws of England*, 21st ed., vol. III (1950), where it is said at p. 337:

> Now the great constitutional lawyer Dicey, writing in 1885 was so deeply impressed by the absence of arbitrary . . . governments present and past, that he coined the phrase "the rule of law" to express the regime under which Englishmen lived; and he tried to give precision to it in the following words which have exercised a profound influence on all subsequent thought and conduct.
>
> "That the rule of law, which forms a fundamental principle of the constitution has three meanings, or may be regarded from three different points of view."

The second meaning proposed by Dicey is the one with which we are here concerned and it was stated in the following terms:

> It means again equality before the law or the equal subjection of all classes

to the ordinary law of the land administered by the ordinary courts; the "rule of law" in this sense excludes the idea of any exemption of officials or others from the duty of obedience to the law which governs other citizens or from the jurisdiction of the ordinary courts.

"Equality before the law" in this sense is frequently invoked to demonstrate that the same law applies to the highest official of Government as to any other ordinary citizen, and in this regard Professor F. R. Scott, in delivering the Plaunt Memorial Lectures on Civil Liberties and Canadian Federalism (1959), speaking of the case of Roncarelli v. Duplessis (1959), 16 D.L.R. (2d) 689, [1959] S.C.R. 121, had occasion to say:

> . . . it is always a triumph for the law to show that it is applied equally to all without fear or favour. This is what we mean when we say that all are equal before the law.

The relevance of these quotations to the present circumstances is that "equality before the law" as recognized by Dicey as a segment of the rule of law, carries the meaning of equal subjection of all classes to the ordinary law of the land as administered by the ordinary Courts, and in my opinion the phrase "equality before the law" as employed in s. 1(b) of the Bill of Rights is to be treated as meaning equality in the administration or application of the law by the law enforcement authorities and the ordinary Courts of the land. This construction is, in my view, supported by the provisions of paras. (a) to (g) of s. 2 of the Bill which clearly indicate to me that it was equality in the administration and enforcement of the law with which Parliament was concerned when it guaranteed the continued existence of "equality before the law".

Turning to the Indian Act itself, it should first be observed that by far the greater part of that Act is concerned with the internal regulation of the lives of Indians on reserves and that the exceptional provisions dealing with the conduct of Indians off reserves and their contracts with other Canadian citizens fall into an entirely different category.

It was, of course necessary for Parliament, in the exercise of s. 91 (24) authority, to first define what Indian meant, and in this regard s.2(1) of the Act provides that:

> "Indian" means a person who pursuant to this Act is registered as an Indian or is entitled to be registered as an Indian;

It is therefore clear that registration is a necessary prerequisite to Indian status and in order to fully appreciate the nature of the issue raised by the respondents, I think it desirable to consider s. 12(1) (b) in the context of ss. 11 and 12 of the Act which provide:

> 11(1) Subject to section 12, a person is entitled to be registered if that person
>
> > (a) on the 26th day of May 1874 was, for the purposes of An Act providing for the organization of the Department of the Secretary of State of Canada, and for the management of Indian and Ordinance Lands, being chapter 42 of the Statues of Canada, 1868, as amended by section 6 of chapter 6 of the Statues of Canada, 1869, and section

8 of chapter 21 of the Statutes of Canada, 1874, considered to be entitled to hold, use or enjoy the lands and other immovable property belonging to or appropriated to the use of the various tribes, bands or bodies of Indians in Canada;
(b) is a member of a band
    (i) for whose use and benefit, in common, lands have been set apart or since the 26th day of May 1874, have been agreed by treaty to be set apart, or
    (ii) that has been declared by the Governor in Council to be a band for the purposes of this Act;
(c) is a male person who is a direct descendent in the male line of a male person described in paragraph (a) or (b);
(d) is the legitimate child of
    (i) a male person described in paragraph (a) or (b), or
    (ii) a person described in paragraph (c);
(e) is the illegitimate child of a female person described in paragraph (a), (b) or (d); or
(f) is the wife or widow of a person who is entitled to be registered by virtue of paragraph (a), (b), (c), (d) or (e).

(2) Paragraph (1)(e) applies only to persons born after the 13th day of August 1956.
12(1) The following persons are not entitled to be registered, namely,
  (a) a person who
    (i) has received or has been allotted half-breed lands or money scrip,
    (ii) is a descendant of a person described in subparagraph (i),
    (iii) is enfranchised, or
    (iv) is a person born of a marriage entered into after the 4th day of September 1951 and has attained the age of twenty-one years, whose mother and whose father's mother are not persons described in paragraph 11(1) (a), (b) or (d) or entitled to be registered by virtue of paragraph 11 (1)(e),
unless, being a woman, that person is the wife or widow of a person described in section 11, and
(b) a woman who married a person who is not an Indian, unless that woman is subsequently the wife or widow of a person described in section 11.

Provision for the loss of status by women who marry non-Indians was first introduced in 1869 by s. 6 of c. 6 of the Statutes of Canada of that year [amending s. 15, 1868 (Can.), c. 4] which reads as follows:

Provided always that any Indian woman marrying any other than an Indian, shall cease to be an Indian within the meaning of this Act, nor shall the children issue of such marriage be considered as Indians within the meaning of this Act; Provided also, that any Indian woman marrying an Indian of another tribe, band or body shall cease to be a member of the tribe, band or body to which she formerly belonged, and become a member of the tribe, band or body of which her husband is a member, and the children, issue of this marriage, shall belong to their father's tribe only.

It is thus apparent that the marital status of Indian women who marry non-Indians has been the same for at least one hundred years and that their loss of band status on marriage to a member of another band and acquisition of status in that band, for which provision is made under s. 14 of the Indian Act, has been in effect for the same period.

The first 41 sections of the Indian Act are concerned with the status of Indians and the administration of Indian reserves, including the detailed provisions to which I have referred with respect to the status of those entitled to the use and benefit of the lands of which they are composed.

The Act then proceeds to the enactment of laws governing the use and disposition of all property of Indians whether real or personal (see ss. 12 to 86), and s. 87 deals with conditions under which property of Indians on reserves is exempt from taxation.

Relations between Indians and non-Indians are first considered under the following headings: "Legal Rights of Indians" (ss. 88 to 90); "Trading with Indians" (ss. 91 to 92); "Removal of materials from reserves" (s. 93); "Sale of intoxicants to and possession thereof by Indians" (ss. 94 to 97); and forfeitures and penalties for breach of these sections are dealt with in ss. 103 and 104. The remainder of the statute is concerned almost exclusively with the topic of enfranchisement, ss. 109 to 113, and schools, ss. 114 to 123.

A careful reading of the Act discloses that s. 95 (formerly s. 94, R.S.C. 1952, c. 149) is the only provision therein made which creates an offence for any behaviour of an Indian off a reserve and it will be plain that there is a wide difference between legislation such as s. 12(1)(b) governing the civil rights of designated persons living on Indian reserves to the use and benefits of Crown lands, and criminal legislation such as s.95 which creates an offence punishable at law for Indians to act in a certain fashion when off a reserve. The former legislation is enacted as a part of the plan devised by Parliament, under s. 91(24) for the regulation of the internal domestic life of Indians on reserves. The latter is criminal legislation exclusively concerned with behaviour of Indians off a reserve.

Section 95 (formerly s. 94) reads, in part, as follows:

95. An Indian who
   (b) is intoxicated . . .
off a reserve, is guilty of an offence and is liable on summary conviction to a fine of not less than ten dollars and not more than fifty dollars or to imprisonment for a term not exceeding three months or to both fine and imprisonment.

These were the provisions that were at issue in the case of R. v. Drybones (1969), 9 D.L.R. (3d) 473, [1970] 3 C.C.C. 355, [1970] S.C.R. 282, where this Court held that they could not be construed and applied without exposing Indians as a racial group to a penalty in respect of conduct as to which the Parliament of Canada had imposed no sanctions on other Canadians who were subject to

Canadian laws regulating their conduct, which were of general application in the Northwest Territories where the offence was allegedly committed and in which there are no Indian reserves.

In that case the decision of the majority of this Court was that the provisions of s. 94(b), as it then was, could not be enforced without bringing about inequality between one group of citizens and another and that this inequality was occasioned by reason of the race of the accused. It was there said, at pp. 484-5:

> ... I am ... of opinion that an individual is denied equality before the law if it is made an offence punishable at law, on account of his race, for him to do something which his fellow Canadians are free to do without having committed any offence or having been made subject to any penalty.

> It is only necessary for the purpose of deciding this case for me to say that in my opinion s. 94(b) of the Indian Act is a law of Canada which creates such an offence and that it can only be construed in such manner that its application would operate so as to abrogate, abridge or infringe one of the rights declared and recognized by the Bill of Rights. For the reasons which I have indicated, I am therefore of opinion that s. 94(b) is inoperative.

> For the purpose of determining the issue raised by this appeal it is unnecessary to express any opinion respecting the operation of any other section of the Indian Act.

And it was later said, at pp. 485-6:

> The present case discloses laws of Canada which abrogate, abridge and infringe the right of an individual Indian to equality before the law and in my opinion if those laws are to be applied in accordance with the express language used by Parliament in s. 2 of the Bill of Rights, then s. 94(b) of the Indian Act must be declared to be inoperative.

> It appears to me to be desirable to make it plain that these reasons for judgment are limited to a situation in which, under the laws of Canada, it is made an offence punishable at law on account of race, for a person to do something which all Canadians who are not members of that race may do with impunity; in my opinion the same considerations do not by any means apply to all the provisions of the Indian Act.

Having regard to the express reservations contained in these passages, I have difficulty in understanding how that case can be construed as having decided that any sections of the Indian Act, except s. 94(b) are rendered inoperative by the Bill of Rights.

The Drybones case can, in my opinion, have no application to the present appeals as it was in no way concerned with the internal regulation of the lives of Indians on reserves or their right to the use and benefit of Crown lands thereon, but rather deals exclusively with the effect of the Bill of Rights on a section of the Indian Act creating a crime with attendant penalties for the conduct by Indians off a reserve in an area where non-Indians, who were also governed by federal law, were not subject to any such restriction.

The fundamental distinction between the present case and that of Drybones, however, appears to me to be that the impugned section in the latter case could not be enforced without denying equality of treatment in the administration and enforcement of the law before the ordinary Courts of the land to a racial group, whereas no such inequality of treatment between Indian men and women flows as a necessary result of the application of s. 12(1)(b) of the Indian Act.

To summarize the above, I am of opinion:

1. that the Bill of Rights is not effective to render inoperative legislation, such as s. 12(1)(b) of the Indian Act, passed by the Parliament of Canada in discharge of its constitutional function under s. 91(24) of the British North America Act, 1867, to specify how and by whom Crown lands reserved for Indians are to be used;
2. that the Bill of Rights does not require federal legislation to be declared inoperative unless it offends against one of the rights specifically guaranteed by s. 1, but where legislation is found to be discriminatory, this affords an added reason for rendering it ineffective;
3. that equality before the law under the Bill of Rights means equality of treatment in the enforcement and application of the laws of Canada before the law enforcement authorities and the ordinary Courts of the land, and no such inequality is necessarily entailed in the construction and application of s. 12(1)(b).

I would allow the appeal of the Attorney-General of Canada v. Lavell, reverse the judgment of the Federal Court of Appeal and restore the decision of Judge B. W. Grossberg. In accordance with the terms of the order of the Federal Court of Appeal granting leave to appeal to this Court, the appellant will pay to the respondent her solicitor-and-client costs of the appeal and the application for leave. There should be no further order as to costs.

On the appeal of Isaac et al. v. Bedard, a question was raised in this Court as to the jurisdiction of the trial Court. In view of the conclusion reached on the merits, no decision is now necessary on that question. The appeal to this Court should be allowed, the judgment at trial should be reversed and the action dismissed. Under the circumstances, there should be no order as to costs in that case in any Court.

* * *

HALL and SPENCE, JJ., concur with LASKIN, J.

* * *

PIGEON, J.: I agree in the result with Ritchie, J. I certainly cannot disagree with the view I did express in R. v. Drybones (1969), 9 D.L.R. (3d) 473 at pp. 489-90, [1970] 3 C.C.C. 355, [1970] S.C.R. 282, that the enactment of the Canadian Bill of Rights was not intended to effect a virtual suppression of federal legislation over Indians. My difficulty is Laskin, J.'s strongly reasoned opinion that, unless we are to depart from what was said by the majority in Drybones, these appeals should be dismissed because, if discrimination by reason of race makes certain statutory provisions inoperative, the same result must follow as to statutory provisions which exhibit discrimination by reason of sex. In the end, it appears to me that, in the circumstances, I need not reach a firm conclusion on that point. Assuming the situation is such as Laskin, J., says, it cannot be improper for me

inequality before the law when the respondent was in no different position than other fellow Canadians who were married females. This decision was reversed by the Federal Court of Appeal which held that because the Indian Act prescribed a different result in the case of an Indian woman who married a non-Indian man from that which followed when an Indian man married a non-Indian woman, there was discrimination by reason of sex in violation of the Canadian Bill of Rights; and, further, that this discrimination infringed the respondent's right to equality with other Indians before the law.

In Isaac et al. v. Bedard, Osler, J., of the Ontario Supreme Court also held that s. 12(1)(b) of the Indian Act was inoperative, agreeing with the decision of the Federal Court of appeal in the Lavell case which he considered to be in accordance with the Drybones case [see 25 D.L.R. (3d) 551, [1972] 2 O.R. 391]. In the Bedard case, as in the Lavell case, the respondent, born a full-blooded Indian, had married a non-Indian man in 1964 but she separated from him in 1970 and returned with the two children of the marriage to the Six Nations Reserve where she had been born and took possession of a house which had been left to her under her mother's will, the terms of which had been approved, as required by the Indian Act, by the Council of the Six Nations and by an official on behalf of the Minister of Indian Affairs. The defendants, members of the Council, passed a number of resolutions purporting to give the respondent permission for successive limited periods to reside on the reserve, but she was to dispose of the property during that time. On September 7, 1971, after having previously informed the respondent that there would be no further permission, the Council passed a resolution requesting the District Supervisor to serve a notice to quit on the respondent. Thereupon the respondent sued to enjoin her expulsion and also sought declaratory relief. The application for an injunction was later withdrawn and counsel agreed that a declaration only would be sought as against the members of the Band Council, the appellants in this Court. The respondent's name was removed from the membership list of her band after she brought action but before delivery of her statement of claim.

Osler, J., determined [at pp. 556-7] that "there is plainly discrimination by reason of sex with respect to the rights of an individual to the enjoyment of property"; and further that "the loss of status as an Indian and the loss of the right to be registered and to occupy property upon a reserve is discrimination which is adverse to the interest of Indian women" and is in contravention of the Canadian Bill of Rights. He declared that all acts of the Council of the Band and of the District Supervisor purportedly based on s. 12(1)(b) were without effect.

In both cases, which were argued together, leave was given to various bodies and organizations and to a number of individuals to intervene by representation and by submissions to this Court. The position of the Attorney-General of Canada in the Lavell case was supported by counsel appearing on behalf of the Indian Association of Alberta, the Union of British Columbia Indian Chiefs, the Manitoba Indian Brotherhood Inc., the Union of New Brunswick Indians, the Indian Brotherhood of the Northwest Territories, the Union of Nova Scotia Indians, the Union of Ontario Indians, the Federation of Saskatchewan Indians, the Indian Association of Quebec, the Yukon Native Brotherhood and the National Indian Brotherhood, by counsel appearing on behalf of the Six Nations Band and by counsel appearing on behalf of the Treaty Voice of Alberta Association. The position of the respondent was supported by counsel appearing for the Native Council of Canada, by counsel appearing for Rose Wilhelm, Alberta Committee on Indian Rights for Indian Women Inc., Viola Shannacappo, University Women's Club of Toronto and University Women Graduates Limited, the North Toronto Business and Professional Women's Club Inc. and Monica Agnes Turner, and by counsel for Anishnarvbekwek of Ontario Incorporated. There was the same division of support for the appellants and the respondent in the Bedard case, in which the Attorney-General of Canada also intervened to support the position of the appellants.

An issue of jurisdiction was raised in the Bedard case with which it will be convenient to deal at this point. That issue is whether it was open to Osler, J., as a member of a provincial superior Court, to entertain an action for declaratory relief in this case, or whether exclusive jurisdiction resided in the Federal Court by virtue of s. 18 of the Federal Court Act. Osler, J., was of the opinion that his jurisdiction as a Superior Court Judge was not clearly taken away by s. 18 of the Federal Court Act, and he doubted also whether the Band Council was a "federal board, commission or other tribunal" within s. 2(g) of that Act.

I share the doubt of Osler, J., whether a Band Council, even an elected one under s. 74 of the Indian Act (the Act also envisages that a Band Council may exist by custom of the band), is the type of tribunal contemplated by the definition in s. 2(g) of the Federal Court Act which embraces "any body or any person or persons having, exercising or purporting to exercise jurisdiction or powers conferred by or under an Act of the Parliament of Canada". A Band Council has some resemblance to the board of directors of a corporation, and if the words of s. 2(g) are taken literally, they are broad enough to embrace boards of directors in respect of powers given to them under such federal statutes as the Bank Act, R.S.C. 1970, c. B-1, as amended, the Canada Corporations Act, R.S.C. 1970, c. C-32, as amended, and the Canadian and British Insurance Companies Act, R.S.C. 1970, c. I-15, as amended. It is to me an open question whether private authorities (if I may so categorize boards of directors of banks and other companies) are contemplated by the Federal Court Act under s. 18 thereof. However, I do not find it necessary to come to a definite conclusion here on whether jurisdiction should have been ceded to the Federal Court to entertain the declaratory action brought by Mrs. Bedard against the members of the Band Council. There is another ground upon which, in this case, I would not interfere with the exercise of jurisdiction by Osler, J.

Although the Indian Act by s. 81, confers authority upon the Council of a band to make by-laws for specified purposes, and it may also be given authority under s. 83 to make by-laws for additional specified purposes, there is nothing in the record here that indicates that the members of the Band Council proceeded under any by-law. The by-law powers include in para. (p) of s. 81 the removal and punishment of persons trespassing upon the reserve, but in the cross-examination of the appellant Isaac on his affidavit he stated that the Band Council did not purport to remove Mrs. Bedard from the reserve. Nor was any charge laid against her by any member of the Band Council under s. 30 of the Indian Act which makes it an offence to trespass on a reserve. The Band Council was content to request the District Supervisor to give her a notice to quit and to leave any legal proceedings to the administrative authorities under the Indian Act. Such proceedings might have consisted of a charge of trespass or might also have been taken under s. 31 of the Indian Act which empowers the Attorney-General to exhibit an information in respect of any alleged trespass upon a reserve.

What the Band Council did do was to assume to exercise permit power in respect of Mrs. Bedard's residence on the reserve. I use the word "assume" because in his affidavit the [appellant] Isaac stated that the Band Council "has at all times assumed jurisdiction to grant, refuse and revoke permission for persons who are not members of the Six Nations Band to reside upon or occupy property upon the Six Nations Reserve". The record does not disclose any statutory basis for this assumption of authority which was exercised against Mrs. Bedard by the various resolutions already referred to. Section 25 of the Indian Act, relating to the re-quired disposition of land by an Indian who ceases to be entitled to reside thereon on a reserve, itself specifies the period within which the disposition must be made and confers upon the responsible Minister and not upon the Band Council the power to extend the period.

I am not satisfied that the Band Council was purporting to exercise powers conferred by the Indian Act rather than powers which it felt it had apart from the Act. It was open to the appellants to establish their authority if it was drawn from the Act, but they did not do so. This leaves the question whether in such circum-stances the respondent should have been allowed to proceed by way of a decla-ration in the light of the fact that the Band Council's resolutions were in themselves, on the record in the case, of no legal force. They did threaten Mrs. Bedard and could have been followed up by invocation of s. 31 or by the laying of a charge under s. 30. In these circumstances, I am disposed to support the broad view taken by Osler, J., in exercising his discretion to entertain Mrs. Bedard's claim for declaratory relief so that her rights could be ascertained: see Vine v. National Dock Labour Board, [1957] A.C. 488.

The contentions of the appellants in both cases in appeal, stripped of their detail, amount to a submission that the Canadian Bill of Rights does not apply to Indians on a reserve, nor to Indians in their relations to one another whether or not on a reserve. This submission does not deny that the effect of s. 12(1)(b) of the Indian Act is to prescribe substantive discrimination by reason of sex, a differentiation in the treatment of Indian men and Indian women when they marry nonIndians, this differentiation being exhibited in the loss by the women of their status as Indians under the Act. It does, however, involve the assertion that the particular discrimination upon which the two appeals are focused is not offensive to the relevant provisions of the Canadian Bill of Rights; and it also involves the assertion that the Drybones case is distinguishable or, if not, that it has been overcome by the re-enactment of the Indian Act in the Revised Statutes of Canada, 1970, including the then s. 94 (now s. 95) which was in issue in that case. I regard this last-mentioned assertion, which is posited on the fact that the Canadian Bill of Rights was not so re-enacted, as simply an oblique appeal for the overruling of the Drybones case.

The Drybones case decided two things. It decided first—and this decision was a necessary basis for the second point in it—that the Canadian Bill of Rights was more than a mere interpretation statute whose terms would yield to a contrary intention; it had paramount force when a federal enactment conflicted with its terms, and it was the incompatible federal enactment which had to give way. This was the issue upon which the then Chief Justice of this Court, Chief Justice Cartwright, and Justices Abbott and Pigeon, dissented. Pigeon, J., fortified his view on this main point by additional observations, bringing into consideration, inter alia, s. 91(24) of the British North America Act, 1867. The second thing decided by Drybones was that the accused in that case, an Indian under the Indian Act, was denied equality before the law, under s. 1(b) of the Canadian Bill of Rights, when it was made a punishable offence for him, on account of his race, to do something which his fellow Canadians were free to do without being liable to punishment for an offence. Ritchie, J., who delivered the majority opinion of the Court, reiterated this basis of decision by concluding his reasons as follows [at pp. 485-6]:

> It appears to me to be desirable to make it plain that these reasons for judgment are limited to a situation in which, under the laws of Canada, it is made an offence punishable at law on account of race, for a person to do something which all Canadians who are not members of that race may do with impunity . . .

It would be unsupportable in principle to view the Drybones case as turning on the fact that the challenged s. 94 of the Indian Act created an offence visited by punishment. The gist of the judgment lay in the legal disability imposed upon a person by reason of his race when other persons were under no similar restraint. If for the words "on account of race" there are substituted the words "on account of sex" the result must surely be the same where a federal enactment imposes disabilities or prescribed disqualifications for members of the female sex which are not imposed upon members of the male sex in the same circumstances.

It is said, however, that although this may be so as between males and females in general, it does not follow where the distinction on the basis of sex is limited as here to members of the Indian race. This, it is said further, does not offend the guarantee of "equality before the law" upon which the Drybones case proceeded. I wish to deal with these two points in turn and to review, in connection with the first point, the legal consequences for an Indian woman under the Indian Act when she marries a non-Indian.

It appears to me that the contention that a differentiation on the basis of sex is not offensive to the Canadian Bill of Rights where that differentiation operates only among Indians under the Indian Act is one that compounds racial inequality even beyond the point that the Drybones case found unacceptable. In any event, taking the Indian Act as it stands, as a law of Canada whose various provisions fall to be assessed under the Canadian Bill of Rights, I am unable to appreciate upon what basis the command of the Canadian Bill of Rights, that laws of Canada shall operate without discrimination by reason of sex, can be ignored in the operation of the Indian Act.

The Indian Act defines an Indian as a person who is registered as an Indian pursuant to the Act or is entitled to be so registered. It is registration or registrability upon a band list or upon a general list that is the key to the scheme and application of the Act. The Registrar, charged with keeping the membership records, is the person to whom protests may be made by a Band Council or by an affected person respecting the inclusion or deletion of a name from the Indian Register. By s. 9(2) his decision on a protest is final subject to a reference to a

Judge under s. 9(3). The Lavell case arose in this way. Section 11 of the Act enumerates the persons entitled to be registered, and it is common ground that both Mrs. Lavell and Mrs. Bedard were so entitled prior to their respective marriages. Section 12 lists the classes of persons not entitled to be registered, and the only clause thereof relevant here is s-s. (1)(b) which I have already quoted. Section 14 has a peripheral relevance to the present case in its provision that a woman member of a band who marries a person outside that band ceases to be a member thereof but becomes a member of the band of which her husband is a member. There is no absolute disqualification of an Indian woman from registrability on the Indian Register (that is, as a member on the general list) by marrying outside a band unless the marriage is to a non-Indian.

Registration or registrability entitles an Indian as a member of a band (and that was the status of both Mrs. Lavell and Mrs. Bedard prior to their respective marriages) to the use and benefit of the reserve set aside for the band. This may take the form of possession or occupation of particular land in the reserve under an allotment by the Council of the Band with the approval of the responsible Minister, and it may be evidenced by a certificate of possession or a certificate of occupation, the latter representing possession for a limited period only. Indians may make wills disposing of their property, and it may also pass on intestacy, in either case subject to approval or control of the Minister or of a competent Court; and in the case of a devise or descent of land in a reserve the claimant's possession must be approved by the Minister under s. 49. Section 50 has only a remote bearing on the Bedard case in providing that a person who is not entitled to reside on a reserve does not by devise or descent acquire a right to possession or occupation of land in that reserve. It begs the question in that the issue here is whether or not Mrs. Bedard became disentitled to reside on the land in the reserve which was left to her by her mother upon the latter's death in 1969. The fact that the respondent's brother now holds a certificate of possession of all the land formerly possessed by the mother, that certificate having been issued after the respondent transferred her interest to her brother in February, 1971, does not affect the overriding question of the respondent's right to reside on the land, having her brother's consent to residence thereon.

Indians entitled to be registered and to live on a reserve are members of a society in which, through Band Councils, they share in the administration of the reserve subject to overriding governmental authority. There is provision for election of councillors by band members residing on a reserve, and I note that there is no statutory discrimination between Indian men and women either as qualified electors or as qualified candidates for election as councillors. Other advantages that come from membership in the social unit relate to farm operations and to eligibility for governmental loans for various enumerated purposes.

Section 12(1)(b) effects a statutory excommunication of Indian women from this society but not of Indian men. Indeed, as was pointed out by counsel for the Native Council of Canada, the effect of ss. 11 and 12(1)(b) is to excommunicate the children of a union of an Indian woman with a non-Indian. There is also the invidious distinction, invidious at least in the light of the Canadian Bill of Rights, that the Indian Act creates between brothers and sisters who are Indians and who respectively marry non-Indians. The statutory banishment directed by s. 12(1)(b) is not qualified by the provision in s. 109(2) for a governmental order declaring an Indian woman who has married a non-Indian to be enfranchised. Such an order is not automatic and no such order was made in relation to Mrs. Bedard; but when made the woman affected is, by s. 110, deemed not to be an Indian within the Indian Act or any other statute of law. It is, if anything, an additional legal instrument of separation of an Indian woman from her native society and from kin, a separation to which no Indian man who marries a non-Indian is exposed.

It was urged, in reliance in part on history, that the discrimination embodied in the Indian Act under s. 12(1)(b) is based upon a reasonable classification of Indians as a race, that the Indian Act reflects this classification and that the paramount purpose of the Act to preserve and protect the members of the race is promoted by the statutory preference for Indian men. Reference was made in this connection to various judgments of the Supreme Court of the United States to illustrate the adoption by the Court of reasonable classifications to square with the due process clause of the Fifth Amendment and with due process and equal protection under the Fourteenth Amendment. Those cases have at best a marginal relevance because the Canadian Bill of Rights itself enumerates prohibited classifications which the judiciary is bound to respect; and, moreover, I doubt whether discrimination on account of sex, where as here it has no biological or physiological rationale, could be sustained as a reasonable classification even if the direction against it was not as explicit as it is in the Canadian Bill of Rights.

I do not think it is possible to leap over the telling words of s. 1, "without discrimination by reason of race, national origin, colour, religion or sex", in order to explain away any such discrimination by invoking the words "equality before the law" in para. (b) and attempting to make them alone the touchstone of reasonable classification. That was not done in the Drybones case; and this Court made it clear in Curr v. The Queen (1972), 26 D.L.R. (3d) 603, 7 C.C.C. (2d) 181, [1972] S.C.R. 889, that federal legislation, which might be compatible with the command of "equality before the law" taken alone may none the less be inoperative if it manifests any of the prohibited forms of discrimination. In short, the proscribed discriminations in s. 1 have a force either independent of the subsequently enumerated paras. (a) to (f) or, if they are found in any federal legislation, they offend those clauses because each must be read as if the prohibited forms of discrimination were recited therein as a part thereof.

This seems to me an obvious construction of s. 1 of the Canadian Bill of Rights. When that provision states that the enumerated human rights and fundamental freedoms shall continue to exist "without discrimination by reason of race, national origin, colour, religion or sex" it is expressly adding these words to para. (a) to (f). Section 1(b) must read therefore as "the right of the individual to equality before the law and the protection of the law without discrimination by reason of race, national origin, colour, religion or sex". It is worth repeating that this is what emerges from the Drybones case and what is found in the Curr case.

There is no clear historical basis for the position taken by the appellant, certainly not in relation to Indians in Canada as a whole, and this was in effect conceded during the hearing in this Court. In any event, history cannot avail against the clear words of ss. 1 and 2 of the Canadian Bill of Rights. It is s. 2 that gives this enactment its effective voice, because without it s. 1 would remain a purely declaratory provision. Section 2 brings the terms of s. 1 into its orbit, and its reference to "every law of Canada" is a reference, as set out in s. 5(2), to any Act of the Parliament of Canada enacted before or after the effective date of the Canadian Bill of Rights. Pre-existing Canadian legislation as well as subsequent Canadian legislation is expressly made subject to the commands of the Canadian Bill of Rights, and those commands, where they are as clear as the one which is relevant here, cannot be diluted by appeals to history. Ritchie, J., in his reasons in the Drybones case touched on this very point when he rejected the contention that the terms of s. 1 of the Canadian Bill of Rights must be circumscribed by the provisions of Canadian statutes in force at the date of the enactment of the Canadian Bill of Rights: see 9 D.L.R. (3d) 473 at pp. 483-4. I subscribe fully to the rejection of that contention. Clarity here is emphasized by looking at the French version of the Canadian Bill of Rights which speaks in s. 1 of the enumerated human rights and fundamental freedoms "pour tout individu au Canada quels que soient sa race, son origine nationale, sa couleur, sa religion ou son sexe".

In my opinion, the appellants' contentions gain no additional force because the Indian Act, including the challenged s. 12(1)(b) thereof, is a fruit of the exercise of Parliament's exclusive legislative power in relation to "Indians, and Lands reserved for the Indians" under s. 91(24) of the British North America Act, 1867. Discriminatory treatment on the basis of race or colour or sex does not inhere in that grant of legislative power. The fact that its exercise may be attended by forms of discrimination prohibited by the Canadian Bill of Rights is no more a justification for a breach of the Canadian Bill of Rights than there would be in the case of the exercise of any other head of federal legislative power involving provisions offensive to the Canadian Bill of Rights. The majority opinion in the Drybones case dispels any attempt to rely on the grant of legislative power as a ground for escaping from the force of the Canadian Bill of Rights. The latter does not differentiate among the various heads of legislative power; it embraces all exercises under whatever head or heads they arise. Section 3 which directs the Minister of Justice to scrutinize every Bill to ascertain whether any of its provisions are inconsistent with ss. 1 and 2 is simply an affirmation of this fact which is evident enough from ss. 1 and 2.

There was an intimation during the argument of these appeals that the Canadian Bill of Rights is properly invoked only to resolve a clash under its terms between two federal statutes, and the Drybones case was relied on in that connection. It is a spurious contention, if seriously advanced, because the Canadian Bill of Rights is itself the indicator to which any Canadian statute or any provision thereof must yield unless Parliament has declared that the statute or the particular provision is to operate notwithstanding the Canadian Bill of Rights. A statute may in itself be offensive to the Canadian Bill of Rights, or it may be by relation to another statute that it is so offensive.

I would dismiss both appeals with costs.

*   *   *

Appeals allowed.

CHAPTER 6

Guerin

THIS CASE is cited as Guerin v. The Queen, S.C.C. (1984). In January of 1958 a lease was signed through which lands of the Musqueam Indian Band were leased to the Shaughnessy Heights Golf Club of Vancouver. Members of the Department of Indian Affairs strongly influenced the band's acceptance of the terms of the lease, which were well below market standards at the time. The band did not receive a copy of the lease until 1970, and sued the government for damages in 1975.

The case raised the question of the nature of Aboriginal title and the question of the nature of the government's legal responsibility towards Aboriginal peoples. The trial judge held that the Crown had not lived up to its responsibility, and awarded the band ten million dollars in damages. The Federal Court of Appeal overturned this decision, which was then appealed to the Supreme Court of Canada. The Supreme Court justices were unanimous in allowing the band's appeal, although for significantly different reasons. Laskin, then Chief Justice, did not take part in the decision.

The decision written by Dickson (with Beetz, Chouinard, and Lamer concurring) stressed that "Indians have a legal right to occupy and possess certain lands, the ultimate title to which is in the Crown" and characterized that title as follows: "the nature of the Indians' interest is therefore best characterized by its general inalienability, coupled with the fact that the Crown is under obligation to deal with the land on the Indians' behalf when the interest is surrendered" (163). Dickson argued that the Crown did not act as an agent for or in a trust relation to Indians, though its relationship bore a "certain resemblance" (166) to both these legal concepts.

Wilson (with Ritchie and McIntyre concurring), while agreeing with Dickson in the final outcome of the case, focused on interpreting section 18 of the Indian Act, which stated that "reserves shall be held by Her Majesty for the use and benefit of the respective bands for which they are set apart" (175). The section also gave the Crown some discretion: "the Governor in Council may determine whether any purpose for which lands in a reserve are used or are to be used is for the use and benefit of the band" (175). While Dickson held that the trust-like relation between the Crown and Indians was created by the nature of Aboriginal title, he also thought that section 18 acted to confirm the relation and transform it into a fiduciary duty. Wilson argued that section 18 recognized an obligation created by the existence of Aboriginal title. Wilson also argued that the Governor in Council's discretionary power regarding Indian lands had to be understood within the context of dealing with the lands "for the use and benefit of the band" (177). Justice Estey also concurred in the final decision.

The decisions contain careful readings of the Royal Proclamation of 1763, St. Catherine's Milling, and Calder, as well as relying on the Marshall decisions. In awarding the band the damages arrived at in the initial hearing, the Supreme Court confirmed both that Aboriginal title was a valuable asset and that the Crown's responsibility for First Nations, while not falling precisely within existing legal categories, is enforceable and trust-like.

A battery of lawyers for Guerin and the National Indian Brotherhood included M.R.V. Storrow, J.J. Reynolds, L.F. Harvey, B.A. Crone, W. Badcock and A.C. Pape. W.I.C. Binnie, M.R. Taylor, and M. Freeman acted for the Crown. As well as comments quoted more than once, some arguments related to the issue of the measure of damages have been edited.

P.K.

DICKSON J. (BEETZ, CHOUINARD and LAMER JJ. concurring): The question is whether the appellants, the chief and councillors of the Musqueam Indian band, suing on their own behalf and on behalf of all other members of the band, are entitled to recover damages from the federal Crown in respect of the leasing to a golf club of land on the Musqueam Indian Reserve. Collier J., of the Trial Division of the Federal Court, declared that the Crown was in breach of trust [reported at [1982] 2 F.C. 385, 10 E.T.R. 61, [1982] 2 C.N.L.R. 83]. He assessed damages at $10,000,000. The Federal Court of Appeal allowed a Crown appeal, set aside the judgment of the Trial Division and dismissed the action [reported at [1983] 2 F.C. 656, [1983] 2 W.W.R. 686, 13 E.T.R. 245, 143 D.L.R. (3d) 416, [1983] 1 C.N.L.R. 20, 45 N.R. 181].

GENERAL

Before adverting to the facts, reference should be made to several of the relevant sections of the Indian Act, R.S.C. 1952, c. 149 [now R.S.C. 970, c. I-6], as amended. Section 18(1) provides in part that reserves shall be held by Her Majesty for the use of the respective Indian bands for which they were set apart. Generally, lands in a reserve shall not be sold, alienated, leased or otherwise disposed of until they have been surrendered to Her Majesty by the band for whose use and benefit in common the reserve was set apart (s. 37). A surrender may be absolute or qualified, conditional or unconditional (s. 38(2)). To be valid, a surrender must be made to Her Majesty, assented to by a majority of the electors of the band, and accepted by the Governor in Council (s. 39(1) [re-en. 1956, c. 40, s. 11]).

The gist of the present action is a claim that the federal Crown was in breach of its trust obligations in respect of the leasing of approximately 62 acres of reserve land to the Shaughnessy Heights Golf Club of Vancouver. The band alleged that a number of the terms and conditions of the lease were different from those disclosed to them before the surrender vote and that some of the lease terms were not disclosed to them at all. The band also claimed failure on the part of the federal Crown to exercise the requisite degree of care and management as a trustee.

THE FACTS

The Crown does not attack the findings of fact made by the trial judge. The Crown simply says that on those facts no cause of action has been made out. The following summary of the facts derives directly from the judgment at trial. Musqueam Indian Reserve (No. 2) in 1955 contained 416.53 acres, situated within the charter area of the city of Vancouver. The Indian Affairs Branch recognized that the reserve was a valuable one, "the most potentially valuable 400 acres in Vancouver today". In 1956 the Shaughnessy Heights Golf Club was interested in obtaining land on the Musqueam Reserve. There were others interested in developing the land, although the band was never told of the proposals for development.

On 4th April 1957 the president of the golf club wrote to Mr. Anfield, District Superintendent of the Indian Affairs Branch, setting forth a proposal for the lease of 160 acres of the Indian Reserve, the relevant terms of which were as follows:

1. The club was to have the right to construct on the leased area a golf course and country club and such other buildings and facilities as it considered appropriate for its membership.
2. The initial term of the lease was to be for 15 years commencing 1st May 1957, with the club to have options to extend the term for four successive periods of 15 years each, giving a maximum term of 75 years.
3. The rental for the first 15-year term was to be $25,000 per annum.
4. The rental for each successive 15-year period was to be determined by mutual agreement between the department and the club and failing agreement, by arbitration, but the rental for any of the 15-year renewal periods was in no event to be increased or decreased over that payable for the preceding 15-year period by more than 15 per cent of the initial rent.
5. At any time during the term of the lease, and for a period of up to six months after termination, the club was to have the right to remove any buildings and other structures it had constructed or placed upon the leased area, and any course improvements and facilities.

On 7th April 1957 a band council meeting was held. Mr. Anfield presided. The trial judge accepted evidence on behalf of the plaintiffs that not all of the terms of the Shaughnessy proposal were put before the band council at the meeting. William Guerin, a councillor, said copies of the proposal were not given to them; he did not recall any mention of $25,000 per year for rental; he described it as a vague general presentation with reference to 15-year periods. Chief Edward Sparrow said he did not recall the golf club proposal being read out in full. At the meeting the band council passed a resolution which the trial judge presumed to have been drawn up by Mr. Anfield. The relevant part of the resolution reads:

That we do approve the leasing of unrequired lands on our Musqueam I.R. 2 and that in connection with the application of the Shaughnessy Golf Club, we do approve the submission to our Musqueam Band of surrender documents for leasing 160 acres approximately as generally outlined on the McGuigan survey in red pencil.

These events followed the band council meeting:

(a) Mr. Bethune, Superintendent of Reserves and Trusts of the Indian Affairs Branch, in Ottawa, questioned the adequacy of the $25,000 annual rental for the first 15 years. At an investment return of 5-6 per cent, the annual rental value would be between $40,000 and $48,000 per year for the first 15 years. The golf club proposal meant an investment return of approximately 3 per cent. Mr. Bethune suggested that the opinion of Mr. Alfred Howell be obtained. Mr. Howell, with the Veterans Land Act Administration, had earlier made an appraisal of the reserve lands at the request of the Indian Affairs Branch.

(b) On 16th May 1957 Mr. Anfield wrote to Mr. Howell asking for the latter's opinion as to whether the $25,000 per year rental for the first 15 years was "just and equitable". Mr. Howell was not given all the details of the Shaughnessy proposal. He was not told that rent increases would be limited to 15 per cent. Nor was he made aware that the golf club proposed to have the right to remove any buildings or improvements.

(c) In his reply to Mr. Anfield, Mr. Howell expressed the view that a 75-year lease, adjustable over 15 years and made with a financially sound tenant, eliminated any risk factor. On that basis he felt the then government bond rate of 3.75 per cent was the most that could be expected.

At trial Mr. Howell said that if he had known the improvements would not revert to the band, he would have recommended a rate of return of 4-6 per cent. He expressed shock at the 15 per cent clause. He had assumed that at the end of the initial term the rental could be renegotiated on the basis of "highest and best use" without any limitation on rental increase.

(d) On 27th September 1957 a band council meeting was held at the reserve, attended by members of the band council, Mr. Anfield, two other officials of the Department of Indian Affairs and representatives of the golf club. Chief Sparrow stipulated for 5 per cent income on the value of 162 acres, amounting to $44,000 per annum. The golf club people balked. They were asked to step outside while the band council and the Indian Affairs personnel had a private discussion. Mr. Anfield said the demand of $44,000 was unreasonable. Eventually, the band council reluctantly agreed to a figure of $29,000. William Guerin testified the councillors agreed to $29,000 because they understood the first lease period was to be 10 years; subsequent rental negotiations would be every five years; and the band council felt it could negotiate for 5 per cent of the subsequent values.

Mr. Grant, officer in charge of the Vancouver agency of the Department of Indian Affairs, testified that there was "absolutely no question that the vote was for a specific lease to a specific tenant on specific terms" and that the band did not give Mr. Anfield "authority to change things around".

(e) On 6th October 1957 a meeting of members of the band was held at the reserve, the so-called "surrender meeting". The trial judge made these findings:
(i) those present assumed or understood the golf club lease would be, aside from

the first term, for 10-year periods, not 15 years; (ii) those present assumed or understood there would be no 15 per cent limitation on rental increases; (iii) the meeting was not told that the golf club had proposed that it should have the right to remove any buildings, structures, course improvements and facilities.

The trial judge found further that two matters which subsequently found their way into the lease were not even put before the surrender meeting. They were not in the original golf club proposal. They first appeared in draft leases, after the meeting. The first of these terms was the method of determining future rents; failing mutual agreement, the matter was to be submitted to arbitration; the new rent would be the fair rent as if the land were still in an uncleared and unimproved condition and used as a golf club. The second term gave the golf club, but not the Crown, the right at the end of each 15-year period to terminate the lease on six month's prior notice. These two terms were not subsequently brought before the band council or the band for comment or approval.

The surrender, which was approved by a vote of 41 to 2, gave the land in question to Her Majesty the Queen on the following terms:

TO HAVE AND TO HOLD the same unto Her said Majesty the Queen, her Heirs and Successors forever in trust to lease the same to such person or persons, and upon such terms as the Government of Canada may deem most conducive to our Welfare and that of our people.

AND upon the further condition that all monies received from the leasing thereof, shall be credited to our revenue trust account at Ottawa.

AND WE, the said Chief and Councillors of the said Musqueam Band of Indians do on behalf of our people and for ourselves, hereby ratify and confirm, and promise to ratify and confirm, whatever the said Government may do, or cause to be lawfully done, in connection with the leasing thereof.

(f) On 6th December 1957 the surrender of the lands was accepted by the federal Crown by Order-in-Council P.C. 1957-1606, "in order that the lands covered thereby may be leased".

(g) On 9th January 1958 a band council meeting was held. A letter was read regarding the proposed golf club lease. The letter indicated the renewal periods were to be 15 years instead of 10 years. Chief Sparrow pointed out that the band had demanded 10-year periods. William Guerin said the council members were "flabbergasted" to learn about the 15-year terms. Guerin testified the band was told it was "stuck" with the 15-year terms. The band council then passed a resolution agreeing the first term should be 15 years, but insisting the renewal periods be 10-year terms.

(h) The lease was signed 22nd January 1958. It provided, inter alia:

1. The term is for 75 years, unless sooner terminated.

2. The rent for the first 15 years is $29,000 per annum.

3. For the succeeding 15-year periods, annual rent is to be determined by mutual agreement, or failing such agreement, by arbitration, such rent to be equal to the fair rent for the demised premises as if the same were still in an uncleared and unimproved condition and used as a golf course.

4. The maximum increase in rent for the second 15-year period (January 1, 1973 to January 1, 1988) is limited to 15% of $29,000, that is $4350 per annum.

5. The golf club can terminate the lease at the end of any 15-year period by giving 6 months' prior notice.

6. The golf club can at any time during the lease and up to 6 months after termination, remove any buildings or other structures, and any course improvements and facilities.

The band was not given a copy of the lease, and did not receive one until 12 years later, in March 1970.

(i) Mr. Grant testified that the terms of the lease ultimately entered into bore little resemblance to what was discussed at the surrender meeting. The judge agreed. He found that the majority of those who voted on 6th October 1957 would not have assented to a surrender of the 162 acres if they had known all the terms of the lease of 22nd January 1958.

ASSESSMENT AT TRIAL AND ON APPEAL OF THE LEGAL EFFECT OF THE FACTS AS FOUND

The plaintiffs based their case on breach of trust. They asserted that the federal Crown was a trustee of the surrendered lands. The trial judge agreed.

The Crown attempted to argue that if there was a trust it was, at best, a "political trust", enforceable only in Parliament and not a "true trust", enforceable in the courts. This distinction was recognized in two leading English cases dealing with the position of the Crown as trustee: Tito v. Waddell; Tito v. A.G., [1977] Ch. 106, [1977] 2 W.L.R. 496, [1977] 3 All E.R. 129; Kinloch v. Secretary of State for India in Council (1882), 7 App. Cas. 619 (H.L.).

In Kinloch Lord Selbourn L.C. said at pp. 625-26:

> Now the words "in trust for" are quite consistent with, and indeed are the proper manner of expressing, every species of trust—a trust not only as regards those matters which are the proper subjects for an equitable jurisdiction to administer, but as respects higher matters, such as might take place between the Crown and public officers discharging, under the directions of the Crown, duties or functions belonging to the prerogative and to the authority of the Crown. In the lower sense they are matters within the jurisdiction of, and to be administered by, the ordinary Courts of Equity; in the higher sense they are not. What their sense is here, is the question to be determined, looking at the whole instrument and at its nature and effect.

Counsel for the band objected to any argument on the "political trust" defence because the Crown had failed to plead it. Collier J. gave leave, on terms, to amend the defence to raise the point but the Crown chose not to take advantage of the opportunity to amend. Collier J. therefore refused to consider the point.

The Crown then argued that if there were a legally enforceable trust its terms were those set out in the surrender document, permitting it to lease the 162 acres to anyone, for any purpose, and upon any terms which the Crown deemed most conducive to the welfare of the band. In the Crown's submission the surrender document imposed on it no obligation to lease to the golf club on the terms discussed at the surrender meeting; nor did it impose any duty on the Crown to obtain the approval of the band in respect of the terms of the lease ultimately entered into.

The trial judge rejected these submissions. He held, citing the Tito case, supra, that the Crown can, if it chooses, act as a trustee. He held also that the surrender of 6th October 1957 imposed on the Crown, as trustee, a duty as of that date, to lease the surrendered land to the golf club on the conditions contemplated by the band. Substantial changes were made to these conditions, in respect of which no instruction or authorization was sought by the Crown, as trustee, from the members of the band, the cestuis que trust. The judge found the Crown liable for breach of trust.

In respect of damages, there was a great deal of evidence at trial, most of it by experts. Citing Fales v. Can. Permanent Trust Co., [1977] 2 S.C.R. 302 at 320, [1976] 6 W.W.R. 10, 70 D.L.R. (3d) 257 (sub nom. Wohlleben v. Can. Permanent Trust Co.), 11 N.R. 487, the judge held that the measure of damages is the actual loss which the acts or omissions have caused to the trust estate, the plaintiffs being entitled to be placed in the same position so far as possible as if there had been no breach of trust. The judge proceeded on the basis that the band would not have agreed to the terms of the lease as signed and the club would not have agreed to a lease on the terms found by the judge to be the terms of the trust. Therefore it would have been possible for the band at some point to have leased the land for residential purposes on a 99-year leasehold basis on extremely favourable terms. In quantifying the award, the judge confessed to being unable to set out a precise rationale or approach, mathematical or otherwise. He said that the award was obviously a "global" figure: a considered reaction based on the evidence, the opinions, the arguments and, in the end, his own conclusions of fact. The judge assessed the plaintiffs' damages at $10,000,000.

The Federal Court of Appeal speaking through Le Dain J., proceeded on the premise that the case presented on behalf of the band rested on the existence of a statutory trust in the private law sense based primarily on the terms of s.18(1) of the Indian Act. Section 18(1) reads:

> 18.(1) Subject to the provisions of this Act, reserves shall be held by Her Majesty for the use and benefit of the respective bands for which they were set apart; and subject to this Act and to the terms of any treaty or surrender, the Governor in Council may determine whether any purpose for which lands in a reserve are used or are to be used is for the use and benefit of the band.

Le Dain J. scrutinized this section and concluded that it was not consistent with a "true trust" in the sense of an equitable obligation enforceable in a court of law. Especially telling, in his opinion, was the discretion vested by s. 18(1) in the Governor in Council to determine whether a particular purpose to which reserve land is being put, or is proposed to be put, is "for the use and benefit of the band". In his view this discretion indicated it was for the government, not the courts, to determine what was for the use and benefit of the band. Such a discretion, in his opinion, was incompatible with an intention to impose an equitable obligation, enforceable in court, to deal with the land in a certain manner. Section 18(1) was therefore incapable of making the Crown a true trustee of those lands [p. 750 W.W.R., p. 75 C.N.L.R.]:

> The extent to which the government assumes an administrative or man-

agement responsibility for the reserves of some positive scope is a matter of governmental discretion, not legal or equitable obligation. I am, therefore, of the opinion that section 18 of the Indian Act does not afford a basis for an action for breach of trust in the management or disposition of reserve lands.

Le Dain J. also rejected the alternative contention on behalf of the band that a trust was created by the terms of the surrender document, especially the words "in trust to lease the same . . .", and that the Crown was in breach of that trust by its alleged failure to exercise ordinary skill and prudence in leasing the land [pp. 751-52 W.W.R., p. 77 C.N.L.R.]:

> . . . it is my opinion that the words "in trust" in the surrender document were intended to do no more than indicate that the surrender was for the benefit of the Indians and conferred an authority to deal with the land in a certain manner for their benefit. They were not intended to impose an equitable obligation or duty to deal with the land in a certain manner. For these reasons, I am of the opinion that the surrender did not create a true trust and does not, therefore, afford a basis for liability based on a breach of trust.

Even if he had been able to find a "true trust", Le Dain J. would have refused to follow Collier J. in concluding that the terms of such a trust were defined by the Indians' understanding of conditions the Crown was to secure in the lease. These conditions did not appear in the surrender document and they did not comply with ss. 37-41 of the Indian Act, governing the conditions of a surrender [p. 732 W.W.R., pp. 60-1 C.N.L.R.].

> From these provisions it is argued that the conditions of a surrender, in order to be valid, must be voted on and approved by a majority of the electors of a band, be certified by the superintendent or other officer who attended the meeting and by the chief or a member of the council of the band, and be submitted to and approved by the Governor in Council, all of which presuppose that the conditions will be in written form. I agree with these contentions. These solemn formalities have been prescribed as a matter of public policy for the protection of a band and the proper discharge of the government's responsibility for the Indians. They are also important as ensuring certainty as to the effect of a surrender and the validity of a subsequent disposition of surrendered land. It is to be noted that they are the only provisions of the Act excluded from the power of the Governor in Council under s. 4(2) to declare by proclamation that particular provisions of the Act shall not apply in certain cases. The oral terms found by the trial judge were not voted on and approved by a majority of the band. They were deduced by the trial judge from the testimony of three members of the band and a former official of the Indian Affairs Branch as to what was said at the meetings, and in some cases as to what was not said. The oral terms of the surrender found by the trial judge were not accepted by the Governor in Council, as required by the Act. What was accepted by Order in Council P.C. 1957-1060 of 6th December 1957 was the "attached surrender dated the sixth day of October, 1957". It was an unqualified

acceptance of the written surrender with no reference, express or implied, to other terms or conditions.

Le Dain J. concluded that the oral conditions of the surrender found by the trial judge could not afford a basis in law for finding liability and awarding damages.

Having found no basis for the trust alleged, the Federal Court of Appeal allowed the Crown's appeal.

FIDUCIARY RELATIONSHIP

The issue of the Crown's liability was dealt with in the courts below on the basis of the existence or non-existence of a trust. In dealing with the different consequences of a "true" trust, as opposed to a "political" trust, Le Dain J. noted that the Crown could be liable only if it were subject to an "equitable obligation enforceable in a court of law". I have some doubt as to the cogency of the terminology of "higher" and "lower" trusts, but I do agree that the existence of an equitable obligation is the sine qua non for liability. Such an obligation is not, however, limited to relationships which can be strictly defined as "trusts". As will presently appear, it is my view that the Crown's obligations vis-à-vis the Indians cannot be defined as a trust. That does not, however, mean that the Crown owes no enforceable duty to the Indians in the way in which it deals with Indian land.

In my view, the nature of Indian title and the framework of the statutory scheme established for disposing of Indian land places upon the Crown an equitable obligation, enforceable by the courts, to deal with the land for the benefit of the Indians. This obligation does not amount to a trust in the private law sense. It is rather a fiduciary duty. If, however, the Crown breaches this fiduciary duty it will be liable to the Indians in the same way and to the same extent as if such a trust were in effect.

The fiduciary relationship between the Crown and the Indians has its roots in the concept of aboriginal, native or Indian title. The fact that Indian bands have a certain interest in lands does not, however, in itself give rise to a fiduciary relationship between the Indians and the Crown. The conclusion that the Crown is a fiduciary depends upon the further proposition that the Indian interest in the land is inalienable except upon surrender to the Crown.

An Indian band is prohibited from directly transferring its interest to a third party. Any sale or lease of land can only be carried out after a surrender has taken place, with the Crown then acting on the band's behalf. The Crown first took this responsibility upon itself in the Royal Proclamation of 1763 [see R.S.C. 1970, App.II]. It is still recognized in the surrender provisions of the Indian Act. The surrender requirement, and the responsibility it entails, are the source of a distinct fiduciary obligation owed by the Crown to the Indians. In order to explore the character of this obligation, however, it is first necessary to consider the basis of aboriginal title and the nature of the interest in land which it represents.

(a) The Existence of Indian Title

In Calder v. A.G. B.C., [1973] S.C.R. 313, [1973] 4 W.W.R. 1, 34 D.L.R. (3d) 145, this court recognized aboriginal title as a legal right derived from the Indians' historic occupation and possession of their tribal lands. With Judson and Hall JJ.

writing the principal judgments, the court split three-three on the major issue of whether the Nishga Indians' aboriginal title to their ancient tribal territory had been extinguished by general land enactments in British Columbia. The court also split on the issue of whether the Royal Proclamation of 1763 was applicable to Indian lands in that province. Judson and Hall JJ. were in agreement, however, that aboriginal title existed in Canada (at least where it had not been extinguished by appropriate legislative action) independently of the Royal Proclamation. Judson J. stated expressly that the Proclamation was not the "exclusive" source of Indian title (pp. 322-23, 328). Hall J. said (at p. 390) that "aboriginal Indian title does not depend on treaty, executive order or legislative enactment".

The Royal Proclamation of 1763 reserved "under our Sovereignty, Protection, and Dominion, for the use of the said Indians, all the Lands and Territories not included within the Limits of Our said Three new Governments, or within the Limits of the Territory granted to the Hudson's Bay Company, as also all the Lands and Territories lying to the Westward of the Sources of the Rivers which fall into the Sea from the West and North West as aforesaid" (at p. 127). In recognizing that the Proclamation is not the sole source of Indian title the Calder decision went beyond the judgment of the Privy Council in St. Catherine's Milling & Lbr. Co. v. R. (1888), 14 App. Cas. 46, 4 Cart. 107 (P.C.). In that case Lord Watson acknowledged the existence of aboriginal title but said it had its origin in the Royal Proclamation. In this respect Calder is consistent with the position of Marshall C.J. in the leading American cases of Johnson v. M'Intosh, 21 U.S. (8 Wheat.) 543, 5 L. Ed. 681 (1823), and Worcester v. Georgia, 31 U.S. (6 Pet.) 515, 8 L.Ed. 483 (1832), cited by Judson and Hall JJ. in their respective judgments.

In Johnson v. M'Intosh Marshall C.J., although he acknowledged the Proclamation of 1763 as one basis for recognition of Indian title, was nonetheless of opinion that the rights of Indians in the lands they traditionally occupied prior to European colonization both predated and survived the claims to sovereignty made by various European nations in the territories of the North American continent. The principle of discovery which justified these claims gave the ultimate title in the land in a particular area to the nation which had discovered and claimed it. In that respect at least the Indians' rights in the land were obviously diminished; but their rights of occupancy and possession remained unaffected. Marshall C.J. explained this principle as follows, at pp. 573-74:

> The exclusion of all other Europeans, necessarily gave to the nation making the discovery the sole right of acquiring the soil from the natives, and establishing settlements upon it . . . . It was a right which all asserted for themselves, and to the assertion of which, by others, all assented.
>
> Those relations which were to exist between the discoverer and the natives, were to be regulated by themselves. The rights thus acquired being exclusive, no other power could interpose between them.
>
> In the establishment of these relations, the rights of the original inhabitants were, in no instance, entirely disregarded; but were necessarily, to a considerable extent, impaired. *They were admitted to be the rightful occupants of the soil, with a legal as well as just claim to retain possession of it,* and to use it according to their own discretion; but their rights to complete sovereignty, as independent nations, were necessarily diminished, and

their power to dispose of the soil at their own will, to whomsoever they pleased, was denied by the original fundamental principle, that discovery gave exclusive title to those who made it. (The emphasis is mine.)

The principle that a change in sovereignty over a particular territory does not in general affect the presumptive title of the inhabitants was approved by the Privy Council in Amodu Tijani v. Southern Nigeria (Secretary), [1921] 2 A.C. 399. That principle supports the assumption implicit in Calder that Indian title is an independent legal right which, although recognized by the Royal Proclamation of 1763, nonetheless predates it. For this reason Kinloch v. Secretary of State for India, supra; Tito v. Waddell, supra, and the other "political trust" decisions are inapplicable to the present case. The "political trust" cases concerned essentially the distribution of public funds or other property held by the government. In each case the party claiming to be beneficiary under a trust depended entirely on statute, ordinance or treaty as the basis for its claim to an interest in the funds in question. The situation of the Indians is entirely different. Their interest in their lands is a pre-existing legal right not created by Royal Proclamation, by s. 18(1) of the Indian Act, or by any other executive order or legislative provision.

It does not matter, in my opinion, that the present case is concerned with the interest of an Indian band in a reserve rather than with unrecognized aboriginal title in traditional tribal lands. The Indian interest in the land is the same in both cases: see A.G. Que. v. A.G. Can., [1921] 1 A.C. 401 at 410-11, 56 D.L.R. 373 (P.C.) (the "Star Chrome" case). It is worth noting, however, that the reserve in question here was created out of the ancient tribal territory of the Musqueam band by the unilateral action of the colony of British Columbia, prior to Confederation.

(b) The Nature of Indian Title

In the St. Catherine's Milling case, supra, the Privy Council held that the Indians had a "personal and usufructuary right" [p. 54] in the lands which they had traditionally occupied. Lord Watson said that "there has been all along vested in the Crown a substantial and paramount estate, underlying the Indian title, which became a plenum dominium whenever that title was surrendered or otherwise extinguished" (at p. 55). He reiterated this idea, stating that the Crown "has all along had a present proprietary estate in the land, upon which the Indian title was a mere burden" (at p. 58). This view of aboriginal title was affirmed by the Privy Council in the Star Chrome case. In Amodu Tijani, supra, Viscount Haldane, adverting to the St. Catherine's Milling and Star Chrome decisions, explained the concept of a usufructuary right as "a mere qualification of or burden on the radical or final title of the Sovereign" (p. 403). He described the title of the Sovereign as a pure legal estate, but one which could be qualified by a right of "beneficial user" that did not necessarily take the form of an estate in land. Indian title in Canada was said to be one illustration "of the necessity for getting rid of the assumption that the ownership of land naturally breaks itself up into estates, conceived as creatures of inherent legal principle" (p. 403). Marshall C.J. took a similar view in Johnson v. M'Intosh, supra, saying, "All our institutions recognize the absolute title of the Crown, subject only to the Indian right of occupancy" (p. 588).

It should be noted that the Privy Council's emphasis on the personal nature of aboriginal title stemmed in part from constitutional arrangements peculiar to Canada . The Indian territory at issue in St. Catherine's Milling was land which in 1867 had been vested in the Crown subject to the interest of the Indians . The Indians' interest was an "Interest other than that of the Province", within the meaning of s.109 of the Constitution Act, 1867. Section 109 provides:

> 109. All Lands, Mines, Minerals, and Royalties belonging to the several Provinces of Canada, Nova Scotia, and New Brunswick at the Union, and all Sums then due or payable for such Lands, Mines, Minerals, or Royalties, shall belong to the several Provinces of Ontario, Quebec, Nova Scotia, and New Brunswick in which the same are situate or arise subject to any Trusts existing in respect thereof, and to any Interest other than that of the Province in the same.

When the land in question in St. Catherine's Milling was subsequently disencumbered of the native title upon its surrender to the federal government by the Indian occupants in 1873, the entire beneficial interest in the land was held to have passed, because of the personal and usufructuary nature of the Indians' right, to the province of Ontario under s.109 rather than to Canada. The same constitutional issue arose recently in this court in Can. v. Smith, [1983] 1 S.C.R. 554, 147 D.L.R. (3d) 237 (sub nom. R. v. Smith), [1983] 3 C.N.L.R. 161, 47 N.R. 132, in which the court held that the Indian right in a reserve, being personal, could not be transferred to a grantee, whether an individual or the Crown. Upon surrender the right disappeared "in the process of release".

No such constitutional problem arises in the present case, since in 1938 the title to all Indian reserves in British Columbia was transferred by the provincial government to the Crown in right of Canada.

It is true that in contexts other than the constitutional the characterization of Indian title as "a personal and usufructuary right" has sometimes been questioned. In Calder, supra, for example, Judson J. intimated at p. 328 that this characterization was not helpful in determining the nature of Indian title. In A.G. Can. v. Giroux (1916), 53 S.C.R. 172, 30 D.L.R. 123, Duff J., speaking for himself and Anglin J., distinguished St. Catherine's Milling on the ground that the statutory provisions in accordance with which the reserve in question in Giroux had been created conferred beneficial ownership on the Indian band which occupied the reserve. In Cardinal v. A.G. Alta., [1974] S.C.R. 695, [1973] 6 W.W.R. 205, 13 C.C.C. (2d) 1, 40 D.L.R. (3d) 553, Laskin J., dissenting on another point, accepted the possibility that Indians may have a beneficial interest in a reserve. The Alberta Court of Appeal in Western Int. Contractors Ltd. v. Sarcee Dev. Ltd., [1979] 3 W.W.R. 631, 98 D.L.R. (3d) 424, [1979] 2 C.N.L.R. 107 (sub nom. Western Indust. Contractors Ltd. v. Sarcee Dev. Ltd.), 15 A.R. 309, accepted the proposition that an Indian band does indeed have a beneficial interest in its reserve. In the present case this was the view as well of Le Dain J. in the Federal Court of Appeal. See also the judgment of Kellock J. in Miller v. R., [1950] S.C.R. 168, [1950] 1 D.L.R. 513, in which he seems implicitly to adopt a similar position. None of these judgments mentioned the Star Chrome case, however, in which the Indian interest in land specifically set aside as a reserve was held to be the same as the "personal and usufructuary right" which was discussed in St. Catherine's Milling.

It appears to me that there is no real conflict between the cases which characterize Indian title as a beneficial interest of some sort, and those which characterize it a personal, usufructuary right. Any apparent inconsistency derives from the fact that in describing what constitutes a unique interest in land the courts have almost inevitably found themselves applying a somewhat inappropriate terminology drawn from general property law. There is a core of truth in the way that each of the two lines of authority has described native title, but an appearance of conflict has nonetheless arisen because in neither case is the categorization quite accurate.

Indians have a legal right to occupy and possess certain lands, the ultimate title to which is in the Crown. While their interest does not, strictly speaking, amount to beneficial ownership, neither is its nature completely exhausted by the concept of a personal right. It is true that the sui generis interest which the Indians have in the land is personal in the sense that it cannot be transferred to a grantee, but it is also true, as will presently appear, that the interest gives rise upon surrender to a distinctive fiduciary obligation on the part of the Crown to deal with the land for the benefit of the surrendering Indians. These two aspects of Indian title go together, since the Crown's original purpose in declaring the Indians' interest to be inalienable otherwise than to the Crown was to facilitate the Crown's ability to represent the Indians in dealings with third parties. The nature of the Indians' interest is therefore best characterized by its general inalienability, coupled with the fact that the Crown is under an obligation to deal with the land on the Indians' behalf when the interest is surrendered. Any description of Indian title which goes beyond these two features is both unnecessary and potentially misleading.

(c) The Crown's Fiduciary Obligation

The concept of fiduciary obligation originated long ago in the notion of breach of confidence, one of the original heads of jurisdiction in Chancery. In the present appeal its relevance is based on the requirement of a "surrender" before Indian land can be alienated.

The Royal Proclamation of 1763 provided that no private person could purchase from the Indians any lands that the Proclamation had reserved to them, and provided further that all purchases had to be by and in the name of the Crown, in a public assembly of the Indians held by the governor or commander-in-chief of the colony in which the lands in question lay. As Lord Watson pointed out in St. Catherine's Milling, supra, at p. 54, this policy with respect to the sale or transfer of the Indians' interest in land has been continuously maintained by the British Crown, by the governments of the colonies when they became responsible for the administration of Indian affairs, and, after 1867, by the federal government of Canada. Successive federal statutes, predecessors to the present Indian Act, have all provided for the general inalienability of Indian reserve land except upon surrender to the Crown, the relevant provisions in the present Act being ss. 37-41.

The purpose of this surrender requirement is clearly to interpose the Crown between the Indians and prospective purchasers or lessees of their land, so as to prevent the Indians from being exploited. This is made clear in the Royal Proclamation itself, which prefaces the provision making the Crown an intermediary with a declaration that [at p. 128] "great Frauds and Abuses have been committed in puchasing Lands of the Indians, to the great Prejudice of our Interests, and to the great Dissatisfaction of the said Indians . . . ." Through the confirmation in the Indian Act of the historic responsibility which the Crown has undertaken, to act on behalf of the Indians so as to protect their interests in transactions with third parties, Parliament has conferred upon the Crown a discretion to decide for itself where the Indians' best interests really lie. This is the effect of s. 18(1) of the Act.

This discretion on the part of the Crown, far from ousting, as the Crown contends, the jurisdiction of the courts to regulate the relationship between the Crown and the Indians, has the effect of transforming the Crown's obligation into a fiduciary one. Professor Ernest J. Weinrib maintains in his article "The Fiduciary Obligation" (1975), 25 U.T.L.J. 1, at p. 7, that "the hallmark of a fiduciary relation is that the relative legal positions are such that one party is at the mercy of the other's discretion". Earlier, at p.4, he puts the point in the following way:

> [Where there is a fiduciary obligation] there is a relation in which the principal's interests can be affected by, and are therefore dependent on, the manner in which the fiduciary uses the discretion which has been delegated to him. The fiduciary obligation is the law's blunt tool for the control of this discretion.

I make no comment upon whether this description is broad enough to embrace all fiduciary obligations. I do agree, however, that where by statute, agreement, or perhaps by unilateral undertaking, one party has an obligation to act for the benefit of another, and that obligation carries with it a discretionary power, the party thus empowered becomes a fiduciary. Equity will then supervise the relationship by holding him to the fiduciary's strict standard of conduct.

It is sometimes said that the nature of fiduciary relationships is both established and exhausted by the standard categories of agent, trustee, partner, director, and the like. I do not agree. It is the nature of the relationship, not the specific category of actor involved that gives rise to the fiduciary duty. The categories of fiduciary, like those of negligence, should not be considered closed: see, e.g., Laskin v. Bache & Co., [1972] 1 O.R. 465, 23 D.L.R. (3d) 385 at 392 (C.A.); Goldex Mines Ltd. v. Revill; Probe Mines Ltd. v. Goldex Mines Ltd. (1974), 7 O.R. (2d) 216, 54 D.L.R. (3d) 672 at 224 (C.A.).

It should be noted that fiduciary duties generally arise only with regard to obligations originating in a private law context. Public law duties, the performance of which requires the exercise of discretion, do not typically give rise to a fiduciary relationship. As the "political trust" cases indicate, the Crown is not normally viewed as a fiduciary in the exercise of its legislative or administrative function. The mere fact, however, that it is the Crown which is obligated to act on the Indians' behalf does not of itself remove the Crown's obligation from the scope of the fiduciary principle. As was pointed out earlier, the Indians' interest in land is an independent legal interest. It is not a creation of either the legislative or executive branches of government. The Crown's obligation to the Indians with respect to that interest is therefor not a public law duty. While it is not a private law duty in the strict sense either, it is nonetheless in the nature of a private law duty. Therefore in this sui generis relationship, it is not improper to regard the Crown as a fiduciary.

Section 18(1) of the Indian Act confers upon the Crown a broad discretion in dealing with surrendered land. In the present case, the document of surrender, set out in part earlier in these reasons, by which the Musqueam band surrendered the land at issue, confirms this discretion in the clause conveying the land to the Crown "in trust to lease . . . upon such terms as the Government of Canada may deem most conducive to our Welfare and that of our people". When, as here, an Indian band surrenders its interest to the Crown, a fiduciary obligation takes hold to regulate the manner in which the Crown exercises its discretion in dealing with the land on the Indians' behalf.

I agree with Le Dain J. that before surrender the Crown does not hold the land in trust for the Indians. I also agree that the Crown's obligation does not somehow crystallize into a trust, express or implied, at the time of surrender. The law of trusts is a highly developed, specialized branch of the law. An express trust requires a settlor, a beneficiary, a trust corpus, words of settlement, certainty of object and certainty of obligation. Not all of these elements are present here. Indeed, there is not even a trust corpus. As the Smith decision, supra, makes clear upon unconditional surrender the Indians' right in the land disappears. No property interest is transferred which could constitute the trust res, so that even if the other indicia of an express or implied trust could be made out, the basic requirement of a settlement of property has not been met. Accordingly, although the nature of Indian title coupled with the discretion vested in the Crown are sufficient to give rise to a fiduciary obligation, neither an express nor an implied trust arises upon surrender.

Nor does surrender give rise to a constructive trust. As was said by this court in Pettkus v. Becker, [1980] 2 S.C.R. 834 at 847, 19 R.F.L. (2d) 165, 8 E.T.R. 143, 117 D.L.R. (3d) 257, 34 N.R. 384, "The principle of unjust enrichment lies at the heart of the constructive trust". See also Rathwell v. Rathwell, [1978] 2 S.C.R. 436, [1978] 2 W.W.R. 101, 1 E.T.R. 307, 1 R.F.L. (2d) 1, 83 D.L.R. (3d) 289. Any similarity between a constructive trust and the Crown's fiduciary obligation to the Indians is limited to the fact that both arise by operation of law; the former is an essentially restitutionary remedy, while the latter is not. In the present case, for example, the Crown has in no way been enriched by the surrender transaction, whether unjustly or otherwise, but the fact that this is so cannot alter either the existence or the nature of the obligation which the Crown owes.

The Crown's fiduciary obligation to the Indians is therefore not a trust. To say as much is not to deny that the obligation is trust-like in character. As would be the case with a trust, the Crown must hold surrendered land for the use and benefit of the surrendering band. The obligation is thus subject to principles very similar to those which govern the law of trusts concerning, for example, the measure of damages for breach. The fiduciary relationship between the Crown and the Indians also bears a certain resemblance to agency, since the obligation can be characterized as a duty to act on behalf of the Indian bands who have surrendered lands, by negotiating for the sale or lease of the land to third parties. But just as the Crown is not a trustee for the Indians, neither is it their agent; not only does the Crown's authority to act on the band's behalf lack a basis in contract, but the band is not a party to the ultimate sale or lease, as it would be if it were the Crown's principal. I repeat, the fiduciary obligation which is owed to the Indians by the Crown is sui generis. Given the unique character both of the Indians' interest in land and of their historical relationship with the Crown, the fact that this is so should occasion no surprise.

The discretion which is the hallmark of any fiduciary relationship is capable of being considerably narrowed in a particular case. This is as true of the Crown's discretion vis-à-vis the Indians as it is of the discretion of trustees, agents, and other traditional categories of fiduciary. The Indian Act makes specific provision for such narrowing in ss. 18(1) and 38(2). A fiduciary obligation will not, of course, be eliminated by the imposition of conditions that have the effect of restricting the fiduciary's discretion. A failure to adhere to the imposed conditions will simply itself be a prima facie breach of the obligation. In the present case both the surrender and the Order-in-Council accepting the surrender referred to the Crown leasing the land on the band's behalf. Prior to the surrender the band had also been given to understand that a lease was to be entered into with the Shaughnessy Heights Golf Club upon certain terms, but this understanding was not incorporated into the surrender document itself. The effect of these so-called oral terms will be considered in the next section.

(d) Breach of the Fiduciary Obligation

The trial judge found that the Crown's agents promised the band to lease the land in question on certain specified terms and then, after surrender, obtained a lease on different terms. The lease obtained was much less valuable. As already mentioned, the surrender document did not make reference to the "oral" terms. I would not wish to say that those terms had nonetheless somehow been incorporated as conditions into the surrender. They were not formally assented to by a majority of the electors of the band, nor were they accepted by the Governor in Council, as required by s. 39(1)(b) and (c). I agree with Le Dain J. that there is no merit in the appellants' submission that for purposes of s. 39 a surrender can be considered independently of its terms. This makes no more sense than would a claim that a contract can have an existence which in no way depends on the terms and conditions that comprise it.

Nonetheless, the Crown, in my view, was not empowered by the surrender document to ignore the oral terms which the band understood would be embodied in the lease. The oral representations form the backdrop against which the Crown's conduct in discharging its fiduciary obligation must be measured. They inform and confine the field of discretion within which the Crown was free to act. After the Crown's agents had induced the band to surrender its land on the understanding that the land would be leased on certain terms, it would be unconscionable to permit the Crown simply to ignore those terms. When the promised lease proved impossible to obtain, the Crown, instead of proceeding to lease the land on different, unfavourable terms, should have returned to the band to explain what had occurred and seek the band's counsel on how to proceed. The existence of such unconscionability is the key to a conclusion that the Crown breached its fiduciary duty. Equity will not countenance unconscionable behaviour in a fiduciary, whose duty is that of utmost loyalty to his principal.

While the existence of the fiduciary obligation which the Crown owes to the

Indians is dependent on the nature of the surrender process, the standard of conduct which the obligation imports is both more general and more exacting than the terms of any particular surrender. In the present case the relevant aspect of the required standard of conduct is defined by a principle analogous to that which underlies the doctrine of promissory or equitable estoppel. The Crown cannot promise the band that it will obtain a lease of the latter's land on certain stated terms, thereby inducing the band to alter its legal position by surrendering the land, and then simply ignore that promise to the band's detriment: see, e.g., Central London Property Trust Ltd. v. High Trees House Ltd., [1947] 1 K.B. 130, [1956] 1 All E.R. 256n; Robertson v. Min. of Pensions, [1949] 1 K.B. 227, [1948] 2 All E.R. 767 (C.A.).

In obtaining without consultation a much less valuable lease than that promised, the Crown breached the fiduciary obligation it owed the band. It must make good the loss suffered in consequence.

LIMITATION OF ACTION AND LACHES

The Crown contends that the band's claim is barred by the Statute of Limitations, R.S.B.C. 1960, c. 370 [repealed and substituted by Limitations Act, S.B.C. 1975, c. 37; now the Limitation Act, R.S.B.C. 1979, c. 236], because it was not filed by 22nd January 1964, six years from the date the lease was signed. The trial judge, however, found that the band and its members were not aware of the actual terms of the lease, and therefore of the breach of fiduciary duty, until March 1970. This was not for lack of effort on the band's part. The Indian Affairs Branch, in conformity with its then policy, had refused to give a copy of the lease to the band, despite repeated requests.

It is well established that where there has been a fraudulent concealment of the existence of a cause of action, the limitation period will not start to run until the plaintiff discovers the fraud, or until the time when, with reasonable diligence, he ought to have discovered it. The fradulent concealment necessary to toll or suspend the operation of the statute need not amount to deceit or common law fraud. Equitable fraud, defined in Kitchen v. Royal Air Force Assn., [1958] 1 W.L.R. 563, [1958] 3 All E.R. 241 (C.A.), as [p. 573] "conduct which, having regard to some special relationship between the two parties concerned, is an unconscionable thing for the one to do towards the other", is sufficient. I agree with the trial judge that the conduct of the Indian Affairs Branch toward the band amounted to equitable fraud. Although the branch officials did not act dishonestly or for improper motives in concealing the terms of the lease from the band, in my view their conduct was nevertheless unconscionable, having regard to the fiduciary relationship between the branch and the band. The limitations period did not therefore start to run until March 1970. The action was thus timely when filed on 22nd December 1975. . . .

MEASURE OF DAMAGES

In my opinion the quantum of damages is to be determined by analogy with the principles of trust law: see, e.g., Re West of England and South Wales Dist. Bank; Ex parte Dale & Co. (1879), 11 Ch. D. 772 at 778. Reviewing the record it seems apparent that the judge at trial considered all the relevant evidence. His judgment, as I read it, discloses no error in principle. I am content to adopt the quantum of damages awarded by the judge, rejecting, as he did, any claim for exemplary or punitive damages.

I would therefore allow the appeal, set aside the judgment in the Federal Court of Appeal and reinstate without variation the trial judge's award, with costs to the present appellants in all courts.

*   *   *

Estey J. (concurring in the result): The facts and issues in this appeal [from judgment reported at [1983] 2 F.C. 656, [1983] 2 W.W.R. 686, 13 E.T R. 245, 143 D.L.R. (3d) 416, [1983] 1 C.N.L.R. 20, 45 N.R. 181, reversing [1982] 2 F.C. 385, 10 E.T.R. 1, [1982] 2 C.N.L.R. 83] are fully dealt with in the reasons for judgment of my colleague, Wilson J., and need no repetition by me. I hasten to say at the outset that I respectfully agree with the disposition proposed by each of them. This action, in my respectful view, however, should be disposed of on the very simple basis of the law of agency.

There is no difference between the parties on the factual relationship between them. The only issue is, what is the appropriate juridical basis upon which the remedy and consequential relief should be founded. The nature of the interests of the Indian band, the Federal Crown and the Crown in right of the province has been long ago settled in St. Catherine's Milling & Lbr. Co. v. R. (1888), 14 App. Cas. 46, 4 Cart. 107 (P.C.), and in Ont. Mining Co. v. Seybold, [1903] A.C. 73, affirming 32 S.C.R. 1, which affirmed 32 O.R. 301, which affirmed 31 O.R. 386; all of which was, only in 1982, re-examined and affirmed in the unanimous decision of this court in Can. v. Smith, [1983] 1 S.C.R. 554, 147 D.L.R. (3d) 237 (sub nom. R. v. Smith), [1983] 3 C.N.L.R. 161, 47 N.R. 132. In 1938, prior to the surrender in question, the title to the Indian reservation land in British Columbia was transferred to the Crown in the right of Canada by British Columbia Orders-in-Council 208 and 1036 pursuant to art. 13 of the Terms of Union of 1871 [see R.S.C. 1970, App. II]. Consequently, the primary constitutional issue discussed in the Smith and St. Catherine's Milling cases, supra, do not arise.

The Indian Act, R.S.C. 1952, c. 149 [now R.S.C. 1970, c. I-6], as amended, the Constitution, the pre-Confederation laws of the colonies in British North America, and the Royal Proclamation of 1763 [see R.S.C. 1970, App. II] all reflect a strong sense of awareness of the community interest in protecting the rights of the native population in those lands to which they had a longstanding connection. One common feature in all these enactments is reflected in the present-day provision in the Indian Act, s. 37, which requires anyone interested in acquiring ownership or some lesser interest in lands set aside for native populations, from a willing grantor, to do so through the appropriate level of government, now the federal government. This section has already been set out by my colleagues. In the elaborate provisions in the Indian Act, there are many alternative ways of protecting the interests of the Indians and of reflecting the community interest in that protection. The statute and the cases make provision for a surrender of the Indian interest in Indian lands as defined in the Act. And cases such as St. Catherine's indicate the extent to which the Indian band must go in order to sever entirely the connection of the native population from the lands in question. This type of surrender would be better described as a release, in the modern lexicon.

Unfortunately, the statute employs the word "surrender" in another connotation. In order to deal with what has been found to be the personal interest of the Indian population in Indian lands, the Act requires the band to "surrender" the land to the Crown in the right of Canada in order to effect the proposed alternate use of the land for the benefit of the Indians. The Act, in short, does not require the Indian to limit his interest in Indian lands to present and continuous occupation. The band may vicariously occupy the lands, or part of such lands, through the medium of a lease or licence. The marketing of the personal interest is not only permitted by the statute, but the machinery is provided for the proper exploitation of this interest by the Indians, subject always to compliance with the statute: vide St. Ann's Island Shooting & Fishing Club Ltd. v. R., [1950] S.C.R. 211, [1950] 2 D.L.R. 225. The step to be taken by the Indian band in seeking to avail itself of the benefits of their right of possession in this manner is, unhappily, also referred to in the statute and in the cases as a "surrender" of the lands and their interest therein to the Crown. This is not a release in the sense of that term in the general law. Indeed, it is quite the opposite. It is a retention of interest and the exploitation of that interest in the manner and to the extent permitted by statute law. The Crown becomes the appointed agent of the Indians to develop and exploit, under the direction of the Indians and for their benefit, the usufructuary interest as described in St. Catherine's.

The appellants clearly, and beyond any argument here, did not release their interest in the lands in the St. Catherine's sense but appointed the Crown in the right of Canada to carry out the commercial exploitation of the Indian interest in the manner prescribed in detail in Surrey v. Peace Arch Ent. Ltd. (1970), 74 W.W.R. 380 (B.C.C.A.); R. v. McMaster, [1926] Ex. C.R. 68; and St. Ann's, supra.

On the facts here, there is no issue but that the Indian band had determined to exercise their interest in the land through the medium of a lease to the golf club. There is no serious issue with the findings of fact by the learned trial judge as to the detailed instructions given by the Indians to the representatives of the Government of Canada on the terms of the lease, including the rent, the term, rights of renewal, removal of fixtures, and many other features common to the preparation of a lease. There is no issue but that the government representatives, for whatever reason, did not carry out these instructions. Nor did those officials keep the Indian band apprised of the program of negotiations in the final stages. Most seriously of all, the respondent did not give the instructing Indians a copy of the final lease or a written description of its contents for many years after the lease was executed.

One need turn no further than 1 Hals. (4th) 418, para.701, to determine the application to these clear and relatively straightforward facts of the principles of the law of agency:

> Whether that relation exists in any situation depends not on the precise terminology employed by the parties to describe their relationship, but on the true nature of the agreement or the exact circumstances of the relationship between the alleged principal and agent . . .

The essence of the agent's position is that he is only an intermediary between two other parties.

The fact that the agent is prescribed by statute in no way detracts in law from the legal capacity of the agent to act as such. The further consideration that the principal (the Indian band as holder of the personal interest in the land) is constrained by statute to act through the agency of the Crown, in no way reduces the rights of the instructing principal to call upon the agent to account for the performance of the mandate. The measure of damages applied by the learned trial judge is in no way affected by ascribing the resultant rights in the plaintiff to a breach of agency. Indeed, it is consonant with the purpose of the statutory agency as prescribed by Parliament, now and historically, that the agent (the Crown), in all its actions, shall serve only the interests of the native population whose rights alone are the subject of the protective measures of the statute. If anything, the principal in this relationship is more secure in his rights than in the absence of a statutorily prescribed agency. The principal is restricted in the selection of the agent, but the agent is nowhere protected in the statute from the consequences in law of a breach of that agency.

For these reasons, I would, with great respect to all who hold a contrary view, hesitate to resort to the more technical and far-reaching doctrines of the law of trusts and the concomitant law attaching to the fiduciary. The result is the same but, in my respectful view, the future application of the Act and the common law to native rights is much simpler under the doctrines of the law of agency.

I therefore share with my colleagues the conclusion that this appeal should be allowed with costs.

*　　*　　*

WILSON J. (concurring in the result) (RITCHIE and McINTYRE JJ. concurring): The appellant, Delbert Guerin, is the chief of the Musqueam Indian Band, the members of which are descended from the original inhabitants of Greater Vancouver. The other appellants are band councillors. In 1955 there were 235 members in the band and they lived on a reserve located within the charter area of the city of Vancouver which contained approximately 416.53 acres of very valuable land.

The subject of the litigation is a lease of 162 acres of the reserve land entered into on 22nd January 1958 on behalf of the band by the Indian Affairs Branch of the federal government with the Shaughnessy Heights Golf Club as lessee. The trial judge found that the Crown was in breach of trust in entering into this lease and awarded the band $10 million in damages [reported at [1982] 2 F.C. 385, 10 E.T.R. 61, [1982] 2 C.N.L.R. 83]. The Crown appealed to the Federal Court of Appeal to have the trial judgment set aside and the band cross-appealed seeking an interest in the award of damages. By a unanimous judgment the Crown's appeal was allowed and the cross-appeal dismissed [reported at [1983] 2 F.C. 656, [1983] 2 W.W.R. 686, 13 E.T.R. 245, 143 D.L.R. (3d) 416, [1983] 1 C.N.L.R. 20, 45 N.R. 81]. The band sought and was granted leave to appeal to this court.

There are four main grounds on which the appellants submit that the trial judge's finding of liability should have been upheld in the Court of Appeal. I paraphrase them from the appellants' factum as follows:

1. Section 18(1) of the Indian Act, R.S.C. 1952, c.149 [now R.S.C. 1970, c. I-6], imposes a trust or, at a minimum, fiduciary duties on the Crown with respect to reserve lands held by it for the use and benefit of Indian

bands. This trust or those fiduciary duties are not merely political in nature but are enforceable in the courts like any other trust or fiduciary duty.

2. The Federal Court of Appeal should not have allowed the Crown to put forward the concept of "political trust" as a defence to the band's claim since, as the learned trial judge pointed out, it was not specifically pleaded as required by R.409 of the Federal Court Rules, C.R.C. 1978, c. 663.

3. The lease lands were surrendered by the band to the Crown in trust for lease to the golf club on very specific terms and those terms were not obtained. The terms which were obtained were much less favourable to the band and the band would not have surrendered the land for lease on those terms.

4. The Crown, by misrepresenting the terms it could and would obtain on the lease, induced the band to surrender its land and thereby committed the tort of deceit.

In any case of alleged breach of trust the facts are extremely important and none more so than in this case. We are fortunate, however, in having very careful and extensive findings by the learned trial judge and, although counsel on both sides roamed at large through the transcript for evidence in support of their various propositions, I have considered it desirable to confine myself very closely to the trial judge's findings.

THE FACTS

There can be little doubt that by the mid 1950s the Indian Affairs Branch was well aware that the appellants' reserve was a very valuable one because of its location. Indeed, offers to lease or buy large tracts of the reserve had already been received. We know this from a report dated 11th October 1955 made by Mr. Anfield who was in charge of the Vancouver agency at the time to Mr. Arneil, the Indian Commissioner for British Columbia. Both these men are since deceased, which is unfortunate since Mr. Anfield played a lead role in the impugned lease transaction. In a later report to Mr. Arneil, Mr. Anfield suggested that a detailed study should be made of the band's requirements of its reserve lands so that the surplus, if any, could be identified and turned to good account for the band's benefit. He suggested that not only should they obtain an appraisal of land values but that a land use planning survey should be prepared aimed at maximum development in order to provide long-term revenue for the band. He continued:

> It seems to me that the real requirement here is the service of an expert estate planner with courage and vision and whose interest and concern would be as much the future of the Musqueam Indians as the revenue use of the lands unrequired by these Indians. It is essential that any new village be a model community. The present or any Agency staff set up could not possibly manage a project like this, and some very realistic and immediate plans must be formulated to bring about the stated wish of these Musqueam people, the fullest possible use and development for their benefit, of what is undoubtedly the most potentially valuable 400 acres in Metropolitan Vancouver today.

Mr. Anfield went on to speak in terms of "another potential British Properties" and suggested that all parties interested in the land should be advised that the land not required by the band for its own uses, when defined and surrendered, would be publicly advertised.

About this time the Shaughnessy Heights Golf Club was looking for a new site. Its lease from the Canadian Pacific Railway was due to expire in 1960 and the club had been told that it would not be renewed. The club turned its attention therefore to the Musqueam Reserve. At the same time an active interest in the reserve was being displayed by a representative of a prominent Vancouver real estate firm on behalf of a developer client interested in a long-term lease. Although his contact had been directly with the Indian Affairs Branch in Ottawa, Messrs. Arneil and Anfield were both aware of it. Indeed, when he suggested to them that he meet with the chief and councillors of the band to try to work out some arrangement, he was told by Mr. Anfield not to do so but to deal only through Indian Affairs personnel. That he followed this advice is made clear from the evidence of the band members who testified. They were told of no interest in their land other than that expressed by the golf club.

The learned trial judge dealt specifically with the issue of the credibility of the members of the band because he was very conscious of the fact that neither Mr. Arneil nor Mr. Anfield was alive to testify. He found the band members to be "honest, truthful witnesses" and accepted their testimony.

The band agreed that its surplus land should be leased and authorized a land appraisal to be made and paid for out of band funds. In fact the appraisal was done by Mr. Howell of the Veterans Land Act Administration. Although he was a qualified appraiser, he was not a land use expert. He divided the reserve for valuation purposes into four areas, the first of which included the 162 acres leased to the golf club. This area comprised 220 acres classified by Mr. Howell as "first-class residential area" and valued at $5,500 per acre making a total of $1,209,120. The other three areas which were all low-lying he valued at $625 per acre. The band was not given a copy of his report and indeed Mr. Arneil and Mr. Anfield had difficulty getting copies. They were very anxious to get the report because they were considering a lease of 150 acres to the golf club at "a figure of say $20,000 to $25,000 a year". The documentary evidence at trial showed that meetings and discussions had taken place between Mr. Anfield and the president of the golf club in 1956 and in the early part of 1957. It is of interest to note that Mr. Anfield had told the president of the golf club about the appraisal which was being carried out and had subsequently reviewed Mr. Howell's report with them. The golf club was, of course, advised that any proposal made by it would have to be laid before the band for its approval.

On 7th April 1957 the band council met, Mr. Anfield presiding. The trial judge found that the golf club proposal was put to the chief and councillors only in the most general terms. They were told the lease would be of approximately 160 acres, that it would be for an initial term of 15 years with options to the club for additional 15-year periods and that it would be "on terms to be agreed upon". In fact, the rent that had been proposed by the club was $25,000 a year for the first 15 years with the rent for each successive 15-year period being settled by mutual agreement or failing that by arbitration. However, under the proposal the rent for the renewal periods was subject to a ceiling increase of 15 per cent of the initial rent of $25,000.

The learned trial judge found that when Mr. Bethune, the Superintendent of Reserves and Trusts in Ottawa, was advised of the $25,000 rental figure he questioned its adequacy and suggested to Mr. Arneil that he consult with Mr. Howell, the appraiser, as to what a proper return on the 160 acres would be. Unfortunately, Mr. Howell was not given all the facts. He was not told of the 15 per cent ceiling on rent increases. He was not told that the golf club would have the right to remove all improvements on termination of the lease, although he was told that the club proposed to spend up to $1,000,000 in buildings and improvements on the leased land. Mr. Howell therefore recommended acceptance of the golf club's offer, stating: "These improvements will revert to the Band at the end of the lease" and "The Department will be in a much sounder position to negotiate an increase in rental in fifteen years time when the Club will have invested a considerable amount of capital in the property, which they will have to protect". Mr. Howell testified at trial that he would not have recommended acceptance of the golf club's offer had he known that the improvements would not revert to the band and that the rental on renewal periods was subject to a 15 per cent ceiling increase. Mr. Howell's letter was forwarded to Ottawa with the request that surrender documents be prepared for submission to the band and this was done. It is interesting to note, however, that in the letter forwarding the surrender documents Mr. Bethune indicated to Mr. Arneil that he would like to see the 15 per cent ceiling on rent removed and rent for subsequent periods established either by mutual agreement or by arbitration.

A band council meeting was held on 25th July 1957, again with Mr. Anfield in the chair. There was further discussion of the proposed lease to the golf club and two councillors expressed the view that the renewal period should be at 10-year intervals rather than 15. It was at this meeting that the resolution was passed to hold a general meeting of band members to consider and vote on the surrender of the 162 acres to the Crown for purposes of the lease. The meeting of the band was held 6th October 1957 but prior to that there was another meeting of councillors on 27th September 1957. Mr. Harrison and Mr. Jackson of the Shaughnessy Golf Club attended this meeting and Mr. Anfield, who had in the interval been promoted to Assistant Indian Commissioner for British Columbia, was there along with a Mr. Grant who was described as "Officer in charge—Vancouver Agency". In the presence of the golf club representatives Chief Sparrow took issue with the $25,000 per annum rental figure and stipulated for something in the neighbourhood of $44,000 to $44,500 per annum. The golf club representatives balked at this and they were asked to step outside while the band council and the Indian Affairs personnel had a private discussion.

Mr. Anfield expressed the view that the $44,000 figure was unreasonable and suggested $29,000 to which the councillors agreed on the understanding that the first lease period would be for 10 years and subsequent rental negotiations would take place every five years. Mr. Grant testified that Mr. Anfield advised the council to go ahead with the lease at the $29,000 figure and in ten years demand a healthy increase from the golf club. Mr. Grant also testified that the council objected to any ceiling on future rental and Mr. Anfield said that he would convey their concern to the Department of Indian Affairs. On that basis the council, according to Mr. Grant, reluctantly accepted the $29,000 figure.

At the meeting of the band on 6th October 1957 ("the surrender meeting") Chief Sparrow was present along with the councillors and members. Mr. Anfield presided as usual. The learned trial judge made specific findings as to what transpired at the meeting and I reproduce them from his reasons [pp. 405-407 F.C., pp. 98-9 C.N.L.R.]:

> (a) Before the Band members voted, those present assumed or understood the golf club lease would be, aside from the first term, for 10-year periods, not 15 years.
> (b) Before the Band members voted, those present assumed or understood there would be no 15% limitation on rental increases.
> (c) The meeting was not told the golf club proposed it should have the right, at any time during the lease and for a period of up to six months after termination, to remove any buildings or structures, and any course improvements and facilities.
> (d) The meeting was not told that future rent on renewal periods was to be determined as if the land were still in an uncleared and unimproved condition and used as a golf club.
> (e) The meeting was not told that the golf club would have the right at the end of each 15-year period to terminate the lease on six-month's prior notice.
> [(d) and (e) paraphrased from the trial judge's reasons at p. 407 F.C., p. 99 C.N.L.R.]

Neither (d) nor (e) were in the original golf club proposal and first appeared in the draft lease following the surrender meeting. They were not brought before the band council or the band at any time for comment or approval. The band voted almost unanimously in favour of the surrender.

By the surrender document the chief and councillors of the band acting on behalf of the band surrendered 162 acres to the Crown:

> [see above, p. 155]

It will be noted that there is no reference in the surrender to the proposed lease to the golf club. The position of the Crown at trial was that once the surrender documents were signed the Crown could lease to anyone on whatever terms it saw fit.

After the surrender there was considerable correspondence between Mr. Anfield and personnel in the Indian Affairs Branch in Ottawa, particularly over the more controversial provisions of the lease, but none of this correspondence was communicated to the band council nor were they given a copy of the draft lease which would have drawn these controversial provisions to their attention. The trial judge states [p. 409 F.C., p. 101 C.N.L.R.]:

> Put baldly, the band members, regardless of the whole history of dealings and the limited information imparted at the surrender meeting, were not consulted.

But it was their land. It was their potential investment and revenue. It was their future.

The learned trial judge accepted that the chief, the councillors and the band members were wholly excluded from any further discussions or negotiations among the Indian Affairs personnel, the golf club officers and their respective solicitors with respect to the terms of the lease. The trial judge found an explanation, although not a justification, for this in the possibility that Indian Affairs personnel at the time took a rather paternalistic attitude towards the Indian people whom they regarded as wards of the Crown.

I turn now to the essential terms of the lease as entered into on 22nd January 1958 as described by the learned trial judge [p. 412 F.C., p. 104 C.N.L.R.]:

[see above, pp. 155-6]

Mr. Grant stated in evidence that the terms of the lease ultimately entered into bore little resemblance to what was discussed and approved at the surrender meeting and the learned trial judge agreed. He found that had the band been aware of the terms in fact contained in the lease they would never have surrendered their land.

So much for the facts as found by the learned trial judge. What recourse in law, if any does the band have in such circumstances?

2. SECTION 18 [am. 1956, c. 40, s. 8] OF THE INDIAN ACT

The appellants contend that the Federal Court of Appeal erred in failing to find that s. 18 of the Indian Act imposed on the Crown a fiduciary obligation enforceable in the courts. The section reads as follows:

18.(1) Subject to the provisions of this Act, reserves shall be held by Her Majesty for the use and benefit of the respective bands for which they were set apart; and subject to this Act and to the terms of any treaty or surrender, the Governor in Council may determine whether any purpose for which lands in a reserve are used or are to be used is for the use and benefit of the band.

Le Dain J., after concluding on the authorities that there was nothing in principle to prevent the Crown from having the status of a trustee in equity, found that s. 18 nevertheless did not have that effect. It merely imposed on the Crown a governmental obligation of an administrative nature. It was a public law obligation rather than a private law obligation. Section 18 could not therefore afford a basis for an action for breach of trust.

While I am in agreement that s. 18 does not per se create a fiduciary obligation in the Crown with respect to Indian reserves, I believe that it recognizes the existence of such an obligation. The obligation has its roots in the aboriginal title of Canada's Indians as discussed in Calder v. A.G.B.C., [1973] S.C.R. 313, [1973] 4 W.W.R. 1, 34 D.L.R. (3d) 145. In that case the court did not find it necessary to define the precise nature of Indian title because the issue was whether or not it had been extinguished. However, in St. Catherine's Milling & Lbr. Co. v. R. (1888), 14 App. Cas. 46, 4 Cart. 107, Lord Watson, speaking for the Privy Council, had stated at p. 54 that "the tenure of the Indians [is] a personal and usufructuary right". That description of the Indians' interest in reserve lands was approved by this court most recently in Can. v. Smith, [1983] 1 S.C.R. 554, 147 D.L.R. (3d) 237 (sub nom. R. v. Smith), [1983] 3 C.N.L.R. 161, 47 N.R. 132. It should be noted that no constitutional issue such as arose in the St. Catherine's and Smith cases arises in this case, since title to Indian reserve land in British Columbia was transferred to the Crown in right of Canada in 1938: see British Columbia Orders-in-Council 208 and 1036 passed pursuant to art. 13 of the Terms of Union of 1871 [see R.S.C. 1970, App.II].

I think that when s. 18 mandates that reserves be held by the Crown for the use and benefit of the bands for which they are set apart, this is more than just an administrative direction to the Crown. I think it is the acknowledgement of a historic reality, namely that Indian bands have a beneficial interest in their reserves and that the Crown has a responsibility to protect that interest and make sure that any purpose to which reserve land is put will not interfere with it. This is not to say that the Crown either historically or by s. 18 holds the land in trust for the bands. The bands do not have the fee in the lands; their interest is a limited one. But it is an interest which cannot be derogated from or interfered with by the Crown's utilization of the land for purposes incompatible with the Indian title unless, of course, the Indians agree. I believe that in this sense the Crown has a fiduciary obligation to the Indian bands with respect to the uses to which reserve land may be put and that s. 18 is a statutory acknowledgement of that obligation. It is my view, therefore, that while the Crown does not hold reserve land under s. 18 of the Act in trust for the bands because the bands' interests are limited by the nature of Indian title, it does hold the lands subject to a fiduciary obligation to protect and preserve the bands' interests from invasion or destruction.

The respondent submits, however, that any obligation imposed on the Crown by s. 18(1) of the Indian Act is political only and unenforceable in courts of equity. Section 18, he says, gives rise to a "trust in the higher sense" as discussed in Kinloch v. Secretary of State for India in Council (1882), 7 App. Cas. 619 (H.L.), and Tito v. Waddell; Tito v. A.G., [1977] Ch. 106, [1977] 2 W.L.R. 496, [1977] 3 All E.R. 129. Le Dain J., delivering the judgment of the Federal Court of Appeal, adopted this approach. He expressed the view [at p. 747 W.W.R., p. 74 C.N.L.R.] that these cases indicate that "in a public law context neither the use of the words 'in trust' nor the fact that the property is to be held or dealt with in some manner for the benefit of others is conclusive of an intention to create a true trust." He found that the discretion conferred on the Crown by s. 18(1) evidenced an intention to exclude the equitable jurisdiction of the courts.

With respect, while I agree with the learned justice that s. 18 does not go so far as to create a trust of reserve lands for the reasons I have given, it does not in my opinion exclude the equitable jurisdiction of the courts. The discretion conferred on the Governor in Council is not an unfettered one to decide the use to which reserve lands may be put. It is to decide whether any use to which they are proposed to be put is "for the use and benefit of the band". This discretionary power must be exercised on proper principles and not in an arbitrary fashion. It is not, in my opinion, open to the Governor in Council to determine that a use of the land which defeats Indian title and affords the band nothing in return is a "purpose" which could be "for the use and benefit of the band". To so interpret the concluding part of s. 18 is to deprive the opening part of any substance.

Moreover, I do not think we are dealing with a purely public law context here. Le Dain J. agrees that a band has a beneficial interest in its reserve. I believe it is clear from s. 18 that that interest is to be respected and this is enough to make the so-called "political trust" cases inapplicable.

In Kinloch, supra, in which Lord Selborne L.C. first advanced the idea of the political trust, the issue was whether a royal warrant that "granted" booty of war to the respondent Secretary of State for India "in trust" for the officers and men of certain forces created a trust enforceable in the courts. It was held that it did not, the effect of the warrant being to constitute the Secretary of State an agent of the Crown for the distribution of the booty rather than a trustee. . . .

It seems to me that the "political trust" line of authorities is clearly distinguishable from the present case because Indian title has an existence apart altogether from s.18(1) of the Indian Act. It would fly in the face of the clear wording of the section to treat that interest as terminable at will by the Crown without recourse by the band.

Continuing with the analysis of s. 18, it seems to me quite clear from the wording of the section that the Governor in Council's authority to determine in good faith whether any purpose to which reserve lands are proposed to be put is for the use and benefit of the band is "subject . . . to the terms of any treaty or surrender". I take this to mean that if a band surrenders its beneficial interest in reserve lands for a specific purpose, then the Governor in Council's authority under the section to decide whether or not the purpose is for the use and benefit of the band is pre-empted. The band had itself agreed to the purpose and the Crown may rely upon that agreement. It will be necessary to consider this in greater detail in connection with the surrender which in fact took place in this case.

3. THE FAILURE TO PLEAD THE DEFENCE OF "POLITICAL TRUST"

The second ground of appeal put forward by the appellants concerns the fact that the defence of "political trust" which was accepted by the Federal Court of Appeal and formed the basis of its decision was not specifically pleaded as required by R. 409 of the Federal Court Rules.

I need say very little about this ground since I think the case falls to be decided on the substantive rather than the procedural issues. However, I agree with the appellants' submission that the Crown's tactics in this regard left a lot to be desired. It is quite apparent that when the trial judge indicated a willingness to permit an amendment at trial but went on to order discovery on the issue, the Crown renounced the defence both at trial and through ministerial statements made out of court. It nevertheless went ahead and sought and obtained leave to raise it in the Federal Court of Appeal. Even although, as the Court of Appeal pointed out, the defence is a strictly legal one and the band was probably not prejudiced by the absence of discovery, the Crown's behaviour does not, in my view, exemplify the high standard of professionalism we have come to expect in the conduct of litigation.

4. THE SURRENDER

Reference has already been made to the language of s. 18 and in particular to the fact that the Crown's fiduciary duty under it is "subject . . . to the terms of any . . . surrender". The implications of this have to be considered in the context of the learned trial judge's finding that the band surrendered the 162 acres to the Crown for lease to the golf club on specific terms which were not obtained. The trial judge found that the surrender itself created a trust relationship between the Crown and the band. The subject of the trust, the trust res, was not the band's beneficial interest in the land but the land itself. The Crown prior to the surrender had title to the land subject to the Indian title. When the band surrendered the land to the Crown, the band's interest merged in the fee. The Crown then held the land free of the Indian title but subject to the trust for lease to the golf club on the terms approved by the band at its meeting on 6th October 1957. This trust was breached by the Crown when it leased the land to the club on terms much less favourable to the band.

It was submitted on behalf of the Crown that even if the surrender gave rise to a trust between the Crown and the band, the terms of the trust must be found in the surrender document and it was silent both as to the lessee and the terms of the lease. Indeed, it expressly gave the government complete discretion both as to the lessee and the terms of the lease and contained a ratification by the band of any lease the government might enter into.

I cannot accept the Crown's submission. The Crown was well aware that the terms of the lease were important to the band. Indeed, we have the trial judge's finding that the band would not have surrendered the land for the purpose of a lease on the terms obtained by the Crown. It ill becomes the Crown, therefore, to obtain a surrender of the band's interest for lease on terms voted on and approved by the band members at a meeting specially called for the purpose and then assert an overriding discretion to ignore those terms at will: see Robertson v. Min. of Pensions, [1949] 1 K.B. 227, [1948] 2 All E.R. 767; Lever Fin. Ltd. v. Westminster (City) London Borough Council, [1971] 1 Q.B. 222, [1970] 3 W.L.R. 732, [1970] 3 All E.R. 496 (C.A.). It makes a mockery of the band's participation. The Crown well knew that the lease it made with the golf club was not the lease the band surrendered its interest to get. Equity will not permit the Crown in such circumstances to hide behind the language of its own document.

I return to s. 18. What effect does the surrender of the 162 acres to the Crown in trust for lease on specific terms have on the Crown's fiduciary duty under the section? It seems to me that s.18 presents no barrier to a finding that the Crown became a full-blown trustee by virtue of the surrender. The surrender prevails over the s.18 duty but in this case there is no incompatibility between them. Rather the fiduciary duty which existed at large under the section to hold the land in the reserve for the use and benefit of the band crystallized upon the surrender into an express trust of specific land for a specific purpose.

There is no magic to the creation of a trust. A trust arises, as I understand it, whenever a person is compelled in equity to hold property over which he has control for the benefit of others (the beneficiaries) in such a way that the benefit of the property accrues not to the trustee, but to the beneficiaries. I think that in the circumstances of this case as found by the learned trial judge the Crown was compelled in equity upon the surrender to hold the surrendered land in trust for the purpose of the lease which the band members had approved as being for their benefit. The Crown was no longer free to decide that a lease on some other terms would do. Its hands were tied.

What then should the Crown have done when the golf club refused to enter into a lease on the approved terms? It seems to me that it should have returned to the band and told them. It was certainly not open to it at that point of time to go ahead with the less favourable lease on the basis that the Governor in Council considered it for the benefit of the band. The Governor in Council's discretion in that regard was pre-empted by the surrender. I think the learned trial judge was right in finding that the Crown acted in breach of trust when it barrelled ahead with a lease on terms which, according to the learned trial judge, were wholly unacceptable to its cestui que trust.

5. THE CLAIM IN DECEIT

The appellants base their claim against the Crown in deceit as well as in trust. They were unsuccessful on this aspect of their claim at trial but have raised it again on appeal to this court. While the learned trial judge found that the conduct of the Indian Affairs personnel amounted to equitable fraud, it was not such as to give rise to an action for deceit at common law. He found no dishonesty or moral turpitude on the part of Mr. Anfield, Mr. Arneil and the others. Their failure to go back to the band and indicate that the terms it had approved were unobtainable, their entry into the lease on less favourable terms and their failure to report to the band what those terms were all flowed, he found, from their paternalistic attitude to the band rather than from any intent to deceive them or cause them harm.

Nevertheless, there was a concealment amounting to equitable fraud. It was "conduct which, having regard to some special relationship between the two parties concerned, is an unconscionable thing for the one to do towards the other": Kitchen v. Royal Air Force Assn., [1958] 1 W.L.R. 563 at 573, [1958] 3 All E.R. 241 (C.A.), per Lord Evershed M.R. The effect of the finding of equitable fraud was to disentitle the Crown to relief for breach of trust under s. 98 of the Trustee Act, R.S.B.C. 1960, c. 390 [now R.S.B.C. 1979, c.414]. A trustee cannot be exonerated from liability for breach of trust under that section unless he has acted "honestly and reasonably".

The trial judge's findings on this aspect of the band's claim are, I believe, sufficient to dispose of this ground of appeal.

6. THE MEASURE OF DAMAGES

I come now to one of the most difficult issues on the appeal, namely the principles applicable to determine the measure of damages. No assistance is to be derived on this issue from the Federal Court of Appeal which exonerated the Crown from any liability. I turn therefore to the approach taken by the learned trial judge.

The trial judge stated as general principles that the measure of damages is "the actual loss which the acts or omissions have caused to the trust estate": Fales v. Can. Permanent Trust Co., [1977] 2 S.C.R. 302 at 320, [1976] 6 W.W.R. 10, 70

D.L.R. (3d) 257 (sub nom. Wohlleben v. Can. Permanent Trust Co.), 11 N.R. 487, per Dickson J., and that the beneficiary is "entitled to be placed in the same position so far as is possible as if there had been no breach of trust": T.D. Bank v. Uhren (1960), 32 W.W.R. 61, 24 D.L.R. (2d) 203 (Sask. C.A.), per Gordon J.A. at p. 66 and Culliton J.A. at p. 73. The learned trial judge then considered whether the proper measure of damages might not be the difference in value between a lease on the terms approved by the band and the lease which was in fact obtained from the golf club. He discarded this measure on the basis that the evidence of the witnesses for the golf club satisfied him that the club would never have entered into a lease on the terms approved by the band. It was his conclusion that the difference in the value of the two leases could not be used as the proper measure in face of the evidence of the golf club witnesses that caused the learned trial judge to consider other approaches based on other uses of the land. Was he correct in this? . . .

I cannot find that the learned trial judge committed any error in principle in approaching the damage issue on the basis of a lost opportunity for residential development. It was urged upon us by counsel for the band that the $10,000,000 figure was inordinately low because the learned trial judge took into consideration the contingency that the golf club would decide to exercise its right to terminate the lease which it could do at any time. Counsel for the band submitted that there was no evidence to suggest that the golf club would terminate the lease before the year 2033 and that indeed there was evidence to the contrary. The golf club had only recently expended $750,000 on capital improvements. There was no other land available in Vancouver to which the golf club could move. Even if there was, relocation would require the golf club to spend substantial amounts of money in creating a new golf course quite apart from the cost of acquisition of the land.

Be that as it may, I do not think it is the function of this court to interfere with the quantum of damages awarded by the trial judge if no error in principle in determining the measure of damages has been demonstrated. The trial judge was entitled to treat the termination of the lease by the club as a contingency tending towards diminution of the band's damages and it is not for this court to substitute the value it would have put upon that contingency for his. I would not, therefore, interfere with the quantum. The trial judge's task was not an easy one but I think he "did the best he could": see Penvidic Contracting Co. v. Int. Nickel Co., [1976] 1 S.C.R. 267 at 279-80, 53 D.L.R. (3d) 748, 4 N.R. 1.

7. PUNITIVE DAMAGES, INTEREST AND COSTS

The court advised Crown counsel at the hearing of the appeal that it was not necessary to hear from him on the subject of punitive damages. That claim falls on the same grounds as the claim for damages in deceit.

I would not interfere with the trial judge's refusal to award prejudgment interest. The award was made for breach of trust, not tort. Section 3(1) of the Crown Liability Act, R.S.C. 1970, c.C-38, has therefore no application. Moreover, damages were assessed as of the date of trial and took the form of a global award.

The trial judge committed no error in awarding post-judgment interest at the statutory rate. I would not interfere with the discretion he exercised in relation to costs.

DISPOSITION

For the reasons given, I would allow the appeal, set aside the judgment of the Federal Court of Appeal and reinstate the judgment of the learned trial judge. I would award the appellants their costs both here and in the Federal Court of Appeal.

CHAPTER 7

Sioui

THIS CASE is cited as R. v. Sioui, S.C.C. (1990). The unanimous judgment was delivered on May 24, 1990 and was written by Justice Lamer. Chief Justice Dickson, as well as Lamer, Wilson, La Forest, L'Heureux-Dubé, Sopinka, Gonthier, Cory and McLachlin heard the case. On May 29, 1982 the accused, four members of the Huron Band of the Lorette Indian Reserve in Québec, cut down trees, camped, and made fires in Jacques-Cartier Park, contrary to park rules established in accordance with the provincial Parks Act. The band members were found guilty in the Court of Sessions of the Peace; the conviction was upheld by the Superior Court but overturned in the Court of Appeal. The Crown then appealed to the Supreme Court of Canada.

At issue by the time the case reached the Supreme Court was the question of whether or not a document signed by General Murray in 1760 was a treaty within the meaning of the word in section 88 of the Indian Act. If so, was the treaty still in effect in 1982? Finally, if it was a treaty, was the nature of the treaty such that it made the relevant sections of the park regulations inoperative? In order to answer these questions, the Supreme Court justices had to examine whether or not both the Huron and General Murray had the authority to negotiate a treaty, whether the document itself had the necessary elements of a treaty, and the legal effects and territorial scope of the treaty.

The decision was favourable to the defendants on all counts. Throughout the decision, the approach taken is that "treaties and statutes relating to Indians should be liberally construed and uncertainties resolved in favour of the Indians" (187); the justices adopted a "liberal and generous attitude" both in determining whether a treaty exists and in interpreting the treaty rights promised. Historical context plays a prominent role in the reasons for the decision, which contains extensive discussion of events leading up to the Royal Proclamation of 1763.

There is much in the case of interest to the student of Aboriginal and treaty rights. For example, Justice Lamer notes that "the Indian nations were regarded in their relations with the European nations which occupied North America as independent nations" (198), an argument that implies favouring recognition of an inherent right to Aboriginal self-government. On the question of whether

treaty rights granted in 1760 may have been extinguished by subsequent documents and acts, Lamer notes that "neither the documents nor the legislative
and administrative history to which the appellant referred the court contain any
express statement that the treaty of September 5, 1760, has been extinguished"
(203). Although Lamer expresses no opinion on whether "a treaty can be extinguished implicitly" (203), there is a strong indication that the Supreme Court
is inclined to interpret Justice Hall's argument in Calder that Aboriginal rights
can only be extinguished by a "clear and plain intent" on the Sovereign's part
to do so as meaning an explicit statement to that effect needs to be made.

The primary significance of this case, however, is that it serves to strengthen
the value of treaty rights, writing into Canadian jurisprudence the words "the
treaty must . . . be construed, not according to the technical meaning of its words
by learned lawyers, but in the sense in which they would naturally be understood by the Indians" (188), from a U.S. Supreme Court decision, Jones v.
Meehan (1899). Presumably the oral histories of treaty nations are to be accorded some weight in determining the meaning of treaties. This, combined
with the "liberal and generous attitude" to be adopted in interpreting treaties,
adds up to a significant victory for treaty nations.

R. Decary and R. Morin acted as counsel for the Crown, with J.Larochelle
and G. Dion acting for Sioui. The case has not been edited.

P.K.

The judgment of the Court was delivered by LAMER J.—

I—FACTS AND RELEVANT LEGISLATION

The four respondents were convicted by the Court of Sessions of the Peace of
cutting down trees, camping and making fires in places not designated in Jacques-
Cartier park contrary to ss. 9 and 37 of the Regulation respecting the Parc de la
Jacques-Cartier (Order in Council 3108 - 81 of November 11, 1981, (1981) 113
O.G. I I,3518), adopted pursuant to the Parks Act, R.S.Q., c. P-9. The regulations
state that:

> 9. In the Park, users may not:
> 1. destroy, mutilate, remove or introduce any kind of plant or part thereof.
> However, the collection of edible vegetable products is authorized solely
> for the purpose of consumption as food on the site, except in the preser-
> vation zones where it is forbidden at all times; . . .
> 37. Camping and fires are permitted only in the places designated and
> arranged for those purposes.

The Parks Act, under which the foregoing regulations were adopted, provides
the following penalties for an offence:

> 11. Every person who infringes this act or the regulations is guilty of an
> offence and liable on summary proceedings, in addition to the costs, to a

fine of not less than $50 nor more than $1,000 in the case of an individual and to a fine of not less than $200 nor more than $5,000 in the case of a corporation.

The respondents appealed unsuccessfully to the Superior Court against this judgment by way of trial de novo. However, the Court of Appeal allowed their appeal and acquitted the respondents, Jacques J.A. dissenting.

The respondents are Indians within the meaning of the Indian Act, R.S.C., 1985, c. I-5 (formerly R.S.C. 1970, c. I-6), and are members of the Huron band on the Lorette Indian reserve. They admit that they committed the acts with which they were charged in Jacques-Cartier park, which is located outside the boundaries of the Lorette reserve. However, they alleged that they were practising certain ancestral customs and religious rites which are the subject of a treaty between the Hurons and the British, a treaty which brings s. 88 of the Indian Act into play and exempts them from compliance with the regulations. Section 88 of the Indian Act states that:

> 88. Subject to the terms of any treaty and any other Act of Parliament, all laws of general application from time to time in force in any province are applicable to and in respect of Indians in the province, except to the extent that those laws are inconsistent with this Act or any order, rule, regulation or by-law made thereunder, and except to the extent that those laws make provision for any matter for which provision is made by or under this Act.

The document the respondents rely on in support of their contentions is dated September 5, 1760 and signed by Brigadier General James Murray. It reads as follows:

> THESE are to certify that the CHIEF of the HURON Tribe of Indians, having come to me in the name of His Nation, to submit to His BRITANNICK MAJESTY, and make Peace, has been received under my Protection, with his whole Tribe; and henceforth no English Officer or party is to molest, or interrupt them in returning to their Settlement at LORETTE; and they are received upon the same terms with the Canadians, being allowed the free Exercise of their Religion, their Customs, and Liberty of trading with the English:—recommending it to the Officers commanding the Posts, to treat them kindly.
> Given under my hand at Longueuil, this 5th day of September, 1760.
>
> JA. MURRAY
> By the Genl's Command,
> JOHN COSNAN,
> Adjut. Genl.

The Hurons had been in the Québec area since about 1650, after having had to leave their ancestral lands located in territory which is now in Ontario. In 1760, they were settled at Lorette on land given to them by the Jesuits eighteen years earlier and made regular use of the territory of Jacques-Cartier park at that time.

II—JUDGMENTS

A. Court of Sessions of the Peace

The questions regarding the existence of a treaty, its extinguishment and its scope were not raised before Judge Bilodeau of the Court of Sessions of the Peace: J.E. 83-722. The respondents argued instead that the regulations were adopted without authority, that they were illegal because they were too vague and imprecise and that they had not been infringed, at least as regards the cutting down and mutilation of trees. Judge Bilodeau rejected each of these arguments.

Finally, the respondents contended that as the relevant provincial legislation was not of general application, s. 88 of the Indian Act made them immune to prosecution under this legislation. Judge Bilodeau concluded that the provincial legislation was general in scope and so found the respondents guilty of the offences with which they were charged.

B. Superior Court

The issue which is the subject of the appeal to this Court was considered by Desjardins J.: J.E. 85-947. He rejected the respondents' argument that the document of September 5 was a treaty, on the ground that Murray had neither the powers nor the intention to enter into a treaty giving territorial rights to the Hurons. He concluded that it was actually a certificate of protection or a safe conduct, and based his conclusion on the fact that neither the Huron nation nor the Sovereign ever regarded the document of September 5 as a treaty.

In the Superior Court the respondents also made the following argument, which was then abandoned in the subsequent appeals: an ancestral right to hunt and fish for their sustenance and that of their families was enjoyed by the Hurons over the territory in question and necessarily implied the right to move about and set up their tents. Desjardins J. considered that such a right had not been proven and that, even if it had been, the provincial legislation would nonetheless have regulated its exercise.

C. Court of Appeal

In the Québec Court of Appeal, [1987] R.J.Q. 1722, the respondents abandoned all arguments based on ancestral rights, rights that might result from the Royal Proclamation of October 7, 1763 or s. 35 of the Constitution Act, 1982.

Bisson J.A., as he then was, whose opinion was concurred in by Paré J.A., saw the document of September 5 as a treaty by which the Hurons surrendered to the British and made peace in exchange for British protection and the free exercise of their religion, customs and trade with the English. The presence of this specific mention of free exercise of religion, customs and liberty of trading with the English is, in the view of the majority, the decisive factor making the document at issue a treaty. Bisson J.A. further concluded that the Act of Capitulation of Montréal had not extinguished the treaty. On the question of whether the customary activities or religious rites practised by the Hurons in Jacques-Cartier park were protected by the treaty, Bisson J.A. considered that all the evidence tended to show that the Hurons moved freely in the area in 1760 and carried on religious and customary activities there. Accordingly it followed, he said, that s. 88 of the Indian Act made the respondents immune from any prosecution for the activities with which they were charged, since the latter were the subject of a treaty whose rights could not be limited by provincial legislation.

Jacques J.A., dissenting, considered that the respondents' claim was of an essentially territorial nature and that neither the document at issue nor the Royal Proclamation of October 7, 1763 conferred rights of this kind on the native peoples.

III—POINTS AT ISSUE

The appellants are asking this Court to dispose of the appeal solely on the basis of the document of September 5, 1760 and s. 88 of the Indian Act. The following constitutional questions were stated by the Chief Justice:

> 1. Does the following document, signed by General Murray on 5 September 1760, constitute a treaty within the meaning of s. 88 of the Indian Act (R.S.C. 1970, c. I-6)?

> THESE are to certify that the CHIEF of the HURON Tribe of Indians, having come to me in the name of His Nation, to submit to His BRITANNICK MAJESTY, and make Peace, has been received under my Protection, with his whole Tribe; and henceforth no English Officer or party is to molest, or interrupt them in returning to their Settlement at LORETTE; and they are received upon the same terms with the Canadians, being allowed the free Exercise of their Religion, their Customs, and Liberty of trading with the English:—recommending it to the Officers commanding the Posts, to treat them kindly. Given under my hand at Longueuil, this 5th day of September, 1760.

> JA. MURRAY
> By the Genl's Command,
> JOHN COSNAN,
> Adjut. Genl.

> 2. If the answer to question 1 is in the affirmative, was the "treaty" still operative on 29 May 1982, at the time when the alleged offences were committed?
> 3. If the answers to questions 1 and 2 are in the affirmative, are the terms of the document of such a nature as to make ss. 9 and 37 of the Regulation respecting the Parc de la Jacques-Cartier (Order in Council 3108-81, Gazette officielle du Québec, Part II, November 25, 1981, pp. 3518 et seq.) made under the Parks Act (R.S.Q., c. P-9) unenforceable in respect of the respondents?

To decide the case at bar I will consider first the question of whether Great Britain, General Murray and the Hurons had capacity to sign a treaty, assuming that those parties intended to do so. If they had, I will then consider whether the parties actually did enter into a treaty. Finally, if the document of September 5, 1760 is a treaty, I will analyse its contents to determine the nature of the rights guaranteed therein and establish whether they have territorial application.

IV—ANALYSIS

A. Introduction

Our courts and those of our neighbours to the south have already considered what distinguishes a treaty with the Indians from other agreements affecting them. The task is not an easy one. In Simon v. The Queen, [1985] 2 S.C.R. 387, this Court adopted the comment of Norris J.A. in R. v. White and Bob (1964), 50 D.L.R. (2d) 613 (B.C.C.A.) (affirmed in the Supreme Court (1965), 52 D.L.R. (2d) 481), that the courts should show flexibility in determining the legal nature of a document recording a transaction with the Indians. In particular, they must take into account the historical context and perception each party might have as to the nature of the undertaking contained in the document under consideration. To the question of whether the document at issue in White and Bob was a treaty within the meaning of the Indian Act, Norris J.A. replied (at pp. 648-49):

> The question is, in my respectful opinion, to be resolved not by the application of rigid rules of construction without regard to the circumstances existing when the document was completed nor by the tests of modern day draftsmanship. In determining what the intention of Parliament was at the time of the enactment of s. 87 [now s. 88] of the Indian Act, Parliament is to be taken to have had in mind the common understanding of the parties to the document at the time it was executed.

As the Chief Justice said in Simon, supra, treaties and statutes relating to Indians should be liberally construed and uncertainties resolved in favour of the Indians (at 410). In our quest for the legal nature of the document of September 5, 1760, therefore, we should adopt a broad and generous interpretation of what constitutes a treaty.

In my opinion, this liberal and generous attitude, heedful of historical fact, should also guide us in examining the preliminary question of the capacity to sign a treaty, as illustrated by Simon and White and Bob.

Finally, once a valid treaty is found to exist, that treaty must in turn be given a just, broad and liberal construction. This principle, for which there is ample precedent, was recently reaffirmed in Simon. The factors underlying this rule were eloquently stated in Jones v. Meehan, 175 U.S. 1 (1899), a judgment of the United States Supreme Court, and are I think just as relevant to questions involving the existence of a treaty and the capacity of the parties as they are to the interpretation of a treaty (at pp. 10-11):

> In construing any treaty between the United States and an Indian tribe, it must always . . . be borne in mind that the negotiations for the treaty are conducted, on the part of the United States, an enlightened and powerful nation, by representatives skilled in diplomacy, masters of a written language, understanding the modes and forms of creating the various technical estates known to their law, and assisted by an interpreter employed by themselves; that the treaty is drawn up by them and in their own language; that the Indians, on the other hand, are a weak and dependent people, who have no written language and are wholly unfamiliar with all the forms of legal expression, and whose only knowledge of the terms in which the

treaty is framed is that imparted to them by the interpreter employed by the United States; and that the treaty must therefore be construed, not according to the technical meaning of its words to learned lawyers, but in the sense in which they would naturally be understood by the Indians.

The Indian people are today much better versed in the art of negotiation with public authorities than they were when the United States Supreme Court handed down its decision in Jones. As the document in question was signed over a hundred years before that decision, these considerations argue all the more strongly for the courts to adopt a generous and liberal approach.

B. Question of capacity of parties involved

Before deciding whether the intention in the document of September 5, 1760 was to enter into a treaty within the meaning of s. 88 of the Indian Act, this Court must decide preliminary matters regarding the capacity of Great Britain, General Murray and the Huron nation to enter into a treaty. If any one of these parties was without such capacity, the document at issue could not be a valid treaty and it would then be pointless to consider it further.

As to General Murray's capacity, the appellant argued that Bisson J.A. erred in suggesting that he had admitted Murray's capacity to enter into a treaty. He said he only admitted that the signature on the document was that of Murray and that the document was a safe conduct. As I consider that Murray had the capacity to enter into a treaty, the question of whether or not an admission was made in this regard is of no importance.

I will first examine the capacity of Great Britain to enter into a treaty and then consider that of Murray and the Hurons.

1. CAPACITY OF GREAT BRITAIN

At this preliminary stage of the analysis, and for purposes of discussion, it has to be assumed that the document of September 5, 1760 possesses the characteristics of a treaty and that the only issue that arises concerns the capacity of the parties to create obligations of the kind contained in a treaty.

The appellant argued that the British Crown could not validly enter into a treaty with the Hurons as it was not sovereign in Canada in 1760. The appellant based this argument on the rules of international law, as stated by certain eighteenth and nineteenth century writers, which required that a state should be sovereign in a territory before it could alienate that territory. (See E. de Vattel, *The Law of Nations or Principles of the Law of Nature* (1760), vol. II, book III, para. 197; E. Ortolan, *Des moyens d'acquérir le domaine international ou propriété d'État entre les nations* (1851), para. 167.)

Without deciding what the international law on this point was, I note that the writers to whom the appellant referred the Court studied the rules governing international relations and did not comment on the rules which at that time governed the conclusion of treaties between European nations and native peoples. In any case, the rules of international law do not preclude the document being characterized as a treaty within the meaning of s. 88 of the Indian Act. At the time with which we are concerned relations with Indian tribes fell somewhere between the kind of relations conducted between sovereign states and the relations that such states had with their own citizens. The Simon decision, supra, is clear in this regard:

> an Indian treaty is an agreement sui generis which is neither created nor terminated according to the rules of international law (see p. 404).

Of course, if the document is a treaty, it could not have been binding on France if Canada had remained under its sovereignty at the end of the war. It would be fair to assume that the Hurons knew enough about warfare to understand that a treaty concluded with the enemy would be of little use to them if the French regained de facto control of New France.

Both Simon and White and Bob make it clear that the question of capacity must be seen from the point of view of the Indians at that time, and the Court must ask whether it was reasonable for them to have assumed that the other party they were dealing with had the authority to enter into a valid treaty with them. I conclude without any hesitation that the Hurons could reasonably have believed that the British Crown had the power to enter into a treaty with them that would be in effect as long as the British controlled Canada. France had not hesitated to enter into treaties of alliance with the Hurons and no one ever seemed to have questioned France's capacity to conclude such agreements. From the Hurons' point of view, there was no difference between these two European states. They were both foreigners to the Hurons and their presence in Canada had only one purpose, that of controlling the territory by force.

2. GENERAL MURRAY'S CAPACITY

The appellant disputes Murray's capacity to sign a treaty on behalf of Great Britain on the ground that he was at that time only Governor of the city and district of Québec and a brigadier general in the British Army. As Governor, he was subject to the authority of His Majesty's Secretary of State for the Southern Department, and as a soldier he was the subordinate of General Amherst, the "Commander in Chief of His Britannic Majesty's Troops and Forces in North America". It is true that Murray's capacity to enter into this treaty is less obvious than that of Great Britain to "treat" with the Indians.

In Simon Dickson C.J. cited with approval, at p. 400, N.A.M. MacKenzie in "Indians and Treaties in Law" (1929), 7 Can. Bar Rev. 561, on the question of a person's powers to enter into a treaty with the Indians:

> As to the capacity of the Indians to contract and the authority of Governor Hopson to enter into such an agreement, with all deference to His Honour, both seem to have been present. Innumerable treaties and agreements of a similar character were made by Great Britain, France, the United States of America and Canada with the Indian tribes inhabiting this continent, and these treaties and agreements have been and still are held to be binding. Nor would Governor Hopson require special "powers" to enter into such an agreement. Ordinarily "full powers" specially conferred are essential to the proper negotiating of a treaty, but the Indians were not on a par with a sovereign state and fewer formalities were required in their case. Governor Hopson was the representative of His Majesty and as such had sufficient authority to make an agreement with the Indian tribes.

The Chief Justice went on as follows, at p. 401:

> The Treaty was entered into for the benefit of both the British Crown and the Micmac people, to maintain peace and order as well as to recognize and confirm the existing hunting and fishing rights of the Micmac. In my opinion, both the Governor and the Micmac entered into the Treaty with the intention of creating mutually binding obligations which would be solemnly respected. It also provided a mechanism for dispute resolution. The Micmac Chief and the three other Micmac signatories, as delegates of the Micmac people, would have possessed full capacity to enter into a binding treaty on behalf of the Micmac. Governor Hopson was the delegate and legal representative of His Majesty the King. It is fair to assume that the Micmac would have believed that Governor Hopson, acting on behalf of His Majesty the King, had the necessary authority to enter into a valid treaty with them. I would hold that the Treaty of 1752 was validly created by competent parties.

To arrive at the conclusion that a person had the capacity to enter into a treaty with the Indians, he or she must thus have represented the British Crown in very important, authoritative functions. It is then necessary to take the Indians' point of view and to ask whether it was reasonable for them to believe, in light of the circumstances and the position occupied by the party they were dealing with directly, that they had before them a person capable of binding the British Crown by treaty. To determine whether the Hurons' perception of Murray's capacity to sign a treaty on behalf of Great Britain was reasonable, the importance of the part played by the latter in Canada in 1760 has to be established.

Although during the siege of Québec James Murray was the fourth ranking officer in the British military hierarchy in Canada, after the death of Wolfe and the departure of Townshend and Monckton he became the highest ranking officer in the British Army stationed in Canada. General Amherst was the highest military authority in North America and his authority covered all British soldiers in Canada. Murray received the command of the troops at Québec from him. A very important fact is that since 1759 Murray had also acted as military governor of the Québec district, which included Lorette. He had used his powers to regulate, inter alia, the currency exchange rate and the prices of grain, bread and meat and to create civil courts and appoint judges (Governor Murray's *Journal of the Siege of Québec* (1939), pp. 10, 11, 12, 14, 16 and 17).

At the time the document under consideration was signed, General Amherst and his troops were occupied in crossing the rapids upstream of Montréal and it was not until some days later, probably on September 8, 1760, that they reached that city (see in this regard the work of F. X. Garneau, *Histoire du Canada français* (1969), vol. 3, at pp. 269-72). In my view, therefore, the respondents are correct in stating that on September 5, 1760 Murray was the highest ranking British officer with whom the Hurons could have conferred. The circumstances prevailing at the time, in my view, thus support the respondents' proposition that Murray in fact had the necessary capacity to enter into a treaty. Furthermore, if there is still any doubt, I think it is clear in any event that Murray had such authority in New France that it was reasonable for the Hurons to believe that he had the power to enter into a treaty with them.

It is useful at this point to note a passage from the decision of the British Columbia Court of Appeal in White and Bob, cited with approval by this Court in Simon (at p. 649):

> In the section [88] "Treaty" is not a word of art and in my respectful opinion, it embraces all such engagements made by persons in authority as may be brought within the term "the word of the white man" the sanctity of which was, at the time of British exploration and settlement, the most important means of obtaining the goodwill and co-operation of the native tribes and ensuring that the colonists would be protected from death and destruction. On such assurance the Indians relied.

Murray was one of those persons who could reasonably have been assumed to be capable of giving the word of the white man. Finally, I would even go so far as to say that Murray, as Governor of the Québec district, might reasonably have been regarded by the Hurons living in that district as the person most competent to sign a treaty with them. The fact that they belonged to the territory which was Murray's responsibility and in which he represented His Majesty, in my opinion, entitled them to assume he had the capacity to enter into a valid treaty with them.

In short, even apart from my conclusion with respect to Murray's actual authority to sign a treaty, I am of the view that the Hurons could reasonably have assumed that, as a general, Murray was giving them a safe conduct to return to Lorette, and that as Governor of the Québec district, he was signing a treaty guaranteeing the Hurons the free exercise of their religion, customs and trade with the English. In either case no problems concerning Murray's capacity would invalidate the treaty, if there was one.

For all these reasons, therefore, I conclude that Murray had the necessary powers to enter into a treaty with the Hurons that would be binding on the British.

3. CAPACITY OF THE HURONS

The appellant argues that the Hurons could not enter into a treaty with the British Crown because this Indian nation had no historical occupation or possession of the territory extending from the St-Maurice to the Saguenay. Without going so far as to suggest that there cannot be treaties other than agreements under which the Indians cede land to the Crown, the appellant argues that a treaty could not confer rights on the Indians unless the latter could claim historical occupation or possession of the lands in question. The appellant deduces this requirement from the fact that most of the cases involving treaties between the British and the Indians concern territories which had traditionally been occupied or held at the time in question by the Indian nation which signed the treaty. The academic commentary cited by the appellant also deals with the aspect of historical occupation or possession of land found in treaties with Indians.

There is no basis either in precedent or in the ordinary meaning of the word "treaty" for imposing such a restriction on what can constitute a treaty within the meaning of s. 88 of the Indian Act. In Simon (at p. 410) this Court in fact rejected the argument that s. 88 applied only to land cession treaties. In the Court's opinion that would limit severely the scope of the word "treaty" and run contrary to the principle that Indians treaties should be liberally construed and uncertainties resolved in favour of the Indians. The argument made here must be rejected in the same way. There is no reason why an agreement concerning something other than a territory, such as an agreement about political or social rights, cannot be a treaty within the meaning of s. 88 of the Indian Act. There is also no basis for excluding agreements in which the Crown may have chosen to create, for the benefit of a tribe, rights over territory other than its traditional territory. Accordingly, I consider that a territorial claim is not essential to the existence of a treaty.

I therefore conclude that all the parties involved were competent to enter into a treaty within the meaning of s. 88 of the Indian Act. This leads me to consider the next question: did General Murray and the Hurons in fact enter into such a treaty?

C. Legal nature of the document of September 5, 1760

1. CONSTITUENT ELEMENTS OF A TREATY

In Simon this Court noted that a treaty with the Indians is unique, that it is an agreement sui generis which is neither created nor terminated according to the rules of international law. In that case the accused had relied on an agreement concluded in 1752 between Governor Hopson and the Micmac Chief Cope, and the Crown disputed that this was a treaty. The following are two extracts illustrating the reasons relied on by the Chief Justice in concluding that a treaty had been concluded between the Micmacs and the British Crown (at pp. 401 and 410):

> In my opinion, both the Governor and the Micmac entered into the Treaty with the intention of creating mutually binding obligations which would be solemnly respected. It also provided a mechanism for dispute resolution. . . .
> The Treaty was an exchange of solemn promises between the Micmacs and the King's representative entered into to achieve and guarantee peace. It is an enforceable obligation between the Indians and the white man and, as such, falls within the meaning of the word "treaty" in s. 88 of the Indian Act.

From these extracts it is clear that what characterizes a treaty is the intention to create obligations, the presence of mutually binding obligations and a certain measure of solemnity. In the Court of Appeal Bisson J.A. in fact adopted a similar approach when he wrote (at p. 1726):

> [TRANSLATION] I feel that in order to determine whether document D-7 [the document of September 5, 1760] is a treaty within the meaning of s. 88 of the Indian Act, the fundamental question is as follows: is it an agreement in which the contracting parties . . . intended to create mutual obligations which they intended to observe?

In White and Bob, supra, Norris J.A. also discussed the nature of a treaty under the Indian Act. As he mentioned in the passage I have already quoted, the word "treaty" is not a term of art. It merely identifies agreements in which the "word of the white man" is given and by which the latter made certain of the Indians' co-operation. Norris J.A. also wrote at p. 649:

In view of the argument before us, it is necessary to point out that on numerous occasions in modern days, rights under what were entered into with Indians as solemn engagements, although completed with what would now be considered informality, have been whittled away on the excuse that they do not comply with present day formal requirements and with rules of interpretation applicable to transactions between people who must be taken in the light of advanced civilization to be of equal status. Reliance on instances where this has been done is merely to compound injustice without real justification at law. The transaction in question here was a transaction between, on the one hand, the strong representative of a proprietary company under the Crown and representing the Crown, who had gained the respect of the Indians by his integrity and the strength of his personality and was thus able to bring about the completion of the agreement, and, on the other hand, uneducated savages. The nature of the transaction itself was consistent with the informality of frontier days in this Province and such as the necessities of the occasion and the customs and illiteracy of the Indians demanded . . . The unusual (by the standards of legal draftsmen) nature and form of the document considered in the light of the circumstances on Vancouver Island in 1854 does not detract from it as being a "Treaty".

This lengthy passage brings out the importance of the historical context, including the interpersonal relations of those involved at the time, in trying to determine whether a document falls into the category of a treaty under s. 88 of the Indian Act. It also shows that formalities are of secondary importance in deciding on the nature of a document containing an agreement with the Indians.

The decision of the Ontario Court of Appeal in R. v. Taylor and Williams (1981), 62 C.C.C. (2d) 227, also provides valuable assistance by listing a series of factors which are relevant to analysis of the historical background. In that case the Court had to interpret a treaty, and not determine the legal nature of a document, but the factors mentioned may be just as useful in determining the existence of a treaty as in interpreting it. In particular, they assist in determining the intent of the parties to enter into a treaty. Among these factors are:

1. continuous exercise of a right in the past and at present,
2. the reasons why the Crown made a commitment,
3. the situation prevailing at the time the document was signed,
4. evidence of relations of mutual respect and esteem between the negotiators, and
5. the subsequent conduct of the parties.

2. ANALYSIS OF THE DOCUMENT IN LIGHT OF THESE FACTORS

(a) Wording
Bisson J.A. of the Court of Appeal felt that the document of September 5, 1760 was a treaty because there was no need to include a reference to religion and customs in a mere safe conduct. In view of the presence of protection for certain "fundamental" rights, the document of September 5, 1760 was thus a treaty within the meaning of s. 88 of the Indian Act.

Several aspects of the wording of the document are consistent with the appellant's position that it was an act of surrender and a safe conduct rather than a treaty. The following is a brief review of the appellant's five main arguments in this regard. First, the document opens with the words "These are to certify that . . .", which would suggest that the document in question is a certificate or an acknowledgement of the Hurons' surrender, made official by Murray in order to inform the British troops. Bisson J.A. gave these introductory words an interpretation more favourable to the Hurons: the Hurons did not know how to write and the choice of words only makes it clear that the document of September 5, 1760 recorded an oral treaty.

Second, General Murray used expressions which appear to involve him only personally, which do not suggest that he was acting as a representative of the British Crown. Thus, the following expressions are used:

1. "having come to me",
2. "has been received under my Protection",
3. "By the General's Command"

Although the Hurons had surrendered to His Britannic Majesty, wording the document in this way could tend to show that Murray intended only to give his personal undertaking to protect the Hurons, without thereby binding the British Crown in the long term. Murray, it is argued, had only offered the Hurons military protection and had no intention of entering into a treaty.

Thirdly, the orders given to British soldiers stationed in Canada ("no English Officer or party is to molest, or interrupt them in returning to their Settlement at LORETTE . . . recommending it to the Officers commanding the Posts, to treat them kindly . . . By the Genl's Command") would more naturally form part of a document such as a safe conduct or pass than of a treaty.

These points bring out the unilateral aspect of the document of September 5: it could be an administrative document issued by General Murray, recognizing that the Hurons had laid down their arms and giving orders to British soldiers accordingly. Finally, the document was signed only by the General's representative with no indication that it had been assented to by the Hurons in one way or another. The main purpose of the document is thus, it is argued, to recognize the surrender, and what was more important to the Hurons, allow them to return to Lorette safely without fear of being mistaken for enemies by British soldiers they might meet along the way.

Fourth, the reference to a specific event, namely the return journey to Lorette, as opposed to a document recognizing rights in perpetuity or without any apparent time limit, could show that the purpose of this document was not to settle long-term relations between the Hurons and the British. The temporary and specific nature of the document would indicate that the parties did not intend to enter into a treaty.

Fifth, the document does not possess the formality which is usually to be found in the wording of a treaty. First, it is not the General himself who signed the document, but his adjutant on his behalf. Second, the language used in the document does not have the formalism generally accompanying the signature of a treaty with Indians. Here, for example, are extracts from the treaty at issue in Simon (at pp. 392-93 and 395):

Treaty or
Articles of Peace and Friendship Renewed
between

His Excellency Peregrine Thomas Hopson Esquire Captain General and Governor in Chief in and over His Majesty's Province of Nova Scotia or Acadie. Vice Admiral of the same & Colonel of one of His Majesty's Regiments of Foot, and His Majesty's Council on behalf of His Majesty,

and

Major Jean Baptiste Cope, chief Sachem of the Tribe of Mick Mack Indians Inhabiting the Eastern Coast of the said Province, and Andrew Hadley Martin, Gabriel Martin & Francis Jeremiah, Members and Delegates of the said Tribe, for themselves and their said Tribe their Heirs, and the Heirs of their Heirs forever, Begun made and concluded in the manner, form and Tenor following, viz: . . .

In Faith and Testimony whereof, the Great Seal of the Province is hereunto appended, and the party's to these presents have hereunto interchangeably Set their Hands in the Council Chamber at Halifax this 22nd day of Nov. 1752, in the Twenty sixth Year of His Majesty's Reign.

[signatures deleted]

The appellant argues that the Hurons did not formalize the document either by their signature (which would not be absolutely necessary to make it a treaty) or by the use of necklaces or belts of shells which were the traditional method used by the Hurons to formalize agreements at the time. Clearly, this argument has weight only if the document accurately indicates all the events surrounding the signature. Otherwise, extrinsic proof of solemnities could help to show that the parties intended to enter into a formal agreement and that they manifested this intent in one way or another.

While the analysis thus far seems to suggest that the document of September 5 is not a treaty, the presence of a clause guaranteeing the free exercise of religion, customs and trade with the English cannot but raise serious doubts about this proposition. It seems extremely strange to me that a document which is supposedly only a temporary, unilateral and informal safe conduct should contain a clause guaranteeing rights of such importance. As Bisson J.A. noted in the Court of Appeal judgment, there would have been no necessity to mention the free exercise of religion and customs in a document the effects of which were only to last for a few days. Such a guarantee would definitely have been more natural in a treaty where "the word of the white man" is given.

The appellant and the Attorney General of Canada put forward certain explanations for the presence of such guarantees in the document:

1. the free exercise of religion and customs was part of the protection under which General Murray received the Hurons;
2. the free exercise of religion and customs is mentioned because these benefits had been conferred on Canadians laying down their arms earlier.

As this Court recently noted in R. v. Horse, [1988] 1 S.C.R. 187, at p. 201, extrinsic evidence is not to be used as an aid to interpreting a treaty in the absence of ambiguity or where the result would be to alter its terms by adding words to or subtracting words from the written agreement. This rule also applies in determining the legal nature of a document relating to the Indians. However, a more flexible approach is necessary as the question of the existence of a treaty within the meaning of s. 88 of the Indian Act is generally closely bound up with the circumstances existing when the document was prepared (White and Bob, supra, at pp. 648-49, and Simon, supra, at pp. 409-10). In any case, the wording alone will not suffice to determine the legal nature of the document before the Court. On the one hand, we have before us a document the form of which and some of whose subject-matter suggest that it is not a treaty, and on the other, we find it to contain protection of fundamental rights which supports the opposite conclusion. The ambiguity arising from this document thus means that the Court must look at extrinsic evidence to determine its legal nature.

(b) Extrinsic evidence

It was suggested that the Court examine three types of extrinsic evidence to assist it in determining whether the document of September 5 is a treaty. First, to indicate the parties' intent to enter into a treaty, the Court was offered evidence to present a picture of the historical context of the period. Then, evidence was presented of certain facts closely associated with the signing of the document and relating to the existence of the various constituent elements of a treaty. Finally, still with a view to determining whether the parties intended to enter into a treaty, the Court was told of the subsequent conduct of the parties in respect of the document of September 5, 1760.

I should first mention that the admissibility of certain documents submitted by the intervener the National Indian Brotherhood/Assembly of First Nations in support of its arguments was contested. The intervener was relying on documents that were not part of the record in the lower courts. The appellant agreed that certain of these documents, namely Murray's Journal, letters and instructions, should be included in the record provided this Court considered that their admissibility was justified by the concept of judicial notice. I am of the view that all the documents to which I will refer, whether my attention was drawn to them by the intervener or as a result of my personal research, are documents of a historical nature which I am entitled to rely on pursuant to the concept of judicial knowledge. As Norris J.A. said in White and Bob (at p. 629):

> The Court is entitled "to take judicial notice of the facts of history whether past or contemporaneous" as Lord du Parcq said in Monarch Steamship Co., Ld. v. Karlshamns Oljefabriker (A/B), [1949] A.C. 196 at p. 234, [1949] 1 All E.R. 1 at p. 20, and it is entitled to rely on its own historical knowledge and researches, Read v. Bishop of Lincoln, [1892] A.C. 644, Lord Halsbury, L.C., at pp. 652-4.

The documents I cite all enable the Court, in my view, to identify more accurately the historical context essential to the resolution of this case.

The appellant argues that the historical context at the time the document of September 5 was concluded shows that the parties had no intention to enter into a treaty. The respondents and the intervener the National Indian Brotherhood/Assembly of First Nations, on the other hand, maintain that the historical background to this document supports the existence of a common intent to sign a treaty.

On September 5, 1760, France and England were engaged in a war begun four years earlier, which ended with the Treaty of Paris signed on February 10, 1763. About a year earlier, the battle of the Plains of Abraham had allowed the British to take control of Quebec City and the surrounding area. During the year following this victory, British troops had worked to consolidate their military position in Canada and to solve the supply and other practical problems engendered by the very harsh winter of 1759.

In his work *An Historical Journal of the Campaigns in North-America for the Years 1757, 1758, 1759 and 1760* (1769), at p. 382 (day of September 3, 1760), Capt. Knox also relates the efforts of General Murray to win the loyalty of the Canadians. General Murray at that time invited French soldiers to surrender and Canadians to lay down their arms. He had made it widely known that he would pardon those who surrendered and allow them to keep their land. He had also promised them that he would make larger grants of land and protect them. He gave those who responded to his appeal and took the oath of allegiance to the British Crown safe conducts to return to their parishes. Steps were also taken to inform the Indians who were allies of the British of these changes of allegiance so as to ensure that they would not be attacked on the way back.

As the advantageous position and strength of the British troops became more and more apparent, several groups did surrender and it appears that this movement accelerated in the days preceding that on which the document at issue was signed. In his Historical Journal, supra, at the entries for September 1, 2 and 3, 1760, Knox indicates that:

> The whole parish of Varenne have surrendered, delivered up their arms, and taken the oaths; their fighting-men consisted of five companies of militia: two other parishes, equally numerous, have signified their intentions of submitting to-morrow. . . .
>
> The Canadians are surrendering every-where; they are terrified at the thoughts of Sir William Johnson's Indians coming among them, by which we conjecture they are near at hand. . . .
>
> The regulars now desert to us in great numbers, and the Canadian militia are surrendering by hundreds.

In fact, the total defeat of France in Canada was very near: the Act of Capitulation of Montréal, by which the French troops stationed in Canada laid down their arms, was signed on September 8, 1760 and signalled the end of France's de facto control in Canada.

Great Britain's de jure control of Canada took the form of the Treaty of Paris of February 10, 1763, a treaty which inter alia ensured that the "Inhabitants of Canada" would be free to practise the Roman Catholic religion. Some months later, the Royal Proclamation of October 7, 1763 organized the territories recently acquired by Great Britain and reserved two types of land for the Indians: that located outside the colony's territorial limits and the establishments authorized by the Crown inside the colony.

From the historical situation I have just briefly outlined the appellant deduced that the document at issue is only a capitulation and that the legal nature of such a document should not be construed differently depending on whether it relates to the Indians or to the French. The Court has before it, he submitted, only a capitulation comparable to a capitulation of French soldiers or Canadians, which cannot be elevated to the category of a treaty within the meaning of s. 88 of the Indian Act simply because an Indian tribe was a party to it. In other words, as Murray signed the same kind of document with respect to the Indians, the French or the Canadians his intent could not have been any different. The appellant also maintains that, like the capitulations of the Canadians and the French soldiers, this document was only temporary in nature in that its consequences would cease when the fate of Canada was finally settled at the end of the war.

I consider that, instead, we can conclude from the historical documents that both Great Britain and France felt that the Indian nations had sufficient independence and played a large enough role in North America for it to be good policy to maintain relations with them very close to those maintained between sovereign nations.

The mother countries did everything in their power to secure the alliance of each Indian nation and to encourage nations allied with the enemy to change sides. When these efforts met with success, they were incorporated in treaties of alliance or neutrality. This clearly indicates that the Indian nations were regarded in their relations with the European nations which occupied North America as independent nations. The papers of Sir William Johnson (*The Papers of Sir William Johnson*, 14 vol.), who was in charge of Indian affairs in British North America, demonstrate the recognition by Great Britain that nation-to-nation relations had to be conducted with the North American Indians. As an example, I cite an extract from a speech by Sir Johnson at the Onondaga Conference held in April 1748, attended by the Five Nations (*The Papers of Sir William Johnson*, vol. I, 1921, at p. 157):

> Brethren of the five Nations I will begin upon a thing of a long standing, our first *Brothership*. My Reason for it is, I think there are several among you who seem to forget it; It may seem strange to you how I a *Foreigner* should know this, But I tell you I found out some of the old Writings of our Forefathers which was thought to have been lost and in this old valuable Record I find, that our first *Friendship* Commenced at the Arrival of the first great Canoe or Vessel at Albany . . . [Emphasis added.]

As the Chief Justice of the United States Supreme Court said in 1832 in Worcester v. State of Georgia, 31 U.S. (6 Pet.) 515 (1832), at pp. 548-49, about British policy towards the Indians in the mid-eighteenth century:

> Such was the policy of Great Britain towards the Indian nations inhabiting the territory from which she excluded all other Europeans; such her claims, and such her practical exposition of the charters she had granted: *she considered them as nations capable of maintaining the relations of peace and war; of governing themselves, under her protection; and she made treaties with them, the obligation of which she acknowledged.* [Emphasis added.]

Further, both the French and the English recognized the critical importance of alliances with the Indians, or at least their neutrality, in determining the outcome of the war between them and the security of the North American colonies.

Following the crushing defeats of the English by the French in 1755, the English realized that control of North America could not be acquired without the co-operation of the Indians. Accordingly, from then on they made efforts to ally themselves with as many Indian nations as possible. The French, who had long realized the strategic role of the Indians in the success of any war effort, also did everything they could to secure their alliance or maintain alliances already established (Jack Stagg, *Anglo-Indian Relations in North America to 1763* (1981); "Mr. Nelson's Memorial about the State of the Northern Colonies in America", September 24, 1696, reproduced in O'Callaghan ed., *Documents relative to the Colonial History of New York* (1856), vol. VII, at p. 206; "Letter from Sir William Johnson to William Pitt", October 24, 1760, in *The Papers of Sir William Johnson*, vol. III, 1921, at pp. 269 et seq.; "Mémoire de Bougainville sur l'artillerie du Canada", January 11, 1759, in *Rapport de l'archiviste de la Province de Québec pour 1923-1924* (1924), at p. 58; *Journal du Marquis de Montcalm durant ses campagnes en Canada de 1756 à 1759* (1895), at p. 428).

England also wished to secure the friendship of the Indian nations by treating them with generosity and respect for fear that the safety and development of the colonies and their inhabitants would be compromised by Indians with feelings of hostility. One of the extracts from Knox's work which I cited above reports that the Canadians and the French soldiers who surrendered asked to be protected from Indians on the way back to their parishes. Another passage from Knox, also cited above, relates that the Canadians were terrified at the idea of seeing Sir William Johnson's Indians coming among them. This proves that in the minds of the local population the Indians represented a real and disturbing threat. The fact that England was also aware of the danger the colonies and their inhabitants might run if the Indians withdrew their co-operation is echoed in the following documents: "Letter from Sir William Johnson to the Lords of Trade", November 13, 1763, reproduced in O'Callaghan ed., op. cit., at pp. 574, 579 and 580; "Letter from Sir William Johnson to William Pitt", October 24, 1760, in *The Papers of Sir William Johnson*, vol. III, at pp. 270 and 274; Ratelle, *Contexte historique de la localisation des Attikameks et des Montagnais de 1760 à nos jours* (1987); "Letter from Amherst to Sir William Johnson", August 30, 1760, in *The Papers of Sir William Johnson*, vol. X, 1951, at p. 177; "Instructions from George II to Amherst", September 18, 1758, National Archives of Canada (MG 18 L 4 file 0 20/8); C. Colden, *The History of the Five Indian Nations of Canada* (1747), at p. 180; Stagg, op. cit., at pp. 166-67; and by analogy Murray, *Journal of the Siege of Québec*, supra, entry of December 31, 1759, at pp. 15-16.

This "generous" policy which the British chose to adopt also found expression in other areas. The British Crown recognized that the Indians had certain ownership rights over their land, it sought to establish trade with them which would rise above the level of exploitation and give them a fair return. It also allowed them autonomy in their internal affairs, intervening in this area as little as possible.

Whatever the similarities between a document recording the laying down of arms by French soldiers or Canadians and the document at issue, the analogy does not go so far as to preclude the conclusion that the document was nonetheless a treaty.

Such a document could not be regarded as a treaty so far as the French and the Canadians were concerned because under international law they had no authority to sign such a document: they were governed by a European nation which alone was able to represent them in dealings with other European nations for the signature of treaties affecting them. The colonial powers recognized that the Indians had the capacity to sign treaties directly with the European nations occupying North American territory. The sui generis situation in which the Indians were placed had forced the European mother countries to acknowledge that they had sufficient autonomy for the valid creation of solemn agreements which were called "treaties", regardless of the strict meaning given to that word then and now by international law. The question of the competence of the Hurons and of the French or the Canadians is essential to the question of whether a treaty exists. The question of capacity has to be examined from a fundamentally different viewpoint and in accordance with different principles for each of these groups. Thus, I reject the argument that the legal nature of the document at issue must necessarily be interpreted in the same way as the capitulations of the French and the Canadians. The historical context which I have briefly reviewed even supports the proposition that both the British and the Hurons could have intended to enter into a treaty on September 5, 1760. I rely, in particular, on Great Britain's stated wish to form alliances with as many Indians as possible and on the demoralizing effect for the French, the Canadians and their allies which would result from the loss of this long-standing Indian ally whose allegiance to the French cause had until then been very seldom shaken.

Let us now turn to the second type of extrinsic evidence proposed by the parties, namely evidence relating to facts which were contemporaneous with or which occurred shortly before or after the signing of the document of September 5, 1760.

The respondents first presented evidence that the document of September 5, 1760 was the outcome of negotiations between Murray and certain Indian nations, including the Hurons, who wished to make peace with the British Crown. Knox's Journal, supra, reports the following events for September 6 (at p. 384):

> Eight Sachems, of different nations, lately in alliance with the enemy, have surrendered, for themselves and their tribes, to General Murray: these fellows, after conferring with his Excellency, *and that all matters had been adjusted to their satisfaction*, stepped out to the beach opposite to Montreal, flourished their knives and hatchets, and set up the war-shout; intimating to the French, that they are now become our allies and their enemies. While these Chieftains *were negotiating a peace*, two of our Mohawks entered the apartment where they were with the General and Colonel Burton . . . [Emphasis added.]

Although it is not entirely clear, Knox appears to be relating here events which took place the preceding day, on September 5. This interpretation is confirmed by the fact that Murray makes no reference in his Journal to any meeting with the Indians on the 6th but mentions one on the 5th, while Knox records no meeting with the Indians on the 5th. Both are thus probably speaking of the same meeting on September 5.

The foregoing passage shows that the document of September 5 was not simply an expression of General Murray's wishes, but the result of negotiations between the parties. This document was thus not simply a unilateral act, a simple acknowledgment or safe conduct, but the embodiment of an agreement reached between the representative of the British Crown and the representatives of the Indian nations present, including the representative of the Lorette Hurons.

Knox goes on to say that the Mohawks wanted to turn on the various Indian groups allied with the French who had just concluded peace with the British. Murray and Burton intervened and the Mohawks merely made threats against them. What is significant for purposes of this case is that these threats reflected the Mohawks' perception as to the nature of the agreement which had just been concluded between the eight Sachems and Murray. The Mohawks said the following (at p. 385):

> Do you remember, when you treacherously killed one of our brothers at such a time? Ye shall one day pay dearly for it, ye cowardly dogs,—*let the treaty be as it will:*—I tell you, we will destroy you and your settlement. . . . [Emphasis added.]

The view taken by these Indians was apparently shared by Murray himself. The note written by Murray in his Journal, on September 5, 1760, indicates that he considered that a peace treaty had been concluded with the Indian nations in question.

> Sepr. 5th. March'd with them myself and on the road, met the Inhabitants who were coming to deliver their arms, and take the oaths, there two nations of Indians, of Hurons and Iroquois, came in & *made their Pace*. . . . [Emphasis added.]
>
> (Knox, *Appendix to an Historical Journal or the Campaigns in North America for the Years 1757, 1758, 1759 and 1760* (1916), at p. 831)

The accounts given by Knox and Murray himself of the events on the days that are critical for this case are quite consistent with British policy, which favoured alliance or at least neutrality for the greatest number of the Indian nations in the newly conquered territories. By holding negotiations to conclude a peace treaty between the Hurons and the British, Murray was only giving effect to this clear policy of Great Britain.

The intervener the National Indian Brotherhood/Assembly of First Nations provided the Court with some very interesting evidence in this regard. It submitted the minutes of a conference between Sir William Johnson and the representatives of the Eight Nations, including the Lorette Hurons, held in Montréal on September 16, 1760 (*The Papers of Sir William Johnson*, vol. XIII, 1962, at p. 163). Although the appellant objected to the Court considering this document, I feel it is a reliable source which allows us to take cognizance of a historical fact. Its being submitted by the intervener does not in any way prevent the Court from taking judicial notice of it. Indeed, I can only express my appreciation to the intervener for facilitating my research.

The minutes of this conference refer in several places to the peace recently concluded between the Eight Nations and the English and their allies (at pp. 163-64):

Br. Wy.

You desired of us to [see] deliver up your People who [may be] are still among us—[We] *As you have now settled all matters wth. us & we are become firm Friends.* . .

a Belt

Br. W.

As we have now made a firm Peace wth. the English. & ye. 6 Nats. we shall endeavour all in our Powr. to keep it inviolably.

a large Belt.

[Emphasis added.]

These words were spoken by spokesmen for the Eight Nations and clearly show that the Indians and Sir William Johnson considered that relations between these Indian nations and the British would now take the form of an alliance ("firm friends"). This new situation was undoubtedly the outcome of the peace concluded between the parties, a peace desired by the Eight Nations as well as the British ("We have now made a firm Peace with the English").

Finally, it is worth noting that each of the contributions made by spokesmen at this conference was followed by the presentation of a belt to solemnize the content of the undertakings that had just been made or the words which had just been spoken. As we saw earlier, the appellant contends that the document of September 5, 1760 is not a treaty, inter alia, because the tokens of solemnity that ordinarily accompanied treaties between the Indians and the British are not present. I think it is reasonable to conclude that the circumstances existing on September 5 readily explain the absence of such solemnities. Murray was not given notice of the meeting, and a fortiori its purpose, and it was therefore largely improvised. Murray also had very little time to spend on ceremony: his troops were moving towards Montréal and were on a war footing. He himself was busy organizing the final preparations for a meeting between his army and that of Amherst and Haviland in Montréal, for the purpose of bringing down this last significant French bastion in Canada. Although solemnities are not crucial to the existence of a treaty, I think it is in any case reasonable to regard the presentation of belts at the conference on September 16 as a solemn ratification of the peace agreement concluded a few days earlier.

Lastly, the Court was asked to consider the subsequent conduct of the parties as extrinsic evidence of their intent to enter into a treaty. I do not think this is necessary, since the general historical context of the time and the events closely surrounding the document at issue have persuaded me that the document of September 5, 1760 is a treaty within the meaning of s. 88 of the Indian Act. The fact that the document has allegedly not been used in the courts or other institutions of our society does not establish that it is not a treaty. Non-use may very well be explained by observance of the rights contained in the document or mere oversight. Moreover, the subsequent conduct which is most indicative of the parties' intent is undoubtedly that which most closely followed the conclusion of the document. Eleven days after it was concluded, at the conference to which I have just referred, the parties gave a clear indication that they had intended to conclude a treaty.

I am therefore of the view that the document of September 5, 1760 is a treaty within the meaning of s. 88 of the Indian Act. At this point, the appellant raises two arguments against its application to the present case. First, he argues that the treaty has been extinguished. In the event that it has not been, he argues that the treaty is not such as to render ss. 9 and 37 of the Regulation respecting the Parc de la Jacques-Cartier inoperative. Let us first consider whether on May 29, 1982, the date on which the respondents engaged in the activities which are the subject of the charges, the treaty still had any legal effects.

V—LEGAL EFFECTS OF TREATY OF SEPTEMBER 5, 1760 ON MAY 29, 1982

The appellant argues that, assuming the document of September 5 is a treaty, it was extinguished by the following documents or events:

1. the Act of Capitulation of Montréal, signed on September 8, 1760;
2. the Treaty of Paris signed on February 10, 1763;
3. the Royal Proclamation of October 7, 1763;
4. the legislative and administrative history of the Hurons' land; and
5. the effect of time and non-use of the treaty.

Neither the documents nor the legislative and administrative history to which the appellant referred the Court contain any express statement that the treaty of September 5, 1760 has been extinguished. Even assuming that a treaty can be extinguished implicitly, a point on which I express no opinion here, the appellant was not able in my view to meet the criterion stated in Simon regarding the quality of evidence that would be required in any case to support a conclusion that the treaty had been extinguished. That case clearly established that the onus is on the party arguing that the treaty has terminated to show the circumstances and events indicating it has been extinguished. This burden can only be discharged by strict proof, as the Chief Justice said at pp. 405-6:

> Given the serious and far-reaching consequences of a finding that a treaty right has been extinguished, it seems appropriate to demand strict proof of the fact of extinguishment in each case where the issue arises.

The appellant did not submit any persuasive evidence of extinguishment of the treaty. He argues, first, that the treaty had become obsolete because the Act of Capitulation of Montréal replaced all other acts of capitulation, thereby extinguishing them. This argument is based on article 50 of the Act of Capitulation, which reads as follows:

> The present capitulation shall be inviolably executed in all its articles, and bona fide, on both sides, notwithstanding any infraction, and any other pretence, with regard to the *preceding capitulations*, and without making use of reprisals. [Emphasis added.]

As I have concluded that this is a peace treaty and not a capitulation, art. 50 has no application in this case, so far as extinguishment of the treaty of September 5 is concerned.

That article was designed to ensure that the signatories would comply with the Act of Capitulation, in spite of the existence of reasons for retaliation which the parties might have had as the result of breaches of an earlier act of capitulation. Article 50 can only apply to preceding acts signed on behalf of France, such as the Act of Capitulation of Québec in late 1759. I see nothing here to support the conclusion that this article was also intended to extinguish a treaty between an Indian nation and the British.

The appellant also cites art. 40 of the Act of Capitulation of Montréal, which provides that:

> *The Savages or Indian allies* of his most Christian Majesty, shall be maintained in the Lands they inhabit; if they chuse to remain there; they shall not be molested on any pretence whatsoever, for having carried arms, and served his most Christian Majesty. They shall have, as well as the French, liberty of religion, and shall keep their missionaries. [Emphasis added.]

France could not have claimed to represent the Hurons at the time the Act of Capitulation was made, since the latter had abandoned their alliance with the French some days before. As they were no longer allies of the French, this article does not apply to them. In my opinion, the article can only be interpreted as a condition on which the French agreed to capitulate. Though the Indian allies of the French were its beneficiaries, it was fundamentally an agreement between the French and the British which in no way prevented independent agreements between the British and the Indian nations, whether allies of the French or of the British, being concluded or continuing to exist. Further, I think it is clear that the purpose of art. 40 was to assure the Indians of certain rights, not to extinguish existing rights.

It would be contrary to the general principles of law for an agreement concluded between the English and the French to extinguish a treaty concluded between the English and the Hurons. It must be remembered that a treaty is a solemn agreement between the Crown and the Indians, an agreement the nature of which is sacred: Simon, supra, at p. 410, and White and Bob, supra, at p. 649. The very definition of a treaty thus makes it impossible to avoid the conclusion that a treaty cannot be extinguished without the consent of the Indians concerned. Since the Hurons had the capacity to enter into a treaty with the British, therefore, they must be the only ones who could give the necessary consent to its extinguishment.

The same reasoning applies to the appellant's argument that the Treaty of Paris of February 10, 1763 between France and England terminated the treaty of September 5, 1760 between the Hurons and the English. England and France could not validly agree to extinguish a treaty between the Hurons and the English, nor could France claim to represent the Hurons regarding the extinguishment of a treaty the Hurons had themselves concluded with the British Crown.

The appellant then argued that it follows that the Royal Proclamation of October 7, 1763 extinguished the rights arising out of the treaty of September 5, 1760, because it did not confirm them. I cannot accept such a proposition: the silence of the Royal Proclamation regarding the treaty at issue cannot be interpreted as extinguishing it. The purpose of the Proclamation was first and foremost to organize, geographically and politically, the territory of the new American colonies, namely Québec, East Florida, West Florida and Grenada, and to distribute their possession and use. It also granted certain important rights to the native peoples and was regarded by many as a kind of charter of rights for the Indians: White and Bob, supra, at p. 636; Calder v. Attorney-General of British Columbia, [1973] S.C.R. 313, at p. 395 (Hall J., dissenting); R. v. Secretary of State for Foreign and Commonwealth Affairs, [1982] 2 All E.R. 118 (C.A.), at pp. 124-25 (Lord Denning). The very wording of the Royal Proclamation clearly shows that its objective, so far as the Indians were concerned, was to provide a solution to the problems created by the greed which hitherto some of the English had all too often demonstrated in buying up Indian land at low prices. The situation was causing dangerous trouble among the Indians and the Royal Proclamation was meant to remedy this:

> And whereas it is just and reasonable, and essential to our Interest, and the Security of our Colonies, that the several Nations or Tribes of Indians with whom We are connected, and who live under our Protection, should not be molested or disturbed in the Possession of such Parts of Our Dominions and Territories as, not having been ceded to or purchased by Us, are reserved to them, or any of them, as their Hunting Grounds.— We do therefore, with the Advice of our Privy Council, declare it to be our Royal Will and Pleasure, that no Governor or Commander in Chief in any of our Colonies of Quebec, East Florida or West Florida, do presume, upon any Pretence whatever, to grant Warrants of Survey or pass any Patents for Lands beyond the Bounds of their respective Governments, as described in their Commissions . . .
>
> And We do further declare it to be our Royal Will and Pleasure, for the present as aforesaid, to reserve under our Sovereignty, Protection, and Dominion, for the use of the said Indians, all the Lands and Territories not included within the Limits of Our said Three new Governments, or within the Limits of the Territory granted to the Hudson's Bay Company, as also all the Lands and Territories lying to the Westward of the Sources of the Rivers which fall into the Sea from the West and North West as aforesaid.

I see nothing in these passages which can be interpreted as an intention on the part of the British Crown to extinguish the treaty of September 5. The Proclamation confers rights on the Indians without necessarily thereby extinguishing any other right conferred on them by the British Crown under a treaty.

Legislative and administrative history also provides no basis for concluding that the treaty was extinguished. In 1853, 9,600 acres of land located outside the territory at issue were ceded to the Hurons by the Government of Lower Canada. These lands were within the boundaries of the lands frequented by the Hurons when the treaty of September 5 was concluded. In 1903 the Hurons again ceded these 9,600 acres, without reserving the rights that had been granted to them under the treaty of September 5. The Attorney General of Québec considers that by making this cession without reservation, the Hurons indicated beyond all doubt that this document was not a source of rights so far as they were concerned. This argument cannot stand. Assuming that the 9,600 acres ceded were initially the subject of the treaty, the absence of any reservation in the deed ceding this territory clearly cannot be interpreted as a waiver of the benefits of the treaty in the territory which was not the subject of the cession, whatever the effect of the absence of such a reservation may be with respect to the territory ceded.

The appellant further argues that by adopting the Act to establish the Laurentides National Park, S.Q. 1895, 58 Vict., c. 22, and by making the territory in question a park, the Québec legislator clearly expressed his intention to prohibit the carrying on of certain activities in this territory, whether or not such activities are protected by an Indians treaty.

Section 88 of the Indian Act is designed specifically to protect the Indians from provincial legislation that might attempt to deprive them of rights protected by a treaty. A legislated change in the use of the territory thus does not extinguish rights otherwise protected by treaty. If the treaty gives the Hurons the right to carry on their customs and religion in the territory of Jacques-Cartier park, the existence of a provincial statute and subordinate legislation will not ordinarily affect that right.

Finally, the appellant argues that non-use of the treaty over a long period of time may extinguish its effect. He cites no authority for this. I do not think that this argument carries much weight: a solemn agreement cannot lose its validity merely because it has not been invoked to, which in any case is disputed by the respondents, who maintain that it was relied on in a seigneurial claim in 1824. Such a proposition would mean that a treaty could be extinguished merely because it had not been relied on in litigation, which is untenable.

In view of the liberal and generous approach that must be adopted towards Indians rights and the evidence in the record, I cannot conclude that the treaty of September 5 no longer had any legal effect on May 29, 1982.

The question that arises at this point is as to whether the treaty is capable of rendering ss. 9 and 37 of the Regulations inoperative. To answer this it will now be necessary to consider the territorial scope of the rights guaranteed by the treaty, since the appellant recognizes that the activities with which the respondents are charged are customary or religious in nature.

VI—TERRITORIAL SCOPE OF RIGHTS GUARANTEED BY TREATY OF
    SEPTEMBER 5, 1760

Although the document of September 5 is a treaty within the meaning of s. 88 of the Indian Act, that does not necessarily mean that the respondents are exempt from the application of the Regulation respecting the Parc de la Jacques-Cartier. It is still necessary that the treaty protecting activities of the kind with which the respondents are charged cover the territory of Jacques-Cartier park. The appellant argues that the territorial scope of the treaty does not extend to the territory of the park. The respondents, on the other hand, argue that the treaty confers personal rights on them and that they are in no way seeking to assert rights of a territorial nature.

Although this case does not involve a territorial claim as such, in that the Hurons are not claiming control over territory, I am of the view that exercise of the right they are claiming has an essential territorial aspect. The respondents argue that they have a right to carry on their customs and religious rites in a specific territory, namely that of the park. The substantive content of the right cannot be considered apart from its territorial content. Just as it would distort the nature of a right of way to consider it while ignoring its territorial aspect, one cannot logically disregard the territorial aspect of the substantive rights guaranteed by the treaty of September 5, 1760. The respondents must therefore show that the treaty guaranteed their right to carry on their customs and religious rites in the territory of Jacques-Cartier park.

The treaty gives the Hurons the freedom to carry on their customs and their religion. No mention is made in the treaty itself of the territory over which these rights may be exercised. There is also no indication that the territory of what is now Jacques-Cartier park was contemplated. However, for a freedom to have real value and meaning, it must be possible to exercise it somewhere. That does not mean, despite the importance of the rights concerned, that the Indians can exercise it anywhere. Our analysis will be confined to setting the limits of the promise made in the treaty, since the respondents have at no time based their argument on the existence of aboriginal rights protecting the activities with which they are charged.

The respondents suggest that the treaty gives them the right to carry on their customs and religion in the territory of the park because it is part of the territory frequented by the Hurons in 1760, namely the area between the Saguenay and the St-Maurice. In their submission, customs as they existed at the time of the treaty and as they might reasonably be expected to develop subsequently are what the British Crown undertook to preserve and foster.

The appellant argued in the Court of Appeal that the free exercise of the customs mentioned in the document of September 5, 1760 has to be limited to the Lorette territory, a territory of 40 arpents by 40 arpents. In this Court, he argues that even if the treaty covers the activities with which the respondents are charged, these rights must be exercised in accordance with the legislation designed to protect users of the park and to preserve it. He further argues that, except as regards the cutting of trees, the legislation only affects the way in which the right can be exercised, not the substance of the right. This should be a sufficient basis for requiring the Hurons to observe the legislation. In his intervention the Attorney General of Canada argues that the respondents' claim is essentially a territorial one and that in order to establish their rights, the respondents must show a connection between the rights claimed and their exercise in a given territory. He is of the view that the document in the present case does not connect the freedom of exercise of religion, customs and trade with the English to any territory.

In my view, the treaty essentially has to be interpreted by determining the intention of the parties on the territorial question at the time it was concluded. It is not sufficient to note that the treaty is silent on this point. We must also undertake the task of interpreting the treaty on the territorial question with the same generous approach toward the Indians that applied in considering earlier questions. Now as then, we must do our utmost to act in the spirit of Simon.

The historical context, which has been used to demonstrate the existence of the treaty, may equally assist us in interpreting the extent of the rights contained in it. As MacKinnon J.A. said in Taylor and Williams, supra, at 232:

> Cases on Indian or aboriginal rights can never be determined in a vacuum.
> It is of importance to consider the history and oral traditions of the tribes
> concerned, and the surrounding circumstances at the time of the treaty,
> relied on by both parties, in determining the treaty's effect.

Before I again turn to history, the problems raised by the territorial question should be briefly stated. There are two rights in opposition here: the provincial Crown's right of ownership over the territory of the park and the Hurons' right to exercise their religion and ancestral customs on this land. The ownership right suggests that ordinarily the Crown can do whatever it likes with its land. On the other hand, a very special importance seems to attach to territories traditionally frequented by the Hurons so that their traditional religious rites and ancestral customs will have their full meaning. Further, the Hurons are trying to protect the possibility of carrying on these rites and customs near Lorette on territory which they feel is suited to such purposes.

Bisson J.A., for the majority of the Court of Appeal, adopted the respondents' position that the territory which is the subject of the treaty is that frequented by the Hurons in 1760. In that case one can only note that if the rights of the Hurons are defined without introducing any limiting factor, a vast area would be subject to the rights recognized by the treaty of September 5, 1760. This could mean that persons who moved into the area frequented by the Hurons after 1760 may have limited the rights resulting from the treaty by making their exercise more difficult. This proposition might even lead one to suppose, a priori, that the Hurons could cut down trees and make fires on private property that had been part of the territory frequented by them at that time. With respect, I feel that adopting such a position would go beyond what General Murray intended. Even a generous interpretation of the document, such as Bisson J.A.'s interpretation, must be realistic and reflect the intention of both parties, not just that of the Hurons. The Court must choose from among the various possible interpretations of the common intention the one which best reconciles the Hurons' interests and those of the conqueror.

On the other hand, to accept the argument that the parties intended to limit the scope of the treaty to the Lorette territory would mean introducing a very severe restriction that is not justified by the wording of the document since Lorette is mentioned only as a destination for safe-conduct purposes. Given the nature of Indian religious rites and especially Indian customs at the time, any significant exercise of such rights would require territory extending beyond Lorette.

I consider that both the first and the second positions are unsatisfactory. In my view, neither one succeeds in deducing the common intention of the parties from the historical context. The interpretation which I think is called for when we give the historical context its full meaning is that Murray and the Hurons contemplated that the rights guaranteed by the treaty could be exercised over the entire territory frequented by the Hurons at the time, so long as the carrying on of the customs and rites is not incompatible with the particular use made by the Crown of this territory.

Let us look first at the relationship the Hurons had with the territory the respondents claim is covered by the treaty. No one argued that the area between the Saguenay and the St-Maurice was land over which there was an aboriginal title in favour of the Hurons. In fact, a group of about 300 people had been brought into the area around Québec by the Jesuits in 1650 ("Relation au R.P. Claude de Lingendes par Paul Ragueneau", of September 1, 1650, in *Relations des jésuites contenant ce qui s'est passé de plus remarquable dans les missions des Pères de la Compagnie de Jésus dans la Nouvelle-France* (1858), vol. 2, at pp. 25 et seq.) and its relatively recent presence in the Lorette area suggests that the Hurons did not have historical possession of these lands.

Next, the policy of the British toward the Indians in territorial matters has to be considered. In quite general terms, the evidence shows that during the Seven Years War the British had adopted a conciliatory attitude toward the Indians because of the lesson they had learned from their earlier defeats at the hands of the French. As I mentioned earlier, they had realized the important role the Indians would necessarily play in the war between the mother countries. The British had also understood the importance for the security of the colony of continuing peace with the Indians once the war was over. I adopt the observations of Bisson J.A. in describing Murray's attitude to the Hurons (at p. 1728):

> [TRANSLATION] In this connection, the reference to customs in treaty D-7 takes on particular importance, as Murray held the Hurons in high regard and undoubtedly wanted to be as much help to them as possible.

However, the British Crown's desire to colonize the conquered land and use that land for its benefit also cannot be doubted. Murray had been engaged for years in a war the purpose of which was to expand the wealth, resources and influence of Great Britain. It is unlikely he would have granted, without further details, absolute rights which might paralyze the Crown's use of the newly conquered territories.

Accordingly, I conclude that in view of the absence of express mention of the territorial scope of the treaty, it has to be assumed that the parties to the treaty of September 5 intended to reconcile the Hurons' need to protect the exercise of their customs and the desire of the British conquerors to expand. Protecting the exercise of the customs in all parts of the territory frequented when it is not incompatible with its occupancy is in my opinion the most reasonable way of reconciling the competing interests. This, in my view, is the definition of the common intent of the parties which best reflects the actual intent of the Hurons and of Murray on September 5, 1760. Defining the common intent of the parties on the question of territory in this way makes it possible to give full effect to the spirit of conciliation, while respecting the practical requirements of the British. This gave the English the necessary flexibility to be able to respond in due course to the increasing need to use Canada's resources, in the event that Canada remained under British suzerainty. The Hurons, for their part, were protecting their customs wherever their exercise would not be prejudicial to the use to which the territory concerned would be put. The Hurons could not reasonably expect that the use would forever remain what it was in 1760. Before the treaty was signed, they had carried on their customs in accordance with restrictions already imposed by an occupancy incompatible with such exercise. The Hurons were only asking to be permitted to continue to carry on their customs on the lands frequented to the extent that those customs did not interfere with enjoyment of the lands by their occupier. I readily accept that the Hurons were probably not aware of the legal consequences, and in particular of the right to occupy to the exclusion of others, which the main European legal systems attached to the concept of private ownership. Nonetheless I cannot believe that the Hurons ever believed that the treaty gave them the right to cut down trees in the garden of a house as part of their right to carry on their customs.

Jacques-Cartier park falls into the category of land occupied by the Crown, since the province has set it aside for a specific use. What is important is not so much that the province has legislated with respect to this territory but that it is using it, is in fact occupying the space. As occupancy has been established, the question is whether the type of occupancy to which the park is subject is incompatible with the exercise of the activities with which the respondents were charged, as these undoubtedly constitute religious customs or rites. Since, in view of the situation in 1760, we must assume some limitation on the exercise of rights protected by the treaty, it is up to the Crown to prove that its occupancy of the territory cannot be accommodated to reasonable exercise of the Hurons' rights.

The Crown presented evidence on such compatibility but that evidence did not persuade me that exercise of the rites and customs at issue here is incompatible with the occupancy.

Jacques-Cartier park is a park that falls within the class of conservation parks. The Parks Act describes them in the following way:

> 1. . . .
>
> (c) "conservation park" means a park primarily intended to ensure the permanent protection of territory representative of the natural regions of Quebec, or of natural sites presenting exceptional features, while rendering them accessible to the public for the purposes of education and cross-country recreation;

Cross-country recreation is given the following definition, again in s. 1 of the Act:

> (e) "cross-country recreation" means a type of recreation characterized by the use of little frequented territory and the use of relatively simple equipment;

Under the Regulation respecting the Parc de la Jacques-Cartier, the park is divided into environmental zones, which are portions of the park for moderate use set aside for the discovery and exploration of the environment, and preservation zones, for limited use and set aside for the conservation, observation and enjoyment of the environment.

For the exercise of rites and customs to be incompatible with the occupancy of the park by the Crown, it must not only be contrary to the purpose underlying that occupancy, it must prevent the realization of that purpose. First, we are dealing with Crown lands, lands which are held for the benefit of the community. Exclusive use is not an essential aspect of public ownership. Second, I do not think that the activities described seriously compromise the Crown's objectives in occupying the park. Neither the representative nature of the natural region where the park is located nor the exceptional nature of this natural site are threatened by the collecting of a few plants, the setting up of a tent using a few branches picked up in the area or the making of a fire according to the rules dictated by caution to avoid fires. These activities also present no obstacle to cross-country recreation. I therefore conclude that it has not been established that occupancy of the territory of Jacques-Cartier park is incompatible with the exercise of Huron rites and customs with which the respondents are charged.

VII—CONCLUSION

For all these reasons, I would dismiss the appeal with costs.

I would dispose of the constitutional questions stated by the Chief Justice as follows:

> 1. Does the following document, signed by General Murray on 5 September 1760, constitute a treaty within the meaning of s. 88 of the Indian Act (R.S.C. 1970, c. I-6)?
>
> THESE are to certify that the CHIEF of the HURON Tribe of Indians, having come to me in the name of His Nation, to submit to His BRITANNICK MAJESTY, and make Peace, has been received under my Protection, with his whole Tribe; and henceforth no English Officer or party is to molest, or interrupt them in returning to their Settlement at LORETTE; and they are received upon the same terms with the Canadians, being allowed the free Exercise of their Religion, their Customs, and Liberty of trading with the English:—recommending it to the Officers commanding the Posts, to treat them kindly. Given under my hand at Longueuil, this 5th day of September, 1760.
>
> JA. MURRAY
> By the Genl's Command,
> JOHN COSNAN,
> Adjut. Genl.

Answer: Yes.

> 2. If the answer to question 1 is in the affirmative, was the "treaty" still operative on 29 May 1982, at the time when the alleged offences were committed?

Answer: Yes.

> 3. If the answer to questions 1 and 2 are in the affirmative, are the terms of the document of such a nature as to make ss. 9 and 37 of the Regulation respecting the Parc de la Jacques-Cartier (Order in Council 3108-81, Gazette officielle du Québec, Part II, November 25, 1981, pp. 3518 et seq.) made under the Parks Act (R.S.Q., c. P-9) unenforceable in respect of the respondents?

Answer: Yes.

Appeal dismissed.

CHAPTER 8

Sparrow

THIS CASE is cited as R. v. Sparrow, S.C.C. (1990). The unanimous decision was delivered by Chief Justice Dickson and Justice La Forest on May 31, 1990 (McIntyre, Lamer, Wilson, L'Heureux-Dubé and Sopinka also heard the case), one week after the decision in R. v. Sioui. Reginald Sparrow, a member of the Musqueam Band in British Columbia, was found to have been fishing on 25 May 1984 in Canoe Passage with a drift net that was longer than had been permitted by the band's food fishing licence. Sparrow defended himself by saying he was exercising an "existing Aboriginal right" as protected by section 35 of the Constitution Act (1982). Sparrow was found guilty in provincial court, a decision which was upheld on appeal to the County Court. The British Columbia Court of Appeal rendered an ambiguous decision: while on the one hand they overturned the conviction because they found Sparrow's Aboriginal right to fish had not been extinguished prior to 1982, on the other they limited the protection of section 35 so that the net restriction was not inconsistent with it. Both the Crown and Sparrow, for different reasons, appealed to the Supreme Court of Canada.

While the practical result of the Supreme Court of Canada decision was to order that a new trial be held, the decision was a significant victory for those interested in the affirmation of Aboriginal rights. The decision is significant because it contains an extensive discussion of how the phrase "existing aboriginal and treaty rights of the aboriginal peoples of Canada are hereby recognized and affirmed" is to be interpreted. Particular emphasis is placed on interpreting the word "existing" and the phrase "recognized and affirmed" (s. 35).

The word "existing" is interpreted as meaning "unextinguished rather than exercisable at a certain time in history" (219). As well, "the phrase 'existing aboriginal rights' must be interpreted flexibly so as to permit their evolution over time" (220). The Supreme Court thereby rejected any attempt to fix Aboriginal rights to their position in 1982 or to the way in which they were regulated on that date. This allows for a much broader interpretation of existing Aboriginal rights. In discussing the words "recognized and affirmed" the justices add "the nature of s. 35(1) itself suggests that it be construed in a purposive way. When the purposes of the affirmation of aboriginal rights are considered, it is clear that a generous, liberal interpretation of the words in the constitutional provision is demanded" (228).

On the question of extinguishment, the justices write into their decision Hall's words "that the intention must be clear and plain." In the case at hand, they note that laws which regulate a right do not extinguish it and lean towards the position that an express or explicit statement must be made before an Aboriginal right is extinguished. They write, for example, that the fact that clear provisions were made allowing Indians to fish for food within certain guidelines "in no way shows a clear intention to extinguish" (223). The implication is that laws of general application would not be sufficient to extinguish an Aboriginal right.

There are many other important implications that derive from this decision. For example, the case affirms the findings in Guerin to the effect that "the government has a responsibility to act in a fiduciary capacity with respect to aboriginal peoples. The relationship between the government and aboriginals is trust like, rather than adversarial" (229). Furthermore, they establish a general principle for the allocation of scarce resources where an Aboriginal right remains in effect. In the specific instance, they argue that "the constitutional nature of the Musqueam food fishing rights means that any allocation of priorities after valid conservation measures have been implemented must give top priority to Indian food fishing" (233). Commercial and sport fisheries are to be accorded a lesser priority and bear the brunt of conservation measures.

It is worth noting that just as the Sioui case relied extensively on historical context, the Sparrow decision relies on academic commentary on the nature of Aboriginal rights, frequently quoting leading scholars in the field. The case was heralded by Aboriginal leaders as a major victory. The discussion here of "existing" had improved their chances of continued existence as Aboriginal peoples.

M.R.V. Storrow, L.F. Harvey, and J. Lysyk were lawyers for Sparrow, with T.R. Braidwood and J.E. Dorsey acting for the Crown. As in Lavell/Bedard, there was a long list of intervenors. The case has not been edited.

P.K.

The judgment of the Court was delivered by

DICKSON C.J. and LA FOREST J.: This appeal requires this Court to explore for the first time the scope of s. 35(1) of the Constitution Act, 1982, and to indicate its strength as a promise to the aboriginal peoples of Canada. Section 35(1) is found in Part II of that Act, entitled "Rights of the Aboriginal Peoples of Canada", and provides as follows:

35.(1) The existing aboriginal and treaty rights of the aboriginal peoples of Canada are hereby recognized and affirmed.

The context of this appeal is the alleged violation of the terms of the Musqueam food fishing licence which are dictated by the Fisheries Act, R.S.C.

1970, c. F-14, and the regulations under that Act. The issue is whether Parliament's power to regulate fishing is now limited by s. 35(1) of the Constitution Act, 1982, and, more specifically, whether the net length restriction in the licence is inconsistent with that provision.

FACTS

The appellant, a member of the Musqueam Indian Band, was charged under s. 61(1) of the Fisheries Act of the offence of fishing with a drift net longer than that permitted by the terms of the Band's Indian food fishing licence. The fishing which gave rise to the charge took place on May 25, 1984 in Canoe Passage which is part of the area subject to the Band's licence. The licence, which had been issued for a one-year period beginning March 31, 1984, set out a number of restrictions including one that drift nets were to be limited to 25 fathoms in length. The appellant was caught with a net which was 45 fathoms in length. He has throughout admitted the facts alleged to constitute the offence, but has defended the charge on the basis that he was exercising an existing aboriginal right to fish and that the net length restriction contained in the Band's licence is inconsistent with s. 35(1) of the Constitution Act, 1982 and therefore invalid.

THE COURTS BELOW

Goulet Prov. Ct. J., who heard the case, first referred to the very similar pre-Charter case of R. v. Derriksan (1976), 71 D.L.R. (3d) 159 (S.C.C.), where this Court held that the aboriginal right to fish was governed by the Fisheries Act and regulations. He then expressed the opinion that he was bound by Calder v. Attorney-General of British Columbia (1970), 74 W.W.R. 481 (B.C.C.A.), which held that a person could not claim an aboriginal right unless it was supported by a special treaty, proclamation, contract or other document, a position that was not disturbed because of the divided opinions of the members of this Court on the appeal which affirmed that decision ([1973] S.C.R. 313). Section 35(1) of the Constitution Act, 1982 thus had no application. The alleged right here was not based on any treaty or other document but was said to have been one exercised by the Musqueam from time immemorial before European settlers came to this continent. He, therefore, convicted the appellant, finding it unnecessary to consider the evidence in support of an aboriginal right.

An appeal to Lamperson J. of the County Court of Vancouver was dismissed for similar reasons, [1986] B.C.W.L.D. 599.

The British Columbia Court of Appeal (1986), 9 B.C.L.R. (2d) 300, found that the courts below had erred in deciding that they were bound by the Court of Appeal decision in Calder, supra, to hold that the appellant could not rely on an aboriginal right to fish. Since the pronouncement of the Supreme Court of Canada judgment, the Court of Appeal's decision has been binding on no one. The court also distinguished Calder on its facts.

The court then dealt with the other issues raised by the parties. On the basis of the trial judge's conclusion that Mr. Sparrow was fishing in ancient tribal territory where his ancestors had fished "from time immemorial", it stated that, with the other circumstances, this should have led to the conclusion that Mr.

Sparrow was exercising an existing aboriginal right. It rejected the Crown's contention that the right was no longer existing by reason of its "extinguishment by regulation". An aboriginal right could continue, though regulated. The court also rejected textual arguments made to the effect that s. 35 was merely of a preambular character, and concluded that the right to fish asserted by the appellant was one entitled to constitutional protection.

The issue then became whether that protection extended so far as to preclude regulation (as contrasted with extinguishment which did not arise in this case) of the exercise of that right. In its view, the general power to regulate the time, place and manner of all fishing, including fishing under an aboriginal right, remains. Parliament retained the power to regulate fisheries and to control Indian lands under ss. 91(12) and (24) of the Constitution Act, 1867 respectively. Reasonable regulations were necessary to ensure the proper management and conservation of the resource, and the regulations under the Fisheries Act restrict the right of all persons including Indians. The court observed, at p. 330:

> Section 35(1) of the Constitution Act, 1982 does not purport to revoke the power of Parliament to act under Head 12 or 24. The power to regulate fisheries, including Indian access to the fisheries continues, subject only to the new constitutional guarantee that the aboriginal rights existing on 17th April 1982 may not be taken away.

The court rejected arguments that the regulation of fishing was an inherent aspect of the aboriginal right to fish and that such regulation must be confined to necessary conservation measures. The right had always been and continued to be a regulated right. The court put it this way, at p. 331:

> The aboriginal right which the Musqueam had was, subject to conservation measures, the right to take fish for food and for the ceremonial purposes of the band. It was in the beginning a regulated, albeit self-regulated, right. It continued to be a regulated right, and on 17th April 1982, it was a regulated right. It has never been a fixed right, and it has always taken its form from the circumstances in which it has existed. If the interests of the Indians and other Canadians in the fishery are to be protected then reasonable regulations to ensure the proper management and conservation of the resource must be continued.

The court then went on to particularize the right still further. It was a right for a purpose, not one related to a particular method. Essentially, it was a right to fish for food and associated traditional band activities:

> The aboriginal right is not to take fish by any particular method or by a net of any particular length. It is to take fish for food purposes. The breadth of the right should be interpreted liberally in favour of the Indians. So "food purposes" should not be confined to subsistence. In particular, this is so because the Musqueam tradition and culture involves a consumption of salmon on ceremonial occasions and a broader use of fish than mere day to day domestic consumption.

That right, the court added, has not changed its nature since the enactment of the Constitution Act, 1982. What has changed is that the Indian food fishery right is now entitled to priority over the interests of other user groups, and that that right, by reason of s. 35(1) cannot be extinguished.

The Court of Appeal found that the trial judge's findings of facts were insufficient to lead to an acquittal. Observing that the conviction was based on an erroneous view of the law and could not stand, the court further remarked upon the existence of unresolved conflicts in the evidence, including the question whether a change in the fishing conditions was necessary to reduce the catch to a level sufficient to satisfy reasonable food requirements, as well as for conservation purposes.

THE APPEAL

Leave to appeal to this Court was then sought and granted. On November 24, 1987, the following constitutional question was stated:

> Is the net length restriction contained in the Musqueam Indian Band Indian Food Fishing Licence dated March 30, 1984, issued pursuant to the British Columbia Fishery (General) Regulations and the Fisheries Act, R.S.C. 1970, c. F-14, inconsistent with s. 35(1) of the Constitution Act, 1982?

The appellant appealed on the ground that the Court of Appeal erred (1) in holding that s. 35(1) of the Constitution Act, 1982 protects the aboriginal right only when exercised for food purposes and permits restrictive regulation of such rights whenever "reasonably justified as being necessary for the proper management and conservation of the resource or in the public interest", and (2) in failing to find the net length restriction in the Band's food fish licence was inconsistent with s. 35(1) of the Constitution Act, 1982.

The respondent Crown cross-appealed on the ground that the Court of Appeal erred in holding that the aboriginal right had not been extinguished before April 17, 1982, the date of commencement of the Constitution Act, 1982, and in particular in holding that, as a matter of fact and law, the appellant possessed the aboriginal right to fish for food. In the alternative, the respondent alleged, the Court of Appeal erred in its conclusions respecting the scope of the aboriginal right to fish for food and the extent to which it may be regulated, more particularly in holding that the aboriginal right included the right to take fish for the ceremonial purposes and societal needs of the Band and that the Band enjoyed a constitutionally protected priority over the rights of other people engaged in fishing. Section 35(1), the respondent maintained, did not invalidate legislation passed for the purpose of conservation and resource management, public health and safety and other overriding public interests such as the reasonable needs of other user groups. Finally, it maintained that the conviction ought not to have been set aside or a new trial directed because the appellant failed to establish a prima facie case that the reduction in the length of the net had unreasonably interfered with his right by preventing him from meeting his food fish requirements. According to the respondent, the Court of Appeal had erred in shifting the burden of proof to the Crown on the issue before the appellant had established a prima facie case.

The National Indian Brotherhood Assembly of First Nations intervened in support of the appellant. The Attorneys General of British Columbia, Ontario, Quebec, Saskatchewan, Alberta and Newfoundland supported the respondent, as did the British Columbia Wildlife Federation and others, the Fishery Council of British Columbia and the United Fishermen and Allied Workers Union.

THE REGULATORY SCHEME

The Fisheries Act, s. 34, confers on the Governor in Council broad powers to make regulations respecting the fisheries, the most relevant for our purposes being those set forth in the following paragraphs of that section:

> 34. . . .
> (a) for the proper management and control of the seacoast and inland fisheries;
> (b) respecting the conservation and protection of fish;
> (c) respecting the catching, loading, landing, handling, transporting, possession and disposal of fish; . . .
> (e) respecting the use of fishing gear and equipment;
> (f) respecting the issue, suspension and cancellation of licences and leases;
> (g) respecting the terms and conditions under which a lease or licence may be issued;

Contravention of the Act and the regulations is made an offence under s. 61(1) under which the appellant was charged.

Acting under its regulation-making powers, the Governor in Council enacted the British Columbia Fishery (General) Regulations, SOR/84-248. Under these Regulations (s. 4), everyone is, inter alia, prohibited from fishing without a licence, and then only in areas and at the times and in the manner authorized by the Act or regulations. That provision also prohibits buying, selling, trading or bartering fish other than those lawfully caught under the authority of a commercial fishing licence. Section 4 reads:

> 4.(1) Unless otherwise provided in the Act or in any Regulations made thereunder in respect of the fisheries to which these Regulations apply or in the Wildlife Act (British Columbia), no person shall fish except under the authority of a licence or permit issued thereunder.
> (2) No person shall fish for any species of fish in the Province or in Canadian fisheries waters of the Pacific Ocean except in areas and at times authorized by the Act or any Regulations made thereunder in respect of the fisheries to which these Regulations apply.
> (3) No person who is the owner of a vessel shall operate that vessel or permit it to be operated in contravention of these Regulations.
> (4) No person shall, without lawful excuse, have in his possession any fish caught or obtained contrary to the Act or any Regulations made thereunder in respect of the fisheries to which these Regulations apply.
> (5) No person shall buy, sell, trade or barter or attempt to buy, sell, trade or barter fish or any portions thereof other than fish lawfully caught under the authority of a commercial fishing licence issued by the Minister or the Minister of Environment for British Columbia.

The Regulations make provision for issuing licences to Indians or a band "for the sole purpose of obtaining food for that Indian and his family and for the band", and no one other than an Indian is permitted to be in possession of fish caught pursuant to such a licence. Subsections 27(1) and (4) of the Regulations read:

> 27.(1) In this section "Indian food fish licence" means a licence issued by the Minister to an Indian or a band for the sole purpose of obtaining food for that Indian and his family or for the band. . . .
> (4) No person other than an Indian shall have in his possession fish caught under the authority of an Indian food fish licence

As in the case of other licences issued under the Act, such licences may, by s. 12 of the Regulations, be subjected to restrictions regarding the species and quantity of fish that may be taken, the places and times when they may be taken, the manner in which they are to be marked and, most important here, the type of gear and equipment that may be used. Section 12 reads as follows:

> 12.(1) Subject to these Regulations and any regulations made under the Act in respect of the fisheries to which these Regulations apply and for the proper management and control of such fisheries, there may be specified in a licence issued under these Regulations
> (a) the species of fish and quantity thereof that is permitted to be taken;
> (b) the period during which and the waters in which fishing is permitted to be carried out;
> (c) the type and quantity of fishing gear and equipment that is permitted to be used and the manner in which it is to be used;
> (d) the manner in which fish caught and retained for educational or scientific purposes is to be held or displayed;
> (e) the manner in which fish caught and retained is to be marked and transported; and
> (f) the manner in which scientific or catch data is to be reported.
> (2) No person fishing under the authority of a licence referred to in subsection (1) shall contravene or fail to comply with the terms of the licence.

Pursuant to these powers, the Musqueam Indian Band, on March 31, 1984, was issued an Indian food fishing licence as it had since 1978 "to fish for salmon for food for themselves and their family" in areas which included the place where the offence charged occurred, the waters of Ladner Reach and Canoe Passage therein described. The licence contained time restrictions as well as the type of gear to be used, notably "One Drift net twenty-five (25) fathoms in length".

The appellant was found fishing in the waters described using a drift net in excess of 25 fathoms. He did not contest this, arguing instead that he had committed no offence because he was acting in the exercise of an existing aboriginal right which was recognized and affirmed by s. 35(1) of the Constitution Act, 1982.

ANALYSIS

We will address first the meaning of "existing" aboriginal rights and the content and scope of the Musqueam right to fish. We will then turn to the meaning of "recognized and affirmed", and the impact of s. 35(1) on the regulatory power of Parliament.

"Existing"

The word "existing" makes it clear that the rights to which s. 35(1) applies are those that were in existence when the Constitution Act, 1982 came into effect. This means that extinguished rights are not revived by the Constitution Act, 1982. A number of courts have taken the position that "existing'" means being in actuality in 1982: R. v. Eninew (1983), 7 C.C.C. (3d) 443, at p. 446 (Sask. Q.B.), affd. (1984), 12 C.C.C. (3d) 365 (Sask. C.A.). See also Attorney-General for Ontario v. Bear Island Foundation (1984), 49 O.R. (2d) 353 (H.C.); R. v. Hare and Debassige (1985), 20 C.C.C. (3d) 1 (Ont. C.A.); Re Steinhauer v. The Queen (1985), 15 C.R.R. 175 (Alta. Q.B.); Martin v. The Queen (1985), 17 C.R.R. 375 (N.B.Q.B.); R. v. Agawa (1988), 28 O.A.C. 201.

Further, an existing aboriginal right cannot be read so as to incorporate the specific manner in which it was regulated before 1982. The notion of freezing existing rights would incorporate into the Constitution a crazy patchwork of regulations. Blair J.A. in Agawa, supra, had this to say about the matter, at p. 214:

> Some academic commentators have raised a further problem which cannot be ignored. The Ontario Fishery Regulations contain detailed rules which vary for different regions in the province. Among other things, the Regulations specify seasons and methods of fishing, species of fish which can be caught and catch limits. Similar detailed provisions apply under the comparable fisheries Regulations in force in other provinces. These detailed provisions might be constitutionalized if it were decided that the existing treaty rights referred to in s. 35(1) were those remaining after regulation at the time of the proclamation of the Constitution Act, 1982.

As noted by Blair J.A., academic commentary lends support to the conclusion that "existing" means "unextinguished" rather than exercisable at a certain time in history. Professor Slattery, "Understanding Aboriginal Rights" (1987), 66 Can. Bar Rev. 726, at pp. 781 - 82, has observed the following about reading regulations into the rights:

> This approach reads into the Constitution the myriad of regulations affecting the exercise of aboriginal rights, regulations that differed considerably from place to place across the country. It does not permit differentiation between regulations of long-term significance and those enacted to deal with temporary conditions, or between reasonable and unreasonable restrictions. Moreover, it might require that a constitutional amendment be enacted to implement regulations more stringent than those in existence on 17 April 1982. This solution seems unsatisfactory.

See also Professor McNeil, "The Constitutional Rights of the Aboriginal People of Canada" (1982), 4 Sup. Ct. L. Rev. 25, at p. 258 (q.v.); Pentney, "The Rights of the Aboriginal Peoples of Canada in the Constitution Act, 1982, Part II, Section 35: The Substantive Guarantee" (1987), 22 U.B.C. Law Rev. 207.

The arbitrariness of such an approach can be seen if one considers the recent history of the federal regulation in the context of the present case and the fishing industry. If the Constitution Act, 1982 had been enacted a few years earlier, any right held by the Musqueam Band, on this approach, would have been constitutionally subjected to the restrictive regime of personal licences that had existed since 1917. Under that regime, the Musqueam catch had by 1969 become minor or non-existent. In 1978 a system of band licences was introduced on an experimental basis which permitted the Musqueam to fish with a 75 fathom net for a greater number of days than other people. Under this regime, from 1977 to 1984, the number of Band members who fished for food increased from 19 persons using 15 boats, to 64 persons using 38 boats, while 10 other members of the Band fished under commercial licences. Before this regime, the Band's food fish requirement had basically been provided by Band members who were licensed for commercial fishing. Since the regime introduced in 1978 was in force in 1982, then, under this approach, the scope and content of an aboriginal right to fish would be determined by the details of the Band's 1978 licence.

The unsuitability of the approach can also be seen from another perspective. Ninety-one other tribes of Indians, comprising over 20,000 people (compared with 540 Musqueam on the reserve and 100 others off the reserve) obtain their food fish from the Fraser River. Some or all of these bands may have an aboriginal right to fish there. A constitutional patchwork quilt would be created if the constitutional right of these bands were to be determined by the specific regime available to each of those bands in 1982.

Far from being defined according to the regulatory scheme in place in 1982, the phrase "existing aboriginal rights" must be interpreted flexibly so as to permit their evolution over time. To use Professor Slattery's expression, in "Understanding Aboriginal Rights", supra, at p. 782, the word "existing" suggests that those rights are "affirmed in a contemporary form rather than in their primeval simplicity and vigour". Clearly, then, an approach to the constitutional guarantee embodied in s. 35(1) which would incorporate "frozen rights" must be rejected.

The Aboriginal Right

We turn now to the aboriginal right at stake in this appeal. The Musqueam Indian Reserve is located on the north shore of the Fraser River close to the mouth of that river and within the limits of the City of Vancouver. There has been a Musqueam village there for hundreds of years. This appeal does not directly concern the reserve or the adjacent waters, but arises out of the Band's right to fish in another area of the Fraser River estuary known as Canoe Passage in the South Arm of the river, some 16 kilometres (about 10 miles) from the reserve. The reserve and those waters are separated by the Vancouver International Airport and the Municipality of Richmond.

The evidence reveals that the Musqueam have lived in the area as an organized society long before the coming of European settlers, and that the taking of salmon was an integral part of their lives and remains so to this day. Much of the evidence of an aboriginal right to fish was given by Dr. Suttles, an anthropologist, supported by that of Mr. Grant, the Band administrator. The Court of Appeal thus summarized Dr. Suttles' evidence, at pp. 307-308:

Dr. Suttles was qualified as having particular qualifications in respect of the ethnography of the Coast Salish Indian people of which the Musqueams were one of several tribes. He thought that the Musqueam had lived in their historic territory, which includes the Fraser River estuary, for at least 1,500 years. That historic territory extended from the north shore of Burrard Inlet to the south shore of the main channel of the Fraser River including the waters of the three channels by which that river reaches the ocean. As part of the Salish people, the Musqueam were part of a regional social network covering a much larger area but, as a tribe, were themselves an organized social group with their own name, territory and resources. Between the tribes there was a flow of people, wealth and food. No tribe was wholly self-sufficient or occupied its territory to the complete exclusion of others.

Dr. Suttles described the special position occupied by the salmon fishery in that society. The salmon was not only an important source of food but played an important part in the system of beliefs of the Salish people, and in their ceremonies. The salmon were held to be a race of beings that had, in "myth times", established a bond with human beings requiring the salmon to come each year to give their bodies to the humans who, in turn, treated them with respect shown by performance of the proper ritual. Towards the salmon, as toward other creatures, there was an attitude of caution and respect which resulted in effective conservation of the various species.

While the trial for a violation of a penal prohibition may not be the most appropriate setting in which to determine the existence of an aboriginal right, and the evidence was not extensive, the correctness of the finding of fact of the trial judge "that Mr. Sparrow was fishing in ancient tribal territory where his ancestors had fished from time immemorial in that part of the mouth of the Fraser River for salmon" is supported by the evidence and was not contested. The existence of the right, the Court of Appeal tells us, "was not the subject of serious dispute". It is not surprising, then, that, taken with other circumstances, that court should find that "the judgment appealed from was wrong in . . . failing to hold that Sparrow at the relevant time was exercising an existing aboriginal right".

In this Court, however, the respondent contested the Court of Appeal's finding, contending that the evidence was insufficient to discharge the appellant's burden of proof upon the issue. It is true that for the period from 1867 to 1961 the evidence is scanty. But the evidence was not disputed or contradicted in the courts below and there is evidence of sufficient continuity of the right to support the Court of Appeal's finding, and we would not disturb it.

What the Crown really insisted on, both in this Court and the courts below, was that the Musqueam Band's aboriginal right to fish had been extinguished by regulations under the Fisheries Act.

The history of the regulation of fisheries in British Columbia is set out in Jack v. The Queen, [1980] 1 S.C.R. 294, esp. at pp. 308 et seq., and we need only summarize it here. Before the province's entry into Confederation in 1871, the fisheries were not regulated in any significant way, whether in respect of Indians or other people. The Indians were not only permitted but encouraged to continue fishing for their own food requirements. Commercial and sport fishing were not then of any great importance. The federal Fisheries Act was only proclaimed in force in the province in 1876 and the first Salmon Fishery Regulations for British Columbia were adopted in 1878 and were minimal.

The 1878 regulations were the first to mention Indians. They simply provided that the Indians were at all times at liberty, by any means other than drift nets or spearing, to fish for food for themselves, but not for sale or barter. The Indian right or liberty to fish was thereby restricted, and more stringent restrictions were added over the years. As noted in Jack v. The Queen, supra, at p. 310:

> The federal Regulations became increasingly strict in regard to the Indian fishery over time, as first the commercial fishery developed and then sport fishing became common. What we can see is an increasing subjection of the Indian fishery to regulatory control. First, the regulation of the use of drift nets, then the restriction of fishing to food purposes, then the requirement of permission from the Inspector and, ultimately, in 1917, the power to regulate even food fishing by means of conditions attached to the permit.

The 1917 regulations were intended to make still stronger the provisions against commercial fishing in the exercise of the Indian right to fish for food; see P.C. 2539 of Sept. 22, 1917. The Indian food fishing provisions remained essentially the same from 1917 to 1977. The regulations of 1977 retained the general principles of the previous sixty years. An Indian could fish for food under a "special licence" specifying method, locale and times of fishing. Following an experimental program to be discussed later, the 1981 regulations provided for the entirely new concept of a Band food fishing licence, while retaining comprehensive specification of conditions for the exercise of licences.

It is this progressive restriction and detailed regulation of the fisheries which, respondent's counsel maintained, have had the effect of extinguishing any aboriginal right to fish. The extinguishment need not be express, he argued, but may take place where the sovereign authority is exercised in a manner "necessarily inconsistent" with the continued enjoyment of aboriginal rights. For this proposition, he particularly relied on St. Catherine's Milling and Lumber Co. v. The Queen (1888), 14 App. Cas. 46 (P.C.); Calder v. Attorney-General of British Columbia, [1973] S.C.R. 313; Baker Lake (Hamlet) v. Minister of Indian Affairs and Northern Development, [1980] 1 F.C. 518 (T.D.); and Attorney General of Ontario v. Bear Island Foundation, supra. The consent to its extinguishment before the Constitution Act, 1982 was not required; the intent of the sovereign could be effected not only by statute but by valid regulations. Here, in his view, the regulations had entirely displaced any aboriginal right. There is, he submitted, a fundamental inconsistency between the communal right to fish embodied in the aboriginal right, and fishing under a special licence or permit issued to individual Indians (as was the case until 1977) in the discretion of the Minister and subject to terms and conditions which, if breached, may result in cancellation of the licence. The Fisheries Act and its regulations were, he argued, intended to constitute a complete Code inconsistent with the continued existence of an aboriginal right.

At bottom, the respondent's argument confuses regulation with extinguishment. That the right is controlled in great detail by the regulations does not mean that the right is thereby extinguished. The distinction to be drawn was carefully explained, in the context of federalism, in the first Fisheries case, Attorney-General for Canada v. Attorney-General for Ontario, [1898] A.C. 700. There, the Privy Council had to deal with the interrelationship between, on the one hand, provincial property, which by s. 109 of the Constitution Act, 1867 is vested in the provinces (and so falls to be regulated qua property exclusively by the provinces) and, on the other hand, the federal power to legislate respecting the fisheries thereon under s. 91(12) of that Act. The Privy Council said the following in relation to the federal regulation (at pp. 712-13):

> ... the power to legislate in relation to fisheries does necessarily to a certain extent enable the Legislature so empowered to affect proprietary rights. An enactment, for example, prescribing the times of the year during which fishing is to be allowed, or the instruments which may be employed for the purpose (which it was admitted the Dominion Legislature was empowered to pass) might very seriously touch the exercise of proprietary rights, and the extent, character, and scope of such legislation is left entirely to the Dominion Legislature. The suggestion that the power might be abused so as to amount to a practical confiscation of property does not warrant the imposition by the Courts of any limit upon the absolute power of legislation conferred. The supreme legislative power in relation to any subject-matter is always capable of abuse, but it is not to be assumed that it will be improperly used; if it is, the only remedy is an appeal to those by whom the Legislature is elected.

In the context of aboriginal rights, it could be argued that, before 1982, an aboriginal right was automatically extinguished to the extent that it was inconsistent with a statute. As Mahoney J. stated in Baker Lake, supra, at p. 568:

> Once a statute has been validly enacted, it must be given effect. If its necessary effect is to abridge or entirely abrogate a common law right, then that is the effect that the courts must give it. That is as true of an aboriginal title as of any other common law right.

See also Attorney General of Ontario v. Bear Island Foundation, supra, at pp. 439-40. That in Judson J.'s view was what had occurred in Calder, supra, where, as he saw it, a series of statutes evinced a unity of intention to exercise a sovereignty inconsistent with any conflicting interest, including aboriginal title. But Hall J. in that case stated (at p. 404) that "the onus of proving that the Sovereign intended to extinguish the Indian title lies on the respondent and *that intention must be 'clear and plain'*" (emphasis added). The test of extinguishment to be adopted, in our opinion, is that the Sovereign's intention must be clear and plain if it is to extinguish an aboriginal right.

There is nothing in the Fisheries Act or its detailed regulations that demonstrates a clear and plain intention to extinguish the Indian aboriginal right to fish. The fact that express provision permitting the Indians to fish for food may have applied to all Indians and that for an extended period permits were discretionary and issued on an individual rather than a communal basis in no way shows a clear intention to extinguish. These permits were simply a manner of controlling the fisheries, not defining underlying rights.

We would conclude then that the Crown has failed to discharge its burden of proving extinguishment. In our opinion, the Court of Appeal made no mistake in holding that the Indians have an existing aboriginal right to fish in the area where Mr. Sparrow was fishing at the time of the charge. This approach is consistent with ensuring that an aboriginal right should not be defined by incorporating the ways in which it has been regulated in the past.

The scope of the existing Musqueam right to fish must now be delineated. The anthropological evidence relied on to establish the existence of the right suggests that, for the Musqueam, the salmon fishery has always constituted an integral part of their distinctive culture. Its significant role involved not only consumption for subsistence purposes, but also consumption of salmon on ceremonial and social occasions. The Musqueam have always fished for reasons connected to their cultural and physical survival. As we stated earlier, the right to do so may be exercised in a contemporary manner.

The British Columbia Court of Appeal in this case held that the aboriginal right was to fish for food purposes, but that purpose was not to be confined to mere subsistence. Rather, the right was found to extend to fish consumed for social and ceremonial activities. The Court of Appeal thereby defined the right as protecting the same interest as is reflected in the government's food fish policy. In limiting the right to food purposes, the Court of Appeal referred to the line of cases involving the interpretation of the Natural Resources Agreements and the food purpose limitation placed on the protection of fishing and hunting rights by the Constitution Act, 1930 (see R. v. Wesley, [1932] 2 W.W.R. 337; Prince and Myron v. The Queen, [1964] S.C.R. 81; R. v. Sutherland, [1980] 2 S.C.R. 451).

The Court of Appeal's position was attacked from both sides. The respondent for its part, argued that, if an aboriginal right to fish does exist, it does not include the right to take fish for the ceremonial and social activities of the Band. The appellant, on the other hand, attacked the Court of Appeal's restriction of the right to a right to fish for food. He argued that the principle that the holders of aboriginal rights may exercise those rights according to their own discretion has been recognized by this Court in the context of the protection of treaty hunting rights (Simon v. The Queen, [1985] 2 S.C.R. 387) and that it should be applied in this case such that the right is defined as a right to fish for any purpose and by any non-dangerous method.

In relation to this submission, it was contended before this Court that the aboriginal right extends to commercial fishing. While no commercial fishery existed prior to the arrival of European settlers, it is contended that the Musqueam practice of bartering in early society may be revived as a modern right to fish for commercial purposes. The presence of numerous interveners representing commercial fishing interests, and the suggestion on the facts that the net length restriction is at least in part related to the probable commercial use of fish caught under the Musqueam food fishing licence, indicate the possibility of conflict between aboriginal fishing and the   competitive commercial fishery with respect to economically valuable fish such as salmon. We recognize the existence of this conflict and the probability of its intensification as fish availability drops, demand rises and tensions increase. Government regulations governing the exercise of the Musqueam right to fish, as described above, have only recognized the right to fish for food for over a hundred years. This may have reflected the existing position. However, historical policy on the part of the Crown is not only incapable of extinguishing the existing aboriginal right without clear intention, but is also incapable of, in itself, delineating that right. The nature of government regulations cannot be determinative of the content and scope of an existing aboriginal right. Government policy can however regulate the exercise of that right, but such regulation must be in keeping with s. 35(1).

In the courts below, the case at bar was not presented on the footing of an aboriginal right to fish for commercial or livelihood purposes. Rather, the focus was and continues to be on the validity of a net length restriction affecting the appellant's food fishing licence. We therefore adopt the Court of Appeal's characterization of the right for the purpose of this appeal, and confine our reasons to the meaning of the constitutional recognition and affirmation of the existing aboriginal right to fish for food and social and ceremonial purposes.

"Recognized and Affirmed"

We now turn to the impact of s. 35(1) of the Constitution Act, 1982 on the regulatory power of Parliament and on the outcome of this appeal specifically.

Counsel for the appellant argued that the effect of s. 35(1) is to deny Parliament's power to restrictively regulate aboriginal fishing rights under s. 91(24) ("Indians and Lands Reserved for the Indians"), and s. 91(12) ("Sea Coast and Inland Fisheries"). The essence of this submission, supported by the intervener, the National Indian Brotherhood Assembly of First Nations, is that the right to regulate is part of the right to use the resource in the Band's discretion. Section 35(1) is not subject to s. 1 of the Charter, nor to legislative override under s. 33. The appellant submitted that, if the regulatory power continued, the limits on its extent are set by the word "inconsistent" in s. 52(1) of the Constitution Act, 1982 and the protective and remedial purposes of s. 35(1). This means that aboriginal title entails a right to fish by any non-dangerous method chosen by the aboriginals engaged in fishing. Any continuing governmental power of regulation would have to be exceptional and strictly limited to regulation that is clearly not inconsistent with the protective and remedial purposes of s. 35(1). Thus, counsel for the appellant speculated, "in certain circumstances, necessary and reasonable conservation measures *might* qualify" [emphasis added]—where for example such measures were necessary to prevent serious impairment of the aboriginal rights of present and future generations, where conservation could only be achieved by restricting the right and not by restricting fishing by other users, and where the aboriginal group concerned was unwilling to implement necessary conservation measures. The onus of proving a justification for restrictive regulations would lie with the government by analogy with s. 1 of the Charter.

In response to these submissions and in finding the appropriate interpretive framework for s. 35(1), we start by looking at the background of s. 35(1).

It is worth recalling that while British policy towards the native population was based on respect for their right to occupy their traditional lands, a proposition to which the Royal Proclamation of 1763 bears witness, there was from the outset never any doubt that sovereignty and legislative power, and indeed the underlying title, to such lands vested in the Crown; see Johnson v. M'Intosh (1823), 8

Wheaton 543 (U.S.S.C.); see also the Royal Proclamation itself (R.S.C., 1985, App. II, No. 1, pp. 4-6); Calder, supra, per Judson J. at p. 328, Hall J. at pp. 383, 402. And there can be no doubt that over the years the rights of the Indians were often honoured in the breach (for one instance in a recent case in this Court, see Canadian Pacific Ltd. v. Paul, [1988] 2 S.C.R. 654, 91 N.B.R. (2d) 43). As Mac-Donald J. stated in Pasco v. Canadian National Railway Co., [1986] 1 C.N.L.R. 35, at p. 37 (B.C.S.C.): "We cannot recount with much pride the treatment accorded to the native people of this country."

For many years, the rights of the Indians to their aboriginal lands—certainly as legal rights—were virtually ignored. The leading cases defining Indian rights in the early part of the century were directed at claims supported by the Royal Proclamation or other legal instruments, and even these cases were essentially concerned with settling legislative jurisdiction or the rights of commercial enterprises. For fifty years after the publication of Clement's *The Law of the Canadian Constitution* (3rd ed. 1916), there was a virtual absence of discussion of any kind of Indian rights to land even in academic literature. By the late 1960s, aboriginal claims were not even recognized by the federal government as having any legal status. Thus the *Statement of the Government of Canada on Indian Policy 1969*, although well meaning, contained the assertion (at p. 11) that "aboriginal claims to land . . . are so general and undefined that it is not realistic to think of them as specific claims capable of remedy except through a policy and program that will end injustice to the Indians as members of the Canadian community." In the same general period, the James Bay development by Quebec Hydro was originally initiated without regard to the rights of the Indians who lived there, even though these were expressly protected by a constitutional instrument; see the Québec Boundary Extension Act, 1912, S.C. 1912, c. 45. It took a number of judicial decisions and notably the Calder case in this Court (1973) to prompt a reassessment of the position being taken by government.

In the light of its reassessment of Indian claims following Calder, the federal Government on August 8, 1973 issued "a statement of policy" regarding Indian lands. By it, it sought to "signify the Government's *recognition and acceptance* of its continuing responsibility under the British North America Act for Indians and lands reserved for Indians", which it regarded "as an historic evolution dating back to the Royal Proclamation of 1763, which, whatever differences there may be about its judicial interpretation, stands as a basic declaration of the Indian people's interests in land in this country". [Emphasis added.] See Statement made by the Honourable Jean Chrétien, Minister of Indian Affairs and Northern Development on Claims of Indian and Inuit People, August 8, 1973. The remarks about these lands were intended "as an expression of acknowledged responsibility". But the statement went on to express, for the first time, the government's willingness to negotiate regarding claims of aboriginal title, specifically in British Columbia, Northern Québec, and the Territories, and this without regard to formal supporting documents. "The Government", it stated, "is now ready to negotiate with authorized representatives of these native peoples on the basis that where their traditional interest in the lands concerned can be established, an agreed form of compensation or benefit will be provided to native peoples in return for their interest."

It is obvious from its terms that the approach taken towards aboriginal claims in the 1973 statement constituted an expression of a policy, rather than a legal position; see also Canada, Department of Indian Affairs and Northern Development, *In All Fairness: A Native Claims Policy—Comprehensive Claims* (1981), pp. 11-12; Slattery, "Understanding Aboriginal Rights" (1987), 66 Can. Bar Rev. 726, at p. 730. As recently as Guerin v. The Queen, [1984] 2 S.C.R. 335, the federal government argued in this Court that any federal obligation was of a political character.

It is clear, then, that s. 35(1) of the Constitution Act, 1982, represents the culmination of a long and difficult struggle in both the political forum and the courts for the constitutional recognition of aboriginal rights. The strong representations of native associations and other groups concerned with the welfare of Canada's aboriginal peoples made the adoption of s. 35(1) possible and it is important to note that the provision applies to the Indians, the Inuit and the Métis. Section 35(1), at the least, provides a solid constitutional base upon which subsequent negotiations can take place. It also affords aboriginal peoples constitutional protection against provincial legislative power. We are, of course, aware that this would, in any event, flow from the Guerin case, supra, but for a proper understanding of the situation, it is essential to remember that the Guerin case was decided after the commencement of the Constitution Act, 1982. In addition to its effect on aboriginal rights, s. 35(1) clarified other issues regarding the enforcement of treaty rights (see Sanders, "Pre-existing Rights: The Aboriginal Peoples of Canada", in Beaudoin and Ratushny, eds., *The Canadian Charter of Rights and Freedoms*, 2nd ed., esp. at p. 730).

In our opinion, the significance of s. 35(1) extends beyond these fundamental effects. Professor Lyon in "An Essay on Constitutional Interpretation" (1988), 26 Osgoode Hall L.J. 95, says the following about s. 35(1), at p. 100:

> . . . the context of 1982 is surely enough to tell us that this is not just a codification of the case law on aboriginal rights that had accumulated by 1982. Section 35 calls for a just settlement for aboriginal peoples. It renounces the old rules of the game under which the Crown established courts of law and denied those courts the authority to question sovereign claims made by the Crown.

The approach to be taken with respect to interpreting the meaning of s. 35(1) is derived from general principles of constitutional interpretation, principles relating to aboriginal rights, and the purposes behind the constitutional provision itself. Here, we will sketch the framework for an interpretation of "recognized and affirmed" that, in our opinion, gives appropriate weight to the constitutional nature of these words.

In Reference re Manitoba Language Rights, [1985] 1 S.C.R. 721, this Court said the following about the perspective to be adopted when interpreting a constitution, at p. 745:

> The Constitution of a country is a statement of the will of the people to be governed in accordance with certain principles held as fundamental and certain prescriptions restrictive of the powers of the legislature and government. It is, as s. 52 of the Constitution Act, 1982 declares, the "supreme law" of the nation, unalterable by the normal legislative process,

and unsuffering of laws inconsistent with it. The duty of the judiciary is to interpret and apply the laws of Canada and each of the provinces, and it is thus our duty to ensure that the constitutional law prevails.

The nature of s. 35(1) itself suggests that it be construed in a purposive way. When the purposes of the affirmation of aboriginal rights are considered, it is clear that a generous, liberal interpretation of the words in the constitutional provision is demanded. When the Court of Appeal below was confronted with the submission that s. 35 has no effect on aboriginal or treaty rights and that it is merely a preamble to the parts of the Constitution Act, 1982, which deal with aboriginal rights, it said the following, at p. 322:

> This submission gives no meaning to s. 35. If accepted, it would result in denying its clear statement that existing rights are hereby recognized and affirmed, and would turn that into a mere promise to recognize and affirm those rights sometime in the future. . . . To so construe s. 35(1) would be to ignore its language and the principle that the Constitution should be interpreted in a liberal and remedial way. We cannot accept that that principle applies less strongly to aboriginal rights than to the rights guaranteed by the Charter, particularly having regard to the history and to the approach to interpreting treaties and statutes relating to Indians required by such cases as Nowegijick v. R., [1983] 1 S.C.R. 29. . . .

In Nowegijick v. The Queen, [1983] 1 S.C.R. 29, at p. 36, the following principle that should govern the interpretation of Indian treaties and statutes was set out:

> . . . treaties and statutes relating to Indians should be liberally construed and doubtful expressions resolved in favour of the Indians.

In R. v. Agawa, supra, Blair J.A. stated that the above principle should apply to the interpretation of s. 35(1). He added the following principle to be equally applied, at pp. 215-16:

> The second principle was enunciated by the late Associate Chief Justice MacKinnon in R. v. Taylor and Williams (1981), 34 O.R. (2d) 360. He emphasized the importance of Indian history and traditions as well as the perceived effect of a treaty at the time of its execution. He also cautioned against determining Indian right "in a vacuum". The honour of the Crown is involved in the interpretation of Indian treaties and, as a consequence, fairness to the Indians is a governing consideration. He said at p. 367:
>> The principles to be applied to the interpretation of Indian treaties have been much canvassed over the years. In approaching the terms of a treaty quite apart from the other considerations already noted, the honour of the Crown is always involved and no appearance of "sharp dealing" should be sanctioned.
> This view is reflected in recent judicial decisions which have emphasized the responsibility of Government to protect the rights of Indians arising from the special trust relationship created by history, treaties and legislation: see Guerin v. the Queen, [1984] 2 S.C.R. 335; 55 N.R. 161; 13 D.L.R. (4th) 321.

In Guerin, supra, the Musqueam Band surrendered reserve lands to the Crown for lease to a golf club. The terms obtained by the Crown were much less favourable than those approved by the Band at the surrender meeting. This Court found that the Crown owed a fiduciary obligation to the Indians with respect to the lands. The sui generis nature of Indian title, and the historic powers and responsibility assumed by the Crown constituted the source of such a fiduciary obligation. In our opinion, Guerin, together with R. v. Taylor and Williams (1981), 34 O.R. (2d) 360, ground a general guiding principle for s. 35(1). That is, the Government has the responsibility to act in a fiduciary capacity with respect to aboriginal peoples. The relationship between the Government and aboriginals is trust-like, rather than adversarial, and contemporary recognition and affirmation of aboriginal rights must be defined in light of this historic relationship.

We agree with both the British Columbia Court of Appeal below and the Ontario Court of Appeal that the principles outlined above, derived from Nowegijick, Taylor and Williams and Guerin, should guide the interpretation of s. 35(1). As commentators have noted, s. 35(1) is a solemn commitment that must be given meaningful content (Lyon, supra; Pentney, supra; Schwartz, "Unstarted Business: Two Approaches to Defining s. 35—'What's in the Box?' and 'What Kind of Box?'", Ch. XXIV, in First Principles, Second Thoughts (Montréal: Institute for Research on Public Policy, 1986); Slattery, supra; and Slattery, "The Hidden Constitution: Aboriginal Rights in Canada" (1984), 32 Am. J. of Comp. Law 361).

In response to the appellant's submission that s. 35(1) rights are more securely protected than the rights guaranteed by the Charter, it is true that s. 35(1) is not subject to s. 1 of the Charter. In our opinion, this does not mean that any law or regulation affecting aboriginal rights will automatically be of no force or effect by the operation of s. 52 of the Constitution Act, 1982. Legislation that affects the exercise of aboriginal rights will nonetheless be valid, if it meets the test for justifying an interference with a right recognized and affirmed under s. 35(1).

There is no explicit language in the provision that authorizes this Court or any court to assess the legitimacy of any government legislation that restricts aboriginal rights. Yet, we find that the words "recognition and affirmation" incorporate the fiduciary relationship referred to earlier and so import some restraint on the exercise of sovereign power. Rights that are recognized and affirmed are not absolute. Federal legislative powers continue, including, of course, the right to legislate with respect to Indians pursuant to s. 91(24) of the Constitution Act, 1867. These powers must, however, now be read together with s. 35(1). In other words, federal power must be reconciled with federal duty and the best way to achieve that reconciliation is to demand the justification of any government regulation that infringes upon or denies aboriginal rights. Such scrutiny is in keeping with the liberal interpretive principle enunciated in Nowegijick, supra, and the concept of holding the Crown to a high standard of honourable dealing with respect to the aboriginal peoples of Canada as suggested by Guerin v. The Queen, supra.

We refer to Professor Slattery's "Understanding Aboriginal Rights", supra, with respect to the task of envisioning a s. 35(1) justificatory process. Professor Slattery, at p. 782, points out that a justificatory process is required as a compromise between a "patchwork" characterization of aboriginal rights whereby past regulations would be read into a definition of the rights, and a characterization that would guarantee aboriginal rights in their original form unrestricted by subsequent regulation. We agree with him that these two extreme positions must be rejected in favour of a justificatory scheme.

Section 35(1) suggests that while regulation affecting aboriginal rights is not precluded, such regulation must be enacted according to a valid objective. Our history has shown, unfortunately all too well, that Canada's aboriginal peoples are justified in worrying about government objectives that may be superficially neutral but which constitute de facto threats to the existence of aboriginal rights and interests. By giving aboriginal rights constitutional status and priority, Parliament and the provinces have sanctioned challenges to social and economic policy objectives embodied in legislation to the extent that aboriginal rights are affected. Implicit in this constitutional scheme is the obligation of the legislature to satisfy the test of justification. The way in which a legislative objective is to be attained must uphold the honour of the Crown and must be in keeping with the unique contemporary relationship, grounded in history and policy, between the Crown and Canada's aboriginal peoples. The extent of legislative or regulatory impact on an existing aboriginal right may be scrutinized so as to ensure recognition and affirmation.

The constitutional recognition afforded by the provision therefore gives a measure of control over government conduct and a strong check on legislative power. While it does not promise immunity from government regulation in a society that, in the twentieth century, is increasingly more complex, interdependent and sophisticated, and where exhaustible resources need protection and management, it does hold the Crown to a substantive promise. The government is required to bear the burden of justifying any legislation that has some negative effect on any aboriginal right protected under s. 35(1).

In these reasons, we will outline the appropriate analysis under s. 35(1) in the context of a regulation made pursuant to the Fisheries Act. We wish to emphasize the importance of context and a case-by-case approach to s. 35(1). Given the generality of the text of the constitutional provision, and especially in light of the complexities of aboriginal history, society and rights, the contours of a justificatory standard must be defined in the specific factual context of each case.

SECTION 35(1) AND THE REGULATION OF THE FISHERIES

Taking the above framework as guidance, we propose to set out the test for prima facie interference with an existing aboriginal right and for the justification of such an interference. With respect to the question of the regulation of the fisheries, the existence of s. 35(1) of the Constitution Act, 1982, renders the authority of R. v. Derricksan, supra, inapplicable. In that case, Laskin C.J., for this Court, found that there was nothing to prevent the Fisheries Act and the Regulations from subjecting the alleged aboriginal right to fish in a particular area to the controls thereby imposed. As the Court of Appeal in the case at bar noted, the Derricksan line of cases established that, before April 17, 1982, the aboriginal right to fish was subject to regulation by legislation and subject to extinguishment. The new constitutional status of that right enshrined in s. 35(1) suggests that a different approach must be taken in deciding whether regulation of the fisheries might be out of keeping with constitutional protection.

The first question to be asked is whether the legislation in question has the effect of interfering with an existing aboriginal right. If it does have such an effect, it represents a prima facie infringement of s. 35(1). Parliament is not expected to act in a manner contrary to the rights and interests of aboriginals, and, indeed, may be barred from doing so by the second stage of s. 35(1) analysis. The inquiry with respect to interference begins with a reference to the characteristics or incidents of the right at stake. Our earlier observations regarding the scope of the aboriginal right to fish are relevant here. Fishing rights are not traditional property rights. They are rights held by a collective and are in keeping with the culture and existence of that group. Courts must be careful, then, to avoid the application of traditional common law concepts of property as they develop their understanding of what the reasons for judgment in Guerin, supra, at p. 382, referred to as the "sui generis" nature of aboriginal rights. (See also Little Bear, "A Concept of Native Title", [1982] 5 Can. Legal Aid Bul. 99.)

While it is impossible to give an easy definition of fishing rights, it is possible, and, indeed, crucial, to be sensitive to the aboriginal perspective itself on the meaning of the rights at stake. For example, it would be artificial to try to create a hard distinction between the right to fish and the particular manner in which that right is exercised.

To determine whether the fishing rights have been interfered with such as to constitute a prima facie infringement of s. 35(1), certain questions must be asked. First, is the limitation unreasonable? Second, does the regulation impose undue hardship? Third, does the regulation deny to the holders of the right their preferred means of exercising that right? The onus of proving a prima facie infringement lies on the individual or group challenging the legislation. In relation to the facts of this appeal, the regulation would be found to be a prima facie interference if it were found to be an adverse restriction on the Musqueam exercise of their right to fish for food. We wish to note here that the issue does not merely require looking at whether the fish catch has been reduced below that needed for the reasonable food and ceremonial needs of the Musqueam Indians. Rather the test involves asking whether either the purpose or the effect of the restriction on net length unnecessarily infringes the interests protected by the fishing right. If, for example, the Musqueam were forced to spend undue time and money per fish caught or if the net length reduction resulted in a hardship to the Musqueam in catching fish, then the first branch of the s. 35(1) analysis would be met.

If a prima facie interference is found, the analysis moves to the issue of justification. This is the test that addresses the question of what constitutes legitimate regulation of a constitutional aboriginal right. The justification analysis would proceed as follows. First, is there a valid legislative objective? Here the court would inquire into whether the objective of Parliament in authorizing the department to enact regulations regarding fisheries is valid. The objective of the department in setting out the particular regulations would also be scrutinized. An objective aimed at preserving s. 35(1) rights by conserving and managing a natural resource, for example, would be valid. Also valid would be objectives purporting to prevent the exercise of s. 35(1) rights that would cause harm to the general populace or to aboriginal peoples themselves, or other objectives found to be compelling and substantial.

The Court of Appeal below held, at p. 331, that regulations could be valid if reasonably justified as "necessary for the proper management and conservation of the resource *or in the public interest*" (emphasis added). We find the "public interest" justification to be so vague as to provide no meaningful guidance and so broad as to be unworkable as a test for the justification of a limitation on constitutional rights.

The justification of conservation and resource management, on the other hand, is surely uncontroversial. In Kruger v. The Queen, [1978] 1 S.C.R. 104, the applicability of the B.C. Wildlife Act, S.B.C. 1966, c. 55, to the appellant members of the Penticton Indian Band was considered by this Court. In discussing that Act, the following was said about the objective of conservation (at p. 112):

> Game conservation laws have as their policy the maintenance of wildlife resources. It might be argued that without some conservation measures the ability of Indians or others to hunt for food would become a moot issue in consequence of the destruction of the resource. The presumption is for the validity of a legislative enactment and in this case the presumption has to mean that in the absence of evidence to the contrary the measures taken by the British Columbia Legislature were taken to maintain an effective resource in the Province for its citizens and not to oppose the interests of conservationists and Indians in such a way as to favour the claims of the former.

While the "presumption" of validity is now outdated in view of the constitutional status of the aboriginal rights at stake, it is clear that the value of conservation purposes for government legislation and action has long been recognized. Further, the conservation and management of our resources is consistent with aboriginal beliefs and practices, and, indeed, with the enhancement of aboriginal rights.

If a valid legislative objective is found, the analysis proceeds to the second part of the justification issue. Here, we refer back to the guiding interpretive principle derived from Taylor and Williams and Guerin, supra. That is, the honour of the Crown is at stake in dealings with aboriginal peoples. The special trust relationship and the responsibility of the government vis-à-vis aboriginals must be the first consideration in determining whether the legislation or action in question can be justified.

The problem that arises in assessing the legislation in light of its objective and the responsibility of the Crown is that the pursuit of conservation in a heavily used modern fishery inevitably blurs with the efficient allocation and management of this scarce and valued resource. The nature of the constitutional protection afforded by s. 35(1) in this context demands that there be a link between the question of justification and the allocation of priorities in the fishery. The constitutional recognition and affirmation of aboriginal rights may give rise to conflict with the interests of others given the limited nature of the resource. There is a clear need for guidelines that will resolve the allocational problems that arise regarding the fisheries. We refer to the reasons of Dickson J. in Jack v. The Queen, supra, for such guidelines.

In Jack, the appellants' defence to a charge of fishing for salmon in certain rivers during a prohibited period was based on the alleged constitutional incapacity of Parliament to legislate such as to deny the Indians their right to fish for food. They argued that Art. 13 of the British Columbia Terms of Union imposed a constitutional limitation on the federal power to regulate. While we recognize that the finding that such a limitation had been imposed was not adopted by the majority of this Court, we point out that this case concerns a different constitutional promise that asks this Court to give a meaningful interpretation to recognition and affirmation. That task requires equally meaningful guidelines responsive to the constitutional priority accorded aboriginal rights. We therefore repeat the following passage from Jack, at p. 313:

> Conservation is a valid legislative concern. The appellants concede as much. Their concern is in the allocation of the resource after reasonable and necessary conservation measures have been recognized and given effect to. They do not claim the right to pursue the last living salmon until it is caught. Their position, as I understand it, is one which would give effect to an order of priorities of this nature: (i) conservation; (ii) Indian fishing; (iii) non-Indian commercial fishing; or (iv) non-Indian sports fishing; the burden of conservation measures should not fall primarily upon the Indian fishery.
>
> I agree with the general tenor of this argument. . . . With respect to whatever salmon are to be caught, then priority ought to be given to the Indian fishermen, subject to the practical difficulties occasioned by international waters and the movement of the fish themselves. But any limitation upon Indian fishing that is established for a valid conservation purpose overrides the protection afforded the Indian fishery by art. 13, just as such conservation measures override other taking of fish.

The constitutional nature of the Musqueam food fishing rights means that any allocation of priorities after valid conservation measures have been implemented must give top priority to Indian food fishing. If the objective pertained to conservation, the conservation plan would be scrutinized to assess priorities. While the detailed allocation of maritime resources is a task that must be left to those having expertise in the area, the Indians' food requirements must be met first when that allocation is established. The significance of giving the aboriginal right to fish for food top priority can be described as follows. If, in a given year, conservation needs required a reduction in the number of fish to be caught such that the number equalled the number required for food by the Indians, then all the fish available after conservation would go to the Indians according to the constitutional nature of their fishing right. If, more realistically, there were still fish after the Indian food requirements were met, then the brunt of conservation measures would be borne by the practices of sport fishing and commercial fishing.

The decision of the Nova Scotia Court of Appeal in Denny, Paul and Sylliboy v. The Queen, unreported, judgment rendered March 5, 1990, addresses the constitutionality of the Nova Scotia Micmac Indians' right to fish in the waters of Indian Brook and the Afton River, and does so in a way that accords with our understanding of the constitutional nature of aboriginal rights and the link between allocation and justification required for government regulation of the exercise of the rights. Clarke C.J.N.S., for a unanimous court, found that the Nova Scotia Fishery Regulations enacted pursuant to the federal Fisheries Act were in part inconsistent with the constitutional rights of the appellant Micmac Indians. Section 35(1) of the Constitution Act, 1982, provided the appellants with the right to a top priority allocation of any surplus of the fisheries resource which might exist after the needs of conservation had been taken into account. With respect to the issue of the Indians' priority to a food fishery, Clarke C.J.N.S. noted that the official policy of the federal government recognizes that priority. He added the following, at pp. 22-3:

> I have no hesitation in concluding that factual as well as legislative and policy recognition must be given to the existence of an Indian food fishery in the waters of Indian Brook, adjacent to the Eskasoni Reserve, and the waters of the Afton River after the needs of conservation have been taken into account. . .
>
> To afford user groups such as sports fishermen (anglers) a priority to fish over the legitimate food needs of the appellants and their families is simply not appropriate action on the part of the Federal government. It is inconsistent with the fact that the appellants have for many years, and continue to possess an aboriginal right to fish for food. The appellants have, to employ the words of their counsel, a "right to share in the available resource". This constitutional entitlement is second only to conservation measures that may be undertaken by federal legislation.

Further, Clarke C.J.N.S. found that s. 35(1) provided the constitutional recognition of the aboriginal priority with respect to the fishery, and that the regulations, in failing to guarantee that priority, were in violation of the constitutional provision. He said the following, at p. 25:

> Though it is crucial to appreciate that the rights afforded to the appellants by s. 35(1) are not absolute, the impugned regulatory scheme fails to recognize that this section provides the appellants with a priority of allocation and access to any surplus of the fisheries resource once the needs of conservation have been taken into account. Section 35(1), as applied to these appeals, provides the appellants with an entitlement to fish in the waters in issue to satisfy their food needs, where a surplus exists. To the extent that the regulatory scheme fails to recognize this, it is inconsistent with the Constitution. Section 52 mandates a finding that such regulations are of no force and effect.

In light of this approach, the argument that the cases of R. v. Hare and Debassige (1985), 20 C.C.C. (3d) 1 (Ont. C.A.), and R. v. Eninew, R. v. Bear (1984), 12 C.C.C. (3d) 365 (Sask. C.A.), stand for the proposition that s. 35(1) provides no basis for restricting the power to regulate must be rejected, as was done by the Court of Appeal below. In Hare and Debassige, which addressed the issue of whether the Ontario Fishery Regulations, C.R.C. 1978, c. 849, applied to members of an Indian band entitled to the benefit of the Manitoulin Island Treaty which granted certain rights with respect to taking fish, Thorson J.A.

emphasized the need for priority to be given to measures directed to the management and conservation of fish stocks with the following observation (at p. 17):

> Since 1867 and subject to the limitations thereon imposed by the Constitution, which of course now includes s. 35 of the Constitution Act, 1982, the constitutional authority and responsibility to make laws in relation to the fisheries has rested with Parliament. Central to Parliament's responsibility has been, and continues to be, the need to provide for the proper management and conservation of our fish stocks, and the need to ensure that they are not depleted or imperilled by deleterious practices or methods of fishing.
>
> The prohibitions found in ss. 12 and 20 of the Ontario regulations clearly serve this purpose. Accordingly it need not be ignored by our courts that while these prohibitions place limits on the rights of all persons, they are there to serve the larger interest which all persons share in the proper management and conservation of these important resources.

In Eninew, Hall J.A. found, at p. 368, that "the treaty rights can be limited by such regulations as are reasonable". As we have pointed out, management and conservation of resources is indeed an important and valid legislative objective. Yet, the fact that the objective is of a "reasonable" nature cannot suffice as constitutional recognition and affirmation of aboriginal rights. Rather, the regulations enforced pursuant to a conservation or management objective may be scrutinized according to the justificatory standard outlined above.

We acknowledge the fact that the justificatory standard to be met may place a heavy burden on the Crown. However, government policy with respect to the British Columbia fishery, regardless of s. 35(1), already dictates that, in allocating the right to take fish, Indian food fishing is to be given priority over the interests of other user groups. The constitutional entitlement embodied in s. 35(1) requires the Crown to ensure that its regulations are in keeping with that allocation of priority. The objective of this requirement is not to undermine Parliament's ability and responsibility with respect to creating and administering overall conservation and management plans regarding the salmon fishery. The objective is rather to guarantee that those plans treat aboriginal peoples in a way ensuring that their rights are taken seriously.

Within the analysis of justification, there are further questions to be addressed, depending on the circumstances of the inquiry. These include the questions of whether there has been as little infringement as possible in order to effect the desired result; whether, in a situation of expropriation, fair compensation is available; and, whether the aboriginal group in question has been consulted with respect to the conservation measures being implemented. The aboriginal peoples, with their history of conservation-consciousness and interdependence with natural resources, would surely be expected, at the least, to be informed regarding the determination of an appropriate scheme for the regulation of the fisheries.

We would not wish to set out an exhaustive list of the factors to be considered in the assessment of justification. Suffice it to say that recognition and affirmation requires sensitivity to and respect for the rights of aboriginal peoples on behalf of the government, courts and indeed all Canadians.

APPLICATION TO THIS CASE—IS THE NET LENGTH RESTRICTION VALID?

The Court of Appeal below found that there was not sufficient evidence in this case to proceed with an analysis of s. 35(1) with respect to the right to fish for food. In reviewing the competing expert evidence, and recognizing that fish stock management is an uncertain science, it decided that the issues at stake in this appeal were not well adapted to being resolved at the appellate court level.

Before the trial, defence counsel advised the Crown of the intended aboriginal rights defence and that the defence would take the position that the Crown was required to prove, as part of its case, that the net length restriction was justifiable as a necessary and reasonable conservation measure. The trial judge found s. 35(1) to be inapplicable to the appellant's defence, based on his finding that no aboriginal right had been established. He therefore found it inappropriate to make findings of fact with respect to either an infringement of the aboriginal right to fish or the justification of such an infringement. He did, however, find that the evidence called by the appellant

> . . . casts some doubt as to whether the restriction was necessary as a conservation measure. More particularly, it suggests that there were more appropriate measures that could have been taken if necessary; measures that would not impose such a hardship on the Indians fishing for food. That case was not fully met by the Crown.

According to the Court of Appeal, the findings of fact were insufficient to lead to an acquittal. There was no more evidence before this Court. We also would order a re-trial which would allow findings of fact according to the tests set out in these reasons.

The appellant would bear the burden of showing that the net length restriction constituted a prima facie infringement of the collective aboriginal right to fish for food. If an infringement were found, the onus would shift to the Crown which would have to demonstrate that the regulation is justifiable. To that end, the Crown would have to show that there is no underlying unconstitutional objective such as shifting more of the resource to a user group that ranks below the Musqueam. Further, it would have to show that the regulation sought to be imposed is required to accomplish the needed limitation. In trying to show that the restriction is necessary in the circumstances of the Fraser River fishery, the Crown could use facts pertaining to fishing by other Fraser River Indians.

In conclusion, we would dismiss the appeal and the cross-appeal and affirm the Court of Appeal's setting aside of the conviction. We would accordingly affirm the order for a new trial on the questions of infringement and whether any infringement is nonetheless consistent with s. 35(1), in accordance with the interpretation set out here.

For the reasons given above, the constitutional question must be answered as follows:

Question. Is the net length restriction contained in the Musqueam Indian Band Indian Food Fishing Licence dated March 30, 1984, issued pursuant to the British Columbia Fishery (General) Regulations and the Fisheries

Act, R.S.C. 1970, c. F-14, inconsistent with s. 35(1) of the Constitution Act, 1982?

Answer. This question will have to be sent back to trial to be answered according to the analysis set out in these reasons.

Appeal and cross-appeal dismissed.

Index

Index of Cases